MILESTONES IN MANAGEMENT

Milestones in Management
An Essential Reader

EDITED BY HENRY M. STRAGE,
McKINSEY & COMPANY

Copyright © Basil Blackwell Ltd, 1992

First published 1992

Blackwell Publishers
108 Cowley Road
Oxford, OX4 1JF
UK

Three Cambridge Center
Cambridge, Massachusetts 02142
USA

A CIP catalogue record for this book is available from
the British Library.

Library of Congress Cataloging in Publication Data
Milestones in management: an essential reader / edited by Henry Strage.
    p.   cm.
Includes bibliographical references and index.
ISBN 0–631–17625–X (alk. paper)
ISBN 0–631–18359–0 (pbk. : alk. paper)
1. Management. I. Strage, Henry.
HD31.M4373 1992 658.4 – dc20   91–27567
                                      CIP

Typeset in 11 on 13pt Ehrhardt
by Hope Services (Abingdon) Ltd.
Printed in Great Britain by TJ Press Ltd, Padstow, Cornwall

This book is printed on acid-free paper

To Alberta, with whom every day is a milestone

Contents

Foreword

HUGH PARKER
Chairman of Corporate Renewal Associates, London

When I was invited to write this Foreword to *Milestones in Management*, it was suggested that one reason why I had been chosen was that I had been one of the founders, and then the first manager, of McKinsey & Company's first non-US ('offshore' as we Americans used to say) office in London, and in that capacity had observed or experienced at first hand most of the developments and trends recorded in the 28 selections that make up this fascinating collection. The principal architect and editor of this anthology, Henry Strage, was closely associated with me from the earliest days and throughout the first three decades of the London office's existence. From that perspective, Henry has compiled a truly unique and valuable contribution to the literature of management.

When the partners of McKinsey & Company decided in 1959 to extend our practice into Europe – the opening of the London office was followed almost simultaneously by new offices in Geneva, Paris and Düsseldorf – the state of management in Europe generally was far less advanced than in the United States. It was sometimes said that, in terms of management expertise and technique, 'the Atlantic is five years wide'. And, by and large, this was true throughout the 1950s and 1960s.

McKinsey's opportunity, although perhaps not clearly perceived at the time, was to offer our clients the chance to gain competitive advantage by closing this five-year gap. Significantly, the very term 'competitive advantage' – now such a cliché in current usage – was never heard in Europe in the 1950s and 1960s. For cultural and historical reasons, the very idea of free-market competition was an alien one to European managers in those days. But what was at first seen as an interesting American notion was soon perceived as a growing threat, and alarm bells started to ring. One of the most plangent of these was of course Servan-Schreiber's classic *Le Défi Américain*, included here in Part V under the apt heading of 'Calls to Arms'.

The art/science/practice of management has developed, as this eclectic collection shows, unevenly over time and by nationality. It is interesting that only seven of the 28 writers represented here are non-US nationals, and there is no easily discernible logic or sequence to the development of the ideas and concepts described. Some of the contributions are virtually timeless – e.g. most of the papers on Leadership in Part II. Others are more technical (e.g. those by David Hertz and John Kitching), or conceptual (Ted Levitt), or prophetic (Kenichi Ohmae). Some are essentially philosophical – e.g. *Small is Beautiful* and *The Sources of Invention*.

Because of this great diversity of themes and treatments, it is hard to discover from these selected writings any consistent pattern in the evolution of management thinking or practice – unlike, for example, in the evolution of other branches of science such as physics or mathematics. So perhaps management is not a science after all, even though some of us in the 1950s and later tried to persuade ourselves that it was.

The main aim and object of *Milestones in Management* has been to bring together in one volume the best and most influential general management writing from the past 30 years, much of which is not readily accessible to practising managers today. Some of the pieces here can be truly described as seminal – e.g. 'Organizing a Worldwide Business' – while the theses of others – e.g. *Triad Power* and *The Limits to Growth* – still remain to be proven. But all have one thing in common: they contain original ideas that will repay thoughtful study by serious managers who seek to deepen their understanding of the intellectual base of their activity.

There is one long-neglected element of corporate management that is currently much to the fore: the now frequently discussed subject of 'corporate governance'. This is not referred to, either explicitly or implicitly, by any of the writers included here. Yet it is arguably a more fundamental factor in corporate performance – with which all of these writers are ultimately concerned – than many of the others cited.

My own interest in corporate governance – or in 'boardroom management', as I then called it – dates back to the mid-1960s, when it first dawned on me that the real roots of chronic under-performance were often to be found in corporate boardrooms and not, as was commonly supposed, in the ranks of middle or lower management, or in bloody-minded trade unions. The essence of corporate governance really concerns the basic role and responsibility of boards of directors to 'create tomorrow's company out of today's', as Sir John Harvey-Jones has so ably put it.

Much serious management writing has an unfortunate tendency to turgidity and jargon. Happily, the selections included here are largely free of both. In addition, the Editor has had the inspired idea of including pieces by two British writers – Sir Antony Jay's *Management and Machiavelli* and Professor C. Northcote Parkinson's eponymously titled *Parkinson's Law* – that combine both wit and wisdom. For all these reasons, therefore, *Milestones in Management* is not only 'an essential reader', but also eminently readable.

Preface

HENRY M. STRAGE

Throughout my professional career in management, I have always been amazed at how often, in the course of conversation or discussion, the names of some authors seem to be quoted, and how certain texts seem to be referred to again and again.

What seems to make certain authors appear timeless, and their messages as relevant today as when they were first published? Why do certain writers leave a lasting impression on some of our responsible enterprise leaders? Why, in some cases, were authors' ideas quoted and used to support points of view, when those who were speaking had not even read the material that they were quoting?

Several years ago, I decided that it would be interesting to pursue these questions more formally. To make the task more manageable, I chose to focus on the past three decades. That period seemed meaningful as it happened to coincide with both the number of years that McKinsey & Company has been active in the UK and the number of years that I have been an active management consultant.

My approach would not, I fear, qualify as authentic research by normal standards. However, I felt that it would be interesting to share some of the results of my enquiries with a wider audience. *Milestones in Management* is the product of that process.

The term 'milestones' seemed to be particularly appropriate in this context. When travellers made long, arduous trips along often unfamiliar highways and byways in the seventeenth century, their confidence that they were on the right road was reinforced by regular familiar signs indicating how far they had travelled and how far they had yet to go. In a way, the selections in this book are all markers on the road that we travel as we learn about ourselves, the institutions around us and the people with whom we work. There are many roads. There are many milestones. The texts that appear in this book are some that seemed particularly important to the people with whom I spoke.

No book reaches publication as the work of a single person and this book is no exception. I contacted almost 400 people and asked them to 'nominate' selections for the anthology that it represents. Everyone was most helpful, and I thank all of you for your support and interest. If your choice didn't make it this time, perhaps there will be enough interest for a *Milestones II*!

I am particularly grateful to all the very busy people who agreed to write introductions to the selections that they proposed for inclusion. It is not easy to summarize in a few words why you feel that a particular piece of writing was important to you. I hope that these vignettes will provide some useful insights.

Tim Goodfellow of Blackwell Publishers encouraged me from the first time that I described the project to him. He and his colleague Rosemary Roberts were most understanding when I missed deadline after deadline. I do hope that their patience will be at least partially rewarded. Tim was particularly supportive of the idea of closing *Milestones* with an unencumbered somewhat 'free-form' look at what we might expect in the next 30 years.

Alan Kantrow was particularly helpful in selecting which parts of nominated books should be included. Susan Starks edited some of the longer texts to more readily digestible lengths. And Nicola Montenegri pursued publishers and authors for permission to reproduce their work, and coordinated the keying of all texts into computer-compatible form.

Robert Whiting was the 'sergeant major' on the project, and kept an expert eye on the various texts, both reproduced and original. Catherine Waldren, my secretary, kept her head and temper as we soldiered through yet another draft of the final final text. She managed also to act as the level-headed and calm intermediary between me and the extraordinary number of different constituencies who directly or indirectly found themselves contributing to this project.

Lastly – thank you, Alberta, for your patience and encouragement. I had little idea when I started just how much of our 'discretionary' time together would actually be devoted to making 'just a few corrections', or 'rewriting a few parts', or chasing down 'a small fact that has to be right'. Alberta's early training as a professional editor was a valuable compass for keeping the project on course and finding a way past all the book's milestones to the end of the journey.

October 1991

Introduction

THREE decades set against the timescale of modern history are merely a brief moment. Yet the past three decades have been a period of unprecedented growth, political trauma, social upheaval and economic contradiction. In the realm of business, the period has been no less traumatic.

We have lived through both the births and deaths of major industries. We have watched with fascination as whole industries have physically moved from one continent to another. Unprecedented changes in the productivity of labour have brought the totally automated factory from the pages of science fiction to the reality of Monday morning. Careers in business and commerce, once considered marginal at best, have finally become respectable. A mysterious black box – the computer – has permeated every nook and cranny of our business and personal lives. We have *almost* come to accept the computer as a necessary handmaiden of economic progress.

In this book, I have tried to bring together a cross section of literature that has helped to shape management thinking and practice during the past 30 years. The extracts that it contains are 'milestones in management' selected by today's business leaders and management observers. By definition, any such collection is arbitrary. Nevertheless, I believe that these milestones provide a modest starting point for revisiting some of the most important ideas that have helped to shape and influence our lives.

This collection represents the results of over 400 contacts that I arranged with a random cross section of business leaders and academics in the UK. I freely and humbly plead guilty to being unscientific in my choice of sample, the nature of the actual enquiry and, finally, the interpretation of the results.

Nevertheless, the extracts selected for this volume are the ones that were most often mentioned by those whom I approached. I was frankly surprised to learn that many people knew about an author, about his or her book or something related to this or that 'well known idea', but had never actually read the original material. That, however, in my view, does not make it less important. After all, how many people have actually read the complete Bible from cover to cover?

This is not, then, meant to be a history of management thought over the past 30 years.

While such an objective would be noble, I fear that its execution would produce an arid and turgid scholarly tome, probably with very limited interest. It is, rather, simply a collection of material that today's leaders have suggested has had an influence on business life and enterprise development.

Observers versus influencers

It is useful to stop and reflect on the question of whether or not any of these selections were significantly influential per se, or if what I have gathered together is essentially a collection of the works of thoughtful observers who have captured and reported on changes that have taken place.

Our authors seem to fall broadly into several categories that embrace a range of different objectives.

Firstly, there are the authors who are basically reporters or commentators. They have crystallized, synthesized and diagnosed for us the trends and activities that they have either observed, personally championed or helped to formulate in one way or another. In the main, this group of authors tends to lean more towards a reportorial style, rather than the editorial approach.

Our second group of contributors is largely made up of predicters. After observing changing trends and fashions, they have prepared a well-argued case for why changes will – and in some cases must – come and what the implications for us all will be. At one extreme, authors in this group could be classified as visionaries. Whether they are participants, observers, advisers, academics or professional futurologists, they all want to foretell the future and describe a significant shift, change of direction or emphasis in the way in which business is carried out, resources are deployed or major functions or activities are executed. One needs to distinguish here between the faddist and the truly creative thinker. The faddist all too often is more interested in selling books than in adding to our understanding of what is really going on.

The last group of writers are essentially practitioners. These are individuals who provide recipes for success, blueprints for action, advice on how to behave and guidance on how to deal with generalized challenges.

Each group contributed in different ways to management thinking and changed behaviour patterns during the past 30 years. Each of the topics on which they wrote required a different approach. To describe the future, it was impractical to be too precise. On the other hand, if one were explaining how to carry out an industry competitive analysis, one could not risk being vague and inaccurate. To those writing on such topics, providing meticulously researched 'how to do it' books couched in hypothetical terms hardly seemed as convincing and as interesting as discussing personal experiences with passion and conviction.

Why is it that certain kinds of writing worked for particular topics and others did not? I use the word 'work' in this context to indicate that a book or an article actually became a subject for widespread discussion, a topic for debate, a source of inspiration or, in rare cases, the actual catalyst for change – a changemaker.

In the first place timing was very important. I suspect that if *In Search of Excellence* had been published at a different time, when, for example, the world was not in one of its cyclical downturns, it might not have become the all-time runaway best seller that it in fact became. In order to be successful – i.e. to have an impact – our authors had to produce their contributions at a propitious time.

Secondly, how important was the actual style of writing? I would say important, but not critical. In fact, our contributors are mainly clear, concise and primarily jargon-free authors. Few, however, would probably be nominated for a Pulitzer prize.

In the third place, I found that, to be credible, an author had to be very careful to be factually accurate. Interpretations as such can be, by definition, subjective, personal and even slanted. Facts cannot be. Readers quickly distinguish between observation and imagination!

Commentators such as Sloan explained in detail why they personally chose to approach a particular business problem in a certain way. They influenced their readers by the clarity of their views and an ability to express their perceptions, the creativeness of their approach and a passion for wanting to share their success with a larger audience.

Our predicters and visionaries fell more into the realm of ancient soothsayers. They really were not too concerned about trying to explain or justify the past, but more with foretelling, or warning us about, the future. They were, of course, not always right. But I suspect that their influence must not be judged by the accuracy of their message. The Club of Rome's depressing, Malthusian-like tome has, at least at the time of writing, proved inaccurate. However, would it be totally unfair to suggest that it had a major influence on those who, years after it was written, warned us of the environmental chaos that we are now in danger of unwittingly sponsoring?

Finally, we learned to appreciate and love the concepts of experience curves, risk analysis and shareholder value derived from practitioners who presented their tools in interesting, clear and convincing ways. They were not managerial do-it-yourself kits but, rather, well-argued blueprints for action with messages that could be useful for Monday morning.

There is no doubt that, in the 30 years covered by this collection, both management thinking and practice have changed dramatically. In the following pages, I have tried to provide a summary of the major forces that have had an influence on management thinking and practices. It is difficult – if not impossible – to be exhaustive in preparing such a review.

The final section of this Introduction describes the actual *impact* that these often disparate forces have had on management practices.

Major factors influencing management thinking

In general, it is difficult or impossible to trace a particular new idea about management to one specific cause or event. New ideas about management typically emerge as a consequence of, or a response to, a complex mixture of social, economic and technological forces.

What are some of these forces that have helped to shape management thinking during the past 30 years? How have they influenced a major economy? To see a context in which they have fashioned change we can look at the difference between Britain in the 1960s and Britain in the 1990s.

What kind of country was the UK in 1960?

Demographically, there has been comparatively little change in the past 30 years. In terms, for example, of the total number of people employed (including those in the armed forces and on work-related government training programmes) there has been practically no change – less than a 1 per cent increase.

And, as in most developed countries, improved health care and greater attention to life style and food consumption have caused the age profile of the population to shift towards a much higher percentage of persons over 65. Today they represent almost 16 per cent of the population, compared with less than 12 per cent in 1960.

However, these aggregated figures mask some startling shifts in what people do today compared with 1960. For example:

- There are four times as many women working full time in the workforce today as there were in 1960.
- There are 50 per cent more people employed in the service sector today than there were in 1960.
- The number of people who are self-employed has almost doubled.
- The total number of people presently employed by foreign-owned firms in the UK has increased by a factor of ten.

In addition, we seem to have discovered divorce – which has quadrupled – and concurrently decided to have smaller families – 25 per cent smaller today than 30 years ago.

While the 'pound in your pocket' has lost almost 90 per cent of its 1960 value, in general we are all much better off – at least in terms of material possessions. Basic necessities today – colour TV, washing machines, refrigerators and telephones – were, 30 years ago, regarded as luxuries – reserved only for the best-off.

The Sunday Times published a useful article in October 1989 on 'How Our Lives Have Changed between 1964 and 1989'. It contained the following table:

How our lives have changed

1964	1989
Value of pound: £1	Comparative value of pound: 12.5p
Average London house: £4,867	Average London house: £96,866
Mortgage rate: 6%	Mortgage rate: 14.5%
Average earnings:	Average earnings:
Weekly pay (men): £23 11s 7d (23.57)	Weekly pay (men): £269
Holidays:	Holidays:
Return flight to Los Angeles: £210	Two weeks in Acapulco: from £325
Executive car:	Executive car:
3.3/1. Vauxhall: £859 9s 7d (£859.47)	Vauxhall Carlton 3.0 GSI: £19,248
Washing machines:	Washing machines:
Bendix automatic: 107 guineas (112.35)	Hoover automatic: £294
TV sets: 12.9m (all black-and-white)	TV sets: 18.9m (16.5m colour)
Taylor's vintage port: 22s 6d (£1.13)	Taylor's vintage port: £21 a bottle

During the past three decades, management as a serious, respectable, legitimate occupation has undergone a major metamorphosis. In 1960 management was hardly considered a serious occupational pursuit. In the class of 1959 at Oxford and Cambridge, only 129 people – fewer than 2 per cent of the graduating class – actually chose careers in industry, or 'trade', as it was often referred to in those days.

What were the factors that contributed to changing perceptions about the importance of management? What changes were responsible for slowly but deliberately altering people's perceptions about the role of management in our society? What forces eventually contributed to the recognition that management was going to become a permanent and essential ingredient of the nation's professional landscape?

Decline in economic performance

Britain entered the post-war era as the strongest and richest country in Europe. By 1960 it was beginning to lose its comparative competitive advantage. In March 1964 *The Sunday Times* published a feature article written by a totally unknown American management consultant called William Allen. 'Is Britain a Half-Time Country, Getting Half-Pay for Half-Working under Half-Hearted Management?' This is how the editor chose to introduce this rather unassuming article, using terms that were for years afterwards to become the shorthand for describing and sometimes justifying the spiral of decline into which Britain seemed to have fallen. And management was held accountable!

By 1973 *The Economist* sadly reported that Britain, because of its relatively poor growth rate compared with its neighbours, had become the poorest country in Europe, with the exception of Ireland.

The typical indicators of economic performance were yet to become household terms, but the nation's 'terms of trade' and 'output per man hour' and 'days lost in industrial disputes' all clearly pointed in the wrong direction.

After the UK joined the EEC and the full effect of the 1973 oil crisis began to bite, the management of the country's resources finally became a subject for serious consideration and study. Gradually the country began to recognize that the effective management of its resources was an important prerequisite for rebuilding the country, raising the standard of living and providing economic leadership internationally.

Shift towards a global perspective

In 1959 the Commonwealth was the final destination for 38 per cent of all UK exports. Perhaps the mentality of much of industry was encapsulated in the reaction of an export director of a large British engineering company who was *not* prepared to fit metric measurement devices on export orders, or to provide bilingual instructions.

The well-documented moves towards globalization, a single world market and universal products all forced companies that wanted to survive as world-class enterprises to recognize that they must be able to compete worldwide if they were to survive. By 1989 exports to Commonwealth countries had fallen by 75 per cent, to less than 8 per cent of the total!

Change in the country's perceptions about management

In 1967 a Royal Commission reported – after several years of study – that it was finally time for Britain to recognize graduate business studies as a legitimate educational aspiration – at least for some! In that year, the US produced 21,000 MBAs from a total of 198 business schools – in contrast, there were only 42 in the UK from 3 schools awarding business degrees!

While in America business leaders were clearly seen as folk heroes – often gracing the covers of weekly magazines – in Britain, corporate heads were only just beginning to be recognized as worthwhile citizens. A career in business was, slowly and begrudgingly, becoming acceptable.

In 1960 very few people would have recognized the names of the leaders of even the country's largest and most prestigious enterprises.

It is hard to believe that 30 years later we would be entertained on prime-time television by a respected business leader featuring in a documentary series about life at the top in British business.

Casting away a country's security blanket

In 1960 more than half of Britain's labour force was employed in what was essentially the public sector. The legacy of Clement Attlee's nationalizations persisted for 16 years after he had left power and been replaced by a Conservative government.

Unfortunately, while there were some notable exceptions – Beeching at British Rail and Robens at the National Coal Board – during *at least half* of the three decades covered in this review, the leaders of more than 50 per cent of the workforce were classic public-sector 'grey men' who were much more concerned with, and comfortable at, satisfying their ministerial bosses than at facing the real cut-and-thrust world of global competition.

As denationalization began to take hold, the highly visible differences in the performance of privatized enterprises signalled a dramatic change in the country's perception of the role of managers. And private shareholders and institutional investors began to influence management behaviour via the boardroom!

A revitalized financial centre

Financial institutions, broadly defined, cover a very wide spectrum of services – banks, insurance companies, stockbrokers, venture capitalists, asset managers and many others. Britain's centuries-old preeminent position was, after the Second World War, gradually being whittled away by the Swiss and Americans and subsequently by the French, Germans and Japanese. However, the country's financial institutions were revitalized and managed to regain their relative position throughout the world.

While one might question the quality of their own internal managerial competencies, financial institutions have been an important, but unrecognized, force in strengthening the capabilities of management in this country. Because of their role as investors, lenders, partners and controllers in the context of industrial enterprises, both existing institutions and new entities in the country's financial sector have been an important factor in upgrading managerial skills by demanding better, more purposeful management performance and being prepared to reward the winners handsomely.

Technical breakthroughs clear the way for streamlining management practice

As far as I know, no national association of commerce representing business has ever awarded the technological equivalent of the film world's 'Oscar' for outstanding contributions. Perhaps it would not be such a bad idea.

In thinking about which technological achievements have had the greatest and most direct influence on management during the past 25 years, the National Academy of Engineering recently published its own list of accomplishments, and this provides an interesting framework for testing the hypothesis that technological advances profoundly affect management.

In the following table,* each of the ten selections is listed together with some indication of its impact.

Impact of top engineering achievements on management, 1960–1990

Technological achievement	Typical impact on management organization and practice
1 *Microprocessor* Minute chips run everything from electronic devices to personal computers	• Affected *every* function from basic research to logistics and sales management • Created numerous new industries, revolutionized existing ones, eliminated others
2 *Computer Aided Design and Manufacturing* CAD and CAM are improving the quality of products while reducing production time	• Dramatic reductions in production costs • Opened up opportunities for 'customized' mass production • Provided a dramatic new dimension to marketing activities by giving customers more control of design
3 *Fibre Optic Communications* Four fibres, thinner than a human hair, carry more than 40,000 telephone calls simultaneously	• Faster, more reliable and much less costly capacity to communicate • Electronic databases providing instant access • 24-hour global financial markets
4 *Advanced Composite Materials* New materials adding lightness and strength have replaced materials in almost every industry	• Created opportunities for basic redesign of most industrial products, from aeroplanes to razor blades • Changed economics of construction and engineering industry

* Based on the article *Engineering and the Advancement of Human Welfare: 10 Outstanding Achievements 1964–1989* (Washington: National Academy of Engineering).

Technological achievement	Typical impact on management organization and practice
5 *Lasers* Providing new and better ways of carrying out functions in every segment of industrial activity – e.g. medicine, communications, science, textiles	• Quantum changes in storage, retrieval and manipulation of information • Created new industries • Changed basic economics in many manufacturing and service industries
6 *Genetically Engineered Products* Products created by organisms implanted with a foreign gene have dramatically advanced our knowledge of human welfare	• Brought pure scientists into top management and ownership positions • Created need for enterprise functions to provide sophisticated public relations resources and government relations departments
7 *CAT Scan* Computer Axial Topography has revolutionized medical diagnosis and opened new opportunities in the health service field	• Opened the way for sophisticated medical treatment which raised questions about how to make objective decisions in a scarce resource environment
8 *Application Satellites* Satellite systems provide us with the capacity to watch behaviour on earth, monitor weather, improve navigation, speed up global communications	• 'Shortened' distances among parts of the organization • Provided new sources of information • Created new businesses • Allowed more accurate monitoring of activities
9 *Jumbo Jets* Shrink the globe by carrying passengers enormous distances at low cost without refuelling	• Helped make global business a practical reality • Opened up new markets, created improved supply services
10 *Moon Landing* (1969) The countless number of scientific and engineering problems that were connected with the challenge of landing two men on the moon were the precursors of many technological breakthroughs over the next 20 years	• Introduced the 'can do' era in technology – almost nothing is impossible • Spawned thousands of new industrial applications from subminiaturization to new textile products, to measuring devices and 100% quality control requirements (fail safe)

Macroeconomic forces

All the forces at work discussed so far have been primarily domestic in nature. In addition, the past three decades have been a period of dramatic change at the 'macro' economic level. And, while these changes may not have *directly* affected management thinking, there is no question that these global events have had an increasingly important impact as the world shrinks!

Since 1959 the world's population has doubled. Yet today the percentage of that population that exists below the starvation level has increased. The gap between rich and poor countries continues to widen. While there have been no major world wars in the past 30 years, more people have been killed in these three decades than as a result of both World Wars.

We have somehow managed, despite the Club of Rome's gloomy predictions, not to exhaust the earth's productive capacity. Yet annually 10 per cent of the world's arable land disappears for ever. The number of people who go to bed hungry each night has doubled.

We did not pay too much attention to Schumacher's clarion call of 'small is beautiful'. Today's corporations are bigger than ever. Yet countries in the United Nations with a population of less than 15 million represent more than half the total number of members.

There are more scientists alive and working today than the cumulative total of scientists on this planet during the past 1,000 years. Yet, while we can fly to distant planets and look into 'black holes', we seem to have failed to conquer enough knowledge about human diseases to make even a dent in the array of fatal illnesses. New plagues have predicted impacts that conjure up the days of the Black Death.

There are groups of dedicated people today concerned about the preservation of seals, whales, chimpanzees and pandas, yet our inner cities continue to burst at the seams and the quality of life of only a small proportion of the world's population is better now than it was 30 years ago.

Less than 5 per cent of the population of most developed countries can produce enough food to feed us, and even though our industrial output increases every year, the number of people actually working in factories continues to decline.

Impact on management

In his valedictory address in 1979, Sir Nicholas Henderson felt obliged, as he was about to retire from the foreign service, to review and discuss the causes of Britain's economic decline. A major cause, he concluded, was the 'lack of professionalism in British management'.

This was not the first nor the only criticism of British management – in fact, knocking management was recognized as a popular national pastime for many years.

As long as business in both industry and the service sector was an unattractive and unrecognized career path, it continued to suffer from a long tradition of being marginal to the small, but high-quality, skill pool that each year found more attractive alternatives for its energies! It is interesting that, notwithstanding this, the few companies that were able year after year to attract bright young men and women and provide them with outstanding in-house training opportunities and carefully orchestrated challenging assignments were consistently singled out each year as some of the best managed enterprises in the world.

Yet, in parallel with the unprecedented changes in the economic, social and political fabric, management thinking and practice underwent some extraordinary changes. Some were dramatic and obvious; others were more subtle but in no way less important.

What were the main changes in management thinking and practice during these tumultuous 30 years?

(1)   Management became a respectable career aspiration for the country's 'best and brightest'. Most chief executives of responsible public companies no longer had continually to defend their compensation figures, which sounded to most people more like telephone numbers than take-home pay.

Schools finally – albeit reluctantly – began to sneak some practical economics subjects into their curricula. And, on career days, they even allowed some accountants and marketing executives to explain what they actually did from nine to five.

Sales of management books skyrocketed and management training, executive seminars and business schools boomed. And, from time to time, business news actually found its way onto the front page.

(2)   The traditional hierarchical management structures inherited from the Babylonians, shaped by the Romans, fine tuned by the medieval barons, then firmly carved into our industrial landscape by Alfred P. Sloan, emerged after 30 years relatively unscathed. Line and staff, chain of command, decentralization,

separation of policy formulation from operations execution – all these ideas, well established at the beginning of this period, surprisingly survived with comparatively little change.

Scholars tried to explain why managers behaved in certain ways under certain conditions, and distinctions between leaders and managers became a subject for much discussion and debate. But Alfred P. Sloan's description of how he built and ran General Motors presented a blueprint that fitted most companies in 1990.

(3) A systematic shift in the role and responsibility of the board has transformed it from a necessary evil or a friendly eating club into a responsible body in the life and growth of business institutions.

Corporate boards of directors now have much clearer responsibilities to both shareholders and stakeholders. The idea of monthly meetings in a traditional 'gentlemen's club' atmosphere, solely to rubber stamp management decisions, has been for the most part relegated to managerial history books.

(4) Every business today has ready access to an armoury of business processes that provide basic tools for successful operations and problem-solving. Business and product planning, budgeting, decision-making and management support systems, for example, are all highly developed activities that are learnable skills no longer regarded as some sort of art form, inherited talent or magic.

(5) Managing corporations in 1990 has become a complex and demanding task. Compared with 1960, businesses are much bigger, must usually support global operations, demand the capacity to make important decisions rapidly and the ability to integrate a diversity of specialized skills. As a result:

- Most enterprises are subdivided into some form of profit-accountable business units with varying degrees of autonomy.
- At the centre, an array of highly skilled, specialized resources (legal, technical, financial) supports an executive management team.

(6) Industrial rationalization and restructuring have tended to create much more rational collections of businesses that have had to meet global competitive standards in order to survive. Having, in the main unsuccessfully, tried to create and operate the multi-business industrial conglomerate, corporations took the 'stick to your knitting' message to heart.

(7) An important by-product of the introduction of the microchip and computers has been the far greater sophistication now possible in business functions that, 30 years ago, were often considered rather painful and tedious administrative tasks. Logistics, supply management, asset control, inventory control, manufacturing planning and distribution optimization, for example, are all enterprise skills that have made significant contributions to the effective management of corporate resources.

(8)   The massive shifts from a manufacturing to a service economy have introduced the notion that all human activities need to be managed. The idea, for example, that a hospital or a social service could or should be managed would have been seen as absurd 30 years ago.

Today, after many attempts to create totally independent bodies of knowledge about how service institutions and business enterprises should be managed, there seems to be an acceptance that the basic ground rules for good management apply to any situation where resources are brought together to satisfy an agreed need.

(9)   After several different phases of managerial fashion shifts, the customer seems once again to have gained unanimous recognition as the ultimate factor in deciding whether or not an enterprise will survive and prosper. As a result, managerial skills in marketing and related activities have become highly valued and carefully sculpted resources. Here too, the computer has been an enabling device that has put an often overwhelming amount of information into the hands of marketing managers and sales forces. In addition, by giving them all the capacity to manipulate these data, the marketing function no longer relies solely on the seat-of-the-pants skills as its only weapon.

(10)   The ability – real or apparent – to measure accurately, and compare, the performances of managers, management teams and corporate entities has an impact on almost every aspect of corporate structure and life.

- Objective measurement of performance, usually against a predetermined target or objective, slowly but systematically provided a factual basis for evaluating and rewarding performance. 'Clubability' finally became, by 1990, a rare basis for advancement.
- Organization style, shared values and corporate communication were all directly altered as scorekeeping became more reliable.
- Coupled with dramatic changes in the practices of financial institutions and refinements in what has cynically been called 'financial engineering', measurements of past performance and future promise have provided the underlying basis for developments in a creative array of change of ownership transactions.
- Better measurement has also heightened awareness of the inherently unpredictable nature of our economic system. Such unpredictability, supported by the gradual elimination of system controls such as government regulations, trade barriers and monopolies, has forced management to arrange its resources and systems to be able to respond more quickly, to provide mechanisms for dynamic adjustments, and to seek continually for innovative ways to achieve and maintain sustainable competitive advantage.

Part I
Strategy

Introduction

IN 1967 a massive 2,000-page tome, ambitiously entitled *A Handbook of Business Administration*, brought together specially prepared contributions from over a hundred business leaders, academics and consultants from around the world. Perusal of its Table of Contents and Appendix reveals that 'strategy' had not yet become a discrete subject for management attention and consideration. There was no distinct section devoted to the topic and there was not a single contribution with a title that even suggested that a company's management should be concerned about the formulation of strategic plans for its future.

Ten years later, anyone writing an article for a business journal, preparing a speech for a management seminar or writing a book on a management subject, was virtually obliged to include the word 'strategy' in its title. Was this just a fad, or had something fundamentally changed to focus people's minds on this curious, well-established military notion?

In Great Britain, as elsewhere in the West, several important new, or renewed, perspectives on the role and responsibilities of managers, chief executives and boards of directors emerged during this time. The undelegatable responsibility of the board of directors for establishing a company's longer-term objectives and determining what strategies will best ensure their realization changed the focus of attention from what should be accomplished to how it would be accomplished.

At the same time, the need for business decisions to be founded on fact, as opposed to intuition, tradition or snap judgements, heralded what one of my colleagues, Roger Morrison, called in 1967 'The Quiet Management Revolution'.* And in board rooms and top management offices around the country ideas about market growth, industry structure, market share, competitive analysis and external forces at work

---

* J. Roger Morrison: 'The Quiet Management Revolution', *Management Today*, November 1967.

graduated from being generalized, vague statements to being painfully collected and creatively analysed snapshots of what was actually happening in the marketplace.

It was these early moves that paved the way for Bruce Henderson's *Perspectives on Experience*, which, in turn, inspired the rise of strategy consultants and strategy boutiques and stimulated veritable avalanches of publications − some, but not all, based on research findings − produced by both practitioners and academics. Henderson brushed away the cobwebs from the notion of learning curves developed by a Commander in the US Air Force in 1925 and presented to an un-prepared business community the much heralded two-by-two strategic matrix. Practically overnight, 'dogs', 'stars' and 'cash cows' were incor-porated into the vocabulary of management and the age of strategy was officially launched. Perhaps one of the most controversial 'new' concepts was summarized by Patrick Conley in 'Experience Curves as a Planning Tool'.

In the decade that followed, most companies felt obliged to create a 'strategic planning department'. And those that wished to avoid incurring additional head-office overheads took the simpler route of changing the name of their existing planning functions by adding the ubiquitous adjective 'strategic'.

In 1980 a shy and relatively obscure professor at Harvard Business School introduced a whole new dimension to the already overflowing cornucopia of management knowledge. Michael Porter invented the concept of competitive strategy in his book of that name. Whether or not this was a new concept or simply an old one dressed up is irrelevant. The fact is that Porter challenged businesses to look not only at industry structure but also at competitors' behaviour within a given structure.

With less fanfare, two other HBS professors made significant contributions to the state of the art. Alfred Chandler's *Strategy and Structure* concluded, from the detailed study of a group of large American enterprises, that the structures of companies almost always result from decisions about strategy.

While it was written well before it was thought fashionable for managers to incorporate the 'S word' into their titles, Ted Levitt's 'Marketing Myopia' proved virtually timeless. For many years it enjoyed the distinction of being the most requested reprint from the *Harvard Business Review*.

1

Experience Curves as a Planning Tool

PATRICK CONLEY

L ooking back at the tumultuous enthusiasm for the experience curve and the product portfolio that accompanied the birth of modern strategic planning, two questions stand out: what ignited the chain reaction; and, in hindsight, was it a boon or a burden?

The ideas came from teams of people at The Boston Consulting Group working on two problems in parallel: the seeming chaos of electronics pricing, and the development of a process for managing a company built on disparate acquisitions. The credit, as usual, belongs to client management, who were determined to explore some fundamental business questions.

Are the ideas still useful? The answer, of course, depends on how they are used. Their charm lies in their simplicity: even people who know little about business know about 'cash cows', 'stars' and 'dogs'. But, with all caveats removed, they are indeed too simple. Using them takes thought and insight.

The dominant forces in business over the last ten years continue to demonstrate the power of experience and of portfolio analysis. The Japanese and others have organized their companies to achieve the continuous improvement central to the concept of the experience curve and have become formidable competitors. Leveraged buy-outs of diversified firms have dramatically increased their values by drawing attention to the underlying competitive positions and cash-flow characteristics of the different businesses involved.

As competition comes to depend increasingly on the ability to create organizations capable of learning continuously from experience, harnessing the real power of ideas will inevitably gain in importance.

John Clarkeson,
President and Chief Executive Officer,
The Boston Consulting Group, Inc.,
Boston, Massachusetts

Experience Curves as a Planning Tool

If experience improves performance, it should follow that the company that has produced the most widgets will be the most efficient widget producer. This implies that market share is vital in determining potential profitability and that new products, whether developed internally or acquired outside, are doomed to lackluster financial performance unless they capture a dominant market position.

ANY study tool that can help managers understand and predict industry and company trends in price and cost, and that can also help them explain and predict product profitability, is obviously capable of greatly enriching planning. Like most tools, however, the utility of the experience concept lies in its imaginative application. It is no substitute for management, but it can help managers in determining business strategy.

The experience concept is related to the well-known *learning-curve* effect. Since its discovery by the commander of Wright-Patterson Air Force Base in 1925, the interesting 'learning' effect has been highly developed and widely used in certain segments of industry.[1-3] The aircraft and electronics industries often use it to guide both their cost control decisions for assembly operations and their pricing policies. The Department of Defense procurement officers use the learning-curve effect in setting costs targets in cost-based contracts.

'Experience Curves as a Planning Tool' is the full text of a paper presented at a meeting of the Chemical Marketing Research Association, Houston, Texas, February 23–24, 1970, by Dr Patrick Conley, a Vice President of The Boston Consulting Group.

The article is based on extensive research conducted by The Boston Consulting Group which resulted in the book, *Perspectives on Experience* (Boston, 1968, 1970 and 1972), a detailed examination of the implications of the experience effect.

It is surprising, however, that more companies have not realized the value of the concept. Although it has been observed and applied by the chemical industry and occasionally by other manufacturing enterprises,[4,5] the effect is not always considered by managers in assessing manufacturing performance. It is a vague or totally unfamiliar concept to a surprising number of senior managers who do not have a background in manufacturing or in the defense industry. Unfamiliarity takes on special significance, since the effect appears to depend somewhat on confidence that it exists![3]

The well-known learning curve relates the direct labor hours required to perform a task to the number of times the task has been performed. For a wide variety of activities, this relation has been found to be of the form shown in Exhibit 1.1, in which time to perform decreases by a constant percentage whenever the number of trials is doubled. Plotted on log-log scales, this relation becomes a straight line with a slope characteristic of the rate of 'learning,' such as that shown in Exhibit 1.2.

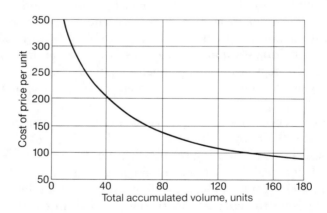

Exhibit 1.1 Representation of experience relationships graphically on a linear scale

A 20 percent reduction in hours for each doubling of performances — or what is called an 80 percent curve — is typical of a very wide variety of tasks. The concept of continuing improvement 'forever,' which is apparent in Exhibit 1.2, is often disturbing. However, one must recall

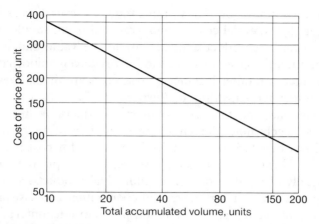

Exhibit 1.2 Representation of experience relationships graphically on a log-log scale

that the base of the curve is *not* time but trials and that the number of trials required to make a given percentage improvement grows enormously as learning occurs. Thus, for all practical purposes, learning in most instances eventually becomes so slow that it appears static.

The experience effect, quantitatively similar to the learning-curve phenomenon, includes all costs, not just direct-labor tasks. It is quite general and seemingly applies to most of the activities undertaken within a corporation. In particular, it applies to the start-up of new plants and even to 'automated' operations.

Cost as a function of learning

Since experience increases the efficiency of an operation, it naturally reduces the cost of that operation. This fact has frequently been used for estimation and prediction.[5] In fact, observers have noted that costs go down *by a fixed percentage* each time the number of units produced doubles. Recent studies by The Boston Consulting Group serve to augment these observations. There is every reason to believe that each element of cost declines in such a way that total cost follows a composite 'experience' curve.

If costs are measured in dollars, it is necessary to eliminate inflation when observations are made over a substantial period of time. Deflation of cost figures thus becomes more important when growth rates are slow, so the doubling of trials or units requires several years. One might also argue that material costs, when large and fixed, should be removed and the experience effect applied only to the value added. However, removing material costs turns out to be a relatively minor correction in most instances; in other instances, these costs are themselves subject to reduction through substitutions ('experience?').

The fact that the total cost of many products declines by a fixed percentage each time the cumulative number of units produced is doubled has been widely recognized and used for cost prediction and control.[3,6] However, cost data are usually proprietary and always mechanically difficult to obtain for individual products, so research on the subject requires a high degree of cooperation and assistance on the part of the manufacturer. A common problem encountered when one examines the historical cost of a particular product is a series of discontinuities in the data. The discontinuities are usually associated with changes in accounting methods and are expensive and tedious to rationalize. Also, since we are considering *total* costs, the method of allocating indirect costs becomes a factor in multiproduct companies, and traditional allocations may have to be adjusted to achieve the desired precision.

Costs and market share

In spite of long-standing awareness of the learning-curve phenomenon and its effect on costs, the broader experience-curve effect and its obvious strategic implication seem until now to have been overlooked. If cost declines predictably with units produced, the competitor who has produced the most units will probably have the lowest cost. Since the products of all competitors have sensibly the same market price, the competitor with the most unit experience should enjoy the greatest profit. Furthermore, it should be clear that very substantial differences in cost and profit can exist between competitors having widely different unit experiences. Of course, this assumes that all competitors have equal access to resources and patents and that the competitors are all reasonably efficient.

Over a period of time when market positions are relatively stable, experience can be equated with market share. Thus market share and profitability are closely related, and competitive positions can become those shown in Exhibit 1.3. In the exhibit, competitor A is the marginal

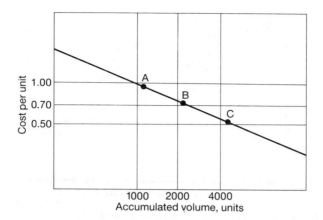

Exhibit 1.3 Market share and costs for three competitors

competitor, whereas competitor C dominates the market. Empirically (and perhaps theoretically), the market share of the dominant competitor in a stable, slowly growing market turns out to be about 50 percent. The next competitor typically has 25 percent; the third has 12 percent, and so on.[7] The 50–25 percent share distribution observed by Cohen may result more from a subconscious agreement among competitors than from the operation of random influences. In a mature market, stability is often in the best interest of all the competitors.

If the market is growing rapidly – say 15 percent or more annually in units – then market shares may be fairly fluid, and the dominant producer may have much more or even less than 50 percent of the market.

Price and experience

Assuming that costs can be made to decline at a predictable rate such as that shown in Exhibit 1.2, we can examine the related price curves for possible correlation. In general, we find most price curves to have either the form shown in Exhibit 1.4 or that shown in Exhibit 1.5, with a strong predominance of the former type. In these idealized examples, as well as in the actual ones to be discussed later, we are plotting industry unit price (or weighted average unit price if several sizes or grades are involved) against total historical industry units on logarithmic scales.

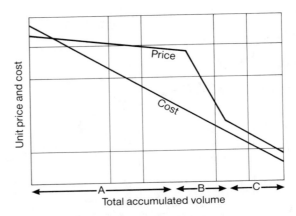

Exhibit 1.4 A characteristic pattern of costs and prices

The costs shown are average industry costs, weighted by the unit production of each competitor. (If these prices are plotted with appropriate costs for the individual competitors' experience, the slope of the price line will *appear* to vary if the competitor is gaining or losing market share substantially.)

In Exhibit 1.4, the constant-dollar price shows little or no decline during phase A, a steep slope of around 60 percent in phase B, and a moderate 70 to 80 percent slope in phase C. The relatively level price exhibited in phase A is associated with the introductory period in which price is set somewhat below initial cost and not changed as volume

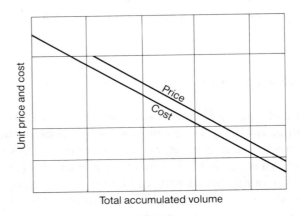

Exhibit 1.5 An alternative pattern of costs and prices

grows. If this price is held too long, competitors enter, and all add capacity until a 'shakeout' price decline occurs in phase B. When prices reach a 'reasonable' level above costs, they continue to decline with cost, as shown in phase C.

Characteristically, the dominant producer is losing his share of the market during phase A. During phase B, market shares may shift considerably as the more aggressive competitors struggle for dominance, using price as a major weapon. In phase C a stable competitive situation is again established with possibly a different dominant competitor than the one in phase A.

In Exhibit 1.5, the price is brought down more nearly in parallel with cost – usually in an attempt to discourage the entry of competition. Although initial margins are less, final margins are usually greater.

There is nothing inherent in the price characteristics shown in Exhibits 1.4 and 1.5 that reveals one to be 'better' than the other. One might expect a wide variety of patterns between the two types shown; however, such variation does not appear to occur in practical instances.

It must be remembered that these idealized curves are typical of those obtaining in uninhibited competition and are exclusive of the influence of inflation. One must also be certain to avoid thinking of them as plots against *time*. Although time increases with experience, the curves are plotted against *units produced* and may be quite irregular with respect to time.

Observations of price behavior

Price data are relatively easy to acquire and, when adjusted by means of the GNP deflator,* they can be plotted as shown in Exhibits 1.6 through 1.10. These exhibits are typical of many, many similar ones for a very wide variety of products. Exhibits 1.6 and 1.7 show the two classical forms of price behavior in semiconductors. Exhibit 1.8 is considered typical of the chemical industry. Exhibit 1.9, for facial tissues, has an unusual break in the price pattern. This break shows what happened when an element in the distribution chain was omitted and the factory picked up the eliminated unit's markup. Exhibit 1.10 shows the behavior of a very slowly growing product, freestanding gas ranges, over a very considerable period. In all of the cases, the data points in any one graph

---

* The GNP deflator is a factor used to correct prices for any given year to what they would have been in the base year by removing the average inflation in the gross national product. See Ref. 8.

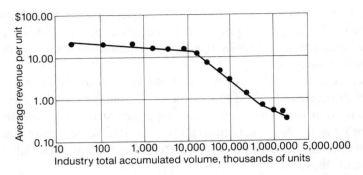

Exhibit 1.6 Revenue curve for silicon transistors during the period from 1954 to 1968

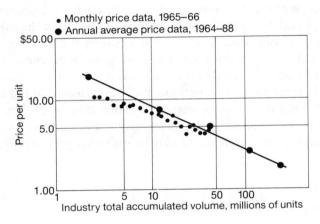

Exhibit 1.7 Price curve for integrated circuits

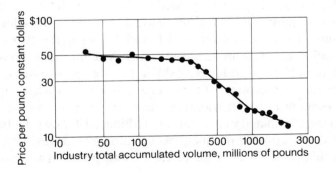

Exhibit 1.8 Polyvinyl chloride price curve (1946–1968)

refer to equal intervals of *time*. Obviously, strong underlying laws are at work.

The 1965–1966 data for integrated circuits in Exhibit 1.7 are particularly remarkable, since each point represents an average *monthly* price. The clustering of points, shown strongly in the progressive data at the high-volume end of Exhibit 1.9, is indicative of declining growth rate in the product. Such a decline (with its resulting cluster) is often the precursor of a price break when it occurs in the location of phase A of Exhibit 1.4.

From the data shown, as well as from the long-acknowledged behavior of costs, one can conclude that prices behave in a remarkably predictable and regular manner and that, in constant dollars, prices tend to decline. Break points are perhaps difficult to foresee, but they are associated with declining growth rates in the presence of a price

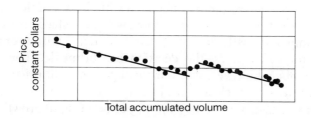

Exhibit 1.9 Price curve for facial tissues (for the years 1933–1955 and 1961–1966)

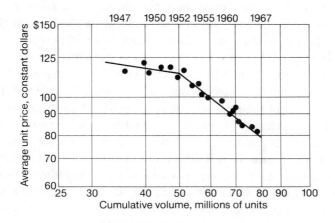

Exhibit 1.10 Price curve for freestanding gas ranges

'umbrella.' Once again, the plots are in terms of total units produced and not in terms of time.

Product strategy implications

Since prices and costs tend to decline with units produced and since the producer with the largest stable market share eventually has the lowest costs and greatest profits, then it becomes vital to have a dominant market share in as many products as possible. However, market share in slowly growing products can be gained only by reducing the share of competitors who are likely to fight back. It may not be worth the cost to wrest shares away from competent competitors in low-growth products. The value – in terms of improved cost and increased volume – of an increase in market share can be calculated with the aid of the experience curve. The investment required to increase one's share in the market can be compared with the calculated value, and, after suitable allowances for risk factors, the decision can be made. The company should remember, however, that most competitors will price at out-of-pocket cost rather than close a facility.

But all products at some time enjoy a period of rapid growth. During rapid growth, a company can gain share by securing most of the *growth*. Thus, while competitors grow, the company can grow even faster and emerge with a dominant share when growth eventually slows. The competitors, pleased with their own growth, may not stage much of a contest even when the company is compounding its market share at their eventual expense. At high growth rates – say 20 to 30 percent in units – it is possible to overtake a competitor in a remarkably few years.

The strategic implication is that a company should strive to dominate the market, either by introducing the product, by segmenting the market, or by discouraging competitors' growth in rapidly growing areas by preemptive pricing or value. Developing and introducing new products, though a good road to dominance, involve considerable cost and uncertainty. Similarly, it is difficult to identify a market segment that can be isolated from those segments in which competitors have more experience and lower costs. However, the history of business abounds with examples of successful segmentation. The key is to find a segment the company can protect over a long period of time. In contrast, the idea of preempting market by price or value concessions is intuitive in most business organizations. Although price competition is usually resisted, it is often cheaper than the more intangible weapon of added value.

The product portfolio

The products of a firm can be categorized into four groups in terms of market share and growth rate. Exhibit 1.11 depicts such a matrix.

	High Market Share	Low Market Share
High growth rate	category 2	category 3
Low growth rate	category 1	category 4

Exhibit 1.11 Product growth and market share

Category 1: Products with a high market share but with low growth. Products in category 1 – those whose growth is equivalent to the growth rate of the GNP – are *not* attractive areas for investment, but they are the main source of reported earnings and cash. They are usually products for which a dominant market share is held. Their good earnings are sometimes used inappropriately to justify continued investment in the hope that growth can be increased, whereas the proper objective is to maximize cash flow consistent with maintaining market share.

Category 2: Products with a high market share and rapid growth. Products in category 2 are those that, if dominant share can be maintained until growth slows, will become the high dollar earners of category 1. These products are heavy consumers of cash and earnings, and those for which leading market position must be maintained. To attempt to extract high earnings from these products during their growth phase will usually blight the growth and sacrifice the dominant position. If continued until growth slows, such 'bleeding' will move the product into category 4 instead of into category 1.

Category 3: Products with a low market share, but rapid growth. Category 3 includes products in which a dominant market share must be achieved before growth slows, or a marginal position will be 'frozen in.' These products demand a heavy commitment of financial and management resources. Since such resources are limited, the number of such products in the portfolio must be limited. If resources are not available to move a product in this category into a dominant market position, then it is usually wise to withdraw from the market.

Category 4: Products with low market shares and slow growth. The final category comprises the 'dogs' – products that consume far more than a just amount of management attention. They can never become satisfactorily profitable and should be liquidated in as clever and as graceful a manner as possible. Outright sale to a buyer with different perceptions can sometimes be accomplished. Often pricing in a manner to upset competitors is a useful adjunct to liquidation. In any event, investment in such areas should be discontinued.

It is useful to examine a corporation's products and try to classify them into the foregoing categories. Lack of balance becomes rapidly evident and plans can be laid to add and drop products to achieve a more nearly satisfactory portfolio. It must be remembered that we are talking of products, not industries, although some industries are sufficiently simple in product diversity that they behave as single products.

An unbalanced product portfolio produces some typical cash-flow symptoms. If the company has too many dominant, slow-growth products, it will usually have a low growth rate coupled with excess cash and inadequate investment opportunity. Having too many high-growth products will produce cash deficiencies as well as rapid growth. Too many low-share, low-growth products will result in inadequate cash *and* inadequate growth. With time, the balance of a product portfolio will automatically change if no deletions or additions are made.

Control implications

Market dominance by product is the key to profitability and it can be achieved by expenditures and investments during the rapid-growth phase for a given product. The source of the funds should be mature or slowly growing products in which dominance has already been achieved and in which expense and investment are no longer intense. It is important to avoid control procedures that stifle the rapid-growth phase; yet when growth slows, it is vital to secure maximum cash flow and avoid investment overshoot.

Budgeting and control systems should be quite different for the two categories, and different objectives should be set for the product managers. Clearly, the main objective in managing the rapidly growing product should be market penetration, whereas the goal for the dominant mature product should be to maximize cash flow. In both cases the total costs should be managed to follow the experience-curve slope appropriate to the industry. A control system that sets appropriately designed goals for market share, cash flow, and cost progress is more likely to produce continuing growth in reported earnings than a system that merely stresses product-line profitability.

To use the experience-curve effect in the control system and the management decision process, the company must have comprehensive data on costs and market share. If such data can be obtained, the company will have a powerful tool.

Needless to say, the successful implementation of a competitive strategy also depends upon the reaction of competitors. The route to a dominant share of a growing market lies in discouraging competitors from adding capacity or increasing their capability to produce the product. An estimate of the key competitors' decision processes is thus invaluable in planning competitive interaction.

Forecasting

The use of the experience curve to forecast prices – both for products and for purchases – is obvious. Again, one must use care to deflate the raw data and reinflate the forecast. Use of the GNP deflator has been most satisfactory and, in particular, better than the sector deflator.* (If the sector deflator is used, one is likely to erase evidence of the effect sought.) Obviously, the resulting forecast carries a forecast of inflation rate that is included in the deflator projections.

The forecast of price-break points is much more difficult than projecting an existing trend – even in the presence of strong inflation. If capacity in the industry seems high and if prices appear soft, it may be wise to initiate the break, since the leader in a severe price decline usually is the gainer in market share.

Conclusions

The fact that manufacturing costs tend to follow an experience curve not only is useful for cost control and forecasting but also has a profound

---

* The sector deflator is a correction factor to be applied to prices in a particular sector of the economy – for example, chemicals – to adjust for the inflation that has occurred in that particular economic sector.

implication for prices and profits. In particular, it is strongly suggested that the producer of a particular product who has made the most units should have the lowest costs and highest profits. The potential profitability of a mature product should be closely related to the market share it enjoys in its particular segment.

The products of a company can be grouped by market share and growth rate in order to prescribe appropriate management of products in each group. Substantially different management objectives should be pursued in each of the four categories described. The important strategic issues of product selection, price policy, investment criteria, and divestment decisions can be more effectively addressed in the context of the experience curve than in other ways – *even if no actual data are ever collected or actual curves plotted.*

References

1 Wright, T. P., 'Factors affecting the cost of airplanes,' *J. Aeron. Sci.*, vol. 3, pp. 122–128, Feb. 1936.
2 Billion, S. A., *Industrial Time Reduction Curves as Tools for Forecasting*. Ann Arbor, Mich.: University Microfilms, 1960.
3 Hirschmann, W. B., 'Profit from the learning curve,' *Harvard Business Rev.*, vol. 42, pp. 125–139. Jan.–Feb. 1964.
4 Perkins, J. H., and Enuendy, G., 'Use of the learning curve to forecast trends of chemical prices,' presented at the American Association of Cost Engineers 10th Annual Meeting, Philadelphia, Pa., June 20–22, 1966.
5 Cole, R. R., 'Increasing utilization of the cost-quantity relationship in manufacturing,' *J. Ind. Eng.*, pp. 173–177, May–June 1958.
6 Andress, F. J., 'The learning curve as a production tool,' *Harvard Business Rev.*, pp. 87–97, Jan.–Feb. 1954.
7 Cohen, J. E., *Model of Simple Competition*. Cambridge: Harvard University Press, 1966.
8 Council of Economic Advisers, 'Economic report to the President,' U.S. Government Printing Office, Washington D.C., 1969.

2

Competitive Strategy

Michael Porter

Competitive Strategy *was first published in 1980, when companies were facing a sharp decline in demand, high interest rates and higher inflation, while governments were committed to using deregulation to ensure that consumers had an ample choice of products and that only the fittest firms survived.*

The transformation of many industries in the past decade has been achieved, I believe, by a generation of managers, often aided and abetted by management consultants, brought up on, or at least heavily influenced by, Professor Porter's book. They did not tamely follow his methodology but became aware through it of the competitive forces that shape their industries. They were therefore equipped with a better understanding of ways to compete.

Creating value for shareholders by meeting the needs of customers can best be accomplished by being among the market leaders that have, or can obtain, a competitive position. A thorough appreciation of the competition shows that, although there may be many attractive markets, the key question is whether the business has, or can acquire, the power to compete effectively. The answer comes from an understanding of Michael Porter's 'five competitive forces'.

A colleague of mine, when carrying out a strategy review of his business, said that the business strategy was not only common sense but also common knowledge. I believe Competitive Strategy *adds substantially to the store of common knowledge and remains one of the most readable introductions to the subject.*

M. H. R. Thompson,
Deputy Chairman, Lloyds Bank Plc,
London

Chapter 1: The Structural Analysis of Industries

THE essence of formulating competitive strategy is relating a company to its environment. Although the relevant environment is very broad, encompassing social as well as economic forces, the key aspect of the firm's environment is the industry or industries in which it competes. Industry structure has a strong influence in determining the competitive rules of the game as well as the strategies potentially available to the firm. Forces outside the industry are significant primarily in a relative sense; since outside forces usually affect all firms in the industry, the key is found in the differing abilities of firms to deal with them.

The intensity of competition in an industry is neither a matter of coincidence nor bad luck. Rather, competition in an industry is rooted in its underlying economic structure and goes well beyond the behavior of current competitors. The state of competition in an industry depends on five basic competitive forces, which are shown in Figure 2.1. The collective strength of these forces determines the ultimate profit potential in the industry, where profit potential is measured in terms of long run return on invested capital. Not all industries have the same potential. They differ fundamentally in their ultimate profit potential as the collective strength of the forces differs; the forces range from intense in industries like tires, paper, and steel – where no firm earns spectacular returns – to relatively mild in industries like oil-field equipment and services, cosmetics, and toiletries – where high returns are quite common.

Reprinted with permission of The Free Press, a Division of Macmillan, Inc. from *Competitive Strategy: Techniques for Analyzing Industries and Competitors* by Michael Porter. Copyright © 1980 by The Free Press. [Published in New York and London; extract abridged.]

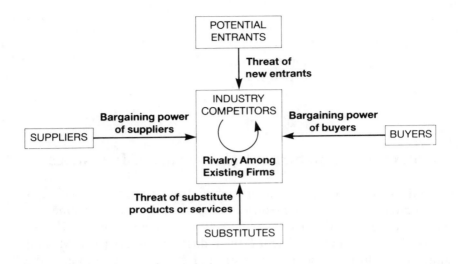

Figure 2.1 Forces driving industry competition

The goal of competitive strategy for a business unit in an industry is to find a position in the industry where the company can best defend itself against these competitive forces or can influence them in its favor. Since the collective strength of the forces may well be painfully apparent to all competitors, the key for developing strategy is to delve below the surface and analyze the sources of each.

The five competitive forces – threat of entry, threat of substitution, bargaining power of buyers, bargaining power of suppliers, and rivalry among current competitors – reflect the fact that competition in an industry goes well beyond the established players. Customers, suppliers, substitutes, and potential entrants are all 'competitors' to firms in the industry and may be more or less prominent depending on the particular circumstances. Competition in this broader sense might be termed *extended rivalry*.

All five competitive forces jointly determine the intensity of industry competition and profitability, and the strongest force or forces are governing and become crucial from the point of view of strategy formulation. For example, even a company with a very strong market position in an industry where potential entrants are no threat will earn low returns if it faces a superior, lower-cost substitute. Even with no substitutes and blocked entry, intense rivalry among existing competitors will limit potential returns. The extreme case of competitive intensity is the economist's perfectly competitive industry, where entry is free, existing firms have no bargaining power against suppliers and customers, and rivalry is unbridled because the numerous firms and products are all alike.

Different forces take on prominence, of course, in shaping competition in each industry. In the ocean-going tanker industry the key force is probably the buyers (the major oil companies), whereas in tires it is powerful original equipment (OEM) buyers coupled with tough competitors. In the steel industry the key forces are foreign competitors and substitute materials.

A number of important economic and technical characteristics of an industry are critical to the strength of each competitive force. These will be discussed in turn.

Threat of entry

New entrants to an industry bring new capacity, the desire to gain market share, and often substantial resources. Prices can be bid down or incumbents' costs inflated as a result, reducing profitability. Companies diversifying through acquisition into the industry from other markets often use their resources to cause a shake-up, as Philip Morris did with Miller beer. Thus acquisition into an industry with intent to build market position should probably be viewed as entry even though no entirely new entity is created.

The threat of entry into an industry depends on the *barriers to entry* that are present, coupled with the *reaction* from existing competitors that the entrant can expect. If barriers are high and/or the newcomer can expect sharp retaliation from entrenched competitors, the threat of entry is low.

Barriers to entry

There are seven major sources of barriers to entry:

Economies of scale. Economies of scale refer to declines in unit costs of a product (or operation or function that goes into producing a product) as the absolute volume *per period* increases. Economies of scale deter entry by forcing the entrant to come in at large scale and risk strong reaction from existing firms or come in at a small scale and accept a cost disadvantage, both undesirable options. Scale economies can be present in nearly every function of a business, including manufacturing, purchasing, research and development, marketing, service network, sales force utilization, and distribution. For example, scale economies in production, research, marketing, and service are probably the key barriers to entry in the mainframe computer industry, as Xerox and General Electric sadly discovered.

Scale economies may relate to an entire functional area, as in the case of a sales force, or they may stem from particular operations or activities that are part of a functional area. For example, in the manufacture of television sets, economies of scale are larger in color tube production, and they are less significant in cabinetmaking and set assembly. It is important to examine each component of costs separately for its particular relationship between unit costs and scale.

Units of multibusiness firms may be able to reap economies similar to those of scale if they are able to *share operations or functions* subject to economies of scale with other businesses in the company. For example, the multibusiness company may manufacture small electric motors, which are then used in producing industrial fans, hairdryers, and cooling systems for electronic equipment. If economies of scale in motor manufacturing extend beyond the number of motors needed in any one market, the multibusiness firm diversified in this way will reap economies in motor manufacturing that exceed those available if it only manufactured motors for use in, say, hairdryers. Thus related diversification around common operations or functions can remove volume constraints imposed by the size of a given industry.[1] The prospective entrant is forced to be diversified or face a cost disadvantage. Potentially shareable activities or functions subject to economies of scale can include sales forces, distribution systems, purchasing, and so on.

The benefits of sharing are particularly potent if there are *joint costs*. Joint costs occur when a firm producing product *A* (or an operation or function that is part of producing *A*) must inherently have the capacity to produce product *B*. An example is air passenger services and air cargo, where because of technological constraints only so much space in the aircraft can be filled with passengers, leaving available cargo space and payload capacity. Many of the costs must be borne to put the plane into the air and there is capacity for freight regardless of the quantity of passengers the plane is carrying. Thus the firm that competes in both passenger and freight may have a substantial advantage over the firm competing in only one market. This same sort of effect occurs in businesses that involve manufacturing processes involving by-products. The entrant who cannot capture the highest available incremental revenue from the by-products can face a disadvantage if incumbent firms do.

A common situation of joint costs occurs when business units can share *intangible* assets such as brand names and know-how. The cost of creating an intangible asset need only be borne once; the asset may then be freely applied to other business, subject only to any costs of adapting or modifying it. Thus situations in which intangible assets are shared can lead to substantial economies.

A type of economies of scale entry barrier occurs when there are economies to vertical integration, that is, operating in successive stages of production or distribution. Here the entrant must enter integrated or face a cost disadvantage, as well as possible foreclosure of inputs or markets for its product *if* most established competitors are integrated. Foreclosure in such situations stems from the fact that most customers purchase from in-house units, or most suppliers 'sell' their inputs in-house. The independent firm faces a difficult time in getting comparable prices and may become 'squeezed' if integrated competitors offer different terms to it than to their captive units. The requirement to enter integrated may heighten the risks of retaliation and also elevate other entry barriers discussed below.

Product Differentiation. Product differentiation means that established firms have brand identification and customer loyalties, which stem from past advertising, customer service, product differences, or simply being first into the industry. Differentiation creates a barrier to entry by forcing entrants to spend heavily to overcome existing customer loyalties. This effort usually involves start-up losses and often takes an extended period of time. Such investments in building a brand name are particularly risky since they have no salvage value if entry fails.

Product differentiation is perhaps the most important entry barrier in baby care products, over-the-counter drugs, cosmetics, investment banking, and public accounting. In the brewing industry, product differentiation is coupled with economies of scale in production, marketing, and distribution to create high barriers.

Capital Requirements. The need to invest large financial resources in order to compete creates a barrier to entry, particularly if the capital is required for risky or unrecoverable up-front advertising or research and development (R&D). Capital may be necessary not only for production facilities but also for things like customer credit, inventories, or covering start-up losses. Xerox created a major capital barrier to entry in copiers, for example, when it chose to rent copiers rather than sell them outright which greatly increased the need for working capital. Whereas today's major corporations have the financial resources to enter almost any industry, the huge capital requirements in fields like computers and mineral extraction limit the pool of likely entrants. Even if capital is available on the capital markets, entry represents a risky use of that capital which should be reflected in risk premiums charged the prospective entrant; these constitute advantages for going firms.[2]

Switching Costs. A barrier to entry is created by the presence of *switching costs*, that is, one-time costs facing the buyer of switching from one supplier's product to another's. Switching costs may include employee retraining costs, cost of new ancillary equipment, cost and time in testing or qualifying a new source, need for technical help as a result of reliance on seller engineering aid, product redesign, or even psychic costs of severing a relationship.[3] If these switching costs are high, then new entrants must offer a major improvement in cost or performance in order for the buyer to switch from an incumbent. For example, in intravenous (IV) solutions and kits for use in hospitals, procedures for attaching solutions to patients differ among competitive products and the hardware for hanging the IV bottles are not compatible. Here switching encounters great resistance from nurses responsible for administering the treatment and requires new investments in hardware.

Access to Distribution Channels. A barrier to entry can be created by the new entrant's need to secure distribution for its product. To the extent that logical distribution channels for the product have already been served by established firms, the new firm must persuade the channels to accept its product through price breaks, cooperative advertising allowances, and the like, which reduce profits. The manufacturer of a new food product, for example, must persuade the retailer to give it space on the fiercely competitive supermarket shelf via promises of promotions, intense selling efforts to the retailer, or some other means.

The more limited the wholesale or retail channels for a product are and the more existing competitors have these tied up, obviously the tougher entry into the industry will be. Existing competitors may have ties with channels based on long relationships, high-quality service, or even exclusive relationships in which the channel is solely identified with a particular manufacturer. Sometimes this barrier to entry is so high that to surmount it a new firm must create an entirely new distribution channel, as Timex did in the watch industry.

Cost Disadvantages Independent of Scale. Established firms may have cost advantages not replicable by potential entrants no matter what their size and attained economies of scale. The most critical advantages are factors such as the following:

- Proprietary product technology: product know-how or design characteristics that are kept proprietary through patents or secrecy.
- Favorable access to raw materials: established firms may have locked up the most favorable sources and/or tied up foreseeable needs early at prices reflecting a lower demand for them than currently exists. For example, Frasch sulphur firms like Texas Gulf Sulphur gained control of some very favorable large salt dome sulphur deposits many years ago, before mineral rightholders were aware of their value as a result of the Frasch mining technology. Discoverers of sulphur deposits were often disappointed oil companies who were exploring for oil and not prone to value them highly.
- Favorable locations: established firms may have cornered favorable locations before market forces bid up prices to capture their full value.
- Government subsidies: preferential government subsidies may give established firms lasting advantages in some businesses.
- Learning or experience curve: in some businesses, there is an observed tendency for unit costs to decline as the firm gains more cumulative experience in producing a product. Costs decline because workers improve their methods and become more efficient (the classic learning curve), layout improves, specialized equipment and processes are developed, better performance is coaxed from equipment, product design changes make manufacturing easier, techniques for measurement arnd control of operations improve, and so on. Experience is just a name for certain kinds of technological change and may apply not only to production but also to

distribution, logistics, and other functions. As is the case with scale economies, cost declines with experience relate not to the entire firm but arise from the individual operations or functions that make up the firm. Experience can lower costs in marketing, distribution, and other areas as well as in production or operations within production, and each component of costs must be examined for the effects of experience.

Cost declines with experience seem to be the most significant in businesses involving a high labor content performing intricate tasks and/ or complex assembly operations (aircraft manufacture, shipbuilding.) They are nearly always the most significant in the early and growth phase of a product's development, and later reach diminishing proportional improvements. Often economies of scale are cited among the reasons that costs decline with experience. Economies of scale are dependent on volume per period, and *not* on cumulative volume, and are very different analytically from experience, although the two often occur together and can be hard to separate.

If costs decline with experience in an industry, and *if the experience can be kept proprietary by established firms*, then this effect leads to an entry barrier. Newly started firms, with no experience, will have inherently higher costs than established firms and must bear heavy start-up losses from below- or near-cost pricing in order to gain the experience to achieve cost parity with established firms (if they ever can). Established firms, particularly the market share leader who is accumulating experience the fastest, will have higher cash flow because of their lower costs to invest in new equipment and techniques. However, it is important to recognize that pursuing experience curve cost declines (and scale economies) may require substantial up-front capital investment for equipment and startup losses. If costs continue to decline with volume even as cumulative volume gets very large, new entrants may never catch up. A number of firms, notably Texas Instruments, Black and Decker, Emerson Electric, and others have built successful strategies based on the experience curve through aggressive investments to build cumulative volume early in the development of industries, often by pricing in anticipation of future cost declines.

The decline in cost from experience can be augmented if there are diversified firms in the industry who *share* operations or functions subject to such a decline with other units in the company, or where there are related activities in the company from which incomplete though useful experience can be obtained. When an activity like the fabrication of raw material is shared by several business units, experience obviously accumulates faster than it would if the activity were used solely to meet the needs in one industry. Or when the corporate entity has related activities within the firm, sister units can receive the benefits of their experience at little or no cost since much experience is an intangible asset. This sort of shared learning accentuates the entry barrier provided by the experience curve, provided the other conditions for its significance are met.

Government Policy. The last major source of entry barriers is government policy. Government can limit or even foreclose entry into industries with such controls as licensing requirements and limits on access to raw materials (like coal lands or mountains on which to build ski areas). Regulated industries like trucking, railroads, liquor retailing, and freight forwarding are obvious examples. Most subtle government restrictions on entry can stem from controls such as air and water pollution standards and product safety and efficacy regulations. For example, pollution control requirements can increase the capital needed for entry and the required technological sophistication and even the optimal scale of facilities. Standards for product testing, common in industries like food and other health-related products, can impose substantial lead times, which not only raise the capital cost of entry but also give established firms ample notice of impending entry and sometimes full knowledge of the new competitor's product with which to formulate retaliatory strategies. Government policy in such areas certainly has direct social benefits, but it often has secondary consequences for entry which are unrecognized.

Expected retaliation

The potential entrant's expectations about the reaction of existing competitors also will influence the threat of entry. If existing competitors are expected to respond forcefully to make the entrant's stay in the industry an unpleasant one, then entry may well be deterred. Conditions that signal the strong likelihood of retaliation to entry and hence deter it are the following:

- a history of vigorous retaliation to entrants;
- established firms with substantial resources to fight back, including excess cash and unused borrowing capacity, adequate excess productive capacity to meet all likely future needs, or great leverage with distribution channels or customers;

- established firms with great commitment to the industry and highly illiquid assets employed in it;
- slow industry growth, which limits the ability of the industry to absorb a new firm without depressing the sales and financial performance of established firms.

Intensity of rivalry among existing competitors

Rivalry among existing competitors takes the familiar form of jockeying for position – using tactics like price competition, advertising battles, product introductions, and increased customer service or warranties. Rivalry occurs because one or more competitors either feels the pressure or sees the opportunity to improve position. In most industries, competitive moves by one firm have noticeable effects on its competitors and thus may incite retaliation or efforts to counter the move; that is, firms are *mutually dependent*. This pattern of action and reaction may or may not leave the initiating firm and the industry as a whole better off. If moves and countermoves escalate, then all firms in the industry may suffer and be worse off than before.

Some forms of competition, notably price competition, are highly unstable and quite likely to leave the entire industry worse off from the standpoint of profitability. Price cuts are quickly and easily matched by rivals, and once matched they lower revenues for all firms unless industry price elasticity of demand is high enough. Advertising battles, on the other hand, may well expand demand or enhance the level of product differentiation in the industry for the benefit of all firms.

Rivalry in some industries is characterized by such phrases as 'warlike', 'bitter', or 'cutthroat', whereas in other industries it is termed 'polite' or 'gentlemanly.' Intense rivalry is the result of a number of interacting structural factors.

Numerous or Equally Balanced Competitors. When firms are numerous, the likelihood of mavericks is great and some firms may habitually believe they can make moves without being noticed. Even where there are relatively few firms, if they are relatively balanced in terms of size and perceived resources, it creates instability because they may be prone to fight each other and have the resources for sustained and vigorous retaliation. When the industry is highly concentrated or dominated by one or a few firms, on the other hand, then there is little mistaking relative strength, and the leader or leaders can impose discipline as well as play a coordinative role in the industry through devices like price leadership.

In many industries foreign competitors, either exporting into the industry or participating directly through foreign investment, play an important role in industry competition. Foreign competitors, although having some differences that will be noted later, should be treated just like national competitors for purposes of structural analysis.

Slow Industry Growth. Slow industry growth turns competition into a market share game for firms seeking expansion. Market share competition is a great deal more volatile than is the situation in which rapid industry growth insures that firms can improve results just by keeping up with the industry, and where all their financial and managerial resources may be consumed by expanding with the industry.

High Fixed or Storage Costs. High fixed costs create strong pressures for all firms to fill capacity which often lead to rapidly escalating price cutting when excess capacity is present. Many basic materials like paper and aluminum suffer from this problem, for example. The significant characteristic of costs is fixed costs relative to value added, and not fixed costs as a proportion of total costs. Firms purchasing a high proportion of costs in outside inputs (low value added) may feel enormous pressures to fill capacity to break even, despite the fact that the absolute proportion of fixed costs is low.

A situation related to high fixed costs is one in which the product, once produced, is very difficult or costly to store. Here firms will also be vulnerable to temptations to shade prices in order to insure sales. This sort of pressure keeps profits low in industries like lobster fishing and the manufacture of certain hazardous chemicals and some service businesses.

Lack of Differentiation or Switching Costs. Where the product or service is perceived as a commodity or near commodity, choice by the buyer is largely based on price and service, and pressures for intense price and service competition result. These forms of competition are particularly volatile, as has been discussed. Product differentiation, on the other hand, creates layers of insulation against competitive warfare because buyers have preferences and loyalties to particular sellers. Switching costs, described earlier, have the same effect.

Capacity Augmented in Large Increments. Where economies of scale dictate that capacity must be added in large increments, capacity additions can be chronically disruptive to the industry supply/demand balance, particularly where there is a risk of bunching capacity additions. The industry may face recurring periods of over-capacity and price cutting, like those that afflict the manufacture of chlorine, vinyl chloride, and ammonium fertilizer.

Diverse Competitors. Competitors diverse in strategies, origins, personalities, and relationships to their parent companies have differing goals and differing strategies for how to compete and may continually run head on into each other in the process. They may have a hard time reading each other's intentions accurately and agreeing on a set of 'rules of the game' for the industry. Strategic choices right for one competitor will be wrong for others.

Foreign competitors often add a great deal of diversity to industries because of their differing circumstances and often differing goals. Owner-operators of small manufacturing or service firms may as well, because they may be satisfied with a subnormal rate of return on their invested capital to maintain the independence of self-ownership, whereas such returns are unacceptable and may appear irrational to a large publicly held competitor. In such an industry, the posture of the small firms may limit the profitability of the large concern. Similarly, firms viewing a market as an outlet for excess capacity (e.g., in the case of dumping) will adopt policies contrary to those of firms viewing the market as a primary one. Finally, differences in the relationship of competing business units to their corporate parents are an important source of diversity in an industry as well. For example, a business unit that is part of a vertical chain of businesses in its corporate organization may well adopt different and perhaps contradictory goals than a free-standing firm competing in the same industry. Or a business unit that is a 'cash cow' in its parent company's portfolio of businesses will behave differently than one that is being developed for long-run growth in view of a lack of other opportunities in the parent.

High Strategic Stakes. Rivalry in an industry becomes even more volatile if a number of firms have high stakes in achieving success there. For example, a diversified firm may place great importance on achieving success in a particular industry in order to further its overall corporate strategy. Or a foreign firm like Bosch, Sony, or Philips may perceive a strong need to establish a solid position in the U.S. market in order to build global prestige or technological credibility. In such situations, the goals of these firms may not only be diverse but even more destabilizing because they are expansionary and involve potential willingness to sacrifice profitability.

High Exit Barriers. Exit barriers are economic, strategic, and emotional factors that keep companies competing in businesses even though they may be earning low or even negative returns on investment. The major sources of exit barriers are the following:

- Specialized assets: assets highly specialized to the particular business or location have low liquidation values or high costs of transfer or conversion.
- Fixed costs of exit: these include labor agreements, resettlement costs, maintaining capabilities for spare parts, and so on.
- Strategic interrelationships: interrelationships between the business unit and others in the company in terms of image, marketing ability, access to financial markets, shared facilities, and so on. They cause the firm to attach high strategic importance to being in the business.
- Emotional barriers: management's unwillingness to make economically justified exit decisions is caused by identification with the particular business, loyalty to employees, fear for one's own career, pride, and other reasons.
- Government and social restrictions: these involve government denial or discouragement of exit out of concern for job loss and regional economic effects; they are particularly common outside the United States.

When exit barriers are high, excess capacity does not leave the industry, and companies that lose the competitive battle do not give up. Rather, they grimly hang on and, because of their weakness, have to resort to extreme tactics. The profitability of the entire industry can be persistently low as a result.

Pressure from substitute products

All firms in an industry are competing, in a broad sense, with industries producing substitute products. Substitutes limit the potential returns of an industry by placing a ceiling on the prices firms in the industry can profitably charge.[4] The more attractive the price-performance alternative offered by substitutes, the firmer the lid on industry profits.

Sugar producers confronted with the large-scale commercialization of high fructose corn syrup, a sugar substitute, are learning this lesson today, as have the producers of acetylene and rayon who faced extreme competition from alternative, lower-cost materials for many of their respective applications. Substitutes not only limit profits in normal times, but they also reduce the bonanza an industry can reap in boom times. In 1978 the producers of fiberglass insulation enjoyed unprecedented demand as a result of high energy costs and severe winter weather. But the industry's ability to raise prices was tempered by the plethora of insulation substitutes, including cellulose, rock wool, and styrofoam. These substitutes are bound to become an ever stronger limit on profitability once the current round of plant additions has boosted capacity enough to meet demand (and then some).

Identifying substitute products is a matter of searching for other products that can perform the same *function* as the product of the industry. Sometimes doing so can be a subtle task, and one which leads the analyst into businesses seemingly far removed from the industry. Securities brokers, for example, are being increasingly confronted with such substitutes as real estate, insurance, money market funds, and other ways for the individual to invest capital, accentuated in importance by the poor performance of the equity markets.

Position vis-à-vis substitute products may well be a matter of *collective* industry actions. For example, although advertising by one firm may not be enough to bolster the industry's position against a substitute, heavy and sustained advertising by all industry participants may well improve the industry's collective position. Similar arguments apply to collective response in areas like product quality improvement, marketing efforts, providing greater product availability, and so on.

Substitute products that deserve the most attention are those that (1) are subject to trends improving their price-performance tradeoff with the industry's product, or (2) are produced by industries earning high profits. In the latter case, substitutes often come rapidly into play if some development increases competition in their industries and causes price reduction or performance improvement. Analysis of such trends can be important in deciding whether to try to head off a substitute strategically or to plan strategy with it as inevitably a key force. In the security guard industry, for example, electronic alarm systems represent a potent substitute. Moreover, they can only become more important since labor-intensive guard services face inevitable cost escalation, whereas electronic systems are highly likely to improve in performance and decline in costs. Here, the appropriate response of security guard firms is probably to offer packages of guards and electronic systems, based on a redefinition of the security guard as a skilled operator, rather than to try to outcompete electronic systems across the board.

Bargaining power of buyers

Buyers compete with the industry by forcing down prices, bargaining for higher quality or more services, and playing competitors against each other – all at the expense of industry profitability. The power of each of the industry's important buyer groups depends on a number of characteristics of its market situation and on the relative importance of its purchases from the industry compared with its overall business. A buyer group is powerful if the following circumstances hold true:

It is concentrated or purchases large volumes relative to seller sales. If a large proportion of sales is purchased by a given buyer this raises the importance of the buyer's business in results. Large-volume buyers are particularly potent forces if heavy fixed costs characterize the industry – as they do in corn refining and bulk chemicals, for example – and raise the stakes to keep capacity filled.

The products it purchases from the industry represent a significant fraction of the buyer's costs or purchases. Here buyers are prone to expend the resources necessary to shop for a favorable price and purchase selectively. When the product sold by the industry in question is a small fraction of buyers' costs, buyers are usually much less price sensitive.

The products it purchases from the industry are standards or undifferentiated. Buyers, sure that they can always find alternative suppliers, may play one company against another, as they do in aluminum extrusion.

It faces few switching costs. Switching costs, defined earlier, lock the buyer to particular sellers. Conversely, the buyer's power is enhanced if the seller faces switching costs.

It earns low profits. Low profits create great incentives to lower purchasing costs. Suppliers to Chrysler, for example, are complaining that they are being pressured for superior terms. Highly profitable buyers, however, are generally less price sensitive (that is, of course, if the item does not represent a large fraction of their costs) and may take a longer run view toward preserving the health of their suppliers.

Buyers pose a credible threat of backward integration. If buyers either are partially integrated or pose a credible threat of backward integration, they are in a position to demand bargaining concessions.[5] The major automobile producers, General Motors and Ford, are well known for using the threat of self-manufacture as a bargaining lever. They engage in the practice of *tapered integration*, that is, producing some of their needs for a given component in-house and purchasing the rest from outside suppliers. Not only is their threat of further integration particularly credible, but also partial manufacture in-house gives them a detailed knowledge of costs which is a great aid in negotiation. Buyer power can be partially neutralized when firms in the industry offer a threat of forward integration into the buyers' industry.

The industry's product is unimportant to the quality of the buyers' products or services. When the quality of the buyers' products is very much affected by the industry's product, buyers are generally less price sensitive. Industries in which this situation exists include oil-field equipment, where a malfunction can lead to large losses (witness the enormous cost of the recent failure of a blowout preventor in a Mexican offshore oil well), and enclosures for electronic medical and test instruments, where the quality of the enclosure can greatly influence the user's impression about the quality of the equipment inside.

The buyer has full information. Where the buyer has full information about demand, actual market prices, and even supplier costs, this usually yields the buyer greater bargaining leverage than when information is poor. With full information, the buyer is in a greater position to insure that it receives the most favourable prices offered to others and can counter suppliers' claims that their viability is threatened.

Most of these sources of buyer power can be attributed to consumers as well as to industrial and commercial buyers; only a modification of the frame of reference is necessary. For example, consumers tend to be more price sensitive if they are purchasing products that are undifferentiated, expensive relative to their incomes, or of a sort where quality is not particularly important to them.

The buyer of wholesalers and retailers is determined by the same rules, with one important addition. Retailers can gain significant bargaining power over manufacturers when they can *influence consumers' purchasing decisions*, as they do in audio components, jewelry, appliances, sporting goods, and other products. Wholesalers can gain bargaining power, similarly, if they can influence the purchase decisions of the retailers or other firms to which they sell.

Altering buyer power

As the factors described above change with time or as a result of a company's strategic decisions, naturally the power of buyers rises or falls. In the ready-to-wear clothing industry, for example, as the buyers (department stores and clothing stores) have become more concentrated and control has passed to large chains, the industry has come under increasing pressure and has suffered falling margins. The industry has been unable to differentiate its product or engender switching costs that lock in its buyers enough to neutralize these trends, and the influx of imports has not helped.

A company's choice of buyer groups to sell to should be viewed as a crucial strategic decision. A company can improve its strategic posture by finding buyers who possess the least power to influence it adversely – in other words, *buyer selection.* Rarely do all the buyer groups a company sells to enjoy equal power. Even if a company sells to a single industry, segments usually exist within that industry which exercise less power (and that are therefore less price sensitive) than others. For example, the replacement market for most products is less price sensitive than the OEM market.

Bargaining power of suppliers

Suppliers can exert bargaining power over participants in an industry by threatening to raise prices or reduce the quality of purchased goods and services. Powerful suppliers can thereby squeeze profitability out of an industry unable to recover cost increases in its own prices. By raising their prices, for example, chemical companies have contributed to the erosion of profitability of contract aerosol packagers because the packagers, facing intense competition from self-manufacture by their buyers, accordingly have limited freedom to raise their prices.

The conditions making suppliers powerful tend to mirror those making buyers powerful. A supplier group is powerful if the following apply:

It is dominated by a few companies and is more concentrated than the industry it sells to. Suppliers selling to more fragmented buyers will usually be able to exert considerable influence in prices, quality, and terms.

It is not obliged to contend with other substitute products for sale to the industry. The power of even large, powerful suppliers can be checked if they compete with substitutes. For example, suppliers producing alternative sweeteners compete sharply for many applications even though individual firms are large relative to individual buyers.

The industry is not an important customer of the supplier group. When suppliers sell to a number of industries and a particular industry does not represent a significant fraction of sales, suppliers are much more prone to exert power. If the industry is an important customer, suppliers' fortunes will be closely tied to the industry and they will want to protect it through reasonable pricing and assistance in activities like R&D and lobbying.

The suppliers' product is an important input to the buyer's business. Such an input is important to the success of the buyer's manufacturing process or product quality. This raises the supplier power. This is particularly true where the input is not storable, thus enabling the buyer to build up stocks of inventory.

The supplier group's products are differentiated or it has built up switching costs. Differentiation or switching costs facing the buyers cut off their options to play one supplier against another. If the supplier faces switching costs the effect is the reverse.

The supplier group poses a credible threat of forward integration. This provides a check against the industry's ability to improve the terms on which it purchases.

We usually think of suppliers as other firms, but *labor* must be recognized as a supplier as well, and one that exerts great power in many industries. There is substantial empirical evidence that scarce, highly skilled employees and/or tightly unionized labor can bargain away a significant fraction of potential profits in an industry. The principles in determining the potential power of labor as a supplier are similar to those just discussed. The key additions in assessing the power of labor are its *degree of organization*, and whether the supply of scarce varieties of labor can *expand*. Where the labor force is tightly organized or the supply of scarce labor is constrained from growing, the power of labor can be high.

The conditions determining suppliers' power are not only subject to change but also often out of the firm's control. However, as with buyers' power the firm can sometimes improve its situation through strategy. It can enhance its threat of backward integration, seek to eliminate switching costs, and the like.

Structural analysis and competitive strategy

Once the forces affecting competition in an industry and their underlying causes have been diagnosed, the firm is in a position to identify its strengths and weaknesses relative to the industry. From a strategic standpoint, the crucial strengths and weaknesses are the firm's posture vis-à-vis the underlying causes of each competitive force. Where does the firm stand against substitutes? Against the sources of entry barriers? In coping with rivalry from established competitors?

An effective competitive strategy takes offensive or defensive action in order to create a *defendable* position against the five competitive forces. Broadly, this involves a number of possible approaches:

- positioning the firm so that its capabilities provide the best defense against the existing array of competitive forces;
- influencing the balance of forces through strategic moves, thereby improving the firm's relative position; or
- anticipating shifts in the factors underlying the forces and responding to them, thereby exploiting change by choosing a strategy appropriate to the new competitive balance before rivals recognize it.

Positioning

The first approach takes the structure of the industry as given and matches the company's strengths and weaknesses to it. Strategy can be viewed as building defenses against the competitive forces or as finding positions in the industry where the forces are weakest.

Knowledge of the company's capabilities and of the causes of the competitive forces will highlight the areas where the company should confront competition and where avoid it. If the company is a low-cost producer, for example, it may choose to sell to powerful buyers while it takes care to sell them only products not vulnerable to competition from substitutes.

Influencing the balance

A company can devise a strategy that takes the offensive. This posture is designed to do more than merely cope with the forces themselves; it is meant to alter their causes.

Innovations in marketing can raise brand identification or otherwise differentiate the product. Capital investments in large-scale facilities or vertical integration affect entry barriers. The balance of forces is partly a result of external factors and partly within a company's control. Structural analysis can be used to identify the key factors driving competition in the particular industry and thus the places where strategic action to influence the balance will yield the greatest payoff.

Exploiting change

Industry evolution is important strategically because evolution, of course, brings with it changes in the structural sources of competition. In the familiar product life-cycle pattern of industry development, for example, growth rates change, advertising is said to decline as the business becomes more mature, and the companies tend to integrate vertically.

These trends are not so important in themselves; what is critical is whether they affect the structural sources of competition. Consider vertical integration. In the maturing minicomputer industry, extensive integration is taking place, both in manufacturing and in software development. This very significant trend is greatly raising economies of scale as well as the amount of capital necessary to compete in the industry. This in turn is raising barriers to entry and may drive some smaller competitors out of the industry once growth levels off.

Obviously, the trends holding the highest priority from a strategic standpoint are those that affect the most important sources of competition in the industry and those that bring new structural factors to the forefront. In contract aerosol packaging, for example, the trend toward less product differentiation is now dominant. This trend has increased buyers' powers, lowered the barriers to entry, and intensified rivalry.

Structural analysis can be used to predict the eventual profitability of an industry. In long-range planning the task is to examine each competitive force, forecast the magnitude of each underlying cause, and then construct a composite picture of the probable profit potential of the industry.

The outcome of such an exercise may differ a great deal from the existing industry structure. Today, for example, the solar heating business is populated by dozens and perhaps hundreds of companies, none with a major market position. Entry is easy, and competitors are battling to establish solar heating as a superior substitute for conventional heating methods.

The potential of solar heating will depend largely on the shape of the future barriers to entry, the improvement of the industry's position relative to substitutes, the ultimate intensity of competition, and the power captured by buyers and suppliers. These characteristics will, in turn, be influenced by such factors as the likelihood of establishment of brand identities, whether significant economies of scale or experience curves in equipment manufacture will be created by technological change, what will be the ultimate capital costs to enter, and the eventual extent of fixed costs in production facilities.

A large number of factors can potentially have an impact on industry competition. Not all of them will be important in any one industry. Rather the framework can be used to identify rapidly what are the crucial structural features determining the nature of competition in a particular industry. This is where the bulk of the analytical and strategic attention should be focused.

Notes

1 For this entry barrier to be significant it is crucial that the shared operation or function be subject to economies of scale which extend beyond the size of any one market. If this is not the case, cost savings of sharing can be illusory. A company may see its costs decline as overhead is spread, but this depends solely on the presence of *excess capacity* in the operation or function. These economies are short-run economies, and once capacity is fully utilized and expanded the true cost of the shared operation will become apparent.
2 In some industries suppliers are willing to help finance entry in order to increase their own sales (oil tankers, logging equipment). This obviously lowers effective capital barriers to entry.
3 Switching costs may also be present for the seller.
4 The impact of substitutes can be summarized as the industry's overall elasticity of demand.
5 If buyers' motivations to integrate are based more on safety of supply or other non-price factors this may imply that firms in the industry must offer great price concessions to forestall integration.

3

Strategy and Structure

ALFRED D. CHANDLER, JR

A lfred Chandler's Strategy and Structure *examines the evolving strategies of a group of large American industrial enterprises, and their efforts to adapt their organizational structures to pursue these strategies more effectively. Chandler concludes that, while these enterprises employed a functional structure early on to minimize costs, their expanding geographic and product scope eventually demanded a transition to a multidivisional structure characterized by a greater degree of operating decentralization. He also documents, in rich detail, the process whereby these transitions actually occurred.*

Strategy and Structure *has been justly acclaimed by academics for its conceptual and historical originality. I suggested including an excerpt in this anthology because, as I understand it, much of what McKinsey has done (especially in its early years) has been to help large enterprises to reorganize from functional to multidivisional structures. Read in that light, the excerpt should attest to the power of simple, yet deep, ideas – in this case, that structure follows strategy – to transform not only how academics think about the real world, but also how practitioners operate within it.*

Pankaj Ghemawat,
Associate Professor, Harvard Business School,
Boston, Massachusetts

Conclusion – Chapters in the History of the Great Industrial Enterprise

FOUR phases or chapters can be discerned in the history of the large American industrial enterprise: the initial expansion and accumulation of resources; the rationalization of the use of resources; the expansion into new markets and lines to help assure the continuing full use of resources; and finally the development of a new structure to make possible continuing effective mobilization of resources to meet both changing short-term market demands and long-term market trends. Although each company had a distinct and unique history, nearly all followed along this general pattern. Because all of them operated within the same external environment, these chapters in the collective history of the industrial enterprise or the history of the enterprise considered as an economic institution followed roughly the underlying changes in the over-all American economy. Of course, the timing of the chapters for the individual companies varied. In the newer industries based on the internal-combustion and electrical engine and on modern chemistry and physics, they came somewhat later than in the older metals or tobacco, sugar, meat packing, and others that processed agricultural products.

The first chapter – accumulating resources

The large American industrial enterprise was born and nurtured in the rapidly industrializing and urbanizing economy of the post-Civil War years. The great railroad construction boom of those years helped swell the population of the agrarian West. It stimulated even more the swift growth of the older commercial centers that serviced the agrarian economy and of the new industrial cities rising to meet the expanding demand for manufactured goods. The railroad itself created a huge new market for the basic iron and steel and machinery industries. The needs of the railroad for vast sums of capital led to the growth of the modern money market in the United States and with it the modern investment banking house, which made it relatively easy later for industrials to tap a wide pool of European and American capital. The construction of the railroads and the rapid urban growth gave work to the unskilled immigrants and farm boys who poured into the larger cities after 1850. The new working force not only provided a supply of labor for the growing industrial enterprises, but also increased the demand for their products. By the 1880s nearly every existing manufacturing enterprise could reach by railroad a large rural and even more swiftly growing industrial and urban market.

To meet these opportunities, industrial enterprises began to enlarge their productive facilities, labor force, and trained supervisory personnel. Often the new resources were self-generated. The firm's profits provided the funds for further expansion, while the skills of its personnel were developed as the latter carried out their daily tasks. If the enterprise needed outside funds for expansion and combination, it went to the Eastern financial centers. In the 1890s, as railroad expansion leveled off, investment houses that had grown and made their initial reputation in the marketing and handling of railroad securities – firms like J. P. Morgan & Co.; A. M. Kidder & Company; Lee, Higginson & Company; Kuhn, Loeb; Brown Brothers & Company – all began to float and trade in industrial securities. Also as railroad construction declined, the laborers from abroad and from rural America found work in the enlarged steel mills, oil refineries, meat-packing, electrical, farm machinery, and implement plants.

In meeting the new demand, industrialists had more difficulty in obtaining a distribution network than expanding production facilities. The makers of new types of goods, which were often based on technological innovations, created their own distributing and marketing organizations with warehouses, transportation equipment, offices, and even retail outlets. The makers of the older, more staple commodities, however, generally waited until they had combined and consolidated with their fellows before creating marketing organizations. Combination normally proved to be only a temporary expedient, simply because it led to, and indeed demanded, a limited use of the firm's available resources.

Consolidation, on the other hand, permitted the lowering of unit costs through high-volume production for the large market. Even so, the need to keep the consolidated production activities working steadily called for closer coordination with the customer demand through the creation of a marketing organization. Conversely, only firms of large capacity could afford to buy or build and to maintain nationwide marketing facilities.

Consolidation, and with it the formation of a marketing department, was usually followed or accompanied by forming purchasing departments and often by obtaining control of raw materials. Beside making possible the economies of large-scale purchasing, the new department made it easier to coordinate supplies with the needs of the mills for materials. Where there was a possibility of a few outsiders or even of competitors obtaining control of a company's basic raw and semifinished materials, the enterprise often moved into the production and transportation of those materials. The main reason for the purchasing of parts and accessories firms was often to assure the close and steady flow of these parts to the primary assembling or manufacturing activities. Thus, in many key American industries after the 1880s a few great enterprises took over the several different stages of the industrial processes that, up to that time, had always been operated by separate, relatively small wholesalers, manufacturers, transporters, and raw materials producers.

The second chapter – rationalizing the use of resources

The creation of these huge new vertically integrated enterprises was the work of the empire builders of American industry. These men, whose names are among the best known in the folklore of American business, usually turned over the administration of the vast resources they had accumulated to other individuals. Their successors had to develop methods for managing rationally the large agglomerations of men, money, and materials. Often in their eagerness to meet the new market, the empire builders in one industry had collected more facilities and personnel than were really necessary to meet the existing demand. Continuing profits depended on the lowering of costs through the systematizing of operations.

In this second period, this pressing task was twofold. First, unit costs had to be reduced by rationalizing the several functional activities and, second, these functional activities had to be closely integrated to market fluctuations. The first task led to the definition of lines of authority and communication within a single functional department; the second brought a structure for the enterprise as a whole. With the first came the systematizing and improving of the processes and techniques of marketing, manufacturing, and the procurement of raw materials. The final form of the second reflected closely the marketing requirements of the firm's products.

For those enterprises that continued to sell ores or primary metals, the task was the least complicated. Here, the market organization remained small, and the flow could be quickly adjusted to current price. But where fabricated shapes and forms made to exact customer specifications were the products, much closer coordination between the selling and manufacturing activities became necessary. To deliver promptly goods made to a bewildering variety of specifications and at the same time to keep large plants operating fairly steadily necessitated scheduling of a high order of skill. When the line of goods became even more technologically complex, as in the case of electrical apparatus, power machinery, and construction equipment companies, then the coordination of production often became even more difficult than in the steel and metal firms. Also the designing of new or improved products to meet customer needs and to counter the offerings of competitors demanded the close cooperation of the marketing, manufacturing, and engineering departments.

For those companies that also manufactured for the producers' market but whose more standardized products were made in advance of orders, the coordination of resources offered somewhat different challenges. In the companies making explosives, chemicals, industrial rubber, glass, paper, metal containers, trucks and farm implements, small engines, and other power machinery and equipment, the scheduling of the flow through the different departments was more routine than it was for non-standard goods. But because these products were not tailored to specific orders, increasingly accurate estimates of market demand were required so that the different departments would not be caught with either too much or too little inventory of materials, parts, and finished goods. Since the customers' needs varied, technically trained personnel helped coordinate designing, making, and selling so that the standardized product might be made to fit these different needs.

Those enterprises selling products for use by the mass consumer had still another set of problems. Because they tended to have a much larger volume of goods, not based on specific orders, flowing through their various activities than did the enterprises selling to the producers' market, the flow had to be directed still more closely toward the short-term fluctuations of demand if resources were to be used efficiently. Among the first to be faced with this problem of coordinating high-volume flow were the makers of perishable products like meat and fruit. By the turn of the century, the meat packers, with their heavy investment in distributing and purchasing as well as in the processing of all kinds of meats, had pioneered in such coordination by developing telegraphic communications between the branch houses, the packing plants, and the stockyards. Both the branch houses and the buyers in the stockyards were in constant telegraphic communication with the central offices in Chicago. And with such information, the central office could allocate supply to demand almost instantaneously.

The makers of less perishable consumer goods came to require even more than this instantaneous coordination between supply and demand. The processes involved in converting their raw materials into finished goods readily available for customer use were more complex and took more time to accomplish than did those in meat packing and some other food industries. This meant a still larger investment in inventory and greater difficulty in adjusting all activities to short-term shifts in demand. Thus the makers of gasoline, tires, tobacco, and some of the less perishable foods began to rely on long-term as well as short-term estimates of the market in order to coordinate and guide product flow through the several departments, and to determine the use of resources within the functional departments.

For the producers of consumer durables, the need was even more critical. Here the investment was still greater, there were more steps in the process, and each functional activity was more complex. To adjust the flow was more difficult and the failure to adjust more costly. Also, because of the relatively expensive materials involved and the relatively high final unit price, the market changes affected unit cost even more than in other industries; that is, in the automobile and appliance businesses variable unit costs rose and fell more sharply with an increase and decrease of output than in most industries. So it was that General Motors and the electrical companies were among the first to develop statistical methods for estimating long-term and short-term demand on which all current activity became based.

In this way, then, the need to apply resources effectively to changes in short-term demand brought the creation of a centralized, functionally departmentalized administrative structure. The functional activities were departmentalized in order to assure effective and rational coordination, appraisal, and planning in each. The central office, in turn, had to make certain the coordination of these different activities in relation to the market. The resulting structure provided a communication network that linked all the facilities involved in the industrial process with the customer's demand. Such a network rendered easier the accurate compliance with specifications as well as rapid and prompt delivery in the producers' goods industries, and the adjustment of volume of output and the making of minor changes in product necessary to meet the fluctuating demands of the mass-consumer-goods industries.

The senior executives at the central office of the functionally departmentalized structures had to make strategic decisions concerning the future allocation of resources as well as tactical ones to assure their efficient current use. Just as operational activities became tied to the short-term estimates of the market, entrepreneurial ones became increasingly based on estimates and forecasts of long-term changes. As the methods for allotting funds, equipment, and personnel became systematized through the development of formal budgets and capital appropriation procedures, their allocation also came to be based on forecasts of the broader economic and financial conditions as well as of the anticipated performance of the specific market. Through such procedures, these executives were able to review, formulate, and approve plans to maintain and expand their share of the existing market. As the structure was worked out, the allocation of future and the application of present resources became more routinized, and basic entrepreneurial decisions became least frequent. But when the responsible executives decided to move into new markets, the older structure began to hinder the efficient allocation and uses of the firm's resources.

The third chapter – continued growth

At the end of the first chapter in its history, an enterprise had accumulated enough resources to meet the demands of the national market and often those of foreign ones accessible by steamship and railroad. For the large companies in the older American industries – the metals and foods and some consumer goods like rubber boots and shoes – this period came to an end around the turn of the century. For those in the electrical industry, it lasted somewhat longer; while many large automobile, power machinery, gasoline, tire, and chemical companies were still rounding out this first chapter in the 1920s. At the end of the second chapter, administrators had defined, sometimes with great care and at others in more of an *ad hoc* informal manner, structures to assure more efficient use of the accumulated resources. In the older industries, these structural changes usually came before World War I, for the newer ones in the 1920s and 1930s.

Then, as other firms followed the innovators in developing more efficient purchasing, production, distribution, and above all administrative methods, cost differentials between companies lessened and profit margins dropped. More intensive advertising, product differentiation and improvement, and similar strategies might increase one firm's share of the market, but only major changes in technology, population, and national income could expand the over-all market for a single line of products. As the market became more saturated and the opportunities to cut costs through more rational techniques lessened, enterprises began to search for other markets or to develop other businesses that might profitably employ some of their partially utilized resources or even make a more profitable application of those still being fully employed.

The first step was to develop a 'full line' of comparable products. Steel and aluminum firms had 'warehouse' lines and special ones for specific industries beside their orders made to customer specifications. The harvester companies built their full line of agricultural implements. The meat packers moved to eggs, poultry, and dairy products to use the refrigerated facilities of their distributing network. The electrical companies developed everything involved in setting up, operating, and maintaining power and light systems. The gasoline companies had their lubricant line. The tire firms made steel rims as well as rubber tires. There are numerous other examples. At the same time, these enterprises intensified their drive to cover the domestic and international market. Expansion overseas often meant the setting up of manufacturing and purchasing as well as marketing facilities. While some companies like International Harvester, Armour, and Swift had invested more than just marketing resources abroad before World War I, many, particularly the chemical firms, only did so after World War II.

More significant than either the filling out of the major line or the move overseas was the development of new products that were often sold to quite different sets of customers. Either new end products might be fashioned from the existing lines or less often wholly new products developed in research laboratories that still employed some of the company's skills and facilities. Sometimes the enterprise began this move by concentrating more on by-products. Often it turned to a brand new field. In either case, the nature of the company's original line and the resulting accumulation of resources determined the extent to which the new products could be developed and new markets captured. In enterprises whose products and processing were based on a highly complex technology, both skills and facilities were most easily transferred to new lines of goods. On the other hand, in those that were less technologically complex and whose resources were concentrated more in raw materials and manufacturing, such a transfer was far more difficult.

Firms whose resources were concentrated in a single function such as transportation had little to transfer besides surplus funds. When a shipping concern, like W. R. Grace & Company, purchased chemical and petroleum companies, it was acting largely as a Wall Street investment house, for it had very few facilities or personnel to re-employ in its new ventures. Many great multifunctional enterprises with vast resources tied up in men and equipment to handle a single line of products have been more reluctant than Grace even to reinvest profits outside of their single major line. They needed funds from their profits to maintain their very large existing investment. When enterprises with few transferable resources, such as the producers and sellers of steel and other metals, and of tobacco, whisky, sugar, and other goods processed from agricultural products, expanded either through merger, or purchase, or the building of new facilities, they usually did so in order to obtain a full line or occasionally to take on allied products for much the same type of market as their own. For comparable reasons, tire and oil companies with huge resources concentrated on a single line have hesitated to embark on a strategy of broad diversification. For some processors of farm products, the task has been easier. A far wider range of products could be made from wheat and milk than from tobacco, bananas, or even meat.

Where a company's resources are invested more in marketing than in raw materials or producing facilities, the opportunity for diversification seems to have been greater. However the enterprises whose resources were the most transferable remained those whose men and equipment came to handle a range of technology rather than a set of end products. In the chemical, electrical and electronic, and power machinery industries, the same personnel using much the same facilities with much the same supplies of raw materials were able to develop new engines, new machines, new household appliances, new synthetic fibers, new films or plastics, or new electrical and electronic devices. Since the enterprises in these industries required the highest of technological skills, their administrators invested increasingly larger amounts of their total resources in research and development. Such resources became less and less tied to any specific product line. As rubber, petroleum, and food companies began to develop technologically advanced skills and facilities, particularly during World War II, they too started to build more of a diversified product line. For all of them, continued growth and with it the accumulation of resources came in their new lines rather than in the old.

The fourth chapter – rationalizing the use of expanding resources

While the strategy of diversification permitted the continuing and expanded use of a firm's resources, it did not assure their efficient employment. Structural reorganization became necessary. If expansion resulted only in the development of a full line of goods that continued to use much the same type of resources, the reorganization of the marketing department so that it had an office for each major type of customer was usually sufficient. But where business diversified into wholly new lines for quite different customers with quite different wants, then more reorganization was needed. It became increasingly difficult to coordinate through the existing structure the different functional activities to the needs of several quite different markets.

Channels of communication and authority as well as the information flowing through these channels grew more and more inadequate. The wants of different customers varied, and demand and taste fluctuated differently in different markets. Such changing market demands and the actions of competitors brought a growing differentiating of the manufacture and procurement of raw materials for the various product lines. Responsibility for maintaining and expanding the enterprise's share of the markets became harder to pin point. In time, then, each major product line came to be administered through a separate, integrated autonomous division. Its manager became responsible for the major operating decisions involved in the coordination of functional activities to changing demand and taste. Expansion into new regions encouraged the formation of comparable divisions for comparable reasons. Yet, as the different geographical markets became more homogeneous (and this occurred as all parts of the United States became more industrial and more urbanized and suburbanized), the regionally defined divisions in petroleum, dairy products, and container enterprises tended to combine into a single unit for one line of products.

Expansion, primarily through diversification, enlarged the range, number, and complexity of the entrepreneurial activities required of the senior executives. The long-term allocation of resources now involved deciding between the expansion, maintenance, and contraction of personnel, plant, and equipment in several different, large-scale, widespread businesses. The appraisal of existing performance as well as the planning of future uses of resources called for a general office in which the executives were given the time, the information, and the encouragement to develop a broad view, all so necessary for the handling of the new and more complex problems. The multidivisional structure met both the short-term and long-term requirements for the profitable application of resources to the changing markets.

In recent years, the builders of the new organizational structures could look to the model created by du Pont, General Motors, Jersey Standard, and Sears, Roebuck. But before the 1930s, those few firms that had developed lines of business which might have been more effectively administered through a multidivisional structure envisaged only two structural alternatives. To the meat packers, rubber companies, and makers of power machinery, the activities had either to be incorporated into a centralized, functionally departmentalized structure or placed in almost completely independent subsidiaries. In either case, the executives responsible for the destiny of the enterprise had little information about or understanding of how the resources not applied directly to the primary line were being employed. Once the new type of structure became known, as it did during the 1930s, its availability undoubtedly encouraged many enterprises to embark on a strategy of diversification, for the ability to maintain administrative control through such an organizational framework greatly reduced the risks of this new type of expansion.

In fact, the systematizing of strategic decisions through the building of a general office and the routinizing of product development by the formation of a research department have, in a sense, institutionalized this strategy of diversification. Companies whose processes are closely related to the science of chemistry and physics have turned to developing new products steadily in order to assure continuing profitable use of resources that are becoming increasingly based on a technology rather than a product line. The research department develops the products and tests their commercial value. The executives in the general office, freed from all but the most essential entrepreneurial duties, can determine, in something of a rational manner, whether the new product uses enough of the firm's present resources or will help in the development of new ones to warrant its production and sale. If it does and if its market is similar to that of the current line, then its production and sale can be handled through an existing division. If the market is quite different, a new division can and should be formed.

The coming of this new strategy and with it the new structure is of paramount importance to the present health and future growth of the American economy. While some of the new products have been sold in the mass consumer market where, according to some commentators, the technical skills and facilities are sometimes wasted, the largest proportion of the output of the chemical, electronic, electrical, and power machinery enterprises have gone to the producers' market. The industrialist has usually been much more concerned about the performance of what he purchases for his business than the consumer has been in his personal buying, as better performance normally means cutting costs. The institutionalizing of the policy of diversification thus helps to assure continued production of new products to cut costs and raise the efficiency of American industry. Such a development is far more significant to the economy's over-all health than production increases in the older basic industries, such as metals and food. The investment in research and development and in the technical skills and equipment that can handle a range of products within a comparable technology is a far more meaningful index of economic growth in a highly urban and industrial nation than is the output of steel, meat, or even automobiles.

The chapters in the collective history of the American industrial enterprise can be clearly defined. Resources accumulated, resources rationalized, resources expanded, and then once again, resources rationalized. For each individual company, these chapters vary in length, significance, and impact. Some firms never attempted to accumulate the resources essential to meet the demands of a national market. Some of those companies that did expand took longer to rationalize the use of their resources than did others. Some set up new structures very systematically, others more informally. Some began to move into new lines and new markets even before they completed building their initial administrative organization. Again some were much slower than others to join the search for new markets; and again, among those that did, some turned more quickly than others to reshaping the structure necessary for the most profitable employment of the expanded resources. A company like General Motors, by inventing a new type of structure when it first organized its accumulated resources, was able to expand through diversification without requiring further significant structural changes; while Jersey Standard's informal, *ad hoc* mobilization of its resources after 1911 meant that a rapid expansion of facilities and personnel forced a much more difficult and much lengthier reorganization in later years.

Nevertheless, if the great industrial enterprise is considered as a collective entity, then these chapters are more easily identified and examined. And if these chapters have some relation to reality, then they have some significance for the scholar, businessman, and even public officials.

4

Marketing Myopia

Theodore Levitt

This was to me – and, I believe, to many of my contemporaries in manufacturing industry in the UK – a revelationary article. In 1960 many manufacturers were making fairly well-established goods to satisfy a demand that was still fuelled by wartime shortages and post-war austerity. The attention of those in manufacturing industry, and particularly in process industry, was concentrated upon increasing throughput and lowering costs via multi-shift working and the twin tools of method study and work measurement. Technology was producing new profit opportunities, and progress for most companies was manifestly best continued by persisting with these priorities.

Thus, by making the distinciton between satisfying a want and providing a specific type of good, Levitt's article provided a new insight for those of us too preoccupied with the everyday practicalities of business to be able to see beyond the conventional wisdom of the time. He made us appreciate that a need may be satisfied tomorrow, not by an improvement on today's product or price, but by a quite dissimilar product or service; the perception of opportunity in such circumstances comes from a thorough-going orientation towards the customer, rather than a product or process orientation.

Levitt's message was too often, and unwisely, taken to be that a business should be dominated by customer-oriented marketing. In fact, he was telling us that the neglect of marketing was preventing the balanced pursuit of all the critical factors in a business that is vital to its success.

The emphasis laid on different facets of a business properly changes with time and circumstances, but Levitt's message that customer-oriented marketing is one of the most important items remains a precept that we ignore at our peril.

Dr Ingram Lenton,
Chairman, Compass Group Plc,
London

Marketing Myopia

E VERY major industry was once a growth industry. But some that are now riding a wave of growth enthusiasm are very much in the shadow of decline. Others which are thought of as seasoned growth industries have actually stopped growing. In every case the reason growth is threatened, slowed, or stopped is *not* because the market is saturated. It is because there has been a failure of management.

Fateful purposes: The failure is at the top. The executives responsible for it, in the last analysis, are those who deal with broad aims and policies. Thus:

- The railroads did not stop growing because the need for passenger and freight transportation declined. That grew. The railroads are in trouble today not because the need was filled by others (cars, trucks, airplanes, even telephones), but because it was *not* filled by the railroads themselves. They let others take customers away from them because they assumed themselves to be in the railroad business rather than in the transportation business. The reason they defined their industry wrong was because they were railroad-oriented instead of transportation-oriented; they were product-oriented instead of customer-oriented.

- Hollywood barely escaped being totally ravished by television. Actually, all the established film companies went through drastic reorganizations. Some simply disappeared. All of them got into trouble not because of TV's inroads but of because of their own myopia. As with the railroads, Hollywood defined its business incorrectly. It thought it was in the movie business when it was actually in the entertainment business. 'Movies' implied a specific, limited product. This produced a fatuous contentment which from the beginning led producers to view TV as a threat. Hollywood scorned and rejected TV when it should have welcomed it as an opportunity – an opportunity to expand the entertainment business.

Today TV is a bigger business than the old narrowly defined movie business ever was. Had Hollywood been customer-oriented (providing entertainment), rather then product-oriented (making movies), would it have gone through the fiscal purgatory that it did? I doubt it. What ultimately saved Hollywood and accounted for its recent resurgence was the wave of new young writers, producers, and directors whose previous successes in television had decimated the old movie companies and toppled the big movie moguls.

There are other less obvious examples of industries that have been and are now endangering their futures by improperly defining their purposes. I shall discuss some in detail later and analyze the kind of policies that lead to trouble. Right now it may help to show what a thoroughly customer-oriented management *can* do to keep a growth industry growing, even after the obvious opportunities have been exhausted; and here there are two examples that have been around for a long time. They are nylon and glass – specifically, E. I. duPont de Nemours & Company and Corning Glass Works.

Both companies have great technical competence. Their product orientation is unquestioned. But this alone does not explain their success. After all, who was more pridefully product-oriented and product-conscious than the erstwhile New England textile companies that have been so thoroughly massacred? The DuPonts and the Cornings have succeeded not primarily because of their product or research orientation but because they have been thoroughly customer-oriented also. It is constant watchfulness for opportunities to apply their technical know-how to the creation of customer-satisfying uses which accounts for their prodigious output of successful new products. Without a very sophisticated eye on the customer, most of their new products might have been wrong, their sales methods useless.

Aluminum has also continued to be a growth industry, thanks to the efforts of two wartime-created companies which deliberately set about creating new customer-satisfying uses. Without Kaiser Aluminum & Chemical Corporation and Reynolds Metals Company, the total demand for aluminum today would be vastly less.

Error of analysis: Some may argue that it is foolish to set the railroads off against aluminum or the movies off against glass. Are not aluminum and glass naturally so versatile that the industries are bound to have more growth opportunities than the railroads and movies? This view commits precisely the error I have been talking about. It defines an industry, or a product, or a cluster of know-how so narrowly as to guarantee its premature senescence. When we mention 'railroads,' we should make sure we mean 'transportation.' As transporters, the railroads still have a good chance for very considerable growth. They are not limited to the railroad business as such (though in my opinion rail transportation is potentially a much stronger transportation medium than is generally believed).

What the railroads lack is not opportunity, but some of the same managerial imaginativeness and audacity that made them great. Even an amateur like Jacques Barzun can see what is lacking when he says:

> I grieve to see the most advanced physical and social organization of the last century go down in shabby disgrace for lack of the same comprehensive imagination that built it up. [What is lacking is] the will of the companies to survive and to satisfy the public by inventiveness and skill.[1]

Shadow of obsolescence

It is impossible to mention a single major industry that did not at one time qualify for the magic appellation of 'growth industry.' In each case its assumed strength lay in the apparently unchallenged superiority of its product. There appeared to be no effective substitute for it. It was itself a runaway substitute for the product it so triumphantly replaced. Yet one after another of these celebrated industries has come under a shadow. Let us look briefly at a few more of them, this time taking examples that have so far received a little less attention:

- *Dry cleaning* – This was once a growth industry with lavish prospects. In an age of wool garments, imagine being finally able to get them safely and easily clean. The boom was on.

  Yet here we are 30 years after the boom started and the industry is in trouble. Where has the competition come from? From a better way of cleaning? No. It has come from synthetic fibers and chemical additives that have cut the need for dry cleaning. But this is only the beginning. Lurking in the wings and ready to make chemical dry cleaning totally obsolescent is that powerful magician, ultrasonics.

- *Electric utilities* – This is another one of those supposedly 'no-substitute' products that has been enthroned on a pedestal of invincible growth. When the incandescent lamp came along, kerosene lights were finished. Later the water wheel and the steam engine were cut to ribbons by the flexibility, reliability, simplicity, and just plain easy availability of electric motors. The prosperity of electric utilities continues to wax extravagant as the home is converted into a museum of electric gadgetry. How can anybody miss by investing in utilities, with no competition, nothing but growth ahead?

But a second look is not quite so comforting. A score of nonutility companies are well advanced toward developing a powerful chemical fuel cell which could sit in some hidden closet of every home silently ticking off electric power. The electric lines that vulgarize so many neighborhoods will be eliminated. So will the endless demolition of streets and service interruptions during storms. Also on the horizon is solar energy, again pioneered by nonutility companies.

Who says that the utilities have no competition? They may be natural monopolies now, but tomorrow they may be natural deaths. To avoid this prospect, they too will have to develop fuel cells, solar energy, and other power sources. To survive, they themselves will have to plot the obsolescence of what now produces their livelihood.

- *Grocery stores* – Many people find it hard to realize that there ever was a thriving establishment known as the 'corner grocery store.' The super-market has taken over with a powerful effectiveness. Yet the big food chains of the 1930s narrowly escaped being completely wiped out by the aggressive expansion of independent supermarkets. The first genuine supermarket was opened in 1930, in Jamaica, Long Island. By 1933 supermarkets were thriving in California, Ohio, Pennsylvania, and elsewhere. Yet the established chains pompously ignored them. When they chose to notice them, it was with such derisive descriptions as 'cheapy,' 'horse-and-buggy,' 'cracker-barrel storekeeping,' and 'unethical opportunists.'

  The executive of one big chain announced at the time that he found it 'hard to believe that people will drive for miles to shop for foods and sacrifice the personal service chains have perfected and to which Mrs. Consumer is accustomed.'[2] As late as 1936, the National Wholesale Grocers convention and the New Jersey Retail Grocers Association said there was nothing to fear. They said that the supers' narrow appeal to the price buyer limited the size of their market. They had to draw from miles around. When imitators came, there would be wholesale liquidations as volume fell. The current high sales of the supers was said to be partly due to their novelty. Basically people wanted convenient neighborhood grocers. If the neighborhood stores 'cooperate with their suppliers, pay attention to their costs, and improve their service,' they would be able to weather the competition until it blew over.[3]

It never blew over. The chains discovered that survival required going into the supermarket business. This meant the wholesale destruction of their huge investments in corner store sites and in established distribution and merchandising methods. The companies with 'the courage of their convictions' resolutely stuck to the corner store philosophy. They kept their pride but lost their shirts.

Self-deceiving cycle: But memories are short. For example, it is hard for people who today confidently hail the twin messiahs of electronics and chemicals to see how things could possibly go wrong with these galloping industries. They probably also cannot see how a reasonably sensible businessman could have been as myopic as the famous Boston millionaire who 50 years ago unintentionally sentenced his heirs to poverty by stipulating that his entire estate be forever invested exclusively in electric streetcar securities. His posthumous declaration, 'There will always be a big demand for efficient urban transportation,' is no consolation to his heirs who sustain life by pumping gasoline at automobile filling stations.

Yet, in a casual survey I recently took among a group of intelligent business executives, nearly half agreed that it would be hard to hurt their heirs by tying their estates forever to the electronics industry. When I then confronted them with the Boston streetcar example, they chorused unanimously, 'That's different!' But is it? Is not the basic situation identical?

In truth, *there is no such thing* as a growth industry, I believe. There are only companies organized and operated to create and capitalize on growth opportunities. Industries that assume themselves to be riding some automatic growth escalator invariably descend into stagnation. The history of every dead and dying 'growth' industry shows a self-deceiving cycle of bountiful expansion and undetected decay. There are four conditions which usually guarantee this cycle:

1　The belief that growth is assured by an expanding and more affluent population.
2　The belief that there is no competitive substitute for the industry's major product.
3　Too much faith in mass production and in the advantages of rapidly declining unit costs as output rises.
4　Preoccupation with a product that lends itself to carefully controlled scientific experimentation, improvement, and manufacturing cost reduction.

I should like now to begin examining each of these conditions in some detail. To build my case as boldly as possible, I shall illustrate the points with reference to three industries – petroleum, automobiles, and electronics – particularly petroleum, because it spans more years and more vicissitudes. Not only do these three have excellent reputations with the general public and also enjoy the confidence of sophisticated investors, but their managements have become known for progressive thinking in areas like financial control, product research, and management training. If obsolescence can cripple even these industries, it can happen anywhere.

Population myth

The belief that profits are assured by an expanding and more affluent population is dear to the heart of every industry. It takes the edge off the apprehensions everybody understandably feels about the future. If consumers are multiplying and also buying more of your product or service, you can face the future with considerably more comfort than if the market is shrinking. An expanding market keeps the manufacturer from having to think very hard or imaginatively. If thinking is an intellectual response to a problem, then the absence of a problem leads to the absence of thinking. If your product has an automatically expanding market, then you will not give much thought to how to expand it.

One of the most interesting examples of this is provided by the petroleum industry. Probably our oldest growth industry, it has an enviable record. While there are some current apprehensions about its growth rate, the industry itself tends to be optimistic.

But I believe it can be demonstrated that it is undergoing a fundamental yet typical change. It is not only ceasing to be a growth industry, but may actually be a declining one, relative to other business. Although there is widespread unawareness of it, I believe that within 25 years the oil industry may find itself in much the same position of retrospective glory that the railroads are now in. Despite its pioneering work in developing and applying the present-value method of investment evaluation, in employee relations, and in working with backward countries, the petroleum business is a distressing example of how complacency and wrongheadedness can stubbornly convert opportunity into near disaster.

One of the characteristics of this and other industries that have believed very strongly in the beneficial consequences of an expanding population, while at the same time being industries with a generic product for which there has appeared to be no competitive substitute, is that the individual companies have sought to outdo their competitors by improving on what they are already doing. This makes sense, of course, if one assumes that sales are tied to the country's population strings, because the customer can compare products only on a feature-by-feature basis. I believe it is significant, for example, that not since John D. Rockefeller sent free kerosene lamps to China has the oil industry done anything really outstanding to create a demand for its product. Not even in product improvement has it showered itself with eminence. The greatest single improvement - namely, the development of tetraethyl lead - came from outside the industry, specifically from General Motors and DuPont. The big contributions made by the industry itself are confined to the technology of oil exploration, production, and refining.

Asking for trouble: In other words, the industry's efforts have focused on improving the *efficiency* of getting and making its product, not really on improving the generic product or its marketing. Moreover, its chief product has continuously been defined in the narrowest possible terms, namely, gasoline, not energy, fuel, or transportation. This attitude has helped assure that:

● Major improvements in gasoline quality tend not to originate in the oil industry. Also, the development of superior alternative fuels comes from outside the oil industry, as will be shown later.

● Major innovations in automobile fuel marketing are originated by small new oil companies that are not primarily preoccupied with production or refining. These are the companies that have been responsible for the rapidly expanding multipump gasoline stations, with their successful emphasis on large and clean layouts, rapid and efficient driveway service, and quality gasoline at low prices.

Thus, the oil industry is asking for trouble from outsiders. Sooner or later, in this land of hungry inventors and entrepreneurs, a threat is sure to come. The possibilities of this will become more apparent when we turn to the next dangerous belief of many managements. For the sake of continuity, because this second belief is tied closely to the first, I shall continue with the same example.

Idea of indispensability: The petroleum industry is pretty much persuaded that there is no competitive substitute for its major product, gasoline – or if there is, that it will continue to be a derivative of crude oil, such as diesel fuel or kerosene jet fuel.

There is a lot of automatic wishful thinking in this assumption. The trouble is that most refining companies own huge amounts of crude oil reserves. These have value only if there is a market for products into which oil can be converted – hence the tenacious belief in the continuing competitive superiority of automobile fuels made from crude oil.

This idea persists despite all historic evidence against it. The evidence not only shows that oil has never been a superior product for any purpose for very long, but it also shows that the oil industry has never really been a growth industry. It has been a succession of different businesses that have gone through the usual historic cycles of growth, maturity, and decay. Its overall survival is owed to a series of miraculous escapes from total obsolescence, of last-minute and unexpected reprieves from total disaster reminiscent of the Perils of Pauline.

Perils of petroleum: I shall sketch in only the main episodes.

First, crude oil was largely a patent medicine. But even before that fad ran out, demand was greatly expanded by the use of oil in kerosene lamps. The prospect of lighting the world's lamps gave rise to an extravagant promise of growth. The prospects were similar to those the industry nów holds for gasoline in other parts of the world. It can hardly wait for the underdeveloped nations to get a car in every garage.

In the days of the kerosene lamp, the oil companies competed with each other and against gaslight by trying to improve the illuminating characteristics of kerosene. Then suddenly the impossible happened. Edison invented a light which was totally non-dependent on crude oil. Had it not been for the growing use of kerosene in space heaters, the incandescent lamp would have completely finished oil as a growth industry at that time. Oil would have been good for little else than axle grease.

Then disaster and reprieve struck again. Two great innovations occurred, neither originating in the oil industry. The successful development of coal-burning domestic central-heating systems made the space heater obsolescent. While the industry reeled, along came its most magnificent boost yet – the internal combustion engine, also invented by outsiders. Then when the prodigious expansion for gasoline finally began to level off in the 1920s, along came the miraculous escape of a central oil heater. Once again, the escape was provided by an outsider's invention and development. And when that market weakened, wartime demand for aviation fuel came to the rescue. After the war the expansion of civilian aviation, the dieselization of railroads, and the explosive demand for cars and trucks kept the industry's growth in high gear.

Meanwhile, centralized oil heating – whose boom potential had only recently been proclaimed – ran into severe competition from natural gas. While the oil companies themselves owned the gas that now competed with their oil, the industry did not originate the natural gas revolution, nor has it to this day greatly profited from its gas ownership. The gas revolution was made by newly formed transmission companies that marketed the product with an aggressive ardor. They started a magnificent new industry, first against the advice and then against the resistance of the oil companies.

By all the logic of the situation, the oil companies themselves should have made the gas revolution. They not only owned the gas; they also were the only people experienced in handling, scrubbing, and using it, the only people experienced in pipeline technology and transmission, and they understood heating problems. But, partly because they knew that natural gas would compete with their own sale of heating oil, the oil companies pooh-poohed the potentials of gas.

The revolution was finally started by oil pipeline executives who, unable to persuade their own companies to go into gas, quit and organized the spectacularly successful gas transmission companies. Even after their success became painfully evident to the oil companies, the latter did not go into gas transmission. The multibillion dollar business which should have been theirs went to others. As in the past, the industry was blinded by its narrow preoccupation with a specific product and the value of its reserves. It paid little or no attention to its customers' basic needs and preferences.

The postwar years have not witnessed any change. Immediately after World War II the oil industry was greatly encouraged about its future by the rapid expansion of demand for its traditional line of products. In 1950 most companies projected annual rates of domestic expansion of around 6% through at least 1975. Though the ratio of crude oil reserves to demand in the Free World was about 20 to 1, with 10 to 1 being usually considered a reasonable working ratio in the United States, booming demand sent oil men searching for more without sufficient regard to what the future really promised. In 1952 they 'hit' in the Middle East; the ratio skyrocketed to 42 to 1. If gross additions to reserves continue at the average rate of the past five years (37 billion barrels annually), then by 1970 the reserve ratio will be up to 45 to 1. This abundance of oil has weakened crude and product prices all over the world.

Uncertain future: Management cannot find much consolation today in the rapidly expanding petrochemical industry, another oil-using idea that did not originate in the leading firms. The total United States production of petrochemicals is equivalent to about 2% (by volume) of the demand for all petroleum products. Although the petrochemical industry is now expected to grow by about 10% per year, this will not offset other drains on the growth of crude oil consumption. Furthermore, while petrochemical products are many and growing, it is well to remember that there are nonpetroleum sources of the basic raw material, such as coal. Besides, a lot of plastics can be produced with relatively little oil. A 50,000-barrel-per-day oil refinery is now considered the absolute minimum size for efficiency. But a 5,000-barrel-per-day chemical plant is a giant operation.

Oil has never been a continuously strong growth industry. It has grown by fits and starts, always miraculously saved by innovations and developments not of its own making. The reason it has not grown in a smooth progression is that each time it thought it had a superior product safe from the possibility of competitive substitutes, the product turned out to be inferior and notoriously subject to obsolescence. Until now, gasoline (for motor fuel, anyhow) has escaped this fate. But, as we shall see later, it too may be on its last legs.

The point of all this is that there is no guarantee against product obsolescence. If a company's own research does not make it obsolete, another's will. Unless an industry is especially lucky, as oil has been until now, it can easily go down in a sea of red figures – just as the railroads have, as the buggy whip manufacturers have, as the corner grocery chains have, as most of the big movie companies have, and indeed as many other industries have.

The best way for a firm to be lucky is to make its own luck. That requires knowing what makes a business successful. One of the greatest enemies of this knowledge is mass production.

Production pressures

Mass-production industries are impelled by a great drive to produce all they can. The prospect of steeply declining unit costs as output rises is more than most companies can usually resist. The profit possibilities look spectacular. All effort focuses on production. The result is that marketing gets neglected.

John Kenneth Galbraith contends that just the opposite occurs.[4] Output is so prodigious that all effort concentrates on trying to get rid of it. He says this accounts for singing commercials, desecration of the countryside with advertising signs, and other wasteful and vulgar practices. Galbraith has a finger on something real, but he misses the strategic point. Mass production does indeed generate great pressure to 'move' the product. But what usually gets emphasized is selling, not marketing. Marketing, being a more sophisticated and complex process, gets ignored.

The difference between marketing and selling is more than semantic. Selling focuses on the needs of the seller, marketing on the needs of the buyer. Selling is preoccupied with the seller's need to convert his product into cash, marketing with the idea of satisfying the needs of the customer by means of the product and the whole cluster of things associated with creating, delivering, and finally consuming it.

In some industries the enticements of full mass production have been so powerful that for many years top management in effect has told the sales departments, 'You get rid of it; we'll worry about profits.' By contrast, a truly marketing-minded firm tries to create value-satisfying goods and services that consumers will want to buy. What it offers for sale includes not only the generic product or service, but also how it is made available to the customer, in what form, when, under what conditions, and at what terms of trade. Most important, what it offers for sale is determined not by the seller but by the buyer. The seller takes his cues from the buyer in such a way that the product becomes a consequence of the marketing effort, not vice versa.

Lag in Detroit: This may sound like an elementary rule of business, but that does not keep it from being violated wholesale. It is certainly more violated than honored. Take the automobile industry.

Here mass production is most famous, most honored, and has the greatest impact on the entire society. The industry has hitched its fortune to the relentless requirements of the annual model change, a policy that makes customer orientation an especially urgent necessity. Consequently the auto companies annually spend millions of dollars on consumer research. But the fact that the new compact cars are selling so well in their first year indicates that Detroit's vast researches have for a long time failed to reveal what the customer really wanted. Detroit was not persuaded that he wanted anything different from what he had been getting until it lost millions of customers to other small car manufacturers.

How could this unbelievable lag behind consumer wants have been perpetuated so long? Why did not research reveal consumer preferences before consumers' buying decisions themselves revealed the facts? Is that not what consumer research is for – to find out before the fact what is going to happen? The answer is that Detroit never really researched the customer's wants. It only researched his preferences between the kinds of things which it had already decided to offer him. For Detroit is mainly product-oriented, not customer-oriented. To the extent that the customer is recognized as having needs that the manufacturer should try to satisfy, Detroit usually acts as if the job can be done entirely by product changes. Occasionally attention gets paid to financing, too, but that is done more in order to sell than to enable the customer to buy.

As for taking care of other customer needs, there is not enough being done to write about. The areas of the greatest unsatisfied needs are ignored, or at best get stepchild attention. These are at the point of sale and on the matter of automative repair and maintenance. Detroit views these problem areas as being of secondary importance. That is underscored by the fact that the retailing and servicing ends of this industry are neither owned and operated nor controlled by the manufacturers. Once the car is produced, things are pretty much in the dealer's inadequate hands. Illustrative of Detroit's arm's-length attitude is the fact that, while servicing holds enormous sales-stimulating, profit-building opportunities, only 57 of Chevrolet's 7,000 dealers provide night maintenance service.

Motorists repeatedly express their dissatisfaction with servicing and their apprehensions about buying cars under the present selling setup. The anxieties and problems they encounter during the auto buying and maintenance processes are probably more intense and widespread today than 30 years ago. Yet the automobile companies do not seem to listen to or take their cues from the anguished consumer. If they do listen, it must be through the filter of their own preoccupation with production. The marketing effort is still viewed as a necessary consequence of the product, not vice versa, as it should be. That is the legacy of mass production, with its parochial view that profit resides essentially in low-cost full production.

What Ford put first: The profit lure of mass production obviously has a place in the plans and strategy of business management, but it must always *follow* hard thinking about the customer. This is one of the most important lessons that we can learn from the contradictory behavior of Henry Ford. In a sense Ford was both the most brilliant and the most senseless marketer in American history. He was senseless because he refused to give the customer anything but a black car. He was brilliant because he fashioned a production system designed to fit market needs. We habitually celebrate him for the wrong reason, his production genius. His real genius was marketing. We think he was able to cut his selling price and therefore sell millions of $500 cars because his invention of the assembly line had reduced the costs. Actually he invented the assembly line because he had concluded that at $500 he could sell millions of cars. Mass production was the *result* not the cause of his low prices.

Ford repeatedly emphasized this point, but a nation of production-oriented business managers refuses to hear the great lesson he taught. Here is his operating philosophy as he expressed it succinctly:

> Our policy is to reduce the price, extend the operations, and improve the article. You will notice that the reduction of price comes first. We have never considered any costs as fixed. Therefore we first reduce the price to the point where we believe more sales will result. Then we go ahead and try to make the prices. We do not bother about the costs. The new price forces the costs down. The more usual way is to take the costs and then determine the price; and although that method may be scientific in the narrow sense, it is not scientific in the broad sense, because what earthly use is it to know the cost if it tells you that you cannot manufacture at a price at which the article can be sold? But more to the point is the fact that, although one may calculate what a cost is, and of course all of our costs are carefully calculated, no one knows what a cost ought to be. One of the ways of discovering . . . is to name a price so low as to force everybody in the place to the highest point of efficiency. The low price makes everybody dig for profits. We make more discoveries concerning manufacturing and selling under this forced method than by any method of leisurely investigation.[5]

Product provincialism: The tantalizing profit possibilities of low unit production costs may be the most seriously self-deceiving attitude that can afflict a company, particularly a 'growth' company where an apparently assured expansion of demand already tends to undermine a proper concern for the importance of marketing and the customer.

The usual result of this narrow pre-occupation with so-called concrete matters is that instead of growing, the industry declines. It usually means that the product fails to adapt to the constantly changing patterns of consumer needs and tastes, to new and modified marketing institutions and practices, or to product developments in competing or complementary industries. The industry has its eyes so firmly on its own specific product that it does not see how it is being made obsolete.

The classical example of this is the buggy whip industry. No amount of product improvement could stave off its death sentence. But had the industry defined itself as being in the transportation business rather than the buggy whip business, it might have survived. It would have done what survival always entails, that is, changing. Even if it had only defined its business as providing a stimulant or catalyst to an energy source, it might have survived by becoming a manufacturer of, say, fanbelts or air cleaners.

What may some day be a still more classical example is, again, the oil industry. Having let others steal marvelous opportunities from it (e.g., natural gas, as already mentioned, missile fuels, and jet engine lubricants), one would expect it to have taken steps never to let that happen again. But this is not the case. We are now getting extraordinary new developments in fuel systems specifically designed to power automobiles. Not only are these developments concentrated in firms outside the petroleum industry, but petroleum is almost systematically ignoring them, securely content in its wedded bliss to oil. It is the story of the kerosene lamp versus the incandescent lamp all over again. Oil is trying to improve hydrocarbon fuels rather than develop *any* fuels best suited to the needs of their users, whether or not made in different ways and with different raw materials from oil.

Here are some things which nonpetroleum companies are working on:

● Over a dozen such firms now have advanced working models of energy systems which, when perfected, will replace the internal combustion engine and eliminate the demand for gasoline. The superior merit of each of these systems is their elimination of frequent, time-consuming, and irritating refueling stops. Most of these systems are fuel cells designed to create electrical energy directly from chemicals without combustion. Most of them use chemicals that are not derived from oil, generally hydrogen and oxygen.

● Several other companies have advanced models of electric storage batteries designed to power automobiles. One of these is an aircraft producer that is working jointly with several electric utility companies. The latter hope to use off-peak generating capacity to supply overnight plug-in battery regeneration. Another company, also using the battery approach, is a medium-size electronics firm with extensive small-battery experience that it developed in connection with its work on hearing aids. It is collaborating with an automobile manufacturer. Recent improvements arising from the need for high-powered miniature power storage plants in rockets have put us within reach of a relatively small battery capable of withstanding great overloads or surges of power. Germanium diode applications and batteries using sintered-plate and nickel-cadmium techniques promise to make a revolution in our energy sources.

● Solar energy conversion systems are also getting increasing attention. One usually cautious Detroit auto executive recently ventured that solar-powered cars might be common by 1980.

As for the oil companies, they are more or less 'watching developments,' as one research director put it to me. A few are doing a bit of research on fuel cells, but almost always confined to developing cells powered by hydrocarbon chemicals. None of them are enthusiastically researching fuel cells, batteries, or solar power plants. None of them are spending a fraction as much on research in these profoundly important areas as they are on the usual run-of-the-mill things like reducing combustion chamber deposit in gasoline engines. One major integrated petroleum company recently took a tentative look at the fuel cell and concluded that although 'the companies actively working on it indicate a belief in ultimate success . . . the timing and magnitude of its impact are too remote to warrant recognition in our forecasts.'

One might, of course, ask: Why should the oil companies do anything different? Would not chemical fuel cells, batteries, or solar energy kill the present product lines? The answer is that they would indeed, and that is precisely the reason for the oil firms having to develop these power units before their competitors, so they will not be companies without an industry.

Management might be more likely to do what is needed for its own preservation if it thought of itself as being in the energy business. But even that would not be enough if it persists in imprisoning itself in the narrow grip of its tight product orientation. It has to think of itself as taking care of customer needs, not finding, refining, or even selling oil.

Once it genuinely thinks of its business as taking care of people's transportation needs, nothing can stop it from creating its own extravagantly profitable growth.

'Creative destruction': Since words are cheap and deeds are dear, it may be appropriate to indicate what this kind of thinking involves and leads to. Let us start at the beginning – the customer. It can be shown that motorists strongly dislike the bother, delay, and experience of buying gasoline. People actually do not buy gasoline. They cannot see it, taste it, feel it, appreciate it, or really test it. What they buy is the right to continue driving their cars. The gas station is like a tax collector to whom people are compelled to pay a periodic toll as the price of using their cars. This makes the gas station a basically unpopular institution. It can never be made popular or pleasant, only less unpopular, less unpleasant.

To reduce its unpopularity completely means eliminating it. Nobody likes a tax collector, not even a pleasantly cheerful one. Nobody likes to interrupt a trip to buy a phantom product, not even from a handsome Adonis or a seductive Venus. Hence, companies that are working on exotic fuel substitutes which will eliminate the need for frequent refueling are heading directly into the outstretched arms of the irritated motorist. They are riding a wave of inevitability, not because they are creating something which is technologically superior or more sophisticated, but because they are satisfying a powerful customer need. They are also eliminating noxious odors and air pollution.

Once the petroleum companies recognize the customer-satisfying logic of what another power system can do, they will see that they have no more choice about working on an efficient, long-lasting fuel (or some way of delivering present fuels without bothering the motorist) than the big food chains had a choice about going into the supermarket business, or the vacuum tube companies had a choice about making semi-conductors. For their own good the oil firms will have to destroy their own highly profitable assets. No amount of wishful thinking can save them from the necessity of engaging in this form of 'creative destruction.'

I phrase the need as strongly as this because I think management must make quite an effort to break itself loose from conventional ways. It is all too easy in this day and age for a company or industry to let its sense of purpose become dominated by the economies of full production and to develop a dangerously lopsided product orientation. In short, if management lets itself drift, it invariably drifts in the direction of thinking of itself as producing goods and services, not customer satisfactions. While it probably will not descend to the depths of telling its salesmen, 'You get rid of it; we'll worry about profits,' it can, without knowing it, be practicing precisely that formula for withering decay. The historic fate of one growth industry after another has been its suicidal product provincialism.

Dangers of R&D

Another big danger to a firm's continued growth arises when top management is wholly transfixed by the profit possibilities of technical research and development. To illustrate I shall turn first to a new industry – electronics – and then return once more to the oil companies. By comparing a fresh example with a familiar one, I hope to emphasize the prevalence and insidiousness of a hazardous way of thinking.

Marketing shortchanged: In the case of electronics, the greatest danger which faces the glamorous new companies in this field is not that they do not pay enough attention to research and development, but that they pay *too much* attention to it. And the fact that the fastest growing electronics firms owe their eminence to their heavy emphasis on technical research is completely beside the point. They have vaulted to affluence on a sudden crest of unusually strong general receptiveness to new technical ideas. Also, their success has been shaped in the virtually guaranteed market of military subsidies and by military orders that in many cases actually preceded the existence of facilities to make the products. Their expansion has, in other words, been almost totally devoid of marketing effort.

Thus, they are growing up under conditions that come dangerously close to creating the illusion that a superior product will sell itself. Having created a successful company by making a superior product, it is not surprising that management continues to be oriented toward the product rather than the people who consume it. It develops the philosophy that continued growth is a matter of continued product innovation and improvement.

A number of other factors tend to strengthen and sustain this belief:

1 Because electronic products are highly complex and sophisticated, managements become top-heavy with engineers and scientists. This creates a

selective bias in favor of research and production at the expense of marketing. The organization tends to view itself as making things rather than satisfying customer needs. Marketing gets treated as a residual activity, 'something else' that must be done once the vital job of product creation and production is completed.

2   To this bias in favor of product research, development, and production is added the bias in favor of dealing with controllable variables. Engineers and scientists are at home in the world of concrete things like machines, test tubes, production lines, and even balance sheets. The abstractions to which they feel kindly are those which are testable or manipulatable in the laboratory, or, if not testable, then functional, such as Euclid's axioms. In short, the managements of the new glamour-growth companies tend to favor those business activities which lend themselves to careful study, experimentation, and control – the hard, practical realities of the lab, the shop, the books.

What gets shortchanged are the realities of the *market*. Consumers are unpredictable, varied, fickle, stupid, shortsighted, stubborn, and generally bothersome. This is not what the engineer-managers say, but deep down in their consciousness it is what they believe. And this accounts for their concentrating on what they know and what they can control, namely, product research, engineering, and production. The emphasis on production becomes particularly attractive when the product can be made at declining unit costs. There is no more inviting way of making money than by running the plant full blast.

Today the top-heavy science-engineering-production orientation of so many electronics companies works reasonably well because they are pushing into new frontiers in which the armed services have pioneered virtually assured markets. The companies are in the felicitous position of having to fill, not find markets; of not having to discover what the customer needs and wants, but of having the customer voluntarily come forward with specific new product demands. If a team of consultants had been assigned specifically to design a business situation calculated to prevent the emergence and development of a customer-oriented marketing viewpoint, it could not have produced anything better than the conditions just described.

Stepchild treatment: The oil industry is a stunning example of how science, technology, and mass production can divert an entire group of companies from their main task. To the extent the consumer is studied at all (which is not much), the focus is forever on getting information which is designed to help the oil companies improve what they are now doing. They try to discover more convincing advertising themes, more effective sales promotional drives, what the market shares of the various companies are, what people like or dislike about service station dealers and oil companies, and so forth. Nobody seems as interested in probing deeply into the basic human needs that the industry might be trying to satisfy as in probing into the basic properties of the raw material that the companies work with in trying to deliver customer satisfactions.

Basic questions about customers and markets seldom get asked. The latter occupy a stepchild status. They are recognized as existing, as having to be taken care of, but not worth very much real thought or dedicated attention. Nobody gets as excited about the customers in his own backyard as about the oil in the Sahara Desert. Nothing illustrates better the neglect of marketing than its treatment in the industry press.

The centennial issue of the *American Petroleum Institute Quarterly*, published in 1959 to celebrate the discovery of oil in Titusville, Pennsylvania, contained 21 feature articles proclaiming the industry's greatness. Only one of these talked about its achievements in marketing, and that was only a pictorial record of how service station architecture has changed. The issue also contained a special section on 'New Horizons,' which was devoted to showing the magnificent role oil would play in America's future. Every reference was ebulliently optimistic, never implying once that oil might have some hard competition. Even the reference to atomic energy was a cheerful catalogue of how oil would help make atomic energy a success. There was not a single apprehension that the oil industry's affluence might be threatened or a suggestion that one 'new horizon' might include new and better ways of serving oil's present customers.

But the most revealing example of the stepchild treatment that marketing gets was still another special series of short articles on 'The Revolutionary Potential of Electronics.' Under that heading this list of articles appeared in the table of contents:

- 'In the Search for Oil'
- 'In Production Operations'
- 'In Refinery Processes'
- 'In Pipeline Operations'

Significantly, every one of the industry's major functional areas is listed, *except* marketing. Why? Either it is believed that electronics holds no revolutionary potential for petroleum marketing (which is palpably wrong), or the editors forgot to discuss marketing (which is more likely, and illustrates its stepchild status).

The order in which the four functional areas are listed also betrays the alienation of the oil industry from the consumer. The industry is implicitly defined as beginning with the search for oil and ending with its distribution from the refinery. But the truth is, it seems to me, that the industry begins with the needs of the customer for its products. From that primal position its definition moves steadily backstream to areas of progressively lesser importance, until it finally comes to rest at the 'search for oil.'

Beginning & end: The view that an industry is a customer-satisfying process, not a goods-producing process, is vital for all businessmen to understand. An industry begins with the customer and his needs, not with a patent, a raw material, or a selling skill. Given the customer's needs, the industry develops backwards, first concerning itself with the physical *delivery* of customer satisfactions. Then it moves back further to *creating* the things by which these satisfactions are in part achieved. How these materials are created is a matter of indifference to the customer, hence the particular form of manufacturing, processing, or what-have-you cannot be considered as a vital aspect of the industry. Finally, the industry moves back still further to *finding* the raw materials necessary for making its products.

The irony of some industries oriented toward technical research and development is that the scientists who occupy the high executive positions are totally unscientific when it comes to defining their companies' overall needs and purposes. They violate the first two rules of the scientific method – being aware of and defining their companies' problems, and then developing testable hypotheses about solving them. They are scientific only about the convenient things, such as laboratory and product experiments.

The reason that the customer (and the satisfaction of his deepest needs) is not considered as being 'the problem' is not because there is any certain belief that no such problem exists, but because an organizational lifetime has conditioned management to look in the opposite direction. Marketing is a stepchild.

I do not mean that selling is ignored. Far from it. But selling, again, is not marketing. As already pointed out, selling concerns itself with the tricks and techniques of getting people to exchange their cash for your product. It is not concerned with the values that the exchange is all about. And it does not, as marketing invariably does, view the entire business process as consisting of a tightly integrated effort to discover, create, arouse, and satisfy customer needs. The customer is somebody 'out there' who, with proper cunning, can be separated from his loose change.

Actually, not even selling gets much attention in some technologically minded firms. Because there is a virtually guaranteed market for the abundant flow of their new products, they do not actually know what a real market is. It is as if they lived in a planned economy, moving their products routinely from factory to retail outlet. Their successful concentration on products tends to convince them of the soundness of what they have been doing, and they fail to see the gathering clouds over the market.

Conclusion

Less than 75 years ago American railroads enjoyed a fierce loyalty among astute Wall Streeters. European monarchs invested in them heavily. Eternal wealth was thought to be the benediction for anybody who could scrape a few thousand dollars together to put into rail stocks. No other form of transportation could compete with the railroads in speed, flexibility, durability, economy, and growth potentials.

As Jacques Barzun put it, 'By the turn of the century it was an institution, an image of man, a tradition, a code of honor, a source of poetry, a nursery of boyhood desires, a sublimest of toys, and the most solemn machine – next to the funeral hearse – that marks the epochs in man's life.'[6]

Even after the advent of automobiles, trucks, and airplanes, the railroad tycoons remained imperturbably self-confident. If you had told them 60 years ago that in 30 years they would be flat on their backs, broke, and pleading for government subsidies, they would have thought you totally demented. Such a future was simply not considered possible. It was not even a discussable subject, or an askable question, or a matter which any sane person would consider worth speculating about. The very thought was insane. Yet a lot of insane notions now have matter-of-fact acceptance – for example, the idea of 100-ton tubes of metal moving smoothly through the air 20,000 feet above the earth, loaded with 100 sane and solid citizens casually drinking martinis – and they have dealt cruel blows to the railroads.

What specifically must other companies do to avoid this fate? What does customer orientation involve? These questions have in part been answered by the preceding examples and analysis. It would take another article to show in detail what is required for specific industries. In any case, it should be obvious that building an effective customer-oriented company involves far more than good intentions or promotional tricks; it involves profound matters of human organization and leadership. For the present, let me merely suggest what appear to be some general requirements.

Visceral feel of greatness: Obviously the company has to do what survival demands. It has to adapt to the requirements of the market, and it has to do it sooner rather than later. But mere survival is a so-so aspiration. Anybody can survive in some way or other, even the skid-row bum. The trick is to survive gallantly, to feel the surging impulse of commercial mastery; not just to experience the sweet smell of success, but to have the visceral feel of entrepreneurial greatness.

No organization can achieve greatness without a vigorous leader who is driven onward by his own pulsating *will to succeed*. He has to have a vision of grandeur, a vision that can produce eager followers in vast numbers. In business, the followers are the customers.

In order to produce these customers, the entire corporation must be viewed as a customer-creating and customer-satisfying organism. Management must think of itself not as producing products but as providing customer-creating value satisfactions. It must push this idea (and everything it means and requires) into every nook and cranny of the organization. It has to do this continuously and with the kind of flair that excites and stimulates the people in it. Otherwise, the company will be merely a series of pigeonholed parts, with no consolidating sense of purpose or direction.

In short, the organization must learn to think of itself not as producing goods or services but as *buying customers*, as doing the things that will make people *want* to do business with it. And the chief executive himself has the inescapable responsibility for creating this environment, this viewpoint, this attitude, this aspiration. He himself must set the company's style, its direction, and its goals. This means he has to know precisely where he himself wants to go, and to make sure the whole organization is enthusiastically aware of where that is. This is a first requisite of leadership, for *unless he knows where he is going, any road will take him there.*

If any road is okay, the chief executive might as well pack his attaché case and go fishing. If an organization does not know or care where it is going, it does not need to advertise that fact with a ceremonial figurehead. Everybody will notice it soon enough.

References

1 Jacques Barzun, 'Trains and the Mind of Man,' *Holiday*, February 1960, p. 21.
2 For more details see M. M. Zimmerman, *The Super Market: A Revolution in Distribution* (New York, McGraw-Hill Book Company, Inc., 1955), p. 48.
3 Ibid., pp. 45–47.
4 *The Affluent Society* (Boston, Houghton Mifflin Company, 1958), pp. 152–160.
5 Henry Ford, *My Life and Work* (New York, Doubleday, Page & Company, 1923), pp. 146–147.
6 Jacques Barzun, 'Trains and the Mind of Man,' *Holiday*, February 1960, p. 20.

Part II

Leadership

Introduction

OF ALL the topics suggested for inclusion in this volume of management milestones, none was so widely mentioned as the subject of leadership and organization. In this area of management concern, one could hardly expect to find as dramatic developments as one might do in spheres affected by technological breakthroughs such as the development of the computer. Nor would one predict the sort of fundamental changes that might be dictated by major disequilibriums in industry structure and/or political realignments. Rather like the proverbial giant oil tanker that, when rounding the Cape of Good Hope, has to begin its turn as it passes Nigeria, shifts in organization and leadership seem to require long periods of time before they have any impact.

In the early 1960s, with the problems of adjusting to the post-war period successfully behind them, most of the UK's largest corporations became increasingly interested – and sometimes even concerned – about how actually to manage the empires that they were creating. As it became clear that a necessary precondition for the successful implementation of their plans and strategies was an effective organization representing a logical reflection of those strategies, attention began to shift from manufacturing and marketing to organization.

What started out as a typical 'This is how I did it' biography of a successful chief executive, very soon after publication became a universally acclaimed handbook of how to organize large multi-business enterprises. After the publication of *My Years with General Motors*, expressions such as 'divisionalization', 'decentralization', 'profit accountable', and 'individual responsibility' entered the permanent lexicon of management. Soon boards and top management would not ask whether they should 'divisionalize', but rather how quickly they could complete the metamorphosis.

As the momentum for change became clear, scholars, theorists and practitioners all began to be carried along by it, and attention gradually turned to how this new organizational structure would actually work in practice. The word 'matrix' – long used as a noun – soon became an overused adjective. We had matrix organization, matrix management, matrix functions and matrix responsibilities. And with them came suggestions as to how to ensure their efficacy. Chuck Ames dusted off the well-established notion of product managers developed in several gigantic consumer product companies and suggested, in 'Payoff from Product Management', that here was a pragmatic, tried and tested approach for solving some of the more intractable problems of making matrix management work.

There was little dispute that the study of organization, unlike, say, that of finance or manufacturing, could only be based on objective fact-finding analysis and cold hard logic up to a point. Beyond that point, it had to rely on all those comparatively 'soft' disciplines with which so many managers and executives had only a passing acquaintance. This uneasy interface produced a cacophony of voices – some contemporary, some resurrected – all expressing ideas on the subject. And so, authorities such as Maslow, Herzberg, McGregor, Bennis, Zaleznik, Gardner and Mintzberg began to cry out for their share of management attention.

None of these, however, was as widely read, admired and listened to as the most venerated management guru of our times – Peter Drucker. His book *The Effective Executive* made it not only legitimate, but compulsory, for all managers to examine the art of organization in terms of its effect on the lives of actual individuals. Boxes and charts, lines dotted and solid, position descriptions, authority levels – these were merely the armoury that management could deploy in its battle for growth and profits. Its most crucial, and often irreplaceable, resources were its people.

5

The Effective Executive

PETER F. DRUCKER

I have always been interested in the notions of 'what really matters' and 'what really makes a difference', and their inevitable links with one's own effectiveness and the nature of the contribution that one can make to the well-being of an organization.

Peter Drucker goes to the heart of these issues by observing in a challenging manner that 'Effective organizations are not common, they are even rarer than effective executives. There are shining examples here and there but, on the whole, organization performance is still primitive.' Having delivered this challenge, Drucker responds to it in a significant fashion. He develops the idea, as valid today as in 1966 when the passage was first written, that effectiveness can be learned. Furthermore, he shows us how this can be done, whilst acknowledging that there is no substitute for experience and no sure-fire prescription for success.

The attraction for me has been, and remains, that he provides the essential insights into leadership and the means of accomplishing significant goals. In doing so, he elucidates the prior processes that deal with selection and judgement, and highlights the courage that is needed to raise 'the sights of people and the egos from preoccupation with the problems to a vision of opportunity and the concern with weakness to exploitation of strength'.

Colin N. J. Wilks,
Chief Financial Officer, Lloyds Bank Plc,
London

Chapter 5: First Things First

IF THERE is any one 'secret' of effectiveness, it is concentration. Effective executives do first things first and they do one thing at a time.

The need to concentrate is grounded both in the nature of the executive job and in the nature of man.

Several reasons for this should already be apparent:

There are always more important contributions to be made than there is time available to make them. Any analysis of executive contributions comes up with an embarrassing richness of important tasks; and any analysis of executives' time discloses an embarrassing scarcity of time available for the work that really contributes. No matter how well an executive manages his time, the greater part of it will still not be his own. Therefore, there is always a time deficit.

The more an executive focuses on upward contribution, the more will he require fairly big continuous chunks of time. The more he switches from being busy to achieving results, the more will he shift to sustained efforts – efforts which require a fairly big quantum of time to bear fruit. Yet to get even that half-day or those two weeks of really productive time requires self-discipline and an iron determination to say 'No'.

Similarly, the more an executive works at making strengths productive, the more will he become conscious of the need to concentrate the human strengths available to him on major opportunities. This is the only way to get results.

But concentration is dictated also by the fact that most of us find it hard enough to do well even one thing at at time, let alone two. Mankind is indeed capable of doing an amazingly wide diversity of things; humanity is a 'multi-purpose tool'. But the way to apply productively

Peter F. Drucker: *The Effective Executive* (London: Heinemann, 1966). By permission.

mankind's great range is to bring to bear a large number of individual capabilities on one task. It is concentration in which all faculties are focused on one achievement.

We rightly consider keeping many balls in the air a circus stunt. Yet even the juggler does it only for ten minutes or so. If he were to try doing it longer, he would soon drop all the balls.

People do, of course, differ. Some do their best work when doing two tasks in parallel at the same time, thus providing a change of pace. This presupposes, however, that they give each of the two tasks the minimum quantum needed to get anything done. But few people, I think, can perform with excellence three major tasks simultaneously.

There was Mozart, of course. He could, it seems, work on several compositions at the same time, all of them masterpieces. But he is the only known exception. The other prolific composers of the first rank – Bach, for instance, Handel, or Haydn, or Verdi – composed one work at a time. They did not begin the next until they had finished the preceding one, or until they had stopped work on it for the time being and put it away in the drawer. Executives can hardly assume that they are 'executive Mozarts'.

Concentration is necessary precisely because the executive faces so many tasks clamouring to be done. For doing one thing at a time means doing it fast. The more one can concentrate time, effort, and resources, the greater the number and diversity of tasks one can actually perform.

No chief executive of any business I have ever known accomplished as much as the recently retired head of a pharmaceutical firm. When he took over, the company was small and operated in one country only. When he retired eleven years later, the company had become a world-wide leader.

This man worked for the first years exclusively on research direction, research programme, and research personnel. The organization had never been a leader in research and had usually been tardy even as a follower. The new chief executive was not a scientist. But he realized that the company had to stop doing five years later what the leaders had pioneered five years before. It had to decide on its own direction. As a result, it moved within five years into a leadership position in two new important fields. The chief executive then turned to building an international company – years after the leaders, such as the old Swiss pharmaceutical houses, had established themselves as leaders all over the world. Carefully analysing drug consumption, he concluded that health insurance and government health services act as the main stimuli to drug demand. By timing his entry into a new country to coincide with a major expansion of its health services he managed to start big in countries where his company had never been before, and without having to take away markets from the well-entrenched, international drug firms.

The last five years of his tenure he concentrated on working out the strategy appropriate to the nature of modern health care, which is fast becoming a 'public utility' in which public bodies such as governments, non-profit hospitals, and semi-public agencies (such as Blue Cross in the United States) pay the bills although an individual, the physician, decides on the actual purchase. Whether his strategy will work out, it is too early to say – it was only perfected in 1965, shortly before he retired. But his is the only one of the major drug companies that, to my knowledge, has even thought about strategy, pricing, marketing, and the relationships of the industry world-wide.

It is unusual for any one chief executive to do one task of such magnitude during his entire tenure. Yet this man did three – in addition to building a strong, well-staffed, world-wide organization. He did this by single-minded concentration on one task at a time.

This is the 'secret' of those people who 'do so many things' and apparently so many difficult things. They do only one at a time. As a result, they need much less time in the end than the rest of us.

The people who get nothing done often work a great deal harder. In the first place, they under-estimate the time for any one task. They always expect that everything will go right. Yet, as every executive knows, nothing ever goes right. The unexpected always happens – the unexpected is indeed the only thing one can confidently expect. And almost never is it a pleasant surprise. Effective executives therefore allow a fair margin of time beyond what is actually needed. In the second place, the typical (that is, the more or less ineffectual) executive tries to hurry – and that only puts him further behind. Effective executives do not race. They set an easy pace but keep going steadily. Finally, the typical executive tries to do several things at once. Therefore, he never has the minimum time quantum for any of the tasks in his programme. If any one of them runs into trouble, his entire programme collapses.

Effective executives know that they have to get many things done – and done effectively. Therefore, they concentrate – their own time and energy as well as that of their organization – on doing one thing at a time, and on doing first things first.

II Sloughing off yesterday

The first rule for the concentration of executive efforts is to slough off the past that has ceased to be productive. Effective executives periodically review their work programmes – and those of their associates – and ask: 'If we did not already do this, would we go into it *now*?' And unless the answer is an unconditional 'Yes' they drop the activity or curtail it sharply. At the least, they make sure that no more resources are being invested in the no longer productive past. And those first-class resources, especially those scarce resources of human strength which are engaged in these tasks of yesterday, are immediately pulled out and put to work on the opportunities of tomorrow.

Executives, whether they like it or not, are forever bailing out the past. This is inevitable. Today is always the result of actions and decisions taken yesterday. Man, however, whatever his title or rank, cannot foresee the future. Yesterday's actions and decisions, no matter how courageous or wise they may have been, inevitably become today's problems, crises, and stupidities. Yet it is the executive's specific job – whether he works in government, in a business or in any other institution – to commit today's resources to the future. This means that every executive forever has to spend time, energy and ingenuity on patching up or bailing out the actions and decisions of yesterday, whether his own or those of his predecessors. In fact this always takes up more hours of his day than any other task.

But one can at least try to limit one's servitude to the past by cutting out those inherited activities and tasks that have ceased to promise results.

No one has much difficulty getting rid of the total failures. They liquidate themselves. Yesterday's successes, however, always linger on long beyond their productive life.

Even more dangerous are the activities which should do well and which, for some reason or other, do not produce. These tend to become, as I have explained elsewhere* 'investments in managerial ego' and sacred. Yet unless they are pruned, and pruned ruthlessly, they drain the life blood from an organization. It is always the most capable people who are wasted in the futile attempt to obtain for the investment in managerial ego the success it 'deserves'.

* *Managing for Results* (New York: Harper & Row; London: Heinemann, 1964).

Every organization is highly susceptible to these twin diseases. But they are particularly prevalent in government. Government programmes and activities age just as fast as the programmes and activities of other institutions. Yet they are not only conceived as eternal; they are welded into the structure through civil-service rules and immediately become vested interests, with their own spokesmen in the legislature.

This was not too dangerous when government was small and played a minor role in social life as it did up till 1914. Today's government, however, cannot afford the diversion of its energies and resources into yesterday. Yet, at a guess, at least half the bureaus and agencies of the Federal government of the United States either regulate what no longer needs regulation – for example the Interstate Commerce Commission whose main efforts are still directed toward protecting the public from a monopoly of the railroads that disappeared thirty years ago. Or they are directed, as is most of the farm programme, toward investment in politicians' egos and toward efforts that should have had results but never achieved them.

There is serious need for a new principle of effective administration under which every act, every agency, and every programme of government is conceived as temporary and as expiring automatically after a fixed number of years – maybe ten – unless specifically prolonged by new legislation following careful outside study of the programme, its results, and its contributions.

President Johnson in 1965–6 ordered such a study for all government agencies and their programmes, adapting the 'programme review' which Secretary McNamara had developed to rid the Defence Department of the barnacles of obsolete and unproductive work. This is a good first step, and badly needed. But it will not produce results as long as we maintain the traditional assumption that all programmes last forever unless proven to have outlived their usefulness. The assumption should rather be that all programmes outlive their usefulness fast and should be scrapped unless proven productive and necessary. Otherwise modern government while increasingly smothering society under rules, regulations, and forms, will itself be smothered in its own fat.

But while government is particularly endangered by organizational obesity, no organization is immune to the disease. The businessman in the large corporation who complains the loudest about bureaucracy in government may encourage in his own company the growth of 'controls' which do not control anything, the proliferation of studies that are only a cover-up for his own unwillingness to face up to a decision, the inflation of all kinds of staffs for all kinds of research or 'relations'. And he himself may waste his own time and that of his key people on the obsolescent product of yesterday while starving tomorrow's successful product. The academician who is loudest in his denunciation of the horrible wastefulness of big business may fight the hardest in the faculty meeting to prolong the life of an obsolescent subject area by making it a required course.

The executive who wants to be effective and who wants his organization to be effective always polices all programmes, all activities, all tasks. He always asks: 'Is this still worth doing?' And if it isn't, he gets rid of it so as to be able to concentrate on the few tasks that, if done with excellence, will really make a difference in the results of his own job and in the performance of his organization.

Above all, the effective executive will slough off an old activity before he starts on a new one. This is necessary in order to keep organizational 'weight control'. Without it, the organization soon loses shape, cohesion, and manageability. Social organizations need to stay lean and muscular as much as biological organisms.

But also, as every executive has learned, nothing new is easy. It always gets into trouble. Unless one has therefore built into the new endeavour the means for bailing it out when it runs into heavy weather, one condemns it to failure from the start. The only effective means for bailing out the new are people who have proven their capacity to perform. Such people are always already busier than they should be. Unless one relieves one of them of his present burden, one cannot expect him to take on the new task.

The alternative – to 'hire in' new people for new tasks – is too risky. One hires new people to expand an already established and smoothly running activity. But one starts something new with people of tested and proven strength, that is with veterans. Every new task is such a gamble – even if other firms have done the same job many times before – that an experienced and effective executive will not, if humanly possible, add to it the additional gamble of hiring an outsider to take charge. He has learned the hard way how many men who looked like geniuses when they worked elsewhere, show up as miserable failures six months after they have started working 'for us'.

An organization needs to bring in fresh people with fresh points of view fairly often. If it only promotes from within it soon becomes inbred and eventually sterile. But if at all possible, one does not bring in the newcomers where the risk is exorbitant, that is into the top executive positions or into leadership of an important new activity. One brings them in just below the top and into an activity that is already defined and reasonably well understood.

Systematic sloughing off of the old is the one and only way to force the new. There is no lack of ideas in any organization I know. 'Creativity' is not our problem. But few organizations ever get going on their own good ideas. Everybody is much too busy on the tasks of yesterday. Putting all programmes and activities regularly on trial for their lives, and getting rid of those that cannot prove their productivity, works wonders in stimulating creativity even in the most hidebound bureaucracy.

Du Pont has been doing so much better than any other of the world's large chemical companies, largely because Du Pont abandons a product or a process *before* it begins to decline. It does not invest scarce resources of people and money into defending yesterday. Most other businesses, however, inside and outside the chemical industry, are run on different principles, viz: 'There'll always be a market for an efficient buggy-whip plant,' and, 'This product built this company and it's our duty to maintain for it the market it deserves.'

It's those other companies, however, which send their executives to seminars on creativity and which complain about the absence of new products. Du Pont is much too busy making and selling new products to do either.

The need to slough off the outworn old to make possible the productive new is universal. It is reasonably certain that we would still have stage-coaches – nationalized, to be sure, heavily subsidized, and with a fantastic research programme to 'retrain the horse' – had there been ministries of transportation around 1825.

III Priorities and posteriorities

There are always more productive tasks for tomorrow than there is time to do them and more opportunities than there are capable people to take care of them – not to mention the always abundant problems and crises.

A decision therefore has to be made which tasks deserve priority and which are of less importance. The only question is which will make the decision – the executive or the pressures. But somehow the tasks will be adjusted to the available time and the opportunities will become available only to the extent to which capable people are around to take charge of them.

If the pressures rather than the executive are allowed to make the decision, the important tasks will predictably be sacrificed. Typically, there will then be no time for the most time-consuming part of any task, the conversion of decision into action. No task is completed until it has become part of organizational action and behaviour. This almost always means that no task is complete unless other people have taken it on as their own, have accepted new ways of doing old things, or the necessity for doing something new, and have otherwise made the executive's 'completed' project their own daily routine. If this is slighted because there is no time, then all the work and effort have been for nothing. Yet this is the invariable result of the executive's failure to concentrate and to impose priorities.

Another predictable result of leaving control of priorities to the pressures is that the work of top management does not get done at all. That is always postponable work, for it does not try to solve yesterday's crises but to make a different tomorrow. And the pressures always favour yesterday. In particular a top group which lets itself be controlled by the pressures will slight the one job no one else can do. It will not pay attention to the outside of the organization. It will therefore lose touch with the only reality, the only area in which there are results. For the pressures always favour what goes on inside. They always favour what has happened over the future, the crisis over the opportunity, the immediate and visible over the real, and the urgent over the relevant.

The job is, however, not to set priorities. That is easy. Everybody can do it. The reason why so few executives concentrate is the difficulty of setting 'posteriorities' – that is, deciding what tasks not to tackle – and of sticking to the decision.

Most executives have learned that what one postpones, one actually abandons. A good many of them suspect that there is nothing less desirable than to take up later a project one has postponed when it first came up. The timing is almost bound to be wrong, and timing is a most important element in the success of any effort. To do five years later what it would have been smart to do five years earlier, is almost a sure recipe for frustration and failure.

Outside of Victorian novels, happiness does not come to the marriage of two people who almost got married at age 21 and who then, at age 38, both widowed, find each other again. If married at age 21, these people might have had an opportunity to grow up together. But in seventeen years both have changed, grown apart, and developed their own ways.

The man who wanted to become a doctor as a youth but was forced to go into business instead, and who now, at age 50 and successful, goes back to his first love and enrolls in medical school, is not likely to finish, let alone to become a successful physician. He may succeed if he has extraordinary motivation, such as a strong religious drive to become a medical missionary. But otherwise he will find the discipline and rote learning of medical school irksome beyond endurance, and medical practice itself humdrum and a bore.

The merger which looked so right six or seven years earlier, but had to be postponed because one company's president refused to serve under the other, is rarely still the right 'marriage' for either side when the stiff-necked executive has finally retired.

That one actually abandons what one postpones makes executives, however, shy from postponing anything altogether. They know that this or that task is not a first priority, but giving it a posteriority is risky. What one has relegated may turn out to be the competitor's triumph. There is no guarantee that the policy area a politician or an administrator has decided to slight may not explode into the hottest and most dangerous political issue.

Neither President Eisenhower nor President Kennedy, for instance, wanted to give high priority to civil rights. And President Johnson most definitely considered Vietnam – and foreign affairs altogether – a posteriority when he came to power. (This, in large measure, explains the violent reaction against him on the part of the liberals who had supported his original priority choice of the War on Poverty, when events forced him to change his priority schedule.)

Setting a posteriority is also unpleasant. Every posteriority is somebody else's top priority.

It is much easier to draw up a nice list of top priorities and then to hedge by trying to do 'just a little bit' of everything else as well. This makes everybody happy. The only drawback is, of course, that nothing whatever gets done.

A great deal could be said about the analysis of priorities. The most important thing about priorities and posteriorities is, however, not intelligent analysis but courage.

Courage rather than analysis dictates the truly important rules for identifying priorities:

- pick the future as against the past;
- focus on opportunity rather than on problem;
- choose your own direction – rather than climb on the bandwagon; and

- aim high, aim for something that will make a difference, rather than for something that is 'safe' and easy to do.

A good many studies of research scientists have shown that achievement (at least below the genius level of an Einstein, a Niels Bohr, or a Max Planck) depends less on ability in doing research than on the courage to go after opportunity. Those research scientists who pick their projects according to the greatest likelihood of quick success, rather than according to the challenge of the problem, are unlikely to achieve distinction. They may turn out a great many footnotes, but neither a law of physics nor a new concept is likely to be named after them. Achievement goes to the people who pick their research priorities by the opportunity and who consider other criteria only as qualifiers rather than as determinants.

In business similarly, the successful companies are not those that work at developing new products for their existing line but those that aim at innovating new technologies or new businesses.

For as a rule it is just as risky, just as arduous, and just as uncertain to do something small that is new, as it is to do something big that is new. It is more productive to convert an opportunity into results than to solve a problem – which only restores the equilibrium of yesterday.

Priorities and posteriorities always have to be reconsidered and revised in the light of realities. No American president, for instance, has been allowed by events to stick to his original list of priority tasks. In fact accomplishing one's priority tasks always changes the priorities and posteriorities themselves.

The effective executive does not, in other words, truly commit himself beyond the *one* task he concentrates on right now. Then he reviews the situation and picks the next one task that now comes first.

Concentration, that is the courage to impose on time and events his own decision as to what really matters and comes first, is the executive's only hope of becoming master of time and events instead of their whipping boy.

6

One More Time: How Do You Motivate Employees?

FREDERICK HERZBERG

I first read Herzberg's views in 1968 when I moved into the personnel field at ICI. At that time, they presented some thinking which was, to me, quite revolutionary: the separation of hygiene factors from motivational ones. This far from obvious concept proved to be a pivotal point in all my subsequent management thinking.

'Job enrichment' is no longer looked upon with the excitement that it was in those days. I believe, in fact, that the concept has now moved on more to that of 'people enrichment' rather than 'job enrichment', but the basic thinking that leads along this path remains as important today as it was in 1968.

Anyone who has made such a valuable contribution to the development of management over such a prolonged period of time has every reason to feel proud.

Sir John Harvey-Jones,
Former Chairman, Imperial Chemical Industries PLC,
London

One More Time: How Do You Motivate Employees?

HOW many articles, books, speeches, and workshops have pleaded plaintively, 'How do I get an employee to do what I want him to do?'

The psychology of motivation is tremendously complex, and what has been unraveled with any degree of assurance is small indeed. But the dismal ratio of knowledge to speculation has not dampened the enthusiasm for new forms of snake oil that are constantly coming on the market, many of them with academic testimonials. Doubtless this article will have no depressing impact on the market for snake oil, but since the ideas expressed in it have been tested in many corporations and other organizations, it will help – I hope – to redress the imbalance in the aforementioned ratio.

'Motivating' with KITA

In lectures to industry on the problem, I have found that the audiences are anxious for quick and practical answers, so I will begin with a straightforward, practical formula for moving people.

What is the simplest, surest, and most direct way of getting someone to do something? Ask him? But if he responds that he does not want to do it, then that calls for a psychological consultation to determine the reason for his obstinacy. Tell him? His response shows that he does not understand you, and now an expert in communication methods has to be brought in to show you how to get through to him. Give him a monetary incentive? I do not need to remind the reader of the complexity and difficulty involved in setting up and administering an incentive system. Show him? This means a costly training program. We need a simple way.

Every audience contains the 'direct action' manager who shouts, 'Kick him!' And this type of manager is right. The surest and least circumlocuted way of getting someone to do something is to kick him in the pants – give him what might be called the KITA.

There are various forms of KITA, and here are some of them:

● *Negative physical KITA.* This is a literal application of the term and was frequently used in the past. It has, however, three major drawbacks: (1) it is inelegant; (2) it contradicts the precious image of benevolence that most organizations cherish; and (3) since it is a physical attack, it directly stimulates the automatic nervous system, and this often results in negative feedback – the employee may just kick you in return. These factors give rise to certain taboos against negative physical KITA.

The psychologist has come to the rescue of those who are no longer permitted to use negative physical KITA. He has uncovered infinite sources of psychological vulnerabilities and the appropriate methods to play tunes on them. 'He took my rug away'; 'I wonder what he meant by that'; 'The boss is always going around me' – these symptomatic expressions of ego sores that have been rubbed raw are the result of application of:

● *Negative psychological KITA.* This has several advantages over negative physical KITA. First, the cruelty is not visible; the bleeding is internal and comes much later. Second, since it affects the higher cortical centers of the brain with its inhibitory powers, it reduces the possibility of physical backlash. Third, since the number of psychological pains that a person can feel is almost infinite, the direction and site possibilities of the KITA are increased many times. Fourth, the person administering the kick can manage to be above it all and let the system accomplish the dirty work. Fifth, those who practice it receive some ego satisfaction (one-upmanship), whereas they would find drawing blood abhorrent. Finally, if the employee does complain, he can always be accused of being paranoid, since there is no tangible evidence of an actual attack.

Now, what does negative KITA accomplish? If I kick you in the rear (physically or psychologically), who is motivated? *I* am motivated; *you* move! Negative KITA does not lead to motivation, but to movement. So:

• *Positive KITA.* Let us consider motivation. If I say to you, 'Do this for me or the company, and in return I will give you a reward, an incentive, more status, a promotion, all the quid pro quos that exist in the industrial organization,' am I motivating you? The overwhelming opinion I receive from management people is, 'Yes, this is motivation.'

I have a year-old Schnauzer. When it was a small puppy and I wanted it to move, I kicked it in the rear and it moved. Now that I have finished its obedience training, I hold up a dog biscuit when I want the Schnauzer to move. In this instance, who is motivated – I or the dog? The dog wants the biscuit, but it is I who want it to move. Again, I am the one who is motivated, and the dog is the one who moves. In this instance all I did was apply KITA frontally; I exerted a pull instead of a push. When industry wishes to use such positive KITAs, it has available an incredible number and variety of dog biscuits (jelly beans for humans) to wave in front of the employee to get him to jump.

Why is it that managerial audiences are quick to see that negative KITA is *not* motivation, while they are almost unanimous in their judgment that positive KITA *is* motivation? It is because negative KITA is rape, and positive KITA is seduction. But it is infinitely worse to be seduced than to be raped; the latter is an unfortunate occurrence, while the former signifies that you were a party to your own downfall. This is why positive KITA is so popular: it is a tradition; it is in the American way. The organization does not have to kick you; you kick yourself.

Myths about motivation

Why is KITA not motivation? If I kick my dog (from the front or the back), he will move. And when I want him to move again, what must I do? I must kick him again. Similarly, I can charge a man's battery, and then recharge it, and recharge it again. But it is only when he has his own generator that we can talk about motivation. He then needs no outside stimulation. He *wants* to do it.

With this in mind, we can review some positive KITA personnel practices that were developed as attempts to instill 'motivation':

(1) *Reducing time spent at work* – This represents a marvelous way of motivating people to work – getting them off the job! We have reduced (formally and informally) the time spent on the job over the last 50 or 60 years until we are finally on the way to the '6½-day weekend.' An interesting variant of this approach is the development of off-hour recreation programs. The philosophy here seems to be that those who play together, work together. The fact is that motivated people seek more hours of work, not fewer.

(2) *Spiraling wages* – Have these motivated people? Yes, to seek the next wage increase. Some medievalists still can be heard to say that a good depression will get employees moving. They feel that if rising wages don't or won't do the job, perhaps reducing them will.

(3) *Fringe benefits* – Industry has outdone the most welfare-minded of welfare states in dispensing cradle-to-the-grave succor. One company I know of had an informal 'fringe benefit of the month club' going for a while. The cost of fringe benefits in this country has reached approximately 25% of the wage dollar, and we still cry for motivation.

People spend less time working for more money and more security than ever before, and the trend cannot be reversed. These benefits are no longer rewards; they are rights. A 6-day week is inhuman, a 10-hour day is exploitation, extended medical coverage is a basic decency, and stock options are the salvation of American initiative. Unless the ante is continuously raised, the psychological reaction of employees is that the company is turning back the clock.

When industry began to realize that both the economic nerve and the lazy nerve of their employees had insatiable appetites, it started to listen to the behavioral scientists who, more out of a humanist tradition than from scientific study, criticized management for not knowing how to deal with people. The next KITA easily followed.

(4) *Human relations training* – Over 30 years of teaching and, in many instances, of practicing psychological approaches to handling people have resulted in costly human relations programs and, in the end, the same question: How do you motivate workers? Here, too, escalations have taken place. Thirty years ago it was necessary to request, 'Please don't spit on the floor.' Today the same admonition requires three 'please's before the employee feels that his superior has demonstrated the psychologically proper attitudes toward him.

The failure of human relations training to produce motivation led to the conclusion that the supervisor or manager himself was not psychologically true to himself in his practice of interpersonal decency. So an advanced form of human relations KITA, sensitivity training, was unfolded.

(5) *Sensitivity training* – Do you really, really understand yourself? Do you really, really, really trust the other man? Do you really, really, really, really cooperate? The failure of sensitivity training is now being explained, by those who have become opportunistic exploiters of the technique, as a failure to really (five times) conduct proper sensitivity training courses.

With the realization that there are only temporary gains from comfort and economic and interpersonal KITA, personnel managers concluded that the fault lay not in what they were doing, but in the employee's failure to appreciate what they were doing. This opened up the field of communications, a whole new area of 'scientifically' sanctioned KITA.

(6) *Communications* – The professor of communications was invited to join the faculty of management training programs and help in making employees understand what management was doing for them. House organs, briefing sessions, supervisory instruction on the importance of communication, and all sorts of propaganda have proliferated until today there is even an International Council of Industrial Editors. But no motivation resulted, and the obvious thought occurred that perhaps management was not hearing what the employees were saying. That led to the next KITA.

(7) *Two-way communication* – Management ordered morale surveys, suggestion plans, and group participation programs. Then both employees and management were communicating and listening to each other more than ever, but without much improvement in motivation.

The behavioral scientists began to take another look at their conceptions and their data, and they took human relations one step further. A glimmer of truth was beginning to show through in the writings of the so-called higher-order-need psychologists. People, so they said, want to actualize themselves. Unfortunately, the 'actualizing' psychologists got mixed up with the human relations psychologists, and a new KITA emerged.

(8) *Job participation* – Though it may not have been the theoretical intention, job participation often became a 'give them the big picture' approach. For example, if a man is tightening 10,000 nuts a day on an assembly line with a torque wrench, tell him he is building a Chevrolet. Another approach had the goal of giving the employee a *feeling* that he is determining, in some measure, what he does on his job. The goal was to provide a *sense* of achievement rather than a substantive achievement in his task. Real achievement, of course, requires a task that makes it possible.

But still there was no motivation. This led to the inevitable conclusion that the employees must be sick, and therefore to the next KITA.

(9) *Employee counseling* – The initial use of this form of KITA in a systematic fashion can be credited to the Hawthorne experiment of the Western Electric Company during the early 1930's. At that time, it was found that the employees harbored irrational feelings that were interfering with the rational operation of the factory. Counseling in this instance was a means of letting the employees unburden themselves by talking to someone about their problems. Although the counseling techniques were primitive, the program was large indeed.

The counseling approach suffered as a result of experiences during World War II, when the programs themselves were found to be interfering with the operation of the organizations; the counselors had forgotten their role of benevolent listeners and were attempting to do something about the problems that they heard about. Psychological counseling, however, has managed to survive the negative impact of World World II experiences and today is beginning to flourish with renewed sophistication. But, alas, many of these programs, like all the others, do not seem to have lessened the pressure of demands to find out how to motivate workers.

Since KITA results only in short-term movement, it is safe to predict that the cost of these programs will increase steadily and new varieties will be developed as old positive KITAs reach their satiation points.

Hygiene vs. motivators

Let me rephrase the perennial question this way: How do you install a generator in an employee? A brief review of my motivation-hygiene theory of job attitudes is required before theoretical and practical suggestions can be offered. The theory was first drawn from an examination of events in the lives of engineers and accountants. At least 16 other investigations, using a wide variety of populations (including some in the Communist countries), have since been completed, making the original research one of the most replicated studies in the field of job attitudes.

The findings of these studies, along with corroboration from many other investigations using different procedures, suggest that the factors involved in producing job satisfaction (and motivation) are separate and distinct from the factors that lead to job dissatisfaction. Since separate factors need to be considered, depending on whether job satisfaction or job dissatisfaction is being examined, it follows that these two feelings are not opposites of each other. The opposite of job satisfaction is not job dissatisfaction but, rather, *no* job satisfaction; and, similarly, the opposite of job dissatisfaction is not job satisfaction, but *no* job dissatisfaction.

Stating the concept presents a problem in semantics, for we normally think of satisfaction and dissatisfaction as opposites – i.e., what is not satisfying must be dissatisfying, and vice versa. But when it comes to understanding the behavior of people in their jobs, more than a play on words is involved.

Two different needs of man are involved here. One set of needs can be thought of as stemming from his animal nature – the built-in drive to avoid pain from the environment, plus all the learned drives which become conditioned to the basic biological needs. For example, hunger, a basic biological drive, makes it necessary to earn money, and then money becomes a specific drive. The other set of needs relates to that unique human characteristic, the ability to achieve and, through achievement, to experience psychological growth. The stimuli for the growth needs are tasks that induce growth; in the industrial setting, they are the *job content*. Contrariwise, the stimuli inducing pain-avoidance behavior are found in the *job environment*.

The growth or *motivator* factors that are intrinsic to the job are: achievement, recognition for achievement, the work itself, responsibility, and growth or advancement. The dissatisfaction avoidance or *hygiene* (KITA) factors that are extrinsic to the job include: company policy and administration, supervision, interpersonal relationships, working conditions, salary, status, and security.

A composite of the factors that are involved in causing job satisfaction and job dissatisfaction, drawn from samples of 1,685 employees, is shown in Exhibit 6.1. The results indicate that motivators were the primary cause of satisfaction, and hygiene factors the primary cause of

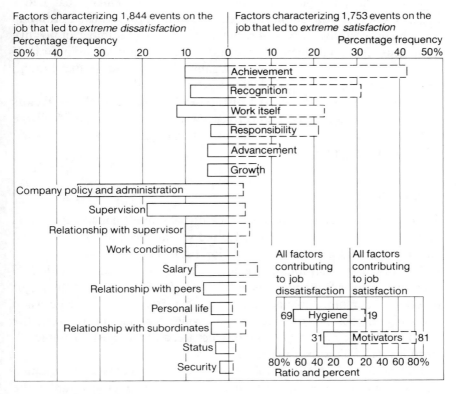

Exhibit 6.1 Factors affecting job attitudes, as reported in 12 investigations

unhappiness on the job. The employees, studied in 12 different investigations, included lower-level supervisors, professional women, agricultural administrators, men about to retire from management positions, hospital maintenance personnel, manufacturing supervisors, nurses, food handlers, military officers, engineers, scientists, house-keepers, teachers, technicians, female assemblers, accountants, Finnish foremen, and Hungarian engineers.

They were asked what job events had occurred in their work that had led to extreme satisfaction or extreme dissatisfaction on their part. Their responses are broken down in the exhibit into percentages of total 'positive' job events and of total 'negative' job events. (The figures total more than 100% on both the 'hygiene' and 'motivators' sides because often at least two factors can be attributed to a single event; advancement, for instance, often accompanies assumption of responsibility.)

To illustrate, a typical response involving achievement that had a negative effect for the employee was, 'I was unhappy because I didn't do the job successfully.' A typical response in the small number of positive job events in the Company Policy and Administration grouping was, 'I was happy because the company reorganized the section so that I didn't report any longer to the guy I didn't get along with.'

As the lower right-hand part of the exhibit shows, of all the factors contributing to job satisfaction, 81% were motivators. And of all the factors contributing to the employees' dissatisfaction over their work, 69% involved hygiene elements.

Eternal triangle

There are three general philosophies of personnel management. The first is based on organizational theory, the second on industrial engineering, and the third on behavioral science.

The organizational theorist believes that human needs are either so irrational or so varied and adjustable to specific situations that the major function of personnel management is to be as pragmatic as the occasion demands. If jobs are organized in a proper manner, he reasons, the result will be the most efficient job structure, and the most favorable job attitudes will follow as a matter of course.

The industrial engineer holds that man is mechanistically oriented and economically motivated and his needs are best met by attuning the individual to the most efficient work process. The goal of personnel management therefore should be to concoct the most appropriate incentive system and to design the specific working conditions in a way that facilitates the most efficient use of the human machine. By structuring jobs in a manner that leads to the most efficient operation, the engineer believes that he can obtain the optimal organization of work and the proper work attitudes.

The behavioral scientist focuses on group sentiments, attitudes of individual employees, and the organization's social and psychological climate. According to his persuasion, he emphasizes one or more of the various hygiene and motivator needs. His approach to personnel management generally emphasizes some form of human relations education, in the hope of instilling healthy employee attitudes and an organizational climate which he considers to be felicitous to human values. He believes that proper attitudes will lead to efficient job and organizational structure.

There is always a lively debate as to the overall effectiveness of the approaches of the organizational theorist and the industrial engineer. Manifestly they have achieved much. But the nagging question for the behavioral scientist has been: What is the cost in human problems that eventually cause more expense to the organization – for instance, turnover, absenteeism, errors, violation of safety rules, strikes, restriction of output, higher wages, and greater fringe benefits? On the other hand, the behavioral scientist is hard put to document much manifest improvement in personnel management, using his approach.

The three philosophies can be depicted as a triangle, as is done in Exhibit 6.2, with each persuasion claiming the apex angle. The motivation-hygiene theory claims the same angle as industrial engineering, but for opposite goals. Rather than rationalizing work to increase efficiency, the theory suggests that work be *enriched* to bring about effective utilization of personnel. Such a systematic attempt to motivate employees by manipulating the motivator factors is just beginning.

The term *job enrichment* describes this embryonic movement. An older term, job enlargement, should be avoided because it is associated with past failures stemming from a misunderstanding of the problem. Job enrichment provides the opportunity for the employee's psychological growth, while job enlargement merely makes a job structurally bigger. Since scientific job enrichment is very new, this article only suggests the principles and practical steps that have recently emerged from several successful experiments in industry.

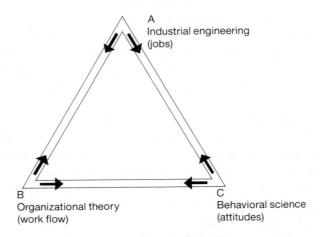

Exhibit 6.2 'Triangle' of philosophies of personnel management

Job loading

In attempting to enrich an employee's job, management often succeeds in reducing the man's personal contribution, rather than giving him an opportunity for growth in his accustomed job. Such an endeavor, which I shall call horizontal job loading (as opposed to vertical loading, or providing motivator factors), has been the problem of earlier job enlargement programs. This activity merely enlarges the meaningless-ness of the job. Some examples of this approach, and their effect, are:

● Challenging the employee by increasing the amount of production expected of him. If he tightens 10,000 bolts a day, see if he can tighten 20,000 bolts a day. The arithmetic involved shows that multiplying zero by zero still equals zero.

● Adding another meaningless task to the existing one, usually some routine clerical activity. The arithmetic here is adding zero to zero.

● Rotating the assignments of a number of jobs that need to be enriched. This means washing dishes for a while, then washing silverware. The arithmetic is substituting one zero for another zero.

● Removing the most difficult parts of the assignment in order to free the worker to accomplish more of the less challenging assignments. This traditional industrial engineering approach amounts to subtraction in the hope of accomplishing addition.

These are common forms of horizontal loading that frequently come up in preliminary brainstorming sessions on job enrichment. The principles

Principle	Motivators involved
A Removing some controls while retaining accountability	Responsibility and personal achievement
B Increasing the accountability of individuals for own work	Responsibility and recognition
C Giving a person a complete natural unit of work (module, division, area, and so on)	Responsibility, achievement, and recognition
D Granting additional authority to an employee in his activity; job freedom	Responsibility, achievement, and recognition
E Making periodic reports directly available to the worker himself rather than to the supervisor	Internal recognition
F Introducing new and more difficult tasks not previously handled	Growth and learning
G Assigning individuals specific or specialized tasks, enabling them to become experts	Responsibility, growth, and advancement

Exhibit 6.3 Principles of vertical job loading

of vertical loading have not all been worked out as yet, and they remain rather general, but I have furnished seven useful starting points for consideration in Exhibit 6.3.

A successful application

An example from a highly successful job enrichment experiment can illustrate the distinction between horizontal and vertical loading of a job. The subjects of this study were the stockholder correspondents employed by a very large corporation. Seemingly, the task required of these carefully selected and highly trained correspondents was quite complex and challenging. But almost all indexes of performance and job attitudes were low, and exit interviewing confirmed that the challenge of the job existed merely as words.

A job enrichment project was initiated in the form of an experiment with one group, designated as an achieving unit, having its job enriched by the principles described in Exhibit 6.3. A control group continued to do its job in the traditional way. (There were also two 'uncommitted' groups of correspondents formed to measure the so-called Hawthorne Effect – that is, to gauge whether productivity and attitudes toward the job changed artificially merely because employees sensed that the company was paying more attention to them in doing something different or novel. The results for these groups were substantially the same as for the control group, and for the sake of simplicity I do not deal with them in this summary.) No changes in hygiene were introduced for either group other than those that would have been made anyway, such as normal pay increases.

The changes for the achieving unit were introduced in the first two months, averaging one per week of the seven motivators listed in Exhibit 6.3. At the end of six months the members of the achieving unit were found to be outperforming their counterparts in the control group, and in addition indicated a marked increase in their liking for the jobs. Other results showed that the achieving group had lower absenteeism and, subsequently, a much higher rate of promotion.

Exhibit 6.4 illustrates the changes in performance, measured in February and March, before the study period began, and at the end of

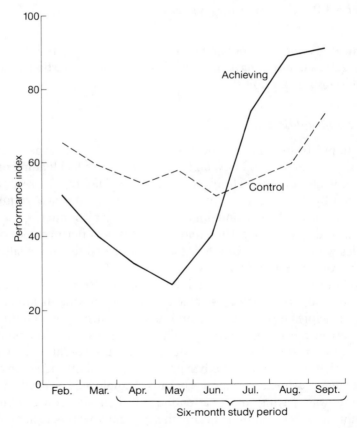

Exhibit 6.4 Shareholder service index in company experiment

each month of the study period. The shareholder service index represents quality of letters, including accuracy of information, and speed of response to stockholders' letters of inquiry. The index of a current month was averaged into the average of the two prior months, which means that improvement was harder to obtain if the indexes of the previous months were low. 'The 'achievers' were performing less well before the six-month period started, and their performance service index continued to decline after the introduction of the motivators, evidently because of uncertainty over their newly granted responsibilities. In the third month, however, performance improved, and soon the members of this group had reached a high level of accomplishment.

Exhibit 6.5 shows the two groups' attitudes toward their job, measured at the end of March, just before the first motivator was introduced, and again at the end of September. The correspondents were asked 16 questions, all involving motivation. A typical one was, 'As you see it, how many opportunities do you feel that you have in your job for making worthwhile contributions?' The answers were scaled from 1 to 5, with 80 as the maximum possible score. The achievers became

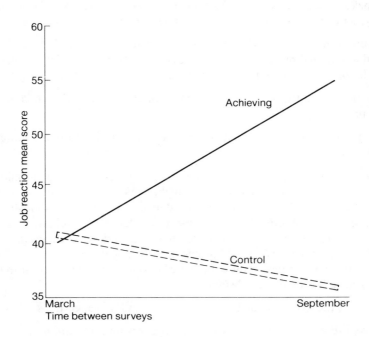

Exhibit 6.5 Changes in attitudes toward tasks in company experiment

much more positive about their job, while the attitude of the control unit remained about the same (the drop is not statistically significant).

How was the job of these correspondents restructured? Exhibit 6.6 lists the suggestions made that were deemed to be horizontal loading, and the actual vertical loading changes that were incorporated in the job of the achieving unit. The capital letters under 'Principle' after 'Vertical loading' refer to the corresponding letters in Exhibit 6.3. The reader will note that the rejected forms of horizontal loading correspond closely to the list of common manifestations of the phenomenon in the left column of Exhibit 6.3.

Steps to job enrichment

Now that the motivator idea has been described in practice, here are the steps that managers should take in instituting the principle with their employees:

(1) Select those jobs in which (a) the investment in industrial engineering does not make changes too costly, (b) attitudes are poor, (c) hygiene is becoming very costly, and (d) motivation will make a difference in performance.

(2) Approach these jobs with the conviction that they can be changed. Years of tradition have led managers to believe that the content of the jobs is sacrosanct and the only scope of action that they have is in ways of stimulating people.

(3) Brainstorm a list of changes that may enrich the jobs, without concern for their practicality.

(4) Screen the list to eliminate suggestions that involve hygiene, rather than actual motivation.

(5) Screen the list for generalities, such as 'give them more responsibility,' that are rarely followed in practice. This might seem obvious, but the motivator words have never left industry; the substance has just been rationalized and organized out. Words like 'responsibility', 'growth', 'achievement', and 'challenge', for example, have been elevated to the lyrics of the patriotic anthem for all organizations. It is the old problem typified by the pledge of allegiance to the flag being more important than contributions to the country – of following the form, rather than the substance.

(6) Screen the list to eliminate any *horizontal* loading suggestions.

(7) Avoid direct participation by the employees whose jobs are to be enriched. Ideas they have expressed previously certainly constitute a valuable source for

Exhibit 6.6 Enlargement vs. enrichment of correspondents' tasks in company experiment

Horizontal loading suggestions (rejected)	Vertical suggestions (adopted)	Principle
Firm quotas could be set for letters to be answered each day, using a rate which would be hard to reach.	Subject matter experts were appointed within each unit for other members of the unit to consult with before seeking supervisory help. (The supervisor had been answering all specialized and difficult questions.)	G
The women could type the letters themselves, as well as compose them, or take on any other clerical functions.	Correspondents signed their own names on letters. (The supervisor had been signing all letters.)	B
All difficult or complex inquiries could be channeled to a few women so that the remainder could achieve high rates of output. These jobs could be exchanged from time to time.	The work of the more experienced correspondents was proofread less frequently by supervisors and was done at the correspondents' desks, dropping verification from 100% to 10%. (Previously, all correspondents' letters had been checked by the supervisor.)	A
	Production was discussed, but only in terms such as 'a full day's work is expected.' As time went on, this was no longer mentioned. (Before, the group had been constantly reminded of the number of letters that needed to be answered.)	D
The women could be rotated through units handling different customers, and then sent back to their own units.	Outgoing mail went directly to the mailroom without going over supervisors' desks. (The letters had always been routed through the supervisors.)	A
	Correspondents were encouraged to answer letters in a more personalized way. (Reliance on the form-letter approach had been standard practice.)	C
	Each correspondent was held personally responsible for the quality and accuracy of letters. (This responsibility had been the province of the supervisor and the verifier.)	B, E

recommended changes, but their direct involvement contaminates the process with human relations *hygiene* and, more specifically, gives them only a *sense* of making a contribution. The job is to be changed, and it is the content that will produce the motivation, not attitudes about being involved or the challenge inherent in setting up a job. That process will be over shortly, and it is what the employees will be doing from then on that will determine their motivation. A sense of participation will result only in short-term movement.

(8) In the initial attempts at job enrichment, set up a controlled experiment. At least two equivalent groups should be chosen, one an experimental unit in which the motivators are systematically introduced over a period of time, and the other one a control group in which no changes are made. For both groups, hygiene should be allowed to follow its natural course for the duration of the experiment. Pre- and post-installation tests of performance and job attitudes are necessary to evaluate the effectiveness of the job enrichment program. The attitude test must be limited to motivator items in order to divorce the employee's view of the job he is given from all the surrounding hygiene feelings that he might have.

(9) Be prepared for a drop in performance in the experimental group the first few weeks. The changeover to a new job may lead to a temporary reduction in efficiency.

(10) Expect your first-line supervisors to experience some anxiety and hostility over the changes you are making. The anxiety comes from their fear that the changes will result in poorer performance for their unit. Hostility will arise when the employees start assuming what the supervisors regard as their own responsibility for performance. The supervisor without checking duties to perform may then be left with little to do.

After a successful experiment, however, the supervisor usually discovers the supervisory and managerial functions he has neglected, or which were never his because all his time was given over to checking the work of his subordinates. For example, in the R&D division of one large chemical company I know of, the supervisors of the laboratory assistants were theoretically responsible for their training and evaluation. These functions, however, had come to be performed in a routine, unsubstantial fashion. After the job enrichment program, during which the supervisors were not merely passive observers of the assistants' performance, the supervisors actually were devoting their time to reviewing performance and administering thorough training.

What has been called an employee-centered style of supervision will come about not through education of supervisors, but by changing the jobs that they do.

Concluding note

Job enrichment will not be a one-time proposition, but a continuous management function. The initial changes, however, should last for a very long period of time. There are a number of reasons for this:

- The changes should bring the job up to the level of challenge commensurate with the skill that was hired.
- Those who have still more ability eventually will be able to demonstrate it better and win promotion to higher-level jobs.
- The very nature of motivators, as opposed to hygiene factors, is that they have a much longer-term effect on employees' attitudes. Perhaps the job will have to be enriched again, but this will not occur as frequently as the need for hygiene.

Not all jobs can be enriched, nor do all jobs need to be enriched. If only a small percentage of the time and money that is now devoted to hygiene, however, were given to job enrichment efforts, the return in human satisfaction and economic gain would be one of the largest dividends that industry and society have ever reaped through their efforts at better personnel management.

The argument for job enrichment can be summed up quite simply: If you have someone on a job, use him. If you can't use him on the job, get rid of him, either via automation or by selecting someone with lesser ability. If you can't use him and you can't get rid of him, you will have a motivation problem.

Author's note: I should like to acknowledge the contributions that Robert Ford of the American Telephone and Telegraph Company has made to the ideas expressed in this paper, and in particular to the successful application of these ideas in improving work performance and the job satisfaction of employees.

7

The Nature of Managerial Work

Henry Mintzberg

I must be a slow learner, for I paid relatively little attention to Henry Mintzberg's book The Nature of Managerial Work when it first appeared in 1973. For me then, as for many others, strategy for the firm was primarily a question of rational analysis of market dynamics and structures of competition. That the way in which managers behaved from day to day critically affected their judgements and their choices of information on which to base those judgements was not immediately obvious to me.

I suspect that Henry himself did not fully comprehend the significance of what he had done until much later. The book reads like yet another text on the behaviour side of management, with relatively few lines of direct connection to strategic choice and the management of the processes by which firms build competitive strength over long periods of time. These are themes that Henry developed later on with his prolific stream of writings on what has come to be called 'emergent' as opposed to 'planned' strategy. Yet, as I have found these ideas and connections to be of increasing importance in my own work, I have also found that I have needed to go back to Henry's starting point to understand why he has been so influential in the field of strategy.

My sense of the book's impact on other people's thinking and behaviour is that it was a 'sleeper' for many years. Not until it had become clear in the late 1970s that all the then new analytical apparatus of strategic planning was not working as well as it should have been did the book rise to prominence. The search for better ways to define the issues, and above all to place people firmly in the set of central considerations, pushed many managers and academics to read with new eyes a book that they had already known about for some time.

One measure of the impact on company behaviour is the frequency with which Henry's terminology is used in planning meetings, even though often without attribution. It is now legitimate in many companies to recognize explicitly the 'soft' issues of the management process. Among academics, the book can be seen to mark one of the starting points for a long-standing and continuing debate about how to blend more adequately the wisdom of the behavioural sciences with the power of economic analysis.

The relevance of the original argument seems to be growing all the time. We are all acutely aware of just how much organizational capability determines long-run competitiveness, especially when the competitive environment changes so quickly. The questions raised in the book still lack good answers, for it is hard to define them clearly in operational terms. Yet, many of those who are currently seeking better answers to the enduring problems of how to improve firms' total performance use Henry's thinking as a critical point of departure.

Professor John M. Stopford,
London Business School,
London

Chapter 7: The Future of Managerial Work

Now this is not the end. It is not even the beginning of the end. But it is, perhaps, the end of the beginning.

Winston Churchill

THIS chapter begins with a definition of the manager and a statement of his basic purposes, from which we see the derivation of ten working roles. These roles indicate the manager's considerable responsibility in his organization; this responsibility in turn gives rise to a number of basic characteristics of the job of managing. It is because of these characteristics that a science of managing has not yet emerged. The second section of this chapter describes the manager in a 'loop.'

This descriptive summary is followed by four sections that present some normative implications of these findings. The third section is addressed to the manager himself, and contains a list of self-study questions as well as ten basic points the manager might consider to improve his effectiveness. In the fourth section the implications of the findings for the teacher of managers are considered, particularly in the area of skill development, and in the fifth section the implications for the management scientist are reviewed briefly. The final section contains some suggestions for further research. These four sections are organized to suggest the order in which change will come to the manager's job. Today's managers can make immediate changes in the way they work, while the teacher of managers will influence the next generation of managers. The management scientist can help the manager in a number of areas today, but it will take considerable time to develop a true science of managing. Finally, to the researcher will fall

Extract from *The Nature of Managerial Work* by Henry Mintzberg. Copyright © 1973 by Henry Mintzberg. Reprinted by permission of Harper & Row, Publishers, Inc. [Published in New Jersey; extract abridged.]

the task of developing the thorough understanding of the manager's job that all participants – managers, teachers, management scientists – will eventually require if they are to make truly profound changes in the work of managing.

A comprehensive description of managerial work

I present below a summary of my basic propositions about managerial work. It should be noted that these are supported by differing amounts of evidence – some are simply hypotheses while others have considerable empirical support. These propositions are presented here in an integrated description to show the interrelationships among the manager's purposes, roles, and characteristics, and the influence these have on the development of a science of managing.

Definition and Basic Purposes. The manager is that person in charge of a formal organization or one of its subunits. He is vested with formal authority over his organizational unit, and this leads to his two basic purposes. First, the manager must ensure that his organization produces its specific goods or services efficiently. He must design, and maintain the stability of, its basic operations, and he must adapt it in a controlled way to its changing environment. Second, the manager must ensure that his organization serves the ends of those persons who control it (the 'influencers'). He must interpret their particular preferences and combine these to produce statements of organizational preference that can guide its decision-making. Because of his formal authority the manager must serve two other basic purposes as well. He must act as the key communication link between his organization and its environment, and he must assume responsibility for the operation of his organization's status system.

Ten Working Roles. These basic purposes are operationalized through ten interrelated roles, performed by all managers. The roles fall into three groupings – three *interpersonal* roles, which derive from the manager's authority and status, three *informational* roles, which derive from the interpersonal roles and the access they provide to information, and four *decisional* roles, which derive from the manager's authority and information.

As *figurehead*, the simplest of managerial roles, the manager is a symbol, required because of his status to carry out a number of social, inspirational, legal, and ceremonial duties. In addition, the manager must be available to certain parties who demand to deal with him because of his status and authority. The *figurehead* role is most significant at the highest levels of the organizational hierarchy.

The *leader* role defines the manager's interpersonal relationships with his subordinates. He must bring together their needs and those of the organization to create a milieu in which they will work effectively. The manager motivates his subordinates, probes into their activities to keep them alert, and takes responsibility for the hiring, training, and promoting of those closest to him. The societal shift toward greater organizational democracy will cause managers to spend more time in the *leader* role.

The *liaison* role focuses on the manager's dealings with people outside his own organizational unit. He develops a network of contacts in which information and favors are traded for mutual benefit. The manager spends a considerable amount of time performing this role, first by making a series of commitments to establish these contacts, and then by engaging in various activities to maintain them. For some managers this role is paramount. In the managerial dyad, for example, the chief executive generally focuses on outside work and the second in command concentrates on internal operations (notably the *leader* and the decisional roles). Line sales managers, because their orientation is external and interpersonal, give special attention to this role, and to the other two interpersonal roles as well.

Through the *leader* and *liaison* roles, the manager gains access to privileged information and he emerges as the 'nerve center' of his organization. He alone has formal access to every subordinate in his own organization, and he has unique access to a variety of outsiders, many of whom are nerve centers of their own organizations. Thus the manager is his organization's information generalist, that person best informed about its operations and environment.

As *monitor* the manager continually seeks and receives internal and external information from a variety of sources to develop a thorough knowledge of his milieu. Because a good part of this information is current and nondocumented, the manager must take prime responsibility for the design of his own information system, which is necessarily informal. Managers in new jobs, particularly, spend considerable time on the *monitor* and *liaison* roles in order to build up their information systems and bring themselves up to the level of knowledge needed for effective strategy-making.

As *disseminator* the manager transmits some of his internal and external information to subordinates. In this way, he maintains their only access to certain privileged information. Some of this information is of a factual nature; some relates to the values of the organization's influencers.

As *spokesman* the manager transmits information to individuals outside his organizational unit. He acts in a public relations capacity, lobbies for his organization, informs key influencers, tells the public about the organization's performance, and sends useful information to his liaison contacts. Furthermore, the manager must serve outsiders as an expert in the industry or function in which his organization operates. Managers of staff groups, because their subunits are highly specialized and oriented to analysis, spend considerable time in this expert capacity as well as giving relatively more attention to the other informational roles.

Because of his formal authority and special information, the manager must take responsibility for his organization's strategy-making system – the means by which decisions important to his organizational unit are made and interrelated. Strategy is made through four decisional roles.

As *entrepreneur* the manager is responsible for the initiation and design of much of the controlled change in his organization. He continually searches for new opportunities and problems and he initiates improve-ment projects to deal with these. Once started, an improvement project may involve the manager in one of three ways. He may delegate all responsibility to a subordinate, implicitly retaining the right to replace him; he may delegate responsibility for the design work but retain responsibility for authorizing the project before implementation; or he may supervise the design work himself. Senior managers appear to maintain supervision at any one time over a large inventory of these projects. Each is worked on periodically, with each step followed by a period of delay during which the senior manager waits for the feedback of information or the occurrence of an event.

As *disturbance handler* the manager is required to take charge when his organization faces a major disturbance. Since each subordinate is charged with a specialized function, only the manager is able to intervene when the organization faces a novel stimulus that is unrelated to any particular function and for which it has no programmed response. In effect, the manager again acts as his organization's generalist – the problem-solver who can deal with any kind of stimulus. Disturbances may reflect an insensitivity to problems, but they may also result from the unanticipated consequences of bold innovation. Hence we may expect to find many disturbances in the work of managers of both innovative and insensitive organizations. One can also expect to find the *disturbance handler* role emphasized following a period of intense innovation; a period of major change must be followed by a period in which the change is consolidated. Furthermore, managers of small companies and those in line production jobs, especially at lower levels in the hierarchy are likely to give the greatest attention to the *disturbance handler* role (and to the other decisional roles) because they tend to be most involved with the day-to-day maintenance of the workflow.

As *resource allocator* the manager oversees the allocation of all his organization's resources and thereby maintains control of its strategy-making process. He does this in three ways. First, by scheduling his own time the manager implicitly sets organizational priorities. Issues that fail to reach him fail to get support. Second, the manager designs the basic work system of his organization and programs the work of subordinates. He decides what will be done, who will do it, and what structure will be used. Third, the manager maintains ultimate control by authorizing, before implementation, all major decisions made by his organization. The authorization decisions are difficult ones to make; the issues are complex, but the time that can be devoted to them is short. The manager can ease the difficulty by choosing the person rather than the proposal. But when he must decide on the proposal, the manager makes use of loose models and plans that he develops implicitly from his nerve-center information. The models describe in a conceptual way a great variety of the internal and external situations that the manager faces. The plans – in the form of anticipated improvement projects – exist as his flexible vision of where the organization might go. Such plans serve as the common frame of reference against which he can evaluate, and hence interrelate, all proposals.

Finally, as *negotiator* the manager takes charge when his organization must have important negotiations with another organization. As *figurehead* he represents his organization, as *spokesman* he speaks for it, and as *resource allocator* he trades resources in real-time with the opposite party.

To summarize, the manager must design the work of his organization, monitor its internal and external environment, initiate change when desirable, and renew stability when faced with a disturbance. The manager must lead his subordinates to work effectively for the organization, and he must provide them with special information, some of which he gains through the network of contacts that he develops. In addition, the manager must perform a number of 'housekeeping' duties, including informing outsiders, serving as *figurehead*, and leading major negotiations.

Thus, the popular view of the manager as the one who must take the broad view, do the unprogrammed work, and buttress the system where it is imperfect is only partly correct. Managers must also do their share of regular work and must involve themselves in certain ongoing organizational activities.

Basic Job Characteristics. It has been noted that the manager must take responsibility for the operation of his organization's strategy-making system, that he alone must find and process a significant amount of its important information, and that he must also perform a number of 'housekeeping' duties. Added to all this is the open-ended nature of his job. There are no clear mileposts in the job of managing, never an indication that nothing more need be done for the moment, always the nagging thought that something could be improved if only the time could be found. Hence the manager's burden of responsibility is inherently great.

His problem is further compounded. The current and speculative nature of so much of the manager's information means that it is verbal. But the dissemination of verbal information is time-consuming. Hence the manager faces a 'dilemma of delegation.' He has unique access to much important information, but he lacks a formal and efficient means of disseminating it. The result is that the manager finds it difficult to delegate certain tasks with confidence, since he has neither the time nor the means to send along all the necessary information.

The net effect of all this is that the manager's time assumes a great opportunity cost. He carries this great burden of responsibility, yet he cannot easily delegate his tasks. As organizations become increasingly large and complex, this burden increases, particularly for senior managers. Unfortunately, these men cannot significantly increase their available time or significantly improve their abilities to manage. Hence the leaders of large complex bureaucracies face the real danger of becoming major obstructions in the flow of decisions and information.

These points explain a number of distinctive characteristics that can be observed in managerial work. The manager feels compelled to perform a great quantity of work and the pace he assumes is unrelenting. The manager seems to have little free time during the workday and he takes few breaks. Senior managers appear unable to escape from their work after hours because of what they take home and because their minds are constantly tuned to their jobs.

The manager's activities are characterized by brevity, variety, and fragmentation. The vast majority are of brief duration, on the order of seconds for foremen and minutes for chief executives. A great variety of activities are performed, but with no obvious patterns. The trivial are interspersed with the consequential so that the manager must shift moods quickly and frequently. There is great fragmentation of work, and interruptions are commonplace. The characteristics of brevity and fragmentation, apparently present in virtually all managers' jobs, are most pronounced for those who are closest to the 'action' – top managers of small organizations, managers at lower levels in the hierarchy, particularly in production jobs, and managers working in the most dynamic environments.

Interestingly, the manager shows signs of preference for brevity and interruption in his work. No doubt, he becomes conditioned by his workload. He develops an appreciation for the opportunity costs of his own time and he lives with the awareness that, no matter what he is doing, there are other, perhaps more important, things that he might do and that he must do. A tendency toward superficiality becomes the prime occupational hazard of the manager.

In choosing activities the manager gravitates where possible to the more active elements in his work – the current, the well-defined, the nonroutine. Very current information – gossip, hearsay, speculation – is favored; routine reports are not. Time scheduling reflects a focus on the definite and the concrete, and activities tend to deal with specific rather than general issues. These characteristics are clearly found in the activities of chief executives and most become even more pronounced at lower levels of the hierarchy. The manager's job is not one that breeds reflective planners; rather, it produces adaptive information manipulators who favor a stimulus-response milieu.

The manager's work is essentially that of communication and his tools are the five basic media – mail, telephone, unscheduled meetings, scheduled meetings, and tours. Managers clearly favor the three verbal media, many spending on the order of 80 percent of their time in verbal contact. Some managers, such as those of staff groups, spend relatively more time alone. But the greatest share of the time of almost all managers is spent in verbal communication. The verbal media are favored because they are the action media, providing current information and rapid feedback. The mail, which moves slowly and contains little 'live action' material, receives cursory treatment. Mail processing tends to be treated as a burden.

The informal media – the telephone and the unscheduled meeting – are generally used for brief contacts when the parties are well known to each other and when information or requests must be transmitted quickly. In contrast, scheduled meetings allow for more formal contacts, of longer duration, with large groups of people, and away from the organization. Of special interest is the flow of incidental, but often important, information at the beginning and end of scheduled meetings. Scheduled meetings are used for the special purposes of ceremony, strategy-making, and negotiation. Managers in large organizations and top managers of public organizations spend more time in scheduled meetings and other formal activities, while the work of lower-level managers and managers in dynamic environments tends to exhibit less formality.

Tours provide the manager with the opportunity to observe activity informally. Yet, managers apparently spend little time in this medium, perhaps because it involves nonspecific activity that is non-action oriented.

An analysis of the characteristics of the manager's interactions with other people shows that he stands between his own organizational unit and an extensive network of contacts. These can include his unit's clients, suppliers, and associates, his peers and colleagues, and their superiors and subordinates. Nonline relationships are a significant component of every manager's job, generally consuming one-third to one-half of his contact time. Managers in large organizations appear to have greater ranges of these contacts and better communication patterns. Much of their horizontal communication, however, appears to be with small cliques of colleagues that serve as centers for specialized information. Subordinates consume about one-third to one-half of the manager's time. He interacts with a wide variety of subordinates, freely bypassing formal channels of authority to get the information he desires. Finally, the evidence suggests that managers spend relatively little time with their superiors, only about one-tenth of their contact hours.

It has been implied in a number of the above conclusions that the burden of his work results in the manager's being carried along by his job to a large extent. The evidence concerning who initiates the manager's contacts and what types of contacts he engages in would appear to bear this out. Nevertheless, the strong incumbent (in any but the most highly structured jobs) can control his own work in subtle ways. In the first place, he is responsible for many of his initial commitments which later lock him into a set of ongoing activities. In the second place, the strong manager can turn to his own advantage those activities in which he must engage; he can extract information, lobby for his causes, or implement changes.

An analysis of the roles further suggests a blend of duties and rights. The duties come with the roles of *figurehead, spokesman, disturbance handler,* and *negotiator.* But in the roles of *leader, entrepreneur,* and *resource allocator,* the manager has the opportunity to put his stamp on his organizational unit and set its course.

Science in the Job. The evidence suggests that there is no science in managerial work. That is to say, managers do not work according to procedures that have been prescribed by scientific analysis. Indeed, the modern manager appears to be basically indistinguishable from his historical counterparts. He may seek different information, but he gets most of it in the same old way, by word of mouth. He may make decisions dealing with modern technology, but he uses the same intuitive (that is, nonexplicit) procedures or 'programs' in making them.

Managers use a whole repertoire of general-purpose programs in their work. Faced with a particular task, the manager chooses, combines, and sequences a set of programs to deal with it. We can identify a number of general-purpose programs – such as information dissemination, alternative selection, and negotiation. There are other general-purpose programs that are more difficult to isolate, such as those associated with the *leader* role. In addition, the manager has some special purpose programs. He uses one – the scheduling program – to control his activities and determine the sequence of tasks to be executed.

The current reality is that all these programs are locked in the manager's brain, not yet described by the management researcher. There can be no science of managing until these programs are demarcated, their contents specified, the set of them linked into a simulation of managerial work, and particular ones subjected to systematic analysis and improvement.

The manager in a 'loop'

To sum up, we find that the manager, particularly at senior levels, is overburdened with work. With the increasing complexity of modern organizations and their problems, he is destined to become more so. He is driven to brevity, fragmentation, and superficiality in his tasks, yet he cannot easily delegate them because of the nature of his information. And he can do little to increase his available time or significantly enhance his power to manage. Furthermore, he is driven to focus on that which is current and tangible in his work, even though the complex problems facing many organizations call for reflection and a far-sighted perspective.

It is these very characteristics of the work that impede attempts to improve it. The researcher has had immense difficulty trying to describe work of this nature. The features of brevity, fragmentation, and verbal communication, adopted by the manager in order to deal with the pressures and complexities of the job, stand in the way of the researcher who attempts to understand it. Hence, we have learned almost nothing about how managers perform their roles – about what programs they use and the contents of these programs.

The evidence from the professions is that the analyst must take a major responsibility for bringing science to bear on the performance of work. The practitioner is busy; his job is to do the work, not to analyze it. The management scientist has so far effected little change in the job of managing. Unable to understand the manager's work and describe his programs and unable to gain access to his information, the management scientist has concentrated his efforts elsewhere in the organization, where activities are explicit, structured, and routine, amenable to analysis.

Hence the manager continues to manage as he always has, receiving little help from the management scientist. But as organizational problems have become more complex, particularly in the public sector, work characteristics – like fragmentation and emphasis on concrete activities and verbal media – have become more pronounced. Such characteristics in turn render the manager less able to cope with difficult problems and further reduce the management scientist's ability to help. In effect, the manager is caught in a 'loop' – work pressures lead to pronounced job characteristics that lead to increased work pressures – and he has been able to do little about it. Society loses, because it looks to its senior managers for solutions to its major problems.

Somehow this vicious circle must be broken. First, managers must better understand the nature of their work and its problems, and they must alter their working habits to deal with them. Second, the classroom must be used to teach the skills of managing and to develop insights into the job and better means of coping with its complexity. Third, the management scientist must help by devoting his energies to those areas where science can be brought to bear on the manager's job. And, finally, the researcher must develop a sufficiently precise understanding of the manager's job to allow the manager, teacher, and management scientist to make significant improvements in the execution of it.

Implications for the manager

Today managing is an art, not a science. Most of the methods managers use are not properly understood; hence they are not taught or analyzed in any formal sense. This means that it will be some time before managers face the dangers of technological obsolescence, in a specific sense. Managing requires first and foremost a set of innate skills. Up to now management science has done very little to supplement these.

The lack of a scientific base for managing has imposed severe pressures on the manager. Basically, he is charged with design of his own information system and operation of his organization's strategy-making system. As organizations grow larger and more complex, the pressures increase. But without any systematic means to disseminate information, the burden of work increases. The manager faces the real danger of becoming a major obstruction in the flow of decisions and information.

The manager can alleviate these problems in a number of ways. First, he can study his own job and come to know the impact he has on his organization. Posed below are a number of self-study questions to aid in such an analysis. Second, the manager can make changes in the way he manages. We shall look at ten points for effective managing that are suggested by our findings.

Self-study

Above all, our study suggests that the way in which the manager works and the specific things he chooses to do have a profound impact on his organization. The more he understands about his job and himself, the more sensitive the manager will be to the needs of his organization and the better will be his performance.

This understanding can come from studying the results of research. But more important, the manager can study his own particular job, either formally or informally. A formal study implies engaging a researcher or staff person to observe the manager at work, record details of his mail and activities, analyze the results, and feed them back to him. Informal analysis can be undertaken by the manager himself (perhaps with the aid of his secretary). He would focus consciously on his own actions, trying to develop an understanding of specifically what he does and why. Perhaps he might collect data systematically, using the diary method.

To stimulate managers to analyze their own work, and to aid in this self-study process, the following 15 groups of guideline questions are presented:

1   Where do I get my information and how? Can I make greater use of my contacts to get information? Can other people do some of my scanning for me? In what areas is my knowledge weakest and how can I get others to provide me with the information I need? Do I have powerful enough mental models of those things within the organization and in its environment that I must understand? How can I develop more effective models?

2   What information do I disseminate into my organization? How important is it that my subordinates get my information? Do I keep too much information to myself because dissemination of it is time-consuming or inconvenient? How can I get more information to others so they can make better decisions?

3   Do I balance information-collecting with action-taking? Do I tend to act prematurely before enough information is in? Or do I wait so long for 'all' the information that opportunities pass me by and I become a bottleneck in my organization?

4   What rate of change am I asking my organization to tolerate? Is this change balanced so that our operations are neither excessively static nor overly disrupted? Have we sufficiently analyzed the impact of this change on the future of our organization?

5   Am I sufficiently well informed to pass judgment on the proposals made by my subordinates? Is it possible to leave final authorization for some of them with subordinates? Do we have problems of coordination because subordinates in fact now make too many of these decisions independently?

6   What is my vision of direction for this organization? Are these 'plans' primarily in my own mind in loose form? Should they be made explicit in order to better guide the decisions of others in the organization? Or do I need flexibility to change them at will?

7   Are we experiencing too many disturbances in this organization? Would they be fewer if we slowed down the rate of change? Do disturbances reflect a delayed reaction to problems? Do we experience infrequent disturbance because we are stagnant? How do I deal with disturbances? Can we anticipate some and develop contingency plans for them?

8   What kind of a leader am I? How do subordinates react to my managerial style? How well do I understand their work? Am I sufficiently sensitive to their reactions to my actions? Do I find an appropriate balance between encouragement and pressure? Do I stifle their initiative?

9   What kind of external relationships do I maintain and how? Are there certain types of people that I should get to know better? Do I spend too much of my time maintaining these relationships?

10   Is there any system to my time scheduling or am I just reacting to the pressures of the moment? Do I find the appropriate mix of activities, or do I tend to concentrate on one particular function or one type of problem just because I find it interesting? Am I more efficient with particular kinds of work at special times of the day or week and does my schedule reflect this? Can someone else (in addition to my secretary) take responsibility for much of my scheduling, and do it more systematically?

11   Do I overwork? What effect does my workload have on my efficiency? Should I force myself to take breaks or to reduce the pace of my activity?

12   Am I too superficial in what I do? Can I really shift moods as quickly and frequently as my work patterns require? Should I attempt to decrease the amount of fragmentation and interruption in my work?

13   Do I orient myself too much toward current, tangible activities? Am I a slave to the action and excitement of my work, so that I am no longer able to concentrate on issues? Do key problems receive the attention they deserve? Should I spend more time reading and probing deeply into certain issues? Could I be more reflective?

14   Do I use the different media appropriately? Do I know how to make the most of written communication? Do I rely excessively on face-to-face communication, thereby putting all but a few of my subordinates at an informational disadvantage? Do I schedule enough of my meetings on a regular basis? Do I spend enough time touring my organization to observe activity at first hand? Am I too detached from the heart of our activities, seeing things only in an abstract way?

15   How do I blend my rights and duties? Do my obligations consume all my time? How can I free myself sufficiently from obligations to ensure that I am taking this organization where I want it to go? How can I turn my obligations to my advantage?

Some of these questions may sound rhetorical. None is meant to be. There are no simple solutions to the complex problems of managerial work. This book can perhaps ask some of the right questions; but if the manager is to improve his work today, he must provide his own answers. For this reason it is crucial that the manager develop a better understanding of his own work.

8

The Human Side of Enterprise

DOUGLAS MCGREGOR

I think that, of all the management books I have read, the one that has influenced me most has been Douglas McGregor's The Human Side of Enterprise. *I discovered it in the early 1960s when I first became exposed to the wider aspects of business, having started my career as an engineer, and then having moved further into the commercial/ marketing stream. Up to that point, I had had only limited experience in managing people. With my scientific background, I was in any event more inclined to the view that management is merely a case of analysing a situation, deciding what the right course of action is and then implementing that decision. Such issues as human behaviour and motivation never entered the calculation.*

But, right away, Douglas McGregor's thesis struck a responsive chord, so that I could immediately empathize with his ideas and recognize in them my own feelings and my own responses. Furthermore, I had an immediate opportunity to put them into practice in the job that I was then doing, with very satisfying and rewarding results. Until then, I had succeeded by my own efforts; from then on, I discovered the much greater thrill of leading and motivating a team to produce more than its members had thought themselves capable of doing.

I believe that McGregor's book in fact marked a watershed in management thinking, which had tended previously to be dominated by an organized and scientific approach to management tasks. Because of the great improvements effected by this scientific management approach, the human side of enterprise had perhaps been ignored. But, with the growing complexity of management, and the need to decentralize and free up organizational structures, McGregor's ideas on how to motivate and involve people really came into their own. They have, in my view, been the foundation on which almost all modern management concepts are built.

The lesson is as valid today as it was when McGregor wrote his book. Without the involvement of the people that it concerns, any decision is not only likely to be impaired, it is also less likely to be fully implemented, because the protagonists are not motivated to make it succeed. The business world is full of examples of marvellous strategic plans that have been drawn up but have never produced results, precisely for this reason.

Given the task that he faces, perhaps we should send Mr Gorbachev a container-load of copies of Dr McGregor's book.

Christopher Hampson,
Executive Director, Imperial Chemical Industries PLC,
London

Chapter 4: Theory Y: The Integration of Individual and Organizational Goals

TO some, the preceding analysis [Theory X: the traditional view of direction and control] will appear unduly harsh. Have we not made major modifications in the management of the human resources of industry during the past quarter century? Have we not recognized the importance of people and made vitally significant changes in managerial strategy as a consequence? Do the developments since the twenties in personnel administration and labor relations add up to nothing?

There is no question that important progress has been made in the past two or three decades. During this period the human side of enterprise has become a major preoccupation of management. A tremendous number of policies, programs, and practices which were virtually unknown thirty years ago have become commonplace. The lot of the industrial employee – be he worker, professional, or executive – has improved to a degree which could hardly have been imagined by his counterpart of the nineteen twenties. Management has adopted generally a far more humanitarian set of values; it has successfully striven to give more equitable and more generous treatment to its employees. It has significantly reduced economic hardships, eliminated the more extreme forms of industrial warfare, provided a generally safe and pleasant working environment, *but it has done all these things without changing its fundamental theory of management*. There are exceptions here and there, and they are important; nevertheless, the assumptions of Theory X remain predominant throughout our economy.

Management was subjected to severe pressures during the Great Depression of the thirties. The wave of public antagonism, the open warfare accompanying the unionization of the mass production industries, the general reaction against authoritarianism, the legislation of the New

Abridged from Douglas McGregor: *The Human Side of Enterprise* (New York: McGraw-Hill, 1960, 2nd edn 1985). Reproduced by kind permission of McGraw-Hill Publishing Company.

Deal produced a wide 'pendulum swing.' However, the changes in policy and practice which took place during that and the next decade were primarily adjustments to the increased power of organized labor and to the pressures of public opinion.

Some of the movement was away from 'hard' and toward 'soft' management, but it was short-lived, and for good reasons. It has become clear that many of the initial strategic interpretations accompanying the 'human relations approach' were as naïve as those which characterized the early stages of progressive education. We have now discovered that there is no answer in the simple removal of control – that abdication is not a workable alternative to authoritarianism. We have learned that there is no direct correlation between employee satisfaction and productivity. We recognize today that 'industrial democracy' cannot consist in permitting everyone to decide everything, that industrial health does not flow automatically from the elimination of dissatisfaction, disagreement, or even open conflict. Peace is not synonymous with organizational health; socially responsible management is not co-extensive with permissive management.

Now that management has regained its earlier prestige and power, it has become obvious that the trend toward 'soft' management was a temporary and relatively superficial reaction rather than a general modification of fundamental assumptions or basic strategy. Moreover, while the progress we have made in the past quarter century is substantial, it has reached the point of diminishing returns. The tactical possibilities within conventional managerial strategies have been pretty completely exploited, and significant new developments will be unlikely without major modifications in theory.

The assumptions of theory Y

There have been few dramatic break-throughs in social science theory like those which have occurred in the physical sciences during the past half century. Nevertheless, the accumulation of knowledge about human behavior in many specialized fields has made possible the formulation of a number of generalizations which provide a modest beginning for new theory with respect to the management of human resources. Some of these, which will hereafter be referred to as Theory Y, are as follows:

1   *The expenditure of physical and mental effort in work is as natural as play or rest.* The average human being does not inherently dislike work.

Depending upon controllable conditions, work may be a source of satisfaction (and will be voluntarily performed) or a source of punishment (and will be avoided if possible).

2 *External control and the threat of punishment are not the only means for bringing about effort toward organizational objectives. Man will exercise self-direction and self-control in the service of objectives to which he is committed.*

3 *Commitment to objectives is a function of the rewards associated with their achievement.* The most significant of such rewards, e.g., the satisfaction of ego and self-actualization needs, can be direct products of effort directed toward organizational objectives.

4 *The average human being learns, under proper conditions, not only to accept but to seek responsibility.* Avoidance of responsibility, lack of ambition, and emphasis on security are generally consequences of experience, not inherent human characteristics.

5 *The capacity to exercise a relatively high degree of imagination, ingenuity, and creativity in the solution of organizational problems is widely, not narrowly, distributed in the population.*

6 *Under the conditions of modern industrial life, the intellectual potentialities of the average human being are only partially utilized.*

These assumptions involve sharply different implications for managerial strategy than do those of Theory X. They are dynamic rather than static: they indicate the possibility of human growth and development; they stress the necessity for selective adaptation rather than for a single absolute form of control. They are not framed in terms of the least common denominator of the factory hand, but in terms of a resource which has substantial potentialities.

Above all, the assumptions of Theory Y point up the fact that the limits on human collaboration in the organizational setting are not limits of human nature but of management's ingenuity in discovering how to realize the potential represented by its human resources. Theory X offers management an easy rationalization for ineffective organizational performance: it is due to the nature of the human resources with which we must work. Theory Y, on the other hand, places the problems squarely in the lap of management. If employees are lazy, indifferent, unwilling to take responsibility, intransigent, uncreative, uncooperative, Theory Y implies that the causes lie in management's methods of organization and control.

The assumptions of Theory Y are not finally validated. Nevertheless, they are far more consistent with existing knowledge in the social sciences than are the assumptions of Theory X. They will undoubtedly be refined, elaborated, modified as further research accumulates, but they are unlikely to be completely contradicted.

On the surface, these assumptions may not seem particularly difficult to accept. Carrying their implications into practice, however, is not easy. They challenge a number of deeply ingrained managerial habits of thought and action.

The principle of integration

The central principle of organization which derives from Theory X is that of direction and control through the exercise of authority – what has been called 'the scalar principle.' The central principle which derives from Theory Y is that of integration: the creation of conditions such that the members of the organization can achieve their own goals *best* by directing their efforts toward the success of the enterprise. These two principles have profoundly different implications with respect to the task of managing human resources, but the scalar principle is so firmly built into managerial attitudes that the implications of the principle of integration are not easy to perceive.

Someone once said that fish discover water last. The 'psychological environment' of industrial management – like water for fish – is so much a part of organizational life that we are unaware of it. Certain characteristics of our society, and of organizational life within it, are so completely established, so pervasive, that we cannot conceive of their being otherwise. As a result, a great many policies and practices and decisions and relationships could only be – it seems – what they are.

Among these pervasive characteristics of organizational life in the United States today is a managerial attitude (stemming from Theory X) toward membership in the industrial organization. It is assumed almost without question that organizational requirements take precedence over the needs of individual members. Basically, the employment agreement is that in return for the rewards which are offered, the individual will accept external direction and control. The very idea of integration and self-control is foreign to our way of thinking about the employment relationship. The tendency, therefore, is either to reject it out of hand (as socialistic, or anarchistic, or inconsistent with human nature) or to twist it unconsciously until it fits existing conceptions.

The concept of integration and self-control carries the implication that the organization will be more effective in achieving its economic objectives if adjustments are made, in significant ways, to the needs and goals of its members.

A district manager in a large, geographically decentralized company is notified that he is being promoted to a policy level position at headquarters. It is a big promotion with a large salary increase. His role in the organization will be a much more powerful one, and he will be associated with the major executives of the firm.

The headquarters group who selected him for this position have carefully considered a number of possible candidates. This man stands out among them in a way which makes him the natural choice. His performance has been under observation for some time, and there is little question that he possesses the necessary qualifications, not only for this opening but for an even higher position. There is genuine satisfaction that such an outstanding candidate is available.

The man is appalled. He doesn't want the job. His goal, as he expresses it, is to be the 'best damned district manager in the company.' He enjoys his direct associations with operating people in the field, and he doesn't want a policy level job. He and his wife enjoy the kind of life they have created in a small city, and they dislike actively both the living conditions and the social obligations of the headquarters city.

He expresses his feelings as strongly as he can, but his objections are brushed aside. The organization's needs are such that his refusal to accept the promotion would be unthinkable. His superiors say to themselves that of course when he has settled in to the new job, he will recognize that it was the right thing. And so he makes the move.

Two years later he is in an even higher position in the company's headquarters organization, and there is talk that he will probably be the executive vice-president before long. Privately he expresses considerable unhappiness and dissatisfaction. He (and his wife) would 'give anything' to be back in the situation he left two years ago.

Within the context of the pervasive assumptions of Theory X, promotions and transfers in large numbers are made by unilateral decision. The requirements of the organization are given priority automatically and almost without question. If the individual's personal goals are considered at all, it is assumed that the rewards of salary and position will satisfy him. Should an individual actually refuse such a move without a compelling reason, such as health or a severe family crisis, he would be considered to have jeopardized his future because of this 'selfish' attitude. It is rare indeed for management to give the individual the opportunity to be a genuine and active partner in such a decision, even though it may affect his most important personal goals. Yet the implications following from Theory Y are that the organization is likely to suffer if it ignores these personal needs and goals. In making unilateral decisions with respect to promotion, management is failing to utilize its human resources in the most effective way.

The principle of integration demands that both the organization's and the individual's needs be recognized. Of course, when there is a sincere joint effort to find it, an integrative solution which meets the needs of the individual *and* the organization is a frequent outcome. But not always – and this is the point at which Theory Y begins to appear unrealistic. It collides head on with pervasive attitudes associated with management by direction and control.

The assumptions of Theory Y imply that unless integration is achieved *the organization will suffer*. The objectives of the organization are *not* achieved best by the unilateral administration of promotions, because this form of management by direction and control will not create the commitment which would make available the full resources of those affected. The lesser motivation, the lesser resulting degree of self-direction and self-control are costs which, when added up for many instances over time, will more than offset the gains obtained by unilateral decisions 'for the good of the organization.'

One other example will perhaps clarify further the sharply different implications of Theory X and Theory Y.

It could be argued that management is already giving a great deal of attention to the principle of integration through its efforts in the field of economic education. Many millions of dollars and much ingenuity have been expended in attempts to persuade employees that their welfare is intimately connected with the success of the free enterprise system and of their own companies. The idea that they can achieve their own goals best by directing their effort toward the objectives of the organization has been explored and developed and communicated in every possible way. Is this not evidence that management is already committed to the principle of integration?

The answer is a definite no. These managerial efforts, with rare exceptions, reflect clearly the influence of the assumptions of Theory X. The central message is an exhortation to the industrial employee to work hard and follow orders in order to protect his job and his standard of living. Much has been achieved, it says, by our established way of running industry, and much more could be achieved if employees would adapt themselves *to management's definition* of what is required. Behind these exhortations lies the expectation that of course the requirements of the organization and its economic success must have priority over the needs of the individual.

Naturally, integration means working together for the success of the enterprise so we all may share in the resulting rewards. But management's implicit assumption is that working together means adjusting to the requirements of the organization *as management perceives them.* In terms of existing views, it seems inconceivable that individuals, seeking their own goals, would further the ends of the enterprise. On the contrary, this would lead to anarchy, chaos, irreconcilable conflicts of self-interest, lack of responsibility, inability to make decisions, and failure to carry out those that were made.

All these consequences, and other worse ones, *would* be inevitable unless conditions could be created such that the members of the organization perceived that they could achieve their own goals *best* by directing their efforts toward the success of the enterprise. If the assumptions of Theory Y are valid, the practical question is whether, and to what extent, such conditions can be created.

The application of theory Y

In the physical sciences there are many theoretical phenomena which cannot be achieved in practice. Absolute zero and a perfect vacuum are examples. Others, such as nuclear power, jet aircraft, and human space flight, are recognized theoretically to be possible long before they become feasible. This fact does not make theory less useful. If it were not for our theoretical convictions, we would not even be attempting to develop the means for human flight into space today. In fact, were it not for the development of physical science theory during the past century and a half, we would still be depending upon the horse and buggy and the sailing vessel for transportation. Virtually all significant technological developments wait on the formulation of relevant theory.

Similarly, in the management of the human resources of industry, the assumptions and theories about human nature at any given time limit innovation. Possibilities are not recognized, innovating efforts are not undertaken, until theoretical conceptions lay a groundwork for them.

Assumptions like those of Theory X permit us to conceive of certain possible ways of organizing and directing human effort, *but not others*. Assumptions like those of Theory Y open up a range of possibilities for new managerial policies and practices. As in the case of the development of new physical science theory, some of these possibilities are not immediately feasible, and others may forever remain unattainable. They may be too costly, or it may be that we simply cannot discover how to create the necessary 'hardware.'

There is substantial evidence for the statement that the potentialities of the average human being are far above those which we typically realize in industry today. If our assumptions are like those of Theory X, we will not even recognize the existence of these potentialities and there will be no reason to devote time, effort, or money to discovering how to realize them. If, however, we accept assumptions like those of Theory Y, we will be challenged to innovate, to discover new ways of organizing and directing human effort, even though we recognize that the perfect organization, like the perfect vacuum, is practically out of reach.

We need not be overwhelmed by the dimensions of the managerial task implied by Theory Y. To be sure, a large mass production operation in which the workers have been organized by a militant and hostile union faces management with problems which appear at present to be insurmountable with respect to the application of the principle of integration. It may be decades before sufficient knowledge will have accumulated to make such an application feasible. Applications of Theory Y will have to be tested initially in more limited ways and under more favorable circumstances. However, a number of applications of Theory Y *in managing managers and professional people* are possible today. Within the managerial hierarchy, the assumptions can be tested and refined, techniques can be invented and skill acquired in their use. As knowledge accumulates, some of the problems of application at the worker level in large organizations may appear less baffling than they do at present.

Perfect integration of organizational requirements and individual goals and needs is, of course, not a realistic objective. In adopting this principle, we seek that degree of integration in which the individual can achieve his goals *best* by directing his efforts toward the success of the organization. 'Best' means that this alternative will be more attractive than the many others available to him: indifference, irresponsibility, minimal compliance, hostility, sabotage. It means that he will continuously be encouraged to develop and utilize voluntarily his capacities, his knowledge, his skill, his ingenuity in ways which contribute to the success of the enterprise.*

Acceptance of Theory Y does not imply abdication, or 'soft' management, or 'permissiveness.' As was indicated above, such notions stem from the acceptance of authority as the *single* means of managerial control, and from attempts to minimize its negative consequences. Theory Y assumes that people will exercise self-direction and self-control in the achievement of organizational objectives *to the degree that they are committed to those objectives.* If that commitment is small, only a slight degree of self-direction and self-control will be likely, and a substantial amount of external influence will be necessary. If it is large, many conventional external controls will be relatively superfluous, and to some extent self-defeating. Managerial policies and practices materially affect this degree of commitment.

Authority is an inappropriate means for obtaining commitment to objectives. Other forms of influence – help in achieving integration, for example – are required for this purpose. Theory Y points to the possibility of lessening the emphasis on external forms of control to the degree that commitment to organizational objectives can be achieved. Its underlying assumptions emphasize the capacity of human beings for self-control, and the consequent possibility of greater managerial reliance on other means of influence. Nevertheless, it is clear that authority *is* an appropriate means for control under certain circumstances – particularly where genuine commitment to objectives cannot be achieved. The assumptions of Theory Y do not deny the appropriateness of authority, but they do deny that it is appropriate for all purposes and under all circumstances.

Many statements have been made to the effect that we have acquired today the know-how to cope with virtually any technological problems which may arise, and that the major industrial advances of the next half

---

* A recent, highly significant study of the sources of job satisfaction and dissatisfaction among managerial and professional people suggests that these opportunities for 'self-actualization' are the essential requirements of both job satisfaction and high performance. The researchers find that 'the wants of employees divide into two groups. One group revolves around the need to develop in one's occupation as a source of personal growth. The second group operates as an essential base to the first and is associated with fair treatment in compensation, supervision, working conditions, and administrative practices. *The fulfillment of the needs of the second group does not motivate the individual to high levels of job satisfaction and . . . to extra performance on the job.* All we can expect from satisfying [this second group of needs] is the prevention of dissatisfaction and poor job performance.' Frederick Herzberg, Bernard Mausner, and Barbara Bloch Snyderman, *The Motivation to Work.* New York: John Wiley & Sons, Inc., 1959, pp. 114–115. (Italics mine.)

century will occur on the human side of enterprise. Such advances, however, are improbable so long as management continues to organize and direct and control its human resources on the basis of assumptions – tacit or explicit – like those of Theory X. Genuine innovation, in contrast to a refurbishing and patching of present managerial strategies, requires first the acceptance of less limiting assumptions about the nature of the human resources we seek to control, and second the readiness to adapt selectively to the implications contained in those new assumptions. Theory Y is an invitation to innovation.

References

Brown, J. A. C., *The Social Psychology of Industry*. Baltimore: Penguin Books, Inc., 1954.
Cordiner, Ralph J., *New Frontiers for Professional Managers*. New York: McGraw-Hill Book Company, Inc., 1956.
Dubin, Robert, *The World of Work: Industrial Society and Human Relations*. Englewood Cliffs, N.J.: Prentice-Hall, Inc., 1958.
Friedmann, Georges, *Industrial Society: The Emergence of the Human Problems of Automation*. Glencoe Ill.: Free Press, 1955.
Herzberg, Frederick, Bernard Mausner, and Barbara Bloch Snyderman, *The Motivation to Work*. New York: John Wiley & Sons, Inc., 1959.
Krech, David, and Richard S. Crutchfield, *Theory and Problems of Social Psychology*. New York: McGraw-Hill Book Company, Inc., 1948.
Leavitt, Harold J., *Managerial Psychology*. Chicago: University of Chicago Press, 1958.
McMurry, Robert N., 'The Case for Benevolent Autocracy,' *Harvard Business Review*, vol. 36, no. 1 (January-February), 1958.
Rice, A. K., *Productivity and Social Organizations: The Ahmedabad Experiment*. London: Tavistock Publications, Ltd., 1958.
Stagner, Ross, *The Psychology of Industrial Conflict*. New York: John Wiley & Sons, Inc., 1956.

9

Payoff from Product Management

B. Charles Ames

IT is hard for me to realize that nearly 30 years have elapsed since I wrote this piece for the Harvard Business Review. *At that time, I was a new Principal with McKinsey and actively involved with several companies struggling for better results through the use of product managers. Since that time, I have consulted with, and managed, a number of companies where the product management concept has been employed. In fact, several companies that I am involved with today rely on product managers to get the necessary focus and emphasis on their key product/market segments.*

What do I see that is new or different? The answer is, not much. The same complaints and problems exist. And attention to the same fundamentals is needed to make the concept work effectively. It is surprising how well the points made in the article still apply. From my admittedly biased point of view, they seem to have stood the test of time pretty well.

Nothing is perfect, however. If I were writing the piece today there are a couple of points that I would make differently.

For one thing, I have learned that a lot more thought should be given to the question of whether to organize around products (with product managers) or markets (with market managers). Both approaches have their rightful places, and the choice depends on the condition of the business and the strategy alternatives available. I discussed this thought more completely in a subsequent article for the Harvard Business Review *called 'Product Managers, Market Managers or Both?'*

Secondly, I have become less patient with age and would take a much tougher stand on holding the product or market manager accountable for profits than I suggested in my comments under 'measuring the manager'. More than one product manager has told me that my new position is patently unfair because he does not have the authority commensurate with this kind of 'general management' responsibility. Maybe so, but I am not as interested in being fair as in getting results, and I have seen at first hand what a powerful motivator the heat of profit responsibility can be.

B. Charles Ames,
Clayton & Dublier, Inc.,
New York

Payoff from Product Management

PRODUCT managers have taken well-earned bows for the success of any outstanding companies. They have received – and they deserve – the credit for steering many well-known products to market-share leadership and high profitability in the face of today's intense, competitive scramble. In many large, complex multiproduct corporations, the product manager has provided the vigorous product-by-product leadership that the top executives of a smaller, more tightly knit company give to its one basic product line.

It comes as no surprise, then, to find a recent survey disclosing that three out of four companies in its sample are using this organizational concept.* What is surprising, however, is the current surge of dissatisfaction with the way product managers and the product manager concept are working out. A sampling of opinion at a recent management conference suggests that the following are by no means atypical reactions:

- The president of a large, diversified company in the consumer package field observes that his product managers are being paid $18,000 to $22,000 a year but spend the bulk of their time servicing a few major accounts. His question: 'What are these men really doing to improve the growth and profitability of our company? Most of their time is spent hand-holding a couple of customers. Why do we have to pay this much for men who are in effect just headquarters account specialists?'
- The chief executive of a company manufacturing heavy equipment has challenged his marketing director to justify the continued cost of the company's four product managers. He complains that they have not lived up to their

* See Michael Schiff and Martin Mellman, *Financial Management of the Marketing Function*, New York, Financial Executives Research Foundation, 1962.

avowed role as 'little general managers,' that their contributions have not been commensurate with the costs that they and their staffs have added to overhead.

● One product manager in a leading textile fabrics company has served notice that he wants to give up that position and return to line sales. He complains that, despite his imposing title, his role is really limited to maintaining sales statistics and performing a variety of high-grade clerical tasks. What really disturbs him most is that top management is not as concerned as he is about this state of affairs.

Do these complaints – and their number is increasing – lead to the conclusion that the product manager concept itself is not practical? Certainly not, for the many instances where it is still working well demonstrate that it is not only a sound concept, but in many ways an indispensable one. It is because of the soundness of the concept that it works in so many cases. Where it fails, the fault, almost invariably, lies in how management has gone about applying - or misapplying - a basically sound management tool.

Mixed record

Why, if the concept is so sound, is the record so mixed? An analysis of the marketing experience of a wide range of companies suggests that there are basically two reasons why product managers pay off in some companies and not in others:

1   The product manager concept was designed to fit a rather special set of corporate circumstances and some specific marketing needs. Under these conditions, it can be highly successful. However, it has been applied in many companies in which, because these special conditions are not present, it could not possibly be effective and where other organizational approaches would be much more productive.

2   The concept is an organizational anomaly in that it violates a proven management precept – i.e., that responsibility should always be matched by equivalent authority – and yet it works, if properly applied. Many companies in which it could pay off handsomely are getting mediocre results simply because they have failed to observe some rigorous requirements that must be respected if this approach is to be effective despite its flying in the face of first principles.

These two reasons are, of course, interrelated. Because it is a difficult concept to apply effectively, product management should be used only when it is really the best way to get the job done. Conversely, even in those situations in which all of the conditions are favorable, the care and feeding of the product manager is still not as simple as some tables of organization make it look, and some of the success stories make it sound.

Wrong churches, right pews

Which companies should use product managers?

An analysis of the concept's history will provide some clues. The product manager's job was created primarily to fill a critical need. In large, multiproduct companies, it had always been difficult to be certain that each product received the attention and support it merited from each of the various functional activities of the business, especially manufacturing, marketing, and sales. Under these circumstances, the task of managing and coordinating all the factors bearing on the success of each of many products had proved too much for any one executive to handle. Also, it had proved unrealistic to expect functional department heads automatically to balance and coordinate the interests of many products, if they were left to do this as well as their other duties. Therefore, to meet this need, the product manager form of organization was created (see Exhibit 9.1).

But, having forgotten this history, many companies have gone astray. Once the product manager concept proved itself in practice and reports

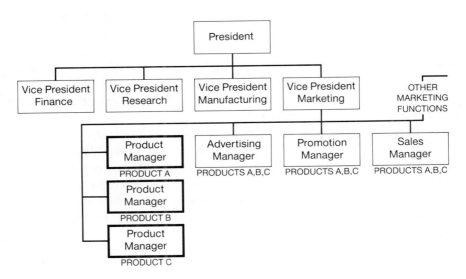

Exhibit 9.1 Product manager organization

of its success spread, some managements concluded that *any* company with many products and many product problems could take this royal route to success. Failing to recognize the real conditions that make it useful, many companies have tried to use this concept under conditions where other approaches would be more applicable. For example:

• In some companies, where the economics and physical setup permit, it would have made more sense to divisionalize the company, setting up separate and self-sustaining units for each major product or product group, as shown in Exhibit 9.2A. (This is usually the preferred organizational approach when each product group really represents a distinct business which is large enough – or potentially large enough – to support its own production and marketing operations.)

• In other companies it would have been better to set up separate product marketing groups, keeping the manufacturing operations centralized, as shown in Exhibit 9.2B. (This makes more organizational sense when complete divisionalization is not feasible, but the marketing requirements, e.g., advertising, promotion, packaging, and sales are significantly different for each product.)

• In still other companies it would have been advantageous to have separate sales operations for each product group, with marketing and manufacturing activities maintained centrally, as shown in Exhibit 9.2C. (This is a more logical approach when separate customer groups must be served, or when the business of each product is too small for divisionalization, or when, finally, the only place product specialization is important and practical is in the sales area.)

These are all valid alternatives to the product manager approach. Furthermore, they are often simpler to apply, so that the product manager concept should be used only when these alternatives are impractical or undesirable. For example, divisionalization or separate marketing groups do not make economic sense when the product businesses involved are small. Likewise, setting up separate product sales forces is usually an awkward, as well as an uneconomical, approach when there is a common set of customers for the products.

Thus, only in multiproduct companies where physically separated operating divisions, marketing groups, or sales units are not practical, is product management the preferred organizational alternative. In these cases the product manager provides a means of ensuring individual attention for all major products without separating off any part of the line operations.

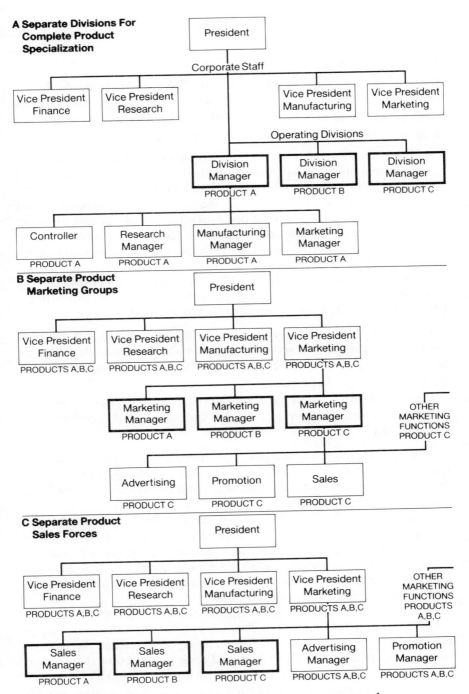

Exhibit 9.2 Some alternatives to the product manager approach

Danger of generalizing

Some of the unhappy experiences stem from the existing confusion about the authority and scope of the product manager's job. On this point management may be misled by those who have tried to generalize from successful company experience. For example:

- Some say the product manager's activity should be limited essentially to advertising and promotion. Others argue that this is far too restrictive, since many other factors contribute to the success of a product.
- Many say the product manager should have full profit responsibility and final authority over many important decisions – for example, pricing, inventory levels, product improvements, and the like. An equal number contend that he should not have final decision-making responsibility in any of these areas, since these are properly line decisions.
- And while some say that he should not be concerned with engineering or other key functions outside the marketing area, many point out that having a hand in these activities may be an essential part of his job.

For the most part, these are arguments that no one can win, because the product manager's responsibilities *should* differ from one company to another, and they *should* be tailored to the particular needs of each company and of each product.

In contrast, three examples of product manager assignments in three different businesses show clearly the spread of responsibilities that actually exists:

- In a leading grocery manufacturing company each product manager spends about 75% of his time on packaging, advertising, and consumer promotion, because these factors more than any others control the growth and profitability of these products.
- On the other hand, a product manager for a fabric manufacturer gets involved in a much broader and more complex set of activities. He finds that he must split his time about equally among styling and design, inventory policies, distribution building, pricing, advertising, and promotion. All of these contribute significantly to the success of the product and are, therefore, essential parts of the product manager's job.
- In a large, broad-based electronics company the product manager for a control systems group spends the bulk of his time working with his counterpart in engineering to (1) evaluate bid opportunities, (2) determine the focus of product development, and (3) coordinate and participate in technical discussions with customer groups. These activities are what make his product a success. Advertising and promotion get relatively little of his time because they are relatively unimportant in building the business.

These three examples make it clear that anyone who tries to strait-jacket the product manager into a universal set of responsibilities is certain to be wrong in most cases. What he does and how he works should depend entirely on the requirements of the particular product and its markets.

The same is true about trying to force the product manager into any standard set of staffline relationships. In his relationships with the rest of the organization, the product manager is clearly not a line executive in the classic sense, for he has no line authority. Nor is he staff in the sense of support staff, as are, for example, the market research or advertising managers. The difference is that he does have the unqualified responsibility for seeing that everything related to his product gets done well and on time. His job is to serve as the focal point for planning and coordinating all of the activities required for the growth and profitability of his product. This does not mean that he does all the planning for his product, but it does mean that he sees that all the activities affecting his product are properly planned.

To carry out this role effectively, he must be an expert on all matters relating to his product, both inside and outside the company. He must be able to rely on his superior knowledge, management skills, and sheer persuasiveness to get things planned and accomplished. He has to do this by working through executives who do have line authority. This unique responsibility and these complex relationships with the rest of the management group are what make the product manager an organizational anomaly – and both his responsibility and his set of relationships will be different in every situation.

Four keys to failure

Looked at this way, the product manager concept is obviously not the easiest organizational approach to use well. The specific difficulties are as varied as the companies themselves. But most breakdowns can be traced to four fundamental failures on the part of top management.

Off-the-shelf approach

Often the product manager concept never gets off the ground in a company because product managers are simply appointed and their jobs set up on the basis of what someone has heard about how some other company has made it work. Little, if any, attempt is made to think through the specific requirements of the company or to spell out the clear-cut responsibility assignments and relationships necessary to make the concept work for a particular product. A surprising number of product managers have been caught in this situation, and most of them will agree that they have been hamstrung in their efforts by organizational blunders that could have been avoided if proper thought had been given to fundamentals. Here are two examples:

● One product manager in the plastics field found that he was organizationally cut off from direct contact with production scheduling or product development. Top management, applying a generalized concept of the job, had restricted the product manager's assignment to the marketing area. Yet the profit for his product depended heavily on maintaining uninterrupted production, even at a sacrifice in margins. And product improvements were the major weapon for entering new markets and capturing the new business that would strengthen his competitive position. He rightfully complained, 'These activities are the heart of this business. Unless I get into these areas with both feet, my role as product manager is a joke.'

● Similarly, a product manager for a packaged-goods item complained that he was virtually excluded from advertising decisions by the advertising manager who, having the ear of the president, was a very powerful figure in the organization. In this case, advertising was a critical factor in product success. No one seemed to think that this was very serious except the product manager, who asked, 'How can I be expected to plan the profitability of my product when I don't have anything to say about the key element in the entire marketing program?'

Problems such as these stem partly from a failure to recognize the built-in difficulties of the product manager's job. With broad responsibilities and little or no line authority, he has an organizational problem under the best of circumstances. To add to this by throwing roadblocks across his efforts can make a difficult job impossible. His success depends largely on how well he is able to develop and maintain a host of complex working relationships with other executives throughout the organization. It is extremely important, therefore, to keep his channels as clear as possible. It is even more important to recognize that each product manager's assignment must be tailored to enable him to focus on the particular activities that are keys to the product's growth and profitability – regardless of what they are or where they fit in the organization.

Obviously this is much easier said than done, for it involves determining what the product manager's specific responsibilities should be, where he should be positioned in the organization's structure, and how he should work with other executives. But unless this thorough analysis is made, the product manager is almost certain to find that he has two strikes against him, or sometimes three, before he even starts to work.

Expecting too much

When management's expectations are excessive, even reasonable success is unlikely. This is especially true in the industrial field, as the frustrating experience of a large electronics company dramatically illustrates:

> This company had serious difficulties marketing many of its products. Noting the accomplishments of product managers in other companies, management clutched at the product manager concept as the answer to its problems. Four product managers were appointed; no other organizational changes or staff additions were made. Within a short time, three of the four were replaced, and there was a general feeling of dissatisfaction with the whole idea.
>
> A closer look at the experience of this company makes it apparent that from the outset far too much was expected of the product managers. They were expected, by some management miracle, to resolve single-handedly an Augean stable load of problems that had plagued the company for a long period of time. For example, inventories and manufacturing costs were way out of line; there was serious slippage on engineering projects; and the sales organization had let the backlog drop below the safety level. These were all difficult problems, rooted deep in the line operations of the company, that could not possibly be tackled on an across-the-board front by a cadre of men. Thus to think that the new product managers – by *themselves* – could solve these problems was totally unrealistic.
>
> Retracing the history of this experience also revealed that, from the very beginning, management, because of its exaggerated idea of what the new concept should be expected to accomplish, blamed the product managers for everything that went wrong. This, in turn, weakened the one weapon they had – the respect of line executives for their competence. Consequently, the product managers were unable to begin to develop the cooperative relationships which they needed with the various functional executives and which were so important to their doing their jobs.
>
> Finally, top management's unrealistic appraisal of the job also helps explain its failure to provide the kind of training that might have helped

the product managers to grow in their jobs. The experience of these men had been, for the most part, in sales. Thus, it was understandably difficult for them to flag potential problems in manufacturing and engineering, and next to impossible for them either to develop appropriate programs of action or to persuade line executives to respect their recommendations. A sound training and development program would have helped to broaden their capabilities and the scope of their contribution. And, with a little help and some patience, they might in time have lived up to expectations.

Reacting to this situation, the product managers unenthusiastically compared their position to 'walking blindfolded on a treadmill.' They recognized that it was impossible to handle all of the problems that management expected them to deal with. They lived, furthermore, in jittery anticipation that management might blame them for almost anything that went wrong, expecting them somehow to be able to make up for the inadequacies of those with line responsibility.

Although this example is admittedly somewhat extreme, it is not as unique as it should be. Far too often, the product manager concept breaks down because of top management's exaggerated preconceptions of what the product manager can do, especially when both the idea and the man are new. Under these conditions, the chances for making the concept work even reasonably well are drastically reduced.

Expecting too little

At the other extreme, when management is reluctant to give its product managers enough responsibility or appropriate status in the organization, the job frequently degenerates into a low-level clerical assignment. The results of this problem were dramatically illustrated recently at a marketing conference. Two product managers from competing companies participated and discovered that while their position descriptions showed their basic responsibilities to be essentially the same, there was a striking contrast in the roles they played in their respective organizations:

● In the one case, the product manager played a very strong role in planning for and managing his assigned product line. He constantly analyzed market conditions and requirements and made sure that his product programs were implemented. He pinpointed target markets for distribution-building programs and obtained approval to increase warehouse stocks for faster delivery. To keep costs down, he got the manufacturing and development departments to program a 10% cost reduction in his product. Once a year he worked up and presented a written plan for his product to top management. As soon as this was approved, he began working with all departments to ensure that their plans were tied into the over-all plan for his product. He had the authority to make many day-to-day operating decisions; for example, he could authorize departures from the approved pricing structure, change priorities on development programs, and approve and implement promotions. Furthermore, he followed up with appropriate line executives to see that decisions beyond the scope of his responsibility were correctly made and carried out. Thus, he was *in fact* a manager for his product line.

● By contrast, his counterpart's job was structured so that he was a combination fact-gatherer for higher level management and correspondence clerk for his product line. He collected information, which he passed on to line executives so that they could make plans or decisions. He made no effort to draw together an over-all plan for his product line, nor was he expected to. He spent much time dealing with routine sales correspondence that should have been handled in the field. And he never followed up on programs to see that they were carried out properly. As a result, both management and the product manager were disillusioned with the whole product management concept.

Obviously, management in the first company took the steps and provided the support necessary to enable a product manager to carry out his role. As a result, the company is getting a payoff from its product managers. The second company clearly is wasting its money.

Assigning the wrong man

The product manager concept, not easy under any circumstances, simply will not work with anything less than outstanding men on the job. More than any one else, the product manager influences the destinies of his product, for while all of the line executives in the company have functional responsibilities, he is the only one with a full-time commitment to a particular product. Moreover, with no authority to order things done, he must convince line executives to act on programs and ideas he develops for his product area. He can do this only if he is the most informed person in his company about his product's needs, if he has imaginative yet practical ideas for meeting these needs, plus the personal skills to get his ideas accepted.

Management often loses sight of these points in setting up or making product manager assignments. Thus:

● In one company, four of the five incumbents were made product managers after they failed to make the grade in the field selling force.

● In another company, the product manager's compensation range was locked into the salary structure at such a low level that it was impossible to attract the caliber of man needed to do the job.

● In still another company, the pattern was to use the product manager position as a training ground for promising younger men to groom them for district sales management assignments.

The results were the same in all these cases: the men appointed to product manager positions were not strong enough to gain the respect and support of line management. Consequently, they were not able to do the job that management intended. In such situations there is little justification for blaming the concept.

By the same token, those companies that have achieved outstanding results from their product managers have succeeded largely because they staffed the job with qualified people. Thus:

● One company in the electronics industry recently effected a major turnaround in its business chiefly as a result of settling for nothing less than recognized leaders in their fields for each of its product manager positions. This required changing the salary structure so that the product managers were paid on a par with the number two man in the marketing department, and in certain cases even providing stock options to attract the very best men for these jobs. This increased costs, but management today is convinced that the company's markedly improved performance is attributable to this action and that it has been well worth the added investment.

● Management in another company, concerned about increasing competition for its major product line, drafted the man generally considered to be 'the best commercial brain in the company' for the product manager position. This move made good sense because the product area contributed nearly 50% of the company's profits.

On the other hand, the difficulty of finding qualified men to fill product manager positions cannot be passed over lightly. One president put this problem in perspective when he said, 'I have no doubt about the usefulness of the product manager concept. However, I do have doubts about our ability to find the paragons who can effectively fill these jobs. We have a hard enough time finding good general managers; now we must uncover men with comparable ability or potential at a starting salary level we can afford to pay.'

Actually, he is overstating the case. A good product manager does not have to be an expert in everything that relates to his product. To start with, he has to have talent and experience in those few functions that are critical for the success of the product. For example, in a consumer product, he has to have a background in advertising and promotion. The rest he can master as part of his on-the-job training. In the last analysis, every product manager is not going to graduate to general manager, but he has to have many of the requisite capabilities, and experience shows that the chances for success are severely hampered if he does not.

Making the concept work

While there are no ready-made rules to guarantee effective product management, there are certain specific steps that can be taken to avoid the common pitfalls.

(1) *Clearly establish the need for product management.* The product manager concept must be weighed against other organization alternatives (for example, divisionalization, separate product marketing groups or sales forces) to make sure that it offers the best means of fulfilling the needs of the operation, and, most important, that it is not being installed simply because it is fashionable. After the pros and cons of each alternative have been considered, the case for product management may not be as clear-cut as it seemed at first glance. And since it is a difficult concept to make work, it should be chosen only when it is demonstrably the *best* alternative.

(2) *Ensure proper attention to organization fundamentals.* First, the major areas of responsibility the product managers will have, and the relationship with the persons whom they will work with most closely, should be carefully defined. Also, management must make sure they are so positioned in the organization structure to have the status and the access to key decision makers required to carry out their assignments.

This latter point needs emphasis, for it is essential to avoid burying the product manager beneath layers of organizational levels if he is to function effectively. In fact, one company that recognized the need for across-the-board attention to its products moved the product managers out of the marketing department up to a position reporting directly to the general manager, so that they would not be restricted by organizational lines. While this is clearly an exceptional case, it underscores the importance of positioning the product managers as high in the organization as practical.

Next, the product manager's specific activities and working relationships should be committed to writing as a basis for gaining agreement and understanding. Here a far more definitive job description is required than for most other positions because of the broad scope and limited authority of the usual product manager assignment. One way of doing this is to spell out the product manager's responsibilities in terms of the way in which he will work with each key man in the organization.

Exhibit 9.3 Specifying the product manager's responsibility

Because of the nature of the product manager's job, his responsibility must be defined in more detail than might otherwise be necessary. This is important not only to guide the product manager, but also to familiarize others in the organization with what management expects of the product manager. The two following examples contrast descriptions of the product manager's role and relationships with one area – product development.

Here is a typical statement taken from a major company that offers inadequate guidance to the product manager:

> *Statement of responsibility*: Works closely with product development
> to ensure adequate plans and programs for his product line.

Now, here is the kind of statement that does provide the product manager with a basis for achieving understanding and building close working relationships. It is taken from the product manager's position description in another company which, understandably, has been outstanding in its use of this concept:

> The critical importance of new-product development in the company's business cannot be overemphasized. It is the mainstream for product improvements and new applications so vital to the company's continuing growth and profitability.
>
> The product development department is responsible basically for developing and testing new products and applications and for improving existing products and processes. The relationships of product managers with this department will be centered on the product development manager who is responsible for his assigned product line. The basic

Exhibit 9.3 shows, first, a typical company's statement of the product manager's responsibility in one area (in this case, product development). The exhibit then goes on to show how a more successful company expanded and clarified the specific responsibilities and relationships of the product manager to the product development group. The latter company, a leader in the textile field, wanted to reshape and upgrade its product management group. With a similar elaboration of each of the product manager's key activities, this company found it much easier to ensure that everyone in the organization understood how the product managers' responsibilities had changed and how they would work under the new concept.

(3) *Develop a manning 'spec' that is realistically geared to the range of skills required to handle the assignment.* Different product manager assignments obviously require different skills. For example, a product manager for a packaged-goods item must be well-grounded in advertising and promotion know-how. On the other

responsibility for recommending applications and product development goals and programs rests with the product development manager. However, in order to ensure a marketing-oriented point of view, the product development manager should rely heavily on the counsel of the product manager in determining the general nature of projects for his product line and the priorities that should be assigned to them.

An important responsibility of the product manager is to guide the efforts of the product development groups into the most profitable channels from a sales standpoint. He does this by keeping these groups closely informed of field needs, important market trends, and his own marketing plans. In effect, the product manager supplies the major part of the commercial intelligence needed by the product development department.

Ultimately, the director of product development and the vice president of marketing must collaborate in establishing the total applications and product development goals of the company, the over-all budget for this activity, and the priorities of major products.

Once project priorities and timetables are established, the product manager is expected to incorporate product development plans for his product line into his over-all product plans. And he is charged with the responsibility for keeping informed on the general status of projects for his product line and seeing that appropriate corrective action is taken when schedules bog down or planned goals are not achieved. To this end, he directs the discussions related to his product line in regularly scheduled development meetings and takes the initiative to secure the involvement of other departments when that is necessary.

---

hand, a product manager in the military electronics field must have a solid technical background in his product area and know the ins and outs of marketing to the government.

As a rule, these basics are not difficult to identify. Nor are they by themselves sufficient to do the job. Even more important are other skills that are frequently overlooked. A demonstrated sense of business judgment, the personal skills to operate effectively on a staff basis, the faculty to deal effectively with a full range of business problems, and the verbal ability to articulate his point of view and persuade others to see it are also requisites for any product manager. In view of this, a special combination of skills is required. The key is to get them down in writing to serve as a checklist in the screening and selection processes.

Once the 'spec' is completed, the important need is to hold to the standard that has been set. Unquestionably, it is difficult to find men who have the range of skills required. And, often, the established compensation range is not adequate to attract them. Consequently, there is an understandable tendency to settle for second best. But the odds are heavy against any company that does not stick to the standards that have been agreed on. For effective product management depends, more than on anything else, on the skills of the individuals appointed to the jobs.

(4) *Provide for the thorough orientation and training of men appointed to product management positions.* Few will disagree that this requirement is essential. Yet the number of cases where it is actually done well could be counted on one hand, for it is not as simple as it sounds.

For one thing, the product manager's job is built around a planning responsibility that is difficult to describe in meaningful terms and even more difficult to teach. For another, there are not texts or handbooks on product management as there are for sales management, advertising, market research, and the like. But these are the very reasons why it is so essential to place major emphasis on training.

Although this task is admittedly difficult, it is far from impossible. Many companies have found that time and effort put into developing a comprehensive program to indoctrinate and to train its product managers have really paid off in improved performance.

Comprehensive program

In the first part of one such company's program, the new product manager is provided with a list of specific first steps he should take when beginning his assignment. The following five tasks (excerpted from the company's written program) illustrate the kind of start-up activities that the much longer list covers:

(a) Study carefully all available descriptive literature about the new product manager position. Pay particular attention to the position description, especially that part which defines the role and relationships of the product manager. It is up to you to become thoroughly familiar with the major responsibilities of the position. Obtain a clear understanding of your working relationships with other executives in the company. Use the 'role and relationships' description as a basis for discussions with other executives to ensure complete understanding and agreement on the way you will work together.

(b) Obtain from the vice president of marketing his major thoughts on management of your assigned product line. In order to behave as an extension of the vice president of marketing, you should become familiar with his ideas on: major problems related to the product line, significant opportunities for strengthening market position, over-all marketing strategy, and internal strengths and weaknesses affecting the marketing of the product line.

(c) Become familiar with the company's marketing planning and control process. Study the principles, elements, and steps in planning described in the planning guide [see description of second part of the company's program]. Discuss with the planning director the technique, format, and timing involved in developing a product marketing plan.

(d) Ensure that you will have adequate product information available to you and that you know how to use it. Read the memorandum, *Interpreting Control Reports to Pinpoint Trouble Spots* [see description of third part of the company's program], using it as a guide to discuss your needs with market research and the controller.

(e) Develop a written marketing plan for your product group. Review it with and obtain the endorsement of the vice president of marketing. Discuss it also with other key executives to ensure their understanding of the plan as the standard for executing programs and measuring performance during the ensuing period.

Thus, the new product manager has a series of specific task assignments, beginning with his first day on the job. And he stands a much better chance of getting the right start than the man who is left on his own to figure out how he should get under way.

In the second part of the program, each product manager is coached in the fundamentals of planning. Here special emphasis is put on showing him:

● What constitutes a good product marketing plan, and what areas for his product deserve major attention.
● How it should be developed and tied together with other departments' plans.
● How it relates to budgeting and other operating procedures.
● How it fits into the management process, including how it should be used once it is completed and approved.
● When and how it should be modified.

In the third and final part of the program, a working guide aimed at helping the product manager carry out his role is developed and continuously updated. This guide focuses on the 'how to' aspects of the product manager's job and covers explanations of such basic activities as these:

● Developing the product strategy and product plan.
● Recommending capital appropriations.
● Keeping abreast of the economics of the product's business.
● Preparing and getting approval of advertising and promotion budgets.
● Interpreting control reports to pinpoint trouble spots.

Such a guide serves as a useful reference document for new and experienced product managers alike. And, as new ideas or improved procedures are developed, a product manager is given the extracurricular assignment of developing a new guideline. The objective is to develop a handbook that will give the product manager a running start in mastering most of the knotty tasks within his sphere of responsibility.

Properly done, any one of the three parts to this program unquestionably requires time and effort. And it would be wrong to think that every company should have a program that is this extensive. However, the example shatters the idea that training the product manager is impossible. Many companies could achieve a much higher level of product manager performance by taking a cue from this program.

Measuring the manager

Because of the wide variances that exist in product manager assignments, it is difficult to agree on standards of performance that will provide a basis for evaluating how well the job is being carried out. Although product profitability and share of market performance are indicators that cannot be overlooked indefinitely (since, after all, the primary role of the product manager is to provide the specialized attention needed to improve these), it is not fair to hold the product manager accountable for these factors on a short-term basis. There are too many influences beyond his control that contribute to profit and market share changes up or down.

In my experience, the following criteria are a fairer and much more realistic basis for evaluating a product manager's effectiveness:

1   Is he on top of varying market conditions and requirements so that he is able to accurately interpret the changing needs of his product's business?

2   Does he draw together complete and imaginative plans for his product area that are acceptable to top management?

3   Do his plans include concrete programs for effecting required improvement in his product's business?

4   Does he follow up and, if necessary, modify approved plans to see that product objectives are achieved?

5   Is he generally regarded by other executives as the most knowledgeable about his product's requirements, and do they look to him for ideas on what they should do to meet the product's needs?

Based on the foregoing, it is clear that the product manager's job, unlike most others, cannot be tied down with easy, common definitions or descriptions. Nor are there any clear-cut bench marks for evaluating

Product manager or market manager?

Almost anything that can be said about the product manager applies equally to his organizational first cousin, the market manager.

There is a difference between the market manager and the product manager, but it resides not in the organizational nature of the job, or in its problems, but rather in the marketing circumstances that make one approach more effective than the other.

As noted in this article, the product manager approach is most appropriate for companies with a number of different products that have to be produced and marketed through the same manufacturing, marketing, or sales divisions. On the other hand, where a company has an essentially homogeneous, or at least closely related, line of products which appeal to different segments of the market, the market manager approach may make more organizational sense, since it may put appropriate focus on each of the marketing opportunities.

What these two have in common is that in each case there is a member of the management group with high-level responsibility for getting a product to market without any direct line authority over the full range of activities required to get the job done. It is this similarity that makes almost everything that can be said about the problems of the product manager valid also for organizing the market manager's job.

---

the product manager's performance. These factors add to the difficulty of making the concept work.

Conclusion

The product manager concept can be made to work, but it will pay off only if top management takes these steps:

● Makes certain that the product manager approach is the one best suited to organizational needs.

● Clearly defines and communicates the role and working relationships of the product manager.

● Selects the right man for the job.

● Provides proper training for the job realistically expected to be done.

● Develops a realistic approach to evaluating and improving the product manager's contribution.

These ground rules alone are the first steps toward making the product manager concept work. A company that has run into problems with its product manager setup would do well to ask how many of these ground rules it has followed. And it is a better-than-even-money bet that attention to these points can be a major contributing factor to better product management.

10

A Theory of Human Motivation

A. H. MASLOW

I must admit at the outset that I have never read 'A Theory of Human Motivation' in its present version and that I have, altogether, only the vaguest knowledge of Professor Maslow's activities. However, I am very familiar with the ideas that he put forward on the motivation theory for which he has been credited, which have been widely acclaimed in an unusually large number of professional disciplines around the world. Obviously, as a psychologist, he is well reputed in this specific field. But, perhaps more interestingly, it is in the field of motivation theories of management that his concept of the hierarchy of needs has succeeded in capturing and retaining the attention of academics, practitioners and observers over a period of many years.

The basic idea that there exists a quantifiable hierarchy of needs for every human being sounds, on the face of it, so simplistic as not to require restating. Yet it took someone of the calibre of Maslow to classify each need and to use his idea of the hierarchy of needs as the foundation for a system defining intrinsic human values and human goals that are self-validating.

As we increasingly began to recognize and acknowledge that human resources were the critical factor in economic and industrial development, a model covering how to motivate people, explain their behaviour and understand their role in a team or group setting became a more and more valuable management tool.

I suppose that, during the past 30 years, hundreds of observers and professionals like myself have, without fully appreciating it, used Maslow's theory in the process of carrying out our responsibilities. Usually, when we invoke Maslow's theories we simply call them common sense. But, as we know, common sense is hardly ever common or even sensible until it has been put into the right context and into a framework that is usable, explainable and reproducible.

It would, perhaps, be interesting to postulate what Maslow would be writing about if he were alive today. Certainly his ideas would still be applicable to the 90 per cent of the world that has come, for better or for worse, to be called the 'have nots'. But it is intriguing to speculate as to whether or not we could expect some new and greater insight into human motivation, greed and the hierarchy of needs when one considers the 10 per cent of the 'haves' who enjoy the fulfilment of many of the needs that were unmet when Maslow first began writing.

Dr James L. Fisher,
Chairman, Fisher, Dillistone and Associates,
London

A Theory of Human Motivation

Dynamics of the basic needs

The 'physiological' needs

THE needs that are usually taken as the starting point for motivation theory are the so-called physiological drives. Two recent lines of research make it necessary to revise our customary notions about these needs: first, the development of the concept of homeostasis, and, second, the finding that appetites (preferential choices among foods) are a fairly efficient indication of actual needs or lacks in the body.

Homeostasis refers to the body's automatic efforts to maintain a constant, normal state of the blood stream. Cannon[1] has described this process for (1) the water content of the blood; (2) salt content; (3) sugar content; (4) protein content; (5) fat content; (6) calcium content; (7) oxygen content; (8) constant hydrogen-ion level (acid-base balance); and (9) constant temperature of the blood. Obviously this list can be extended to include other minerals, the hormones, vitamins, and so on.

Young in a recent article[2] has summarized the work on appetite in its relation to body needs. If the body lacks some chemical, the individual will tend to develop a specific appetite or partial hunger for that food element.

Thus it seems impossible as well as useless to make any list of fundamental physiological needs for they can come to almost any number one might wish, depending on the degree of specificity or description. We cannot identify all physiological needs as homeostatic. That sexual desire, sleepiness, sheer activity, and maternal behavior in

Abridged from A. H. Maslow, 'A Theory of Human Motivation', *Psychological Review* 50 (1943): 370–96. Copyright 1943 by the American Psychological Association, and reproduced by permission. This material is now in the public domain.

animals are homeostatic has not yet been demonstrated. Furthermore, this list would not include the various sensory pleasures (tastes, smells, tickling, stroking) which are probably physiological and which may become the goals of motivated behavior.

In a previous paper[3] it has been pointed out that these physiological drives or needs are to be considered unusual rather than typical because they are isolable and because they are localizable somatically. That is to say, they are relatively independent of each other, of other motivations and of the organism as a whole, and, in many cases, it is possible to demonstrate a localized, underlying somatic base for the drive. This is true less generally than has been thought (exceptions are fatigue, sleepiness, maternal responses), but it is still true in the classic instances of hunger, sex, and thirst.

It should be pointed out again that any of the physiological needs and the consummatory behavior involved with them serve as channels for all sorts of other needs as well. The person who thinks he is hungry may actually be seeking more for comfort or dependence than for vitamins or proteins. Conversely, it is possible to satisfy the hunger need in part by other activities such as drinking water or smoking cigarettes. In other words, these physiological needs are only relatively isolable.

Undoubtedly these physiological needs are the most prepotent of all needs. What this means specifically is that, in the human being who is missing everything in life in an extreme fashion, it is most likely that the major motivation would be the physiological needs rather than any others. A person who is lacking food, safety, love, and esteem would most probably hunger for food more strongly than for anything else.

If all the needs are unsatisfied, and the organism is then dominated by the physiological needs, all other needs may become simply nonexistent or be pushed into the background. It is then fair to characterize the whole organism by saying simply that it is hungry, for consciousness is almost completely preempted by hunger. All capacities are put into the service of hunger-satisfaction, and the organization of these capacities is almost entirely determined by the one purpose of satisfying hunger. The receptors and effectors, the intelligence, memory, habits, all may now be defined simply as hunger-gratifying tools. Capacities that are not useful for this purpose lie dormant or are pushed into the background. The urge to write poetry, the desire to acquire an automobile, the interest in American history, the desire for a new pair of shoes are, in the extreme case, forgotten or become of secondary importance. For the man who is extremely and dangerously hungry, no other interests exist but food. He dreams food, he remembers food, he thinks about food, he emotes only about food, he perceives only food, and he wants only food. The more subtle determinants that ordinarily fuse with the physiological drives in organizing even feeding, drinking, or sexual behavior, may now be so completely overwhelmed as to allow us to speak at this time (but *only* at this time) of pure hunger drive and behavior, with the one unqualified aim of relief.

Another peculiar characteristic of the human organism when it is dominated by a certain need is that the whole philosophy of the future tends also to change. For our chronically and extremely hungry man, utopia can be defined very simply as a place where there is plenty of food. He tends to think that, if only he is guaranteed food for the rest of his life, he will be perfectly happy and will never want anything more. Life itself tends to be defined in terms of eating. Anything else will be defined as unimportant. Freedom, love, community feeling, respect, philosophy, may all be waved aside as fripperies which are useless, since they fail to fill the stomach. Such a man may fairly be said to live by bread alone.

It cannot possibly be denied that such things are true, but their *generality* can be denied. Emergency conditions are, almost by definition, rare in the normally functioning peaceful society. That this truism can be forgotten is due mainly to two reasons. First, rats have few motivations other than physiological ones, and since so much of the research upon motivation has been made with these animals, it is easy to carry the rat picture over to the human being. Second, it is too often not realized that culture itself is an adaptive tool, one of whose main functions is to make the physiological emergencies come less and less often. In most of the known societies, chronic extreme hunger of the emergency type is rare rather than common. In any case, this is still true in the United States. The average American citizen is experiencing appetite rather than hunger when he says, 'I am hungry.' He is apt to experience sheer life-and-death hunger only by accident and then only a few times through his entire life.

Obviously a good way to obscure the 'higher' motivations, and to get a lopsided view of human capacities and human nature, is to make the organism extremely and chronically hungry or thirsty. Anyone who attempts to make an emergency picture into a typical one and who will measure all of man's goals and desires by his behavior during extreme physiological deprivation is certainly being blind to many things. It is quite true that man lives by bread alone – when there is no bread. But what happens to man's desires when there *is* plenty of bread and when his belly is chronically filled?

At once other (and 'higher') needs emerge, and these, rather than physiological hungers, dominate the organism. And when these in turn are satisfied, again new (and still 'higher') needs emerge, and so on. This is what we mean by saying that the basic human needs are organized into a hierarchy of relative prepotency.

One main implication of this phrasing is that gratification becomes as important a concept as deprivation in motivation theory, for it releases the organism from the domination of a relatively more physiological need, permitting thereby the emergence of other more social goals. The physiological needs, along with their partial goals, when chronically gratified cease to exist as active determinants or organizers of behavior. They now exist only in a potential fashion in the sense that they may emerge again to dominate the organism if they are thwarted. But a want that is satisfied is no longer a want. The organism is dominated and its behavior organized only by unsatisfied needs. If hunger is satisfied, it becomes unimportant in the current dynamics of the individual.

This statement is somewhat qualified by a hypothesis to be discussed more fully later, namely, that it is precisely those individuals in whom a certain need has always been satisfied who are best equipped to tolerate deprivation of that need in the future; furthermore, those who have been deprived in the past will react to current satisfactions differently from the one who has never been deprived.

The safety needs

If the physiological needs are relatively well gratified, there then emerges a new set of needs, which we may categorize roughly as the safety needs. All that has been said of the physiological needs is equally true, although in lesser degree, of these desires. The organism may equally well be wholly dominated by them. They may serve as the almost exclusive organizers of behavior, recruiting all the capacities of the organism in their service, and we may then fairly describe the whole organism as a safety-seeking mechanism. Again we may say of the receptors, the effectors, of the intellect and the other capacities that they are primarily safety-seeking tools. Again, as in the hungry man, we find that the dominating goal is a strong determinant not only of his current world outlook and philosophy but also of his philosophy of the future. Practically everything looks less important than safety (even sometimes the physiological needs which being satisfied, are now underestimated). A man, in this state, if it is extreme enough and chronic enough, may be characterized as living almost for safety alone.

Although in this paper we are interested primarily in the needs of the adult, we can approach an understanding of his safety needs perhaps more efficiently by observation of infants and children, in whom these needs are much more simple and obvious. One reason for the clearer appearance of the threat or danger reaction in infants is that they do not inhibit this reaction at all, whereas adults in our society have been taught to inhibit it at all costs. Thus even when adults do feel their safety to be threatened, we may not be able to see this on the surface. Infants will react in a total fashion and as if they were endangered, if they are disturbed or dropped suddenly, startled by loud noises, flashing light, or other unusual sensory stimulation, by rough handling, by general loss of support in the mother's arms, or by inadequate support.[4]

In infants we can also see a much more direct reaction to bodily illnesses of various kinds. Sometimes these illnesses seem to be immediately and per se threatening and seem to make the child feel unsafe. For instance, vomiting, colic, or other sharp pains seem to make the child look at the whole world in a different way. At such a moment of pain, it may be postulated that, for the child, the appearance of the whole world suddenly changes from sunniness to darkness, so to speak, and becomes a place in which anything at all might happen, in which previously stable things have suddenly become unstable. Thus a child who because of some bad food is taken ill may, for a day or two, develop fear, nightmares, and a need for protection and reassurance never seen in him before his illness.

Another indication of the child's need for safety is his preference for some kind of undisrupted routine or rhythm. He seems to want a predictable, orderly world. For instance, injustice, unfairness, or inconsistency in the parents seems to make a child feel anxious and unsafe. This attitude may be not so much because of the injustice per se or any particular pains involved, but rather because this treatment threatens to make the world look unreliable or unsafe or unpredictable. Young children seem to thrive better under a system which has at least a skeletal outline of rigidity, in which there is a schedule of a kind, some sort of routine, something that can be counted upon, not only for the present, but also far into the future. Perhaps one could express this more accurately by saying that the child needs an organized world rather than an unorganized or unstructured one.

The central role of the parents and the normal family setup are indisputable. Quarreling, physical assault, separation, divorce, or death within the family may be particularly terrifying. Also parental outbursts of rage or threats of punishment sometimes elicit such total panic and terror in the child that we must assume more is involved than the physical pain alone. While it is true that in some children this terror may represent also a fear of loss of parental love, it can also occur in completely rejected children, who seem to cling to the hating parents more for sheer safety and protection than because of hope of love.

Confronting the average child with new, unfamiliar, strange, un-manageable stimuli or situations will too frequently elicit the danger or terror reaction, as, for example, getting lost or even being separated from the parents for a short time, being confronted with new faces, new situations, or new tasks, the sight of strange, unfamiliar, or uncontrollable objects, illness, or death. Particularly at such times, the child's frantic clinging to his parents is eloquent testimony to their role as protectors (quite apart from their roles as food-givers and love-givers).

From these and similar observations, we may generalize and say that the average child in our society usually prefers a safe, orderly, predictable, organized world which he can count on and in which unexpected, unmanageable, or other dangerous things do not happen and in which, in any case, he has all-powerful parents who protect and shield him from harm.

That these reactions may so easily be observed in children is in a way a proof of the fact that children in our society feel too unsafe (or, in a word, are badly brought up). Children who are reared in an unthreatening, loving family do *not* ordinarily react as we have described above.[5] In such children the danger reactions are apt to come mostly to objects or situations that adults too would consider dangerous.[6]

The healthy, normal, fortunate adult in our culture is largely satisfied in his safety needs. The peaceful, smoothly running, 'good' society ordinarily makes its members feel safe enough from wild animals, extremes of temperature, criminals, assault and murder, tyranny, and so on. Therefore, in a very real sense, they no longer have any safety needs as active motivators. Just as a sated man no longer feels hungry, a safe man no longer feels endangered. If we wish to see these needs directly and clearly we must turn to neurotic or near-neurotic individuals, and to the economic and social underdogs. In between these extremes, we can perceive the expressions of safety needs only in such phenomena as, for instance, the common preference for a job with tenure and protection, the desire for a savings account, and for insurance of various kinds (medical, dental, unemployment, disability, old age).

Other broader aspects of the attempt to seek safety and stability in the world are seen in the very common preference for familiar rather than unfamiliar things, or for the known rather than the unknown. The tendency to have some religion or world-philosophy that organizes the universe and the men in it into some sort of satisfactorily coherent, meaningful whole is also in part motivated by safety-seeking. Here, too, we may list science and philosophy in general as partially motivated by the safety needs (we shall see later that there are also other motivations to scientific, philosophical, or religious endeavor).

Otherwise the need for safety is seen as an active and dominant mobilizer of the organism's resources only in emergencies, e.g., war, disease, natural catastrophes, crime waves, societal disorganization, neurosis, brain injury, chronically bad situation.

Some neurotic adults in our society are, in many ways, like the unsafe child in their desire for safety, although in the former it takes on a somewhat special appearance. Their reaction is often to unknown, psychological dangers in a world that is perceived to be hostile, overwhelming, and threatening. Such a person behaves as if a great catastrophe were almost always impending, i.e., he is usually responding as if to an emergency. His safety needs often find specific expression in a search for a protector, or a stronger person on whom he may depend, or perhaps a *Führer*.

The neurotic individual may be described in a slightly different way with some usefulness as a grown-up person who retains his childish attitudes toward the world. That is to say, a neurotic adult may be said to behave 'as if' he were actually afraid of a spanking or of his mother's disapproval or of being abandoned by his parents or of having his food taken away from him. It is as if his childish attitudes of fear and threat reaction to a dangerous world had gone underground and, untouched by the growing up and learning processes, were now ready to be called out by any stimulus that would make a child feel endangered and threatened.[7]

The neurosis in which the search for safety takes its clearest form is in the compulsive-obsessive neurosis. Compulsive-obsessives try frantically to order and stabilize the world so that no unmanageable, unexpected, or unfamiliar dangers will ever appear.[8] They hedge themselves about with all sorts of ceremonials, rules and formulas so that every possible contingency may be provided for and so that no new contingencies may appear. They are much like the brain-injured cases, described by Goldstein,[9] who manage to maintain their equilibrium by avoiding everything unfamiliar and strange and by ordering their restricted world in such a neat, disciplined, orderly fashion that everything in the world can be counted upon. They try to arrange the world so that anything unexpected (dangers) cannot possibly occur. If, through no fault of their own, something unexpected does occur, they go into a panic reaction as if this unexpected occurrence constituted a grave danger. What we can see only as a none-too-strong preference in the healthy person, e.g., preference for the familiar, becomes a life-and-death necessity in abnormal cases.

The love needs

If both the physiological and the safety needs are fairly well gratified, then there will emerge the love and affection and belongingness needs, and the whole cycle already described will repeat itself with this new center. Now the person will feel keenly, as never before, the absence of friends or a sweetheart or a wife or children. He will hunger for affectionate relations with people in general, namely, for a place in his group, and he will strive with great intensity to achieve this goal. He will want to attain such a place more than anything else in the world and may even forget that once, when he was hungry, he sneered at love.

In our society the thwarting of these needs is the most commonly found core in cases of maladjustment and more severe psychopathology. Love and affection, as well as their possible expression in sexuality, are generally looked upon with ambivalence and are customarily hedged about with many restrictions and inhibitions. Practically all theorists of psychopathology have stressed thwarting of the love needs as basic in the picture of maladjustment. Many clinical studies have therefore been made of this need, and we know more about it perhaps than any of the other needs except the physiological ones.[10]

One thing that must be stressed at this point is that love is not synonymous with sex. Sex may be studied as a purely physiological need. Ordinarily sexual behavior is multidetermined, that is to say, determined not only by sexual but also by other needs, chief among which are the love and affection needs. Also not to be overlooked is the fact that the love needs involve both giving *and* receiving love.[11]

The esteem needs

All people in our society (with a few pathological exceptions) have a need or desire for a stable, firmly based, (usually) high evaluation of themselves, for self-respect, or self-esteem, and for the esteem of others. By firmly based self-esteem, we mean that which is soundly based upon real capacity, achievement, and respect from others. These needs may be classified into two subsidiary sets. These are, first, the desire for strength, for achievement, for adequacy, for confidence in the face of the world, and for independence and freedom.[12] Second, we have what we may call the desire for reputation or prestige (defining it as respect or esteem from other people), recognition, attention, importance, or appreciation.[13] These needs have been relatively stressed by Alfred Adler and his followers, and have been relatively neglected by Freud and the psychoanalysts. More and more today, however, there is appearing widespread appreciation of their central importance.

Satisfaction of the self-esteem need leads to feelings of self-confidence, worth, strength, capability, and adequacy, of being useful and necessary in the world. But thwarting of these needs produces feelings of inferiority, of weakness, and of helplessness. These feelings in turn give rise to either basic discouragement or else compensatory or neurotic trends. An appreciation of the necessity of basic self-confidence and an understanding of how helpless people are without it, can be easily gained from a study of severe traumatic neurosis.[14]

The need for self-actualization

Even if all these needs are satisfied, we may still often (if not always) expect that a new discontent and restlessness will soon develop, unless the individual is doing what he is fitted for. A musician must make music, an artist must paint, a poet must write, if he is to be ultimately happy. What a man *can* be, he *must* be. This need we may call self-actualization.

This term, first coined by Kurt Goldstein, is being used in this paper in a much more specific and limited fashion. It refers to the desire for self-fulfillment, namely, to the tendency for one to become actualized in what one is potentially. This tendency might be phrased as the desire to become more and more what one is, to become everything that one is capable of becoming.

The specific form that these needs take will of course vary greatly from person to person. In one individual it may be expressed maternally, as the desire to be an ideal mother, in another athletically, in still another aesthetically, in the painting of pictures, and in another inventively in the creation of new contrivances. It is not necessarily a creative urge, although in people who have any capabilities for creation it will take this form.

The clear emergence of these needs rests upon prior satisfaction of the physiological, safety, love, and esteem needs. We shall call people who are satisfied in these needs, basically satisfied people, and it is from these that we may expect the fullest (and healthiest) creativeness.[15] Since, in our society, basically satisfied people are the exception, we do not know much about self-actualization, either experimentally or clinically. It remains a challenging problem for research.

The preconditions for the basic need satisfactions

There are certain conditions which are immediate prerequisites for the basic need satisfactions. Danger to these is reacted to almost as if it were a direct danger to the basic needs themselves. Such conditions as freedom to speak, freedom to do what one wishes so long as no harm is done to others, freedom to express one's self, freedom to investigate and seek for information, freedom to defend one's self, justice, fairness, honesty, orderliness in the group are examples of such preconditions for basic need satisfactions. Thwarting in these freedoms will be reacted to with a threat or emergency response. These conditions are not ends in themselves but they are *almost* so, since they are so closely related to the basic needs, which are apparently the only ends in themselves. These conditions are defended because without them the basic satisfactions are quite impossible, or, at least, very severely endangered.

If we remember that the cognitive capacities (perceptual, intellectual, learning) are a set of adjustive tools, which have, among other functions, that of satisfaction of our basic needs, then it is clear that any danger to them, any deprivation or blocking of their free use, must also be indirectly threatening to the basic needs themselves. Such a statement is a partial solution of the general problems of curiosity, the search for knowledge, truth, and wisdom, and the ever persistent urge to solve the cosmic mysteries.

We must therefore introduce another hypothesis and speak of degrees of closeness to the basic needs, for we have already pointed out that *any* conscious desires (partial goals) are more or less important as they are more or less close to the basic needs. The same statement may be made for various behavior acts. An act is psychologically important if it contributes directly to satisfaction of basic needs. The less directly it so contributes, or the weaker this contribution is, the less important this act must be conceived to be from the point of view of dynamic psychology. A similar statement may be made for the various defense or coping mechanisms. Some are very directly related to the protection or attainment of the basic needs, others are only weakly and distantly related. Indeed, if we wished, we could speak of more basic and less basic defense mechanisms and then affirm that danger to the more basic defenses is more threatening than danger to less basic defenses (always remembering that this is so only because of their relationship to the basic needs).

The desires to know and to understand

So far, we have mentioned the cognitive needs only in passing. Acquiring knowledge and systematizing the universe have been considered as, in part, techniques for the achievement of basic safety in the world, or, for the intelligent man, expressions of self-actualization. Also freedom of inquiry and expression have been discussed as preconditions of satisfactions of the basic needs. True though these formulations may be, they do not constitute definitive answers to the question as to the motivation role of curiosity, learning, philosophizing, experimenting, and so on. They are, at best, no more than partial answers.

This question is especially difficult because we know so little about the facts. Curiosity, exploration, desire for the facts, desire to know may certainly be observed easily enough. The fact that they often are pursued even at great cost to the individual's safety is an example of the partial character of our previous discussion. In addition, the writer must admit that, though he has sufficient clinical evidence to postulate the desire to know as a very strong drive in intelligent people, no data are available for unintelligent people. It may then be largely a function of relatively high intelligence. Rather tentatively, then, and largely in the hope of stimulating discussion and research, we shall postulate a basic desire to know, to be aware of reality, to get the facts, to satisfy curiosity, or as Wertheimer phrases it, to see rather than to be blind.

This postulation, however, is not enough. Even after we know, we are impelled to know more and more minutely and microscopically, on the one hand, and, on the other, more and more extensively in the direction of a world philosophy, religion, and so on. The facts that we acquire, if they are isolated or atomistic, inevitably get theorized about, and either analyzed or organized or both. This process has been phrased by some as the search for 'meaning.' We shall then postulate a desire to understand, to systematize, to organize, to analyze, to look for relations and meanings.

Once these desires are accepted for discussion, we see that they too form themselves into a small hierarchy in which the desire to know is prepotent over the desire to understand. All the characteristics of a hierarchy of prepotency that we have described above seem to hold for this one as well.

We must guard ourselves against the too easy tendency to separate these desires from the basic needs we have discussed above, i.e., to make a sharp dichotomy between 'cognitive' and 'conative' needs. The desire to know and to understand are themselves conative, i.e., having a striving character, and are as much personality needs as the 'basic needs' we have already discussed.[16]

Further characteristics of the basic needs

The degree of fixity of the hierarchy of basic needs

We have spoken so far as if this hierarchy were a fixed order but actually it is not nearly as rigid as we may have implied. It is true that most of the people with whom we have worked have seemed to have these basic needs in about the order that has been indicated. However, there have been a number of exceptions.

(1) There are some people in whom, for instance, self-esteem seems to be more important than love. This most common reversal in the hierarchy is usually due to the development of the notion that the person who is most likely to be loved is a strong or powerful person, one who inspires respect or fear and who is self-confident or aggressive. Therefore, such people who lack love and seek it, may try hard to put on a front of aggressive, confident behavior. But essentially they seek high self-esteem and its behavior expressions more as a means to an end than for its own sake; they seek self-assertion for the sake of love rather than for self-esteem itself.

(2) There are other, apparently innately creative people in whom the drive to creativeness seems to be more important than any other counterdeterminant. Their creativeness might appear as self-actualization released not by basic satisfaction but in spite of lack of basic satisfaction.

(3) In certain people the level of aspiration may be permanently deadened or lowered. That is to say, the less prepotent goals may simply be lost and may disappear forever, so that the person who has experienced life at a very low level, i.e., chronic unemployment, may continue to be satisfied for the rest of his life if only he can get enough food.

(4) The so-called psychopathic personality is another example of permanent loss of the love needs. There are people who, according to the best data available,[17] have been starved for love in the earliest months of their lives and have simply lost forever the desire and the ability to give and to receive affection (as animals lose sucking or pecking reflexes that are not exercised soon enough after birth).

(5) Another cause of reversal of the hierarchy is that when a need has been satisfied for a long time, this need may be underevaluated. People who have never experienced chronic hunger are apt to underestimate its effects and to look upon food as a rather unimportant thing. If they are dominated by a higher need, this higher need will seem to be the most important of all. It then becomes possible, and indeed does actually happen, that they may, for the sake of this higher need, put themselves into the position of being deprived in a more basic need. We may expect that after a long-time deprivation of the more basic need there will be a tendency to reevaluate both needs so that the more prepotent need will actually become consciously prepotent for the individual who may have given it up very lightly. Thus, a man who has given up his job rather than lose his self-respect, and who then starves for six months or so, may be willing to take his job back even at the price of losing his self-respect.

(6) Another partial explanation of *apparent* reversals is seen in the fact that we have been talking about the hierarchy of prepotency in terms of consciously felt wants or desires rather than of behavior. Looking at behavior itself may give us the wrong impression. What we have claimed is that the person will *want* the more basic of two needs when deprived in both. There is no necessary implication here that he will act upon his desires. Let us say again that there are many determinants of behavior other than needs and desires.

(7) Perhaps more important than all these exceptions are the ones that involve ideals, high social standards, high values, and the like. With such values people become martyrs; they will give up everything for the sake of a particular ideal, or value. These people may be understood, at least in part, by reference to one basic concept (or hypothesis) which may be called 'increased frustration-tolerance through early gratification.' People who have been satisfied in their basic needs throughout their lives, particularly in their earlier years, seem to develop exceptional power to withstand present or future thwarting of these needs simply because they have strong, healthy character structure as a result of basic satisfaction. They are the 'strong' people who can easily weather

disagreement or opposition, who can swim against the stream of public opinion, and who can stand up for the truth at great personal cost. It is just the ones who have loved and been well loved and who have had many deep friendships who can hold out against hatred, rejection or persecution.

I say all this in spite of the fact that there is a certain amount of sheer habituation which is also involved in any full discussion of frustration tolerance. For instance, it is likely that those persons who have been accustomed to relative starvation for a long time are partially enabled thereby to withstand food deprivation. What sort of balance must be made between these two tendencies, of habituation on the one hand, and of past satisfaction breeding present frustration tolerance on the other hand, remains to be worked out by further research. Meanwhile we may assume that they are both operative, side by side, since they do not contradict each other. In respect to this phenomenon of increased frustration tolerance, it seems probable that the most important gratifications come in the first two years of life. That is to say, people who have been made secure and strong in the earliest years tend to remain secure and strong thereafter in the face of whatever threatens.

Degrees of relative satisfaction

So far, our theoretical discussion may have given the impression that these five sets of needs are somehow in a stepwise, all-or-none relationship to one another. We have spoken in such terms as the following: 'If one need is satisfied, then another emerges.' This statement might give the false impression that a need must be satisfied 100 percent before the next need emerges. In actual fact, most members of our society who are normal are partially satisfied in all their basic needs and partially unsatisfied in all their basic needs at the same time. A more realistic description of the hierarchy would be in terms of decreasing percentages of satisfaction as we go up the hierarchy of prepotency. For instance, if I may assign arbitrary figures for the sake of illustration, it is as if the average citizen is satisfied perhaps 85 percent in his physiological needs, 70 percent in his safety needs, 50 percent in his love needs, 40 percent in his self-esteem needs, and 10 percent in his self-actualization needs.

As for the concept of emergence of a new need after satisfaction of the prepotent need, this emergence is not a sudden, saltatory phenomenon but rather a gradual emergence by slow degrees from nothingness. For instance, if prepotent need A is satisfied only 10 percent then need B may not be visible at all. However, as this need A becomes satisfied 25 percent, need B may emerge 5 percent; as need A becomes satisfied 75 percent, need B may emerge 90 percent [sic]; and so on.

Unconscious character of needs

These needs are neither necessarily conscious nor unconscious. On the whole, however, in the average person, they are more often unconscious. It is not necessary at this point to overhaul the tremendous mass of evidence which indicates the crucial importance of unconscious motivation. It would by now be expected, on a priori grounds alone, that unconscious motivations would on the whole be rather more important than the conscious motivations. What we have called the basic needs are very often largely unconscious although they may, with suitable techniques and with sophisticated people, become conscious.

The role of gratified needs

It has been pointed out above several times that our higher needs usually emerge only when more prepotent needs have been gratified. Thus gratification has an important role in motivation theory. Apart from this, however, needs cease to play an active determining or organizing role as soon as they are gratified.

What this means, for example, is that a basically satisfied person no longer has the needs for esteem, love, safety, and so on. The only sense in which he might be said to have them is in the almost metaphysical sense that a sated man has hunger or a filled bottle has emptiness. If we are interested in what *actually* motivates us and not in what has, will, or might motivate us, then a satisfied need is not a motivator. It must be considered for all practical purposes simply not to exist, to have disappeared. This point should be emphasized because it has been either overlooked or contradicted in every theory of motivation I know.[18] The perfectly healthy, normal, fortunate man has no sex needs or hunger needs, or needs for safety or for love or for prestige or for self-esteem, except in stray moments of quickly passing threat. If we were to say otherwise, we should also have to aver that every man had all the pathological reflexes, e.g., Babinski, etc., because if his nervous system were damaged, these would appear.

It is such considerations as these that suggest the bold postulation that a man who is thwarted in any of his basic needs may fairly be envisaged simply as a sick man. This is a fair parallel to our designation as 'sick' of the man who lacks vitamins or minerals. Who is to say that a lack of love is less important than a lack of vitamins? Since we know the pathogenic effects of love starvation, who is to say that we are invoking value questions in an unscientific or illegitimate way, any more than the physician does who diagnoses and treats pellagra or scurvy? If I were permitted this usage, I should then say simply that a healthy man is primarily motivated by his needs to develop and actualize his fullest potentialities and capacities. If a man has any other basic needs in any active, chronic sense, then he is simply an unhealthy man. He is as surely sick as if he had suddenly developed a strong salt-hunger or calcium hunger.[19]

If this statement seems unusual or paradoxical the reader may be assured that this is only one among many such paradoxes that will appear as we revise our ways of looking at man's deeper motivations. When we ask what man wants of life, we deal with his very essence.

Summary

(1) There are at least five sets of goals which we may call basic needs. These are briefly physiological, safety, love, esteem, and self-actualization. In addition, we are motivated by the desire to achieve or maintain the various conditions upon which these basic satisfactions rest and by certain more intellectual desires.

(2) These basic goals are related to one another, being arranged in a hierarchy of prepotency. This means that the most prepotent goal will monopolize consciousness and will tend of itself to organize the recruitment of the various capacities of the organism. The less prepotent needs are minimized, even forgotten or denied. But when a need is fairly well satisfied, the next prepotent ('higher') need emerges, in turn to dominate the conscious life and to serve as the center of organization of behavior, since gratified needs are not active motivators.

Thus man is a perpetually wanting animal. Ordinarily the satisfaction of these wants is not altogether mutually exclusive but only tends to be. The average member of our society is most often partially satisfied and partially unsatisfied in all of his wants. The hierarchy principle is usually empirically observed in terms of increasing percentages of nonsatisfaction as we go up the hierarchy. Reversals of the average order of the hierarchy are sometimes observed. Also it has been observed that an individual may permanently lose the higher wants in the hierarchy under special conditions. There are not only ordinarily multiple motivations for usual behavior but, in addition, many determinants other than motives.

(3) Any thwarting or possibility of thwarting of these basic human goals, or danger to the defenses which protect them or to the conditions upon which they rest, is considered to be a psychological threat. With a few exceptions, all psychopathology may be partially traced to such threats. A basically thwarted man may actually be defined as a 'sick' man.

(4) It is such basic threats which bring about the general emergency reactions.

(5) Certain other basic problems have not been dealt with because of limitations of space. Among these are (a) the problem of values in any definitive motivation theory; (b) the relation between appetites, desires, needs, and what is 'good' for the organism; (c) the etiology of the basic needs and their possible derivation in early childhood; (d) redefinition of motivational concepts, i.e., drive, desire, wish, need, goal; (e) implication of our theory for hedonistic theory; (f) the nature of the uncompleted act, of success and failure, and of aspiration-level; (g) the role of association, habit, and conditioning; (h) relation to the theory of interpersonal relations; (i) implications for psychotherapy; (j) implication for theory of society; (k) the theory of selfishness; (l) the relation between needs and cultural patterns; (m) the relation between this theory and Allport's theory of functional autonomy. These as well as certain other less important questions must be considered as motivation theory attempts to become definitive.

Notes

1 W. B. Cannon, *Wisdom of the Body* (New York: Norton, 1932).
2 P. T. Young, 'The Experimental Analysis of Appetite,' *Psychological Bulletin* 38 (1941): 129–64.
3 A. H. Maslow, 'A Preface of Motivation Theory,' *Psychosomatic Medicine* 5 (1943): 85–92.
4 As the child grows up, sheer knowledge and familiarity as well as better motor development make these 'dangers' less and less dangerous and more and more manageable. Throughout life it may be said that one of the main conative functions of education is this neutralizing of apparent dangers through knowledge, e.g., I am not afraid of thunder because I know something about it.
5 M. Shirley, 'Children's Adjustments to a Strange Situation,' *Journal of Abnormal and Social Psychology* 37 (1942): 201–17.
6 A 'test battery' for safety might be confronting the child with a small exploding fire-cracker or with a bewhiskered face, having the mother leave the room, putting him upon a high ladder, giving him a hypodermic injection, having a mouse crawl up to him, and so on. Of course I cannot seriously recommend the deliberate use of such 'tests,' for they might very well harm the child being tested. But these and similar situations come up by the score in the child's ordinary day-to-day living and may be observed. There is no reason why these stimuli should not be used with, for example, young chimpanzees.
7 Not all neurotic individuals feel unsafe. Neurosis may have at its core a thwarting of affection and esteem needs in a person who is generally safe.
8 A. H. Maslow and B. Mittelmann, *Principles of Abnormal Psychology* (New York: Harper & Bros., 1941).
9 K. Goldstein, *The Organism* (New York: American Book Co., 1939).
10 Maslow and Mittelmann, *Principles of Abnormal Psychology*.
11 For further details see A. H. Maslow, 'The Dynamics of Psychological Security-Insecurity,' *Character and Personality* 10 (1942): 331–44; and J. Plant, *Personality and the Cultural Pattern* (New York: Commonwealth Fund, 1937), chap. 5.

12 Whether or not this particular desire is universal we do not know. The crucial question, especially important today, is, 'Will men who are enslaved and dominated inevitably feel dissatisfied and rebellious?' We may assume on the basis of commonly known clinical data that a man who has known true freedom (not paid for by giving up safety and security but rather built on the basis of adequate safety and security) will not willingly or easily allow his freedom to be taken away from him. But we do not know that this is true for the person born into slavery. The events of the next decade should give us our answer. See discussion of this problem in E. Fromm, *Escape from Freedom* (New York: Farrar & Rinehart, 1941), chap. 5.

13 Perhaps the desire for prestige and respect from others is subsidiary to the desire for self-esteem or confidence in one's self. Observation of children seems to indicate that this is so, but clinical data give no clear support of such a conclusion.

14 A. Kardiner, *The Traumatic Neuroses of War* (New York: Hoeber, 1941). For more extensive discussion of normal self-esteem, as well as for reports of various researches, see A. H. Maslow, 'Dominance, Personality, and Social Behavior in Women,' *Journal of Social Psychology* 10 (1939): 3–39.

15 Clearly creative behavior, like painting, is like any other behavior in having multiple determinants. It may be seen in 'innately creative' people whether they are satisfied or not, happy or unhappy, hungry or sated. Also, it is clear that creative activity may be compensatory, ameliorative, or purely economic. It is my impression (as yet unconfirmed) that it is possible to distinguish the artistic and intellectual products of basically satisfied people from those of basically unsatisfied people by inspection alone. In any case, here too we must distinguish, in a dynamic fashion, the overt behavior itself from its various motivations or purposes.

16 M. Wertheimer, unpublished lectures at the New School for Social Research.

17 D. M. Levy, 'Primary Affect Hunger,' *American Journal of Psychiatry* 94 (1937): 643–52.

18 Note that acceptance of this theory necessitates basic revision of the Freudian theory.

19 If we were to use the 'sick' in this way, we should then also have to face squarely the relations of man to his society. One clear implication of our definition would be that (1) since a man is to be called sick who is basically thwarted, and (2) since such basic thwarting is made possible ultimately only by forces outside the individual, the (3) sickness in the individual must come ultimately from a sickness in the society. The 'good' or healthy society would then be defined as one that permitted man's highest purposes to emerge by satisfying all his prepotent basic needs.

11

My Years with General Motors

Alfred P. Sloan

After 23 years as chief executive of the world's largest public corporation, Alfred P. Sloan decided that it would be interesting to document his impressions of the progress of General Motors. He did so because, although there were already many histories of the US automobile industry, no one had tried to explain the origin and development of GM's decentralized organization, its principles of financial control and its approach to some of the fundamentals of management — leadership, motivation and style.

When the book was published, in 1963, the reader — in addition to being treated to an exciting adventure story about how GM had overcome one adversary after another in its growth — was also given the first blow-by-blow account of how GM met and overcame one of the fundamental problems facing modern global enterprises: how to find a balance between centralized and decentralized management authority and responsibility.

But Sloan not only spelled out the 'why' of divisionalization as a response to growth and complexity; he also went on to define with great care and attention the 'how'. No function within the company was left out. No activity was overlooked. No element in the business chain was omitted.

His concern for efficient production and effective decision-making was given equal time to that devoted to his ideas for the encouragement of innovation and entrepreneurial spirit.

When it appeared in the United Kingdom, My Years with General Motors soon became an extraordinarily influential work. It did not compete for a place on the best seller list with Ian Fleming. Nor did it sell as many copies as books on cooking, flowers and animals. But for many years it clearly had a profound influence on the structure and organization design of Britain's largest and most important enterprises.

Sipko Huismans,
Chief Executive, Courtaulds Plc,
London

Chapter 3: Concept of the Organization

A T THE close of the year 1920 the task before General Motors was reorganization. As things stood, the corporation faced simultaneously an economic slump on the outside and a management crisis on the inside.

The automobile market had nearly vanished and with it our income. Most of our plants and those of the industry were shut down or assembling a small number of cars out of semifinished materials in the plants. We were loaded with high-priced inventory and commitments at the old inflated price level. We were short of cash. We had a confused product line. There was a lack of control and of any means of control in operations and finance, and a lack of adequate information about anything. In short, there was just about as much crisis, inside and outside, as you could wish for if you liked that sort of thing.

I wrote the 'Organization Study' for General Motors as a possible solution for the specific problems created by the expansion of the corporation after World War I. I cannot, of course, say for sure how much of my thought on management came from contacts with my associates. Ideas, I imagine, are seldom, if ever, wholly original, but so far as I am aware, this study came out of my experience in Hyatt, United Motors, and General Motors.

In United Motors I met for the first time the problems of operating a multiple-unit organization with different products made by separate divisions. All that held United Motors together in its beginning was the concept of automotive parts and accessories. We made horns, radiators, bearings, rims, and the like, and we sold them to both automobile producers and the public. Certain limited areas of possible co-ordination presented themselves; for example, the servicing of the

Abridged from Alfred P. Sloan: *My Years with General Motors* (London: Sidgwick & Jackson, 1963).
© 1963 by Alfred P. Sloan, Jr. Reprinted by permission of Harold Matson Company, Inc.

numerous small products made by the different divisions. Separate service agencies for such small items were uneconomic. I therefore set up a single, nationwide organization called United Motors Service, Inc., on October 14, 1916, to represent the divisions, with stations in twenty-odd large cities and several hundred dealers at other points. The divisions naturally resisted this move for a while, but I persuaded them of the need for it, and for the first time learned something about getting decentralized management to yield some of its functions for the common good. The service organization is still operating in General Motors and has grown along with the business as a whole. By placing each division on its own profit-making basis, I gave the general office a common measure of efficiency with which to judge the contribution of each division to the whole.

In the great expansion in General Motors between 1918 and 1920, I had been struck by the disparity between substance and form: plenty of substance and little form. I became convinced that the corporation could not continue to grow and survive unless it was better organized, and it was apparent that no one was giving that subject the attention it needed.

An example, close to home for me: When the United Motors group was brought into the General Motors Corporation in late 1918, I found that if I followed the prevailing practice of inter-corporate relations I would no longer be able to determine the rate of return on investment for these accessory divisions individually or as a group. This would necessarily mean that I would lose some degree of managerial control over my area of operations. At that time, material within General Motors was passing from one operating division to another at cost, or at cost plus some predetermined percentage. My divisions in the United Motors Corporation had sold both to outside customers and to their allied divisions at the market price. I knew that I operated a profit-making group, and I wished to continue to be able to demonstrate this performance to the general management, rather than to have my operating results on interdivisional business swallowed up in the extra bookkeeping profits of some other division. It was a case of keeping the information clear.

It was not, however, a matter of interest to me only with respect to my divisions, since as a member of the Executive Committee, I was a kind of general executive and so had begun to think from the corporate viewpoint. The important thing was that no one knew how much was being contributed – plus or minus – by each division to the common good of the corporation. And since, therefore, no one knew, or could prove, where the efficiencies and inefficiencies lay, there was no objective basis for the allocation of new investment. This was one of the difficulties with the expansion program of that time. It was natural for the divisions to compete for investment funds, but it was irrational for the general officers of the corporation not to know where to place the money to best advantage. In the absence of objectivity it was not surprising that there was a lack of real agreement among the general officers. Furthermore, some of them had no broad outlook, and used their membership on the Executive Committee mainly to advance the interest of their respective divisions.

I had taken up the question of interdivisional relations with Mr Durant before I entered General Motors and my views on it were well enough known for me to be appointed chairman of a committee 'to formulate rules and regulations pertaining to interdivisional business' on December 31, 1918. I completed the report by the following summer and presented it to the Executive Committee on December 6, 1919. I select here a few of its first principles, which, though they are an accepted part of management doctrine today, were not so well known then. I think they are still worth attention.

I stated the basic argument as follows:

> The profit resulting from any business considered abstractly, is no real measure of the merits of that particular business. An operation making $100,000.00 per year may be a very profitable business justifying expansion and the use of all the additional capital that it can profitably employ. On the other hand, a business making $10,000,000 a year may be a very unprofitable one, not only not justifying further expansion but even justifying liquidation unless more profitable returns can be obtained. It is not, therefore, a matter of the amount of profit but of the relation of that profit to the real worth of invested capital within the business. Unless that principle is fully recognized in any plan that may be adopted, illogical and unsound results and statistics are unavoidable . . .

There seems to me still to be no question about that. It is as I see it the strategic aim of a business to earn a return on capital, and if in any particular case the return in the long run is not satisfactory, the deficiency should be corrected or the activity abandoned for a more favorable one.

For sales to outside customers, I recognized in the report that the market would determine the actual price, and if this yielded a desirable return, the business in question might justify expansion. For exclusively interdivisional transactions I recommended that the starting point should be cost plus some predetermined rate of return, but only as a guide. To avoid the possibility of protecting a supplying division which might be a high-cost producer, I recommended a number of steps involving analysis of the operation and comparison with outside competitive production where possible. The point I wish to make here relates not to technique – which other people know better than I do – but to the general principle of rate of return as the measure of the worth of a business. That idea was fundamental in my thinking about management problems.

On the influence of rate of return on decentralization and the relation of the part to the whole, I made several points of which the following seem to me to be of interest.

As to its bearing on organization:

. . . [It] Increases the morale of the organization by placing each operation on its own foundation, making it feel that it is a part of the Corporation, assuming its own responsibility and contributing its share to the final result.

As to its bearing on financial control:

. . . [It] Develops statistics correctly reflecting the relation between the net return and the invested capital of each operating division – the true measure of efficiency – irrespective of the number of other divisions contributing thereto and the capital employed within such divisions.

As to its bearing on strategic investment:

. . . [It] Enables the Corporation to direct the placing of additional capital where it will result in the greatest benefit to the Corporation as a whole.

So far as I know, this was the first written statement of the broad principles of financial control in General Motors.

The 'Organization Study' became a kind of 'best seller' in the corporation all during 1920; I received numerous letters from executives requesting copies of it, so many, in fact, that I found it necessary to reproduce it in quantity. It had no competition; that is, no other tangible effort was made, so far as I know, to achieve a general solution of the organization problem.

At the end of November 1920, when Mr Durant went out and Mr du Pont became president, the new administration needed a scheme of organization immediately. Mr Durant had been able to operate the corporation in his own way, as the saying goes, 'by the seat of his pants.' The new administration was made up of men with very different ideas about business administration. They desired a highly rational and objective mode of operation. The 'Organization Study' served the purpose and . . . it was officially adopted, with some revision, as basic corporation policy.

The study was primitive by comparison with present-day knowledge of management. And it was written from the point of view of presenting something that I thought would be acceptable to Mr Durant. So it was not without constraints. It began as follows:

> The object of this study is to suggest an organization for the General Motors Corporation which will definitely place the line of authority throughout its extensive operations as well as to co-ordinate each branch of its service, at the same time destroying none of the effectiveness with which its work has heretofore been conducted.
>
> The basis upon which this study has been made is founded upon two principles, which are stated as follows:-
>
> 1 The responsibility attached to the chief executive of each operation shall in no way be limited. Each such organization headed by its chief executive shall be complete in every necessary function and enable[d] to exercise its full initiative and logical development.
>
> 2 Certain central organization functions are absolutely essential to the logical development and proper control of the Corporation's activities.

This does not need much interpretation. It asks first for a line of authority, co-ordination, and the retention of the effectiveness of the then prevailing total decentralization. But looking back on the text of the two basic principles, after all these years, I am amused to see that the language is contradictory, and that its very contradiction is the crux of the matter. In point 1, I maximize decentralization of divisional operations in the words 'shall in no way be limited.' In point 2, I proceed to limit the responsibility of divisional chief executives in the expression 'proper control.' The language of organization has always suffered some want of words to express the true facts and circumstances of human interaction. One usually asserts one aspect or another of it at different times, such as the absolute independence of the part, and again the need of co-ordination, and again the concept of the whole with a guiding center. Interaction, however, is the thing, and with some reservation about the language and details I still stand on the fundamentals of what I wrote in the study. Its basic principles are in touch with the central problem of management as I have known it to this day.

The next point in the study was how to carry this philosophy into action. I wrote:

> Having established the above principles as fundamental, and it is believed that all interests within the Corporation agree as to such principles, the definite objects which it is hoped to attain by this study, are enumerated as follows:-
>
> 1 To definitely determine the functioning of the various divisions constituting the Corporation's activities, not only in relation to one another, but in relation to the central organization.

That was a big chew, but it is correct. If you can describe the functions of the parts and the whole, you have laid out a complete working organization, for by implication the apportionment of responsibility for decisions at various levels is contained in the description.

I continued with the second objective:

> 2 To determine the status of the central organization and to co-ordinate the operation of that central organization with the Corporation as a whole to the end that it will perform its necessary and logical place.

This is a restatement of the first point, but in reverse – that is, looking from the top down.

The third objective:

> 3 To centralize the control of all the executive functions of the Corporation in the President as its chief executive officer.

Decentralization or not, an industrial corporation is not the mildest form of organization in society. I never minimized the administrative power of the chief executive officer in principle when I occupied that position. I simply exercised that power with discretion; I got better results by selling my ideas than by telling people what to do. Yet the power to act must be located in the chief executive officer.

The fourth and fifth points speak for themselves:

> 4 To limit as far as practical the number of executives reporting directly to the President, the object being to enable the President to better

guide the broad policies of the Corporation without coming in contact with problems that may safely be entrusted to executives of less importance.

5   To provide means within each executive branch whereby all other executive branches are represented in an advisory way to the end that the development of each branch will be along lines constructive to the Corporation as a whole.

In brief, the study presented a specific structure for the corporation as it existed at that time. It recognized the form of the divisions, each of which was a self-contained group of functions (engineering, production, sales, and the like). It grouped the divisions, according to like activities, and . . . proposed to place an executive in charge of each group. The plan provided for advisory staffs, which would be without line authority. It provided for a financial staff. It distinguished policy from administration of policy, and specified the location of each in the structure. It expressed in its way the concept that was later to be formulated as decentralized operations with co-ordinated control.

The principles of organization in the study thus initiated for the modern General Motors the trend toward a happy medium in industrial organization between the extremes of pure centralization and pure decentralization. The new policy asked that the corporation neither remain as it was, a weak form of organization, nor become a rigid, command form. But the actual forms of organization that were to evolve in the future under a new administration – what exactly, for example, would remain a divisional responsibility and what would be co-ordinated, and what would be policy and what would be administration – could not be deduced by a process of logic from the 'Organization Study.' Even mistakes played a large part in the actual events; and if our competitors – Mr. Ford among them – had not made some of their own of considerable magnitude, and if we had not reversed certain of ours, the position of General Motors would be different from what it is today.

Part III
Globalization

Introduction

JUST as human motivation, social pressures and individual needs have complicated the job of top management, so too have what the economists call 'externalities' – those factors usually beyond our control that have, and will continue to have, a major impact on our lives, our institutions and our beliefs.

It is hard to argue with the suggestion that in the coming decade a universal awareness of, and concern for, the environment and what we do to it will be issues that will interject themselves into many, if not most, aspects of our personal, professional and commercial life.

It would be impossible to summarize all the externalities that have affected management in the UK over the past 30 years. Instead, we have selected two extracts, relating to two particular issues, from among the many that were nominated.

It was not until the early 1970s that the breadth, influence and power of the multinational corporation came to the world's attention. While worldwide giants in the automotive, chemical, oil and basic commodity industries grew unimpeded for many years, their influence and impact on the countries in which they operated only became front-page news when their host countries began to be concerned about their influence.

The Canadians, realizing that two-thirds of their country's industrial base was owned by US corporations, passed legislation to limit future US investment. In Chile, the takeovers of Anaconda and Kennecott copper interests were followed by two-year-long US Senate Foreign Relations Committee enquiries into the influence of IT&T on US foreign policy. Guyana took over Alcan's bauxite mining operations, and a completely unknown, newly formed institution – OPEC – began overnight to do battle with the world's international oil companies. Meanwhile, the UN studied and finally published an ambitious tract on how multinational companies should behave and be controlled.

Against this background, without becoming embroiled in the raging debate about whether or not worldwide enterprises were a blessing or a curse, Clee and Sachtjen examined in a fairly clinical fashion the variables that should influence the way in which multinational corporations conduct their 'intense and sophisticated rivalries' around the globe. 'Organizing a Worldwide Business' made a clear distinction at last between domestic companies with interests abroad and true world enterprises that apply their corporate resources on a global scale.

Triad Power describes a global market consisting of less than 20 per cent of the world's population but representing 80 per cent of the world's purchasing power.

12

Organizing a Worldwide Business

GILBERT H. CLEE AND WILBUR M. SACHTJEN

The fundamental problems of worldwide operations discussed in Clee and Sachtjen's article remain with us today. At the time of its publication, it 'struck a chord', elegantly providing a conceptual framework for handling an increasingly important problem for management. The shifts in economic and political power since the 1960s have probably made it even more relevant today for European and Asian enterprises than for those based in the United States.

A key point in the article is the emphasis on the need for a worldwide perspective; today we could couple that with the need to look for 'global products'. Perhaps such products may have variations for local markets (made easier by modern flexible manufacturing methods), but their 'core' characteristics, necessitating the main R&D and productive investment, are the same everywhere. Superior profitability flows from getting the global product right.

But the difficulty of the inherent conflict between geographic area organizations and world product responsibility remains. It means that a conventional, two-dimensional organization chart cannot express the true complexity of the mechanisms actually employed to increase profits in a sophisticated global enterprise. Clee and Sachtjen touched on this, and wisely did not offer any universal solutions – stating that every company is unique, so that any solution must be specific. Optimization is an elusive goal; practical men and women have to be satisfied with something that works, though with evident imperfections. The product/geographic organization tension is something many of them have to live with today.

For today's international managers, the conceptual framework given in the article is a fine basis on which to build. However, they now work in a different world; US dominance has waned, Japan has developed its businesses amazingly, Europe is finding its true strength. US management know-how has been widely disseminated. And now the rapid changes in the Communist world will lead to new problems and opportunities, exceptionally hard to predict with accuracy.

So, this article is a seminal contribution – still relevant in its essence today, still providing a foundation on which to build solutions to the contemporary problems of multinational, worldwide or global enterprises. However, the changes since the 1960s must be recognized in working out practical solutions; once again, the price of liberty (or effectiveness) is eternal vigilance.

Christopher Saunders,
Director, Cambridge Product Innovation Limited,
Cambridge

Organizing a Worldwide Business

BOTH the rise in U.S. financial commitments and the stepped-up foreign competition in our domestic markets reflect a significant change in the nature of international competition. Increasingly, the tempo and character of this competition are being determined by management decisions in a growing group of true world enterprises. Headquartered in London, Brussels, Tokyo, Geneva, or New York, these companies no longer plan their strategy in the manner of domestic companies with interests abroad. Instead, they apply their corporate resources on a global basis to exploit growth and profit opportunities wherever they may be found in the world.

New pressures

In undertaking the commitment to world enterprise, however, U.S. businessmen have found themselves confronting a whole new range of problems. If managing a domestic business is complex, managing an international enterprise is infinitely more so because of the many new variables bearing on crucial management decisions. Consequently, organizational structures and relationships that may have worked smoothly for an export-oriented domestic company soon show signs of strain.

Among the major U.S. companies committed to investment abroad, three basic organizational structures have evolved in response to the growing pressures, and enough experience has now been accumulated to permit some meaningful evaluation of them. Each of the structural patterns – which are, of course, subject to many variations and modifications – has its own distinctive rationale. Each offers advantages for companies in particular situations and at particular stages of their transition to world enterprise.

These basic organizational patterns are:

1   Variants of the traditional *international division* structure, all displaying a shift of responsibility for policy and worldwide strategic planning to the corporate level.

2   The *geographic* structure, replacing the international division with line managers at the top-management level who bear full operating responsibility for subsidiaries in assigned geographic areas.

3   The *product* structure, replacing the international division with executives at the top-management level who bear worldwide responsibility for development of individual product groups.

In the balance of this article, we propose to describe these dominant organizational types, give detailed examples of each, and explore the advantages and problems they raise for top management. Such an analysis, we believe, should be useful to any company entering or experiencing the transition to world enterprise.

International division structure

In some companies, responsibility for broad policy and strategic planning for overseas operations, once in the hands of an international division or actually carried out by affiliates acting independently, has shifted to executives at the corporate level without significant change in the traditional formal structure (see Exhibit 12.1). Operational responsibilities, such as running the overseas plants and developing markets in individual foreign countries, are handled by the subsidiaries and affiliates, with corporate or international division assistance given as required. The international division may continue to coordinate export sales from the U.S. operation to foreign affiliates and export markets. But it may also function as a coordinating 'middle-man' between production facilities anywhere in the world and the corporation's total complex of worldwide markets.

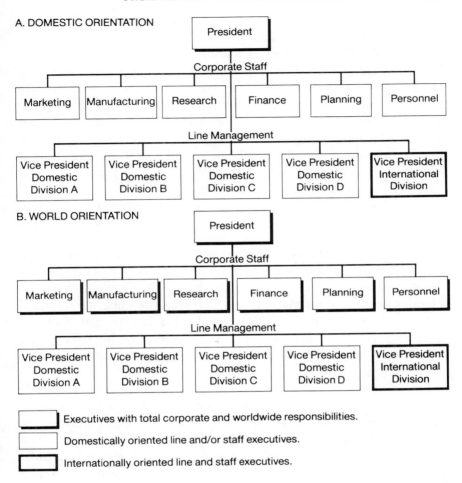

Exhibit 12.1 International division structure

Transition at Alpha

The Alpha Corporation,* a giant automobile manufacturer with plants in 20 countries, its own sales operations in 18 others, and more than 100,000 workers overseas, has approached the problems of managing a world enterprise without any major departure from the international

* Throughout this article, fictitious names have been assigned to the companies whose organizational structures are discussed. Otherwise, no facts have been altered.

division structure. Within that framework, however, its managerial setup has undergone important shifts in recent years.

During the lifetime of Alpha's founder, its foreign affiliates had been handled more in the fashion of personal investments than as extensions of the U.S. operation. To be sure, the founder and a few corporate officers maintained close contact with the foreign affiliates. But in practice – beginning in the late 1920s, when they were given control of foreign sales and assembly – the two big foreign manufacturing affiliates had been making virtually all the key decisions regarding overseas activities.

Need for Tighter Control. In 1948, three years after taking command of the company, Alpha's new chief executive turned his attention to international opportunities and problems. Aware that a potentially huge car and truck market was almost certain to emerge in post-war Europe, he realized that this market could never be won with high-cost U.S. and Canadian output. To wage an effective competitive battle, it was clear, would require European production bases. And this, he reasoned, meant tighter operating control over the big foreign manufacturing affiliates, which were hardly prepared to exploit in an effective, coordinated way the massive opportunities that would soon be developing.

For more than 20 years these two subsidiaries had been virtually autonomous companies with strongly entrenched local managements, exercising ownership control over all the other foreign affiliates. But then the new chief executive made it clear that he wanted ownership control of all foreign activities to rest in the United States, with broad policy and strategic planning for the international activities emanating from a single U.S. office.

Therefore, in addition to supplying the foreign affiliates with technical and management skills to help them recover from the havoc of World War II, corporate headquarters began increasingly to assume control of key management decisions for these operations.

Domestically Oriented Management. Two years before corporate head-quarters 'reached out' for control of the foreign affiliates, an international division had been set up in New York to channel and coordinate the dealings between the domestic company and its foreign affiliates. From 1948 on, however, decisions on policy and strategic planning for the overseas operations were increasingly made directly by top corporate management. The responsibilities of the international division were, and continue to be, mainly confined to coordinating overseas activities, providing advice and assistance to its foreign companies, developing markets in individual countries, and channeling output from producing affiliates to distributors in areas without assembly facilities.

Practically speaking, however, Alpha continues to be a domestically oriented company. The most urgent pressures and preoccupations of corporate headquarters executives involve meeting competition on the domestic front, not overseas. And Alpha's foreign expansion plans are also heavily influenced by the international strategy of its most powerful domestic competitor. Moreover, there has been a discernible tendency to fill key positions in the international division with seasoned domestic managers.

Meanwhile, the overseas activities are being carried on within an increasingly apparent framework of corporate policy and strategy. Corporate headquarters exercises fairly strong worldwide control over all products and planning, and the individual foreign units are functioning much more like operating entities than like the autonomous companies they were in the past. The international division now has responsibility for running the overseas plants, determining minor product modifications from country to country, and increasing penetration in individual markets. At the same time, though, considerable flexibility remains to the overseas operating units. A manager responsible for sales development in a particular market, for example, is free to explore the opportunities for more economical vehicle sourcing for his operations.

Expansion at Beta

Another example of the continued use of the international division pattern in an important world enterprise is Beta, Inc., a large manufacturer of computers and other business machines. Beta's top management has always devoted a great deal of attention to worldwide problems and opportunities. For many years, the overseas activities have been grouped together in a separate corporation, quite apart from Beta's domestic divisions. Historically, this international corporation has operated with considerable autonomy, though most major product-development activity has emanated from the United States divisions.

Unlike Beta's domestic operations, which are laid out along product and functional lines, the operations of the international corporation are organized on a geographic basis. The range of products sold by any one geographic unit in the international corporation is limited only by the state of development of local markets and by local import policies. Some of Beta's foreign units have manufacturing facilities to produce part of the product line, but they depend on the domestic manufacturing operations for items which are not in heavy demand overseas.

As Beta's international operations have expanded – in many cases reaching a level of development comparable to that of its domestic divisions – management has felt a growing need for worldwide policy determination, for effective global product strategy, and for the development of better ways to meet the needs of individual users on a worldwide basis. In response, the corporate staff, which has long had worldwide functional responsibilities, is devoting an increasing share of its time and effort to overseas activities.

Variety of reasons

How is a company such as Alpha able to alter long-standing management decision-making patterns for its foreign operations so completely without making major changes in its basic organizational pattern? Why does Beta's management continue to favor the international division form while setting worldwide policy and controlling the approval of worldwide operating plans at the corporate level? And why do other companies as deeply committed as these two to worldwide activities sometimes prefer to retain the international division form?

Analysis indicates that they may do so for one or more of five reasons:

(1) Formal organizational changes sometimes threaten to disrupt delicate working relationships, particularly in the case of long-established overseas subsidiaries under strong, well-entrenched local managements who are used to running their operations without interference. In this situation, it may be desirable to avoid major organizational realignments while seeking closer coordination between domestic and overseas activities or strengthening corporate control of worldwide policy and strategy. The same considerations are likely to apply where the parent company lacks majority control.

(2) Top management may believe that the foreign activities will get better direction with an international division than with a different organizational form. Under the international division pattern, overseas operations (particularly individual subsidiaries) can benefit from extra management attention that may be needed at the outset. Later on, some other organizational structure may prove more appropriate.

Where the domestic operations are many times larger than those overseas and where corporate management finds it difficult to get a diverse group of domestic divisions to devote adequate effort to their overseas counterparts, the international division form has a good deal of merit. Multiple-product-line companies have the option of organizing the international division on a product, rather than a geographic, basis, thereby encouraging a closer liaison with domestic divisions.

The international division recommends itself with special force in situations where broad-scale international activities are relatively new to a company and where most members of senior operating management lack experience with worldwide problems. Later, as overseas interests become more important to the company and top management gains assurance in handling global problems, a shift in the organizational pattern may become desirable.

(3) Because management views domestic performance as the primary measure of success, the company's key executives may be domestically oriented even though they participate in policy and strategy formulation for the overseas activities. In such a situation, the big foreign affiliates often bypass the international division on major matters and deal directly with corporate management. As long as it achieves tight and effective financial control, top management generally has little inclination to tamper with the existing organizational framework, despite this shortcut in the chain of command.

(4) The company may have worked out special ways, peculiar to its own situation, of deriving the key benefits of another organizational pattern without relinquishing the international division form. If so, it has no compelling motive to make a purely structural realignment.

(5) Finally, the company may not have enough trained, capable executive personnel to staff a worldwide organization effectively.

Problems & disadvantages

The international division form can become ineffective when a company's overseas activities shift significantly from 'exporting' to self-contained operations at many points on the globe. Under these circumstances, too strong an international division can hamper corporate direction of worldwide activities. Ironically, the more independent an international division becomes, the more it tends to insulate corporate management from overseas problems and opportunities.

For a worldwide company with a reasonably diverse product line, the international division form may impede management's efforts to mobilize the resources of the total company to accomplish a global objective. Even with superb coordination at the corporate level, global planning for individual products or product lines is carried out at best awkwardly by two 'semi-autonomous' organizations – the domestic company and the international division. To add a series of country (or area) managements makes the problem still more difficult.

Geographic structure

The second basic organizational form that has emerged as companies evolve toward functioning world enterprises is the geographic structure (see Exhibit 12.2), which is characterized by the assignment of

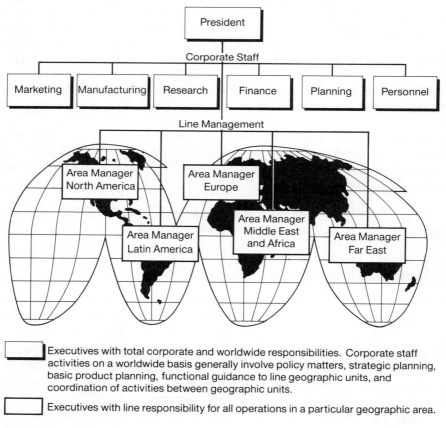

Executives with total corporate and worldwide responsibilities. Corporate staff activities on a worldwide basis generally involve policy matters, strategic planning, basic product planning, functional guidance to line geographic units, and coordination of activities between geographic units.

Executives with line responsibility for all operations in a particular geographic area.

Exhibit 12.2 Geographic structure

operational responsibility for geographic areas of the world to line managers, with corporate headquarters retaining responsibility for worldwide strategic planning and control. (Strategic planning, in this context, includes such critical decisions as the businesses to engage in, the nature of the basic product line, and the location of major facilities. Adaptation of the basic product to meet local need is, in contrast, an area activity.)

In the geographic form of organization, which has replaced the international division form today in many companies, both single-product-line and multiple-product-line, the United States has become simply one of a number of world markets. Producing and selling operations are grouped into geographic units. Sometimes the make-and-sell operations in a given geographic unit are self-contained, with most or all of the company's output in a given area being sold locally. Then again, sometimes there is a substantial flow of semifinished parts or fully assembled units from one area to another.

In the geographic form, responsibility for all products in a particular area is assigned to a single line executive who reports to corporate management. Policy, strategic and logistic planning, and major product development are handled at the corporate level.

Two examples will serve to illustrate the emergence of the geographic structure in varying circumstances.

Homogeneous Gamma

The geographic form has been commonly used by companies with closely related product lines – such as pharmaceuticals, farm implements, soft drinks, home appliances, or packaged food products – which are sold in similar end-use markets around the world.

Some years ago Gamma, Ltd., a huge international farm equipment manufacturer whose operations had been organized along regional lines, adopted an organizational structure built around a series of largely self-contained marketing and manufacturing *operations* units. This grouping is not regional; that is, it is not divided into broad areas (North America, Latin America, or Europe). Rather, it is centered on important individual markets (the United Kingdom, France, Germany, the United States, and Canada). Supplementing these units is an *export marketing* unit to cover sales in parts of the world where Gamma has no manufacturing operations.

Longer-range corporate strategy – determination of the basic worldwide product line, decisions on major facilities, and changes in the logistic product flow from production sources to markets – is set at corporate headquarters. But these decisions are heavily influenced by *operations unit* judgments and recommendations. Each unit is responsible for determining the product lines best suited to its local markets. Besides directing the logistic flow of components and completed machines between countries, corporate-level executives coordinate the operations unit product planning and make strategic decisions on the nature of basic Gamma product development. Then managers at the local level carry out the engineering and product development modifications needed to meet market requirements.

Diversified Delta

Less commonly, the geographic form is also used by companies with reasonably diverse product lines. One example is the Delta Company, a fairly diversified maker of electronics products, which has established a distinctive regional organizational pattern. Four *area* managers (North America; Latin America; Europe/Middle East/Africa; and Far East/ Pacific) are fully responsible for day-to-day operations of all Delta units within their geographical assignments. Regional offices for both North American and Latin American operations are located in New York; for Europe, in Brussels; and for the Far East, in Hong Kong. And reporting to these regional headquarters are individual *country* organizations in more than 30 nations.

Because much of its activity had been carried on overseas for decades, Delta was able to move into the area form unusually fast. In 1959 foreign operating companies, which were previously more or less autonomous, were drawn together for tighter control and closer coordination. Corporate headquarters quickly assumed ultimate responsibility for long-range worldwide strategic planning, and began to exert much tighter direction over the foreign companies. Now both short- and long-range plans are developed locally, reviewed at the *area* manager level, then submitted to corporate management for review and approval. Thus, although planning clearly reflects local needs and requirements, corporate headquarters can closely control capital investment and make other strategic decisions.

The Delta Company, it should be noted, has a special need for local identification in the areas where it operates. Since much of its manufacturing output goes to local governments and telephone companies,

Delta's individual country organizations must try to avoid the appearance of having foreign control. Moreover, their products must be adapted to meet varying local requirements and specifications. Its *area/country* type of geographic organization enables Delta to fit its sales efforts and product specifications closely to local market needs.

Common characteristics

Companies successfully using the geographic organizational structure share two significant characteristics:

(1) The great bulk of sales revenue is derived from similar end-use markets.

(2) Local marketing requirements are critical. (For example, Delta's communications equipment is marketed to telephone companies around the world; but since each foreign government establishes its own product specifications, this equipment is really produced and sold to highly individualized markets.)

The geographic organizational form is well suited to coping with these problems, since variations from market to market in a centrally developed basic product can be dealt with at close range. Normally, such adjustments require only modest technological skills that can easily be provided at the *area* level or below. When greater skills are needed, they can be supplied from corporate headquarters.

The geographic pattern also works well where the product is highly standardized but techniques for penetrating local markets differ. For example:

> A major soft-drink maker ended the separation of its international and domestic operations almost a year ago, placing worldwide direction of marketing, finance, and research at the corporate level. To strengthen their contact with corporate management, the overseas operations have been organized into geographic divisions. Each division is headed by an experienced area manager located at corporate headquarters.

Problems & disadvantages

The tasks of coordinating product variations, transferring new ideas and techniques from one country to another, and optimizing the logistic flow of product from source to worldwide markets frequently prove difficult for companies using the geographic organizational form, particularly those whose products are many or diverse.

One organizational response to these problems, though by no means a universally satisfactory one, has been the creation of a unique type of *product* manager at the corporate level who is assigned worldwide responsibilities for particular products or product lines. Each product manager follows the progress of his assigned product everywhere in the world, acting as an 'exchange desk' to transfer successful developments from area to area and recommending worldwide strategy for individual products with respect to broad markets and basic design changes. But in this arrangement, although the corporate *product* manager's purpose in the organizational structure is easy to describe, his operating relationships with the line *area* managers are liable to be ambiguous.

Product structure

The third basic organizational pattern, more recent in origin than the other two forms, assigns worldwide product *responsibility* to product group executives at the line management level, and coordinates all product *activity* in a given geographical area (see Exhibit 12.3) through area specialists at the corporate staff level.

Thus, over-all goals and strategies for the total enterprise and for each product group are set at corporate headquarters. Within these corporate guidelines, strategic plans for each product group are drawn together by the product group executives for review and approval by top management. Each group, therefore, has primary responsibility for planning and controlling all activities for its products on a worldwide basis. Staff officers at the corporate level provide functional guidance (financial, legal, technical, and so on) to the worldwide product organizations.

Epsilon's answer

A notable example of the product pattern is Epsilon, Inc., whose diverse product line includes man-made fibers, organic intermediates, and plastic resins. By no means a stranger to international operations, Epsilon established a fibers plant in Mexico in the mid-1940s and invested in extensive timber, cellulose pulping, and petrochemical operations in Canada in the late 1940s and early 1950s.

With substantial foreign operations, ambitious plans for further international activities, and a diverse, technologically complex product

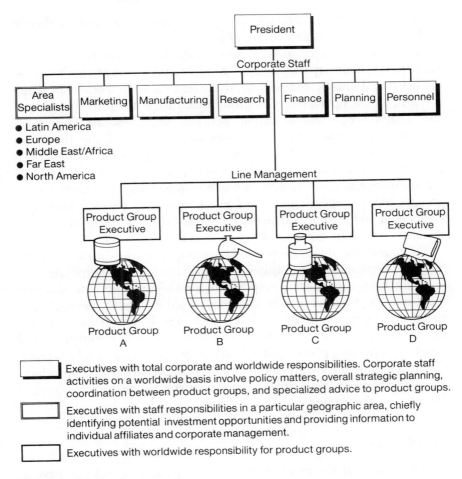

Exhibit 12.3 Product structure

line, Epsilon outgrew the capabilities of its existing organizational pattern and sought a more appropriate form.

The geographic structure offered no real advantages. Practically all of Epsilon's existing foreign operations were in the Western hemisphere. Its products drew on a wide range of complex technologies and went into many different end-use markets. These complexities, top management believed, would seriously overtax either the geographic pattern or an international division form of organization.

The product form promised to be a more appealing alternative, since Epsilon had a group of relatively strong domestic operating companies, each of which could provide essential technological and marketing leadership to present and future affiliates.

Since Epsilon's large and diversified domestic operations overshadow their foreign counterparts, the new group organizations are built around the existing domestic companies. At the heart of each worldwide group is the domestic operation. The group executive is the principal contact and channel of communication between the corporate operations committee (Epsilon's top decision-making body) and the individual foreign subsidiaries and affiliates within his product group. Each product group has a vice president-international, who acts as a deputy for international matters, with as much responsibility for managing the group's foreign operations as his group executive chooses to assign. Functional and technical advice are provided by appropriate staff at the domestic operating company level or the corporate level.

To coordinate the various product-group activities in major world markets, Epsilon has established area managers at the corporate staff level. Each area manager is responsible for keeping corporate management and the product groups informed about economic, political, and social developments in his assigned area. He is also responsible for identifying potential investment opportunities, for stimulating and assisting strategic planning by both corporate- and product-group management, and for developing an *area* plan for all Epsilon's products in a given geographic area to complement the worldwide *product* planning of the groups.

Favoring factors

One limitation of the geographic form is its inherent awkwardness in cases where product lines of great diversity or technological complexity must be sold to various end-use markets. In contrast, the product organization seems made-to-order for these situations. Specifically, there are two situations where the product structure is likely to be advantageous:

1 *The company's product line is widely diversified and the range of products go into a variety of end-use markets.* (Bulk chemicals, for example, are sold on a specification basis to industrial users around the world. On the other hand, fibers require a highly specialized merchandising capability to reach from textile manufacturers to ultimate consumers.)

2 *High shipping costs, tariffs, or other considerations dictate local manufacture of the product, and a relatively high level of technological capability is required.*

(Compare, for example, the technology involved in the production of Nylon 66 with that required for the manufacture of a standard product, such as bar soap, that can be made with comparatively little difficulty.)

At Epsilon, the product organization has brought the foreign operations into close contact with the latest technology in every product field. The foreign operations have gained a tremendous stimulus both from this contact and from the cognition that the domestic organization is really alert to their problems and needs.

Problems & disadvantages

Perhaps the most important problem faced by companies adopting the product organization is the risk involved in turning worldwide product responsibility over to executives whose working experience has been largely domestic and who may either lack sufficient understanding of international problems or be disinclined to devote enough attention to them. Nor is the problem confined to the corporate and product group level. It also applies to key functional managers within the existing domestic operating companies, who are also called on to exercise judgment on international problems and to provide leadership for the foreign activities.

In the multiproduct company, for which the product structure has the strongest appeal, this problem is generally more serious than it is in the predominantly single-product business (automobile, oil, and others), where top management is invariably involved to some degree in worldwide planning for the total enterprise. In the diversified company, top management cannot plan effectively for each of these businesses; the prime responsibility for their direction must be divided into manageable assignments.

Another problem inherent in the product form is coordinating the moves of various product groups in any given part of the world. At Epsilon, where careful provision was made for this situation, there is still the problem of developing satisfactory working relationships and clearly drawing the lines of responsibility between the line product-group executives and the area managers at the corporate level.

Conclusion

To successfully bring about fundamental change in a company's basic organizational structure, even in a purely domestic operation, is no easy accomplishment. In a truly world enterprise, however, it takes on special complexities – just as other management problems do. For this reason alone, it would be unwise to pass general judgments on the three broad organizational patterns that are currently dominant among emerging world enterprises. Even to categorize them as ultimate or transitional forms would presuppose a knowledge of the nature and behavior of world enterprise that we do not as yet possess.

However, one observation does apply with equal force to all the organizational patterns we have examined:

The really decisive point in the transition to world enterprise is top-management recognition that, to function effectively, the ultimate control of strategic planning and policy decisions must shift from decentralized subsidiaries or division locations to corporate headquarters, where a worldwide perspective can be brought to bear on the interests of the total enterprise.

13

Triad Power

KENICHI OHMAE

As the world has continued to shrink, the long-accepted terms used to describe enterprises – whether multinational or international – that looked upon the whole world as their market have become inadequate to describe developments in certain industries. Triad Power *documented for the first time the emergence of the global corporation and global products.*

These global products – be they Big Macs, Sony Walkmans or Otis elevators – were not simply consumer products supported by large-scale, global brand advertising. They were, rather, a whole new generation of goods with clear similarities in demand patterns.

The prosperity of global businesses depends on their success in what Mr Ohmae called 'the Triad' – Japan, Western Europe and the United States. The 600 million consumers in these regions generally have similar needs and preferences. The purchasing power of Triad residents in relation to the relative discretionary income per individual is more than ten times greater than that in the less developed and the newly industrialized countries.

Triad Power *synthesized in a clear, succinct, readable package truths that many of us had previously talked and written about only in isolation. In the pharmaceutical industry, the cost of finding and developing a new product demands that, once developed, the new product must be exploited globally. This situation not only affects the process of developing new technology but also means that every single function in the business chain needs to be reexamined against the new global business realities.*

People, far from disappearing from the success equation, emerge in Triad Power *as the critical factor. And leveraging scarce skills globally is no longer a luxury – it is a necessity.*

Robert P. Bauman,
Chief Executive, SmithKline Beecham,
London

Preface

NOW that we have awakened from the nightmare of the 1973 energy crisis, we have discovered that the pace of technological changes has not only accelerated once again but has in fact exploded. We have seen, too, that the developed nations have become very similar in terms of their sociopolitical behavior.

With Japan's emergence as an industrial power, the combined gross national product (GNP) of Japan and the United States alone accounts for 30 percent of the Free World's total. If the four key countries of the European Community, that is, the United Kingdom, West Germany, France, and Italy, are added to this, the figure reaches 45 percent. In fact, the Organization for Economic Cooperation and Development (OECD) nations, which make up only 15 percent of the total number of countries in the world, account for as much as 54 percent of the global GNP. These countries have very similar problems: a mature and stagnant economy, escalating social costs, an aging population, lack of jobs for skilled workers, and at the same time, dynamic technological developments coupled with the ever-escalating costs of research and development (R&D) and modern production facilities.

Global enterprises that established their modus operandi mainly in the 1960s now are faced with discrepancies between their traditional approach and these new realities. They are out of date. Each age has a form of business organization appropriate to the tempo of its times.

In the field of consumer goods, Unilever (British–Dutch), one of the world's oldest and largest multinational corporations, reflects the colonization period of European dominance. European enterprises such as Philips of the Netherlands have organized each of their businesses around the world to run as independent entities serving the national market where they are situated. Enterprises that operate on this basis usually get their strengths from their strong trade name (for example, Kraft, Nestlé, Kellogg, Coca-Cola, and Pepsi-Cola).

Most American multinationals were shaped in the relatively stable era between the two world wars. The underlying philosophy at this time was that the narrow confines of nationality were outmoded and that great corporate wealth would be amassed by doing business with the world as a single, multinational unit.

Some of the unique circumstances of the post-World War II period favored American companies. The nearly prostrate condition of most European and Japanese industrial firms disqualified them from the technological race. U.S. corporations straddled Latin America, Asia, and Europe, inside and outside the European Community (EC) (apparently unaffected by the political and economic division that seems fundamental to the European psyche) and were organized around the fundamental concept that their technological and competitive edge was virtually unassailable. During the first 20 years of the postwar period, for example, some 2,800 U.S. businesses that had a technological advantage (IBM, Texas Instruments, Xerox), a unique product (Gillette, Kellogg), or a leading position in U.S. industry [International Telephone and Telegraph Corporation (ITT), General Motors] had stakes in 10,000 direct investments abroad.

By and large, subsidiaries were formed along a 'clone' model – producing and selling substantially the same products as the parent company and operating miniature versions of headquarters organizations. The degree of centralization varied, of course, but home country absolutism was the predominant structural mode in industry operations abroad.

Today, all these conditions have altered dramatically. Disparities of size and technical capabilities between American multinationals and their European and Japanese competitors have narrowed or disappeared. In fact, if the sizes of the American corporations were adjusted for their disproportionately larger domestic market, most American multinationals would be equal in size to their Japanese and European counterparts. And the view of the world as a single, homogeneous economic unit no longer holds. Yet, many of today's leading enterprises are still structured around the traditional feudal, absolute, or multinational models.

My own premise challenges the one-world concept and orthodox nationalism. It focuses on cross-cultural alliances and accepts a future in which change is inevitable and in which there is no reward without risk.

Obviously, the most difficult challenge one faces in such an attempt is to overcome misperceptions. In many cases, today's perception is the product of yesterday's truths, or at least half-truths. This is the reason why we tend to dwell on the currently accepted notion for too long. However, in the realistic world of business, such a tendency clearly weakens a corporation's position relative to both domestic and global competitors. In business a manager's oversight is reflected on the profit and loss statement and balance sheet, rather than in the company's glossy annual report.

I travel out of Japan as much as two dozen times per year. On average, I visit the United States 9 to 12 times a year, Europe at least 2 to 3 times, and Southeast Asia a dozen times. This adds up to a lot of tiring traveling. On the other hand, the advantage of moving around is that I develop a feel for what's happening around the world, as opposed to reading scholastic doctrines and analyses of global business and the fate of the multinationals. For some time, particularly through working out of Tokyo both for large Japanese companies in the process of becoming global, and for American and European corporations aiming at increasing their business in Japan, I have come to realize that their perception itself is the biggest hindrance that prevents companies from taking advantage of the dynamic and lucrative international marketplace, particularly in, but not limited to, the OECD.

Let me try to succinctly state three or four new points of view which illustrate the kind of business world in which we live (or, at least, that world as I see it).

(1) Chasing low-labor-cost locations for siting is still in fashion. However, many of these overseas locations are short-lived in terms of their economic competitiveness. Most competitive Japanese companies are pulling out of Southeast Asia and investing in robots and machines.

(2) The traditional mode of operation for a prestigious multinational has been to develop an unchallengeable technology, and exploit its potential on its own or through licensing throughout the world. However, three things have happened:

   (a) The cost of R&D to come up with any sellable technology has become very high.

   (b) Quite a few companies in the OECD possess similar technological competence, and monopoly of any technology has become difficult.

   (c) Diffusion of a new technology to, and its acceptance by, various OECD countries has become very fast – from almost a decade to a year.

The combined impact of these three factors calls for a company's ability to penetrate into major countries of the OECD almost simultaneously and spontaneously. Failing that, it will have to make arrangements with another company to effectively achieve such an objective, at the same time guarding against a sudden attack by untraditional competitors.

(3) There is an emergence of the Triadians, or the residents of Japan, America, and the European Community. We may call them Triadians, or OECDites. These are the people whose academic backgrounds, income levels (both discretionary and nondiscretionary), life-style, use of leisure time, and aspirations are quite similar. In these democratic countries, the national infrastructure, in terms of highways, telephone systems, sewage disposal, power transmission, and governmental systems, is also very similar. From a corporation's point of view, their basic demand patterns enable them to treat this group of people, some 600 million residents, as belonging to virtually the same species. In fact, the behavior of their younger generation is so similar across the national boundaries (and they all behave like California youngsters – we may term this the 'Californianization' of the Free World) that the older generation has difficulty communicating with them. In other words, there is more vertical 'generation gap' than horizontal 'international gap.'

(4) Despite consumers' loss of national identity in each of the OECD countries, the protectionist pressures are mounting. Average consumers want the best and the cheapest, regardless of the origin of the products. But the governmental and 'expressed' public opinions are pushing the whole world toward the bloc economy. This necessitates that any global enterprise must become a true insider, or honorary citizen, in each of the Triad regions.

Despite the glorious success stories of the multinationals in every corner of the world, it has become increasingly difficult to repeat the performance of the early pioneers who knocked out the competition and established an enviable position in any country they entered. Mainly due to the aforementioned protectionist forces at work, today even the most powerful and dominant companies headquartered in any of the Triad regions are having difficulty reproducing their performance abroad, especially in the key countries of Japan, America, and the European Community – a phenomenon of impasse.

A company is more likely to be wiped out by its domestic competitors, rather than a 'foreign invasion,' due mainly to the foreign firms' inability to establish truly profitable and lasting interfaces with the local customers.

The most recent diagnostic results of how the Japanese are doing overseas and how the Western corporations are doing in Japan – in other words, the scorecard of the global business game – again drastically differ from the general perception. For example:

- Most Japanese companies, which have been so successful in the past based on exports out of the highly favorable home ground, are now faced with major problems of running full-size and fully integrated operations in the United States and Europe. Their much-praised management system is faced with cultural challenges of transferability, and success so far has been limited to a handful of truly cautious and thorough companies operating in developing countries.

- Despite the loud public complaints that Japan is closed to foreign businesses, many American and European companies have established a dominant position in Japan. Most of these companies have become true insiders participating with the full spectrum of the Japanese business system, and thus have removed themselves from the 'trade statistics' of imports and exports. As they produce and sell in Japan, they have become less visible to Western eyes. Nonetheless, these companies have several points in common, regardless of their industry of specialization, and give us an insight into the successful 'insiderization' of a global corporation.

[There are three aspects to] becoming a Triad Power:

- There are three ways to establish a de facto insider position in each Triad region. Of the three options, I submit that the consortium formation is the most realistic and productive. The biggest challenge here is to learn and master the language of communication between two corporations that are in partnership.
- The real Triad power actually has equally strong holds in the developing regions immediately south of its geographical region. As a result, a Japanese Triad power is operative primarily in the United States, the European Community, and Southeast Asia. With Japan at the center in its mindset, therefore, the Triad actually becomes a Tetrahedron. Likewise, the American Triad includes the United States, Japan, the European Community and Latin America, and the European Triad consists of Europe, the United States, Japan, and Africa and/or the Middle East. For all of these Triad powers, it is essential that they become truly accepted by, and informed of, these tetrahedral regions (including of course the home region): other regions become less important for survival, and can be treated as marginal and/or opportunistic. Shortcomings of the traditional models, particularly the 'United Nations model' of the multinational corporations, have been that they have neglected the significance of these regions and have treated the world as if it consisted of 150 equally important markets.
- Finally, in order to succeed as a stable Triad power, the viewpoint of a company's headquarters' organization must change, in order to be able to see the critical marketplace at an equidistance regardless of actual physical distance. I call this the 'Anchorage perspective,' or equidistance (that is, seven hours) to Tokyo, New York, and Dusseldorf from Anchorage, Alaska.

These are my observations. While I do not claim academic perfection, I do want to emphasize the importance of these new perspectives for corporations pursuing business around the world. They have been developed over time as embryonic bits and pieces of hypotheses as I move around the world and talk with various business and political figures. However, when I come home, I do verify these hypotheses with analyses based on the data and information available to our Research Department. To the extent that this is possible, I have tried to share a few of these analyses with my readers.

Part IV

Finance

Introduction

MORE capital has probably been raised and invested in the past 30 years than in the previous 300. But, however large that figure may be, it pales into insignificance when one contemplates the much larger number of requests for capital that have had to be evaluated. This capital rationing process among rival investment opportunities is one of the few decisions that is common to all enterprises. And, because these decisions frequently involve irrevocable courses of development, they are in most cases ultimately the responsibility of the board of directors.

Until 'Risk Analysis in Capital Investment' appeared, incorporating the critical dimensions of probability, risk and uncertainty in the decision-making process was, at best, an inexact science. Using computer-based simulation methods, David Hertz developed techniques for measuring and quantifying these variables and thus provided an important tool for making the all-important capital investment decisions.

A significant subset of these decisions comprised decisions either to buy or to sell companies. Eventually this process gave birth to a whole new profession and industry. The M&A business has its own unique cast of characters, a self-inflicted jargon and somewhat loose, but nevertheless comprehensive, ground rules for behaviour.

As the flow of company mergers became a veritable torrent and eventually a waterfall, John Kitching came along and told us what was really happening in 'Why Do Mergers Miscarry?' So popular was this first article, that it was followed by a book, and subsequent updates at periodic intervals. I asked John to write his own introduction and to explain the phenomenon that he has watched so carefully over these last 30 or so years.

Sophisticated analytical tools, faster and faster computer-based concepts for developing strategic plans, and highly qualified and specially trained corporate planning staffs all failed to deliver the

247

promise of surprise-free, stressless life at the corporate 'high table'. Even with the ability to move data at breathless speeds and the almost limitless capacity for asking the 'what if' questions, conventional accounting-oriented approaches for evaluating management's corporate plans did not give all the answers.

A vital contribution to the state of this particular management art was the notion expounded in *Creating Shareholder Value*. In it Rappaport brings together a variety of disparate strands and combines them to form a coherent argument for using shareholder value as the basis for evaluation and decision-making. While introducing some new complications – such as the need to decide on how to calculate the cost of capital – the shareholder value approach has opened the door to much more useful bases for implementing complex strategies.

14

Risk Analysis in Capital Investment

DAVID HERTZ

Twenty-five years ago, risk analysis was just a well-established theoretical tool for mathematicians and statisticians. Then, in 1964, David Hertz, in a lucid article, set out its implications for capital investment decisions. The concept had an immediate impact on a generation of managers of increasing sophistication. They understood it and recognized its potential for enhancing the decision-making process in business and government. Since then, the realization that basic assumptions were unreliable, that all-important input data could be wrong, and that the consequences of a 'less likely' outcome materializing could spell total disaster, frequently resulted in more sensible limits being put on the stakes at risk, and sometimes in the selection of a different course of action altogether.

Today, the same principles and techniques of risk analysis are being widely applied in situations as diverse as damage caused by floods and other natural disasters, competitive bidding, computer fraud, and insurance risks ranging from drugs and pollution to the award of damages in litigation – in fact wherever a risk–reward relationship is involved.

We should all be indebted to David Hertz, as I am, for a contribution of immense value.

Sir Alcon Copisarow,
Council of Lloyd's,
London

Risk Analysis in Capital Investment

O F ALL the decisions that business executives must make, none is more challenging – and none has received more attention – than choosing among alternative capital investment opportunities. What makes this kind of decision so demanding, of course, is not the problem of projecting return on investment under any given set of assumptions. The difficulty is in the assumptions and in their impact. Each assumption involves its own degree – often a high degree – of uncertainty; and, taken together, these combined uncertainties can multiply into a total uncertainty of critical proportions. This is where the element of risk enters, and it is in the evaluation of risk that the executive has been able to get little help from currently available tools and techniques.

There is a way to help the executive sharpen key capital investment decisions by providing him or her with a realistic measurement of the risks involved. Armed with this gauge, which evaluates the risk at each possible level of return, he or she is then in a position to measure more knowledgeably alternative courses of action against corporate objectives.

Need for new concept

The evaluation of a capital investment project starts with the principle that the productivity of capital is measured by the rate of return we expect to receive over some future period. A dollar received next year is worth less to us than a dollar in hand today. Expenditures three years hence are less costly than expenditures of equal magnitude two years from now. For this reason we cannot calculate the rate of return realistically unless we take into account (a) when the sums involved in an investment are spent and (b) when the returns are received.

Comparing alternative investments is thus complicated by the fact that they usually differ not only in size but also in the length of time over which expenditures will have to be made and benefits returned.

These facts of investment life long ago made apparent the short-comings of approaches that simply averaged expenditures and benefits, or lumped them, as in the number-of-years-to-pay-out method. These shortcomings stimulated students of decision making to explore more precise methods for determining whether one investment would leave a company better off in the long run than would another course of action.

It is not surprising, then, that much effort has been applied to the development of ways to improve our ability to discriminate among investment alternatives. The focus of all of these investigations has been to sharpen the definition of the value of capital investments to the company. The controversy and furor that once came out in the business press over the most appropriate way of calculating these values have largely been resolved in favor of the discounted cash flow method as a reasonable means of measuring the rate of return that can be expected in the future from an investment made today.

Thus we have methods which are more or less elaborate mathematical formulas for comparing the outcomes of various investments and the combinations of the variables that will affect the investments. As these techniques have progressed, the mathematics involved has become more and more precise, so that we can now calculate discounted returns to a fraction of a percent.

But the sophisticated executive knows that behind these precise calculations are data which are not that precise. At best, the rate-of-return information he is provided with is based on an average of different opinions with varying reliabilities and different ranges of probability. When the expected returns on two investments are close, he is likely to be influenced by intangibles – a precarious pursuit at best. Even when the figures for two investments are quite far apart, and the choice seems clear, there lurk memories of the Edsel and other ill-fated ventures.

In short, the decision maker realizes that there is something more he ought to know, something in addition to the expected rate of return. What is missing has to do with the nature of the data on which the expected rate of return is calculated and with the way those data are processed. It involves uncertainty, with possibilities and probabilities extending across a wide range of rewards and risks. (For a summary of the new approach, see the ruled insert on pages 268–9.)

The Achilles heel

The fatal weakness of past approaches thus has nothing to do with the mathematics of rate-of-return calculation. We have pushed along this path so far that the precision of our calculation is, if anything, somewhat illusory. The fact is that, no matter what mathematics is used, each of the variables entering into the calculation of rate of return is subject to a high level of uncertainty.

For example, the useful life of a new piece of capital equipment is rarely known in advance with any degree of certainty. It may be affected by variations in obsolescence or deterioration, and relatively small changes in use life can lead to large changes in return. Yet an expected value for the life of the equipment – based on a great deal of data from which a single best possible forecast has been developed – is entered into the rate-of-return calculation. The same is done for the other factors that have a significant bearing on the decision at hand.

Let us look at how this works out in a simple case – one in which the odds appear to be all in favor of a particular decision. The executives of a food company must decide whether to launch a new packaged cereal. They have come to the conclusion that five factors are the determining variables: advertising and promotion expense, total cereal market, share of market for this product, operating costs, and new capital investment.

On the basis of the 'most likely' estimate for each of these variables, the picture looks very bright – a healthy 30% return. This future, however, depends on whether each of these estimates actually comes true. If each of these educated guesses has, for example, a 60% chance of being correct, there is only an 8% chance that all five will be correct (.60 × .60 × .60 × .60 × .60). So the 'expected' return actually depends on a rather unlikely coincidence. The decision maker needs to know a great deal more about the other values used to make each of the five estimates and about what he stands to gain or lose from various combinations of these values.

This simple example illustrates that the rate of return actually depends on a specific combination of values of a great many different variables. But only the expected levels of ranges (worst, average, best; or pessimistic, most likely, optimistic) of these variables are used in formal mathematical ways to provide the figures given to management. Thus predicting a single most likely rate of return gives precise numbers that do not tell the whole story.

The expected rate of return represents only a few points on a continuous curve of possible combinations of future happenings. It is a bit like trying to predict the outcome in a dice game by saying that the most likely outcome is a 7. The description is incomplete because it does not tell us about all the other things that could happen. In Exhibit 14.1, for instance, we see the odds on throws of only two dice having 6 sides. Now suppose that each of eight dice has 100 sides. This is a situation more comparable to business investment, where the company's market share might become any 1 of 100 different sizes and where there are eight factors (pricing, promotion, and so on) that can affect the outcome.

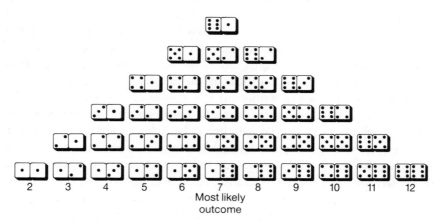

Exhibit 14.1 Describing uncertainty – a throw of the dice

Nor is this the only trouble. Our willingness to bet on a roll of the dice depends not only on the odds but also on the stakes. Since the probability of rolling a 7 is 1 in 6, we might be quite willing to risk a few dollars on that outcome at suitable odds. But would we be equally willing to wager $10,000 or $100,000 at those same odds, or even at better odds? In short, risk is influenced both by the odds on various events occurring and by the magnitude of the rewards or penalties that are involved when they do occur.

To illustrate again, suppose that a company is considering an investment of $1 million. The best estimate of the probable return is $200,000 a year. It could well be that this estimate is the average of three possible returns – a 1-in-3 chance of getting no return at all, a 1-in-3 chance of getting $200,000 per year, a 1-in-3 chance of getting $400,000 per year. Suppose that getting no return at all would put the company out of business. Then, by accepting this proposal, management is taking a 1-in-3 chance of going bankrupt.

If only the best-estimate analysis is used, however, management might go ahead, unaware that it is taking a big chance. If all of the available information were examined, management might prefer an alternative proposal with a smaller, but more certain (that is, less variable) expectation.

Such considerations have led almost all advocates of the use of modern capital-investment-index calculations to plead for a recognition of the elements of uncertainty. Perhaps Ross G. Walker summed up current thinking when he spoke of 'the almost impenetrable mists of any forecast.'*

How can executives penetrate the mists of uncertainty surrounding the choices among alternatives?

Limited improvements

A number of efforts to cope with uncertainty have been successful up to a point, but all seem to fall short of the mark in one way or another:

(1) *More accurate forecasts* – Reducing the error in estimates is a worthy objective. But no matter how many estimates of the future go into a capital investment decision, when all is said and done, the future is still the future. Therefore, however well we forecast, we are still left with the certain knowledge that we cannot eliminate all uncertainty.

(2) *Empirical adjustments* – Adjusting the factors influencing the outcome of a decision is subject to serious difficulties. We would like to adjust them so as to cut down the likelihood that we will make a 'bad' investment, but how can we do that without at the same time spoiling our chances to make a 'good' one? And in any case, what is the basis for adjustment? We adjust, not for uncertainty, but for bias.

For example, construction estimates are often exceeded. If a company's history of construction costs is that 90% of its estimates have been exceeded by

* 'The Judgment Factor in Investment Decisions,' *HBR* March–April 1961, p. 99.

15%, then in a capital estimate there is every justification for increasing the value of this factor by 15%. This is a matter of improving the accuracy of the estimate.

But suppose that new-product sales estimates have been exceeded by more than 75% in one-fourth of all historical cases and have not reached 50% of the estimate in one-sixth of all such cases? Penalties for such overestimating are very real, and so management is apt to reduce the sales estimate to 'cover' the one case in six – thereby reducing the calculated rate of return. In so doing, it is possibly missing some of its best opportunities.

(3) *Revising cutoff rates* – Selecting higher cutoff rates for protecting against uncertainty is attempting much the same thing. Management would like to have a possibility of return in proportion to the risk it takes. Where there is much uncertainty involved in the various estimates of sales, costs, prices, and so on, a high calculated return from the investment provides some incentive for taking the risk. This is, in fact, a perfectly sound position. The trouble is that the decision maker still needs to know explicitly what risks he is taking – and what the odds are on achieving the expected return.

(4) *Three-level estimates* – A start at spelling out risks is sometimes made by taking the high, medium, and low values of the estimated factors and calculating rates of return based on various combinations of the pessimistic, average, and optimistic estimates. These calculations give a picture of the range of possible results but do not tell the executive whether the pessimistic result is more likely than the optimistic one – or, in fact, whether the average result is much more likely to occur than either of the extremes. So, although this is a step in the right direction, it still does not give a clear enough picture for comparing alternatives.

(5) *Selected probabilities* – Various methods have been used to include the probabilities of specific factors in the return calculation. L. C. Grant discussed a program for forecasting discounted cash flow rates of return where the service life is subject to obsolescence and deterioration. He calculated the odds that the investment will terminate at any time after it is made depending on the probability distribution of the service-life factor. After having calculated these factors for each year through maximum service life, he determined an overall expected rate of return.*

Edward G. Bennion suggested the use of game theory to take into account alternative market growth rates as they would determine rate of return for various options. He used the estimated probabilities that specific growth rates would occur to develop optimum strategies. Bennion pointed out:

> Forecasting can result in a negative contribution to capital budget decisions unless it goes further than merely providing a single most probable prediction....[with] an estimated probability coefficient for the

---

* 'Monitoring Capital Investments,' *Financial Executive*, April 1963, p. 19.

forecast, plus knowledge of the payoffs for the company's alternative investments and calculation of indifference probabilities . . . the margin of error may be substantially reduced, and the businessman can tell just how far off his forecast may be before it leads him to a wrong decision.'*

Note that both of these methods yield an expected return, each based on only one uncertain input factor – service life in the first case, market growth in the second. Both are helpful, and both tend to improve the clarity with which the executive can view investment alternatives. But neither sharpens up the range of 'risk taken' or 'return hoped for' sufficiently to help very much in the complex decisions of capital planning.

Sharpening the picture

Since every one of the many factors that enter into the evaluation of a decision is subject to some uncertainty, the executive needs a helpful portrayal of the effects that the uncertainty surrounding each of the significant factors has on the returns he is likely to achieve. Therefore, I use a method combining the variabilities inherent in all the relevant factors under consideration. The objective is to give a clear picture of the relative risk and the probable odds of coming out ahead or behind in light of uncertain foreknowledge.

A simulation of the way these factors may combine as the future unfolds is the key to extracting the maximum information from the available forecasts. In fact, the approach is very simple, using a computer to do the necessary arithmetic. To carry out the analysis, a company must follow three steps:

(1) Estimate the range of values for each of the factors (for example, range of selling price and sales growth rate) and within that range the likelihood of occurrence of each value.

(2) Select at random one value from the distribution of values for each factor. Then combine the values for all of the factors and compute the rate of return (or present value) from that combination. For instance, the lowest in the range of prices might be combined with the highest in the range of growth rate and other factors. (The fact that the elements are dependent should be taken into account, as we shall see later.)

(3) Do this over and over again to define and evaluate the odds of the occurrence of each possible rate of return. Since there are literally millions of

* 'Capital Budgeting and Game Theory,' *HBR* November–December 1956, p. 123.

possible combinations of values, we need to test the likelihood that various returns on the investment will occur. This is like finding out by recording the results of a great many throws what percent of 7s or other combinations we may expect in tossing dice. The result will be a listing of the rates of return we might achieve, ranging from a loss (if the factors go against us) to whatever maximum gain is possible with the estimates that have been made.

For each of these rates we can determine the chances that it may occur. (Note that a specific return can usually be achieved through more than one combination of events. The more combinations for a given rate, the higher the chances of achieving it – as with 7s in tossing dice.) The average expectation is the average of the values of all outcomes weighted by the chances of each occurring.

We can also determine the variability of outcome values from the average. This is important since, all other factors being equal, management would presumably prefer lower variability for the same return if given the choice. This concept has already been applied to investment portfolios.

When the expected return and variability of each of a series of investments have been determined, the same techniques may be used to examine the effectiveness of various combinations of them in meeting management objectives.

Practical test

To see how this new approach works in practice, let us take the experience of a management that has already analyzed a specific investment proposal by conventional techniques. Taking the same investment schedule and the same expected values actually used, we can find what results the new method would produce and compare them with the results obtained by conventional methods. As we shall see, the new picture of risks and returns is different from the old one. Yet the differences are attributable in no way to changes in the basic data – only to the increased sensitivity of the method to management's uncertainties about the key factors.

Investment proposal

In this case, a medium-size industrial chemical producer is considering a $10 million extension to its processing plant. The estimated service life of the facility is ten years; the engineers expect to use 250,000 tons of processed material worth $510 per ton at an average processing cost of $435 per ton. Is this investment a good bet? In fact, what is the return that the company may expect? What are the risks? We need to make the best and fullest use of all the market research and financial analyses that have been developed, so as to give management a clear picture of this project in an uncertain world.

The key input factors management has decided to use are market size, selling prices, market growth rate, share of market (which results in physical sales volume), investment required, residual value of investment, operating costs, fixed costs, and useful life of facilities. These factors are typical of those in many company projects that must be analyzed and combined to obtain a measure of the attractiveness of a proposed capital facilities investment.

Obtaining estimates

How do we make the recommended type of analysis of this proposal? Our aim is to develop for each of the nine factors listed a frequency distribution or probability curve. The information we need includes the possible range of values for each factor, the average, and some idea as to the likelihood that the various possible values will be reached.

It has been my experience that for major capital proposals managements usually make a significant investment in time and funds to pinpoint information about each of the relevant factors. An objective analysis of the values to be assigned to each can, with little additional effort, yield a subjective probability distribution.

Specifically, it is necessary to probe and question each of the experts involved – to find out, for example, whether the estimated cost of production really can be said to be exactly a certain value or whether, as is more likely, it should be estimated to lie within a certain range of values. Management usually ignores that range in its analysis. The range is relatively easy to determine; if a guess has to be made – as it often does – it is easier to guess with some accuracy a range rather than one specific value. I have found from experience that a series of meetings with management personnel to discuss such distributions is most helpful in getting at realistic answers to the a priori questions. (The term *realistic answers* implies all the information management does not have as well as all that it does have.)

The ranges are directly related to the degree of confidence that the estimator has in the estimate. Thus certain estimates may be known to be quite accurate. They would be represented by probability distributions stating, for instance, that there is only 1 chance in 10 that the actual value will be different from the best estimate by more than 10%. Others may have as much as 100% ranges above and below the best estimate.

Thus we treat the factor of selling price for the finished product by asking executives who are responsible for the original estimates these questions:

- Given that $510 is the expected sales price, what is the probability that the price will exceed $550?
- Is there any chance that the price will exceed $650?
- How likely is it that the price will drop below $475?

Managements must ask similar questions for all of the other factors until they can construct a curve for each. Experience shows that this is not as difficult as it sounds. Often information on the degree of variation in factors is easy to obtain. For instance, historical information on variations in the price of a commodity is readily available. Similarly, managements can estimate the variability of sales from industry sales records. Even for factors that have no history, such as operating costs for a new product, those who make the average estimates must have some idea of the degree of confidence they have in their predictions, and therefore they are usually only too glad to express their feelings. Likewise, the less confidence they have in their estimates, the greater will be the range of possible values that the variable will assume.

This last point is likely to trouble businessmen. Does it really make sense to seek estimates of variations? It cannot be emphasized too strongly that the less certainty there is in an average estimate, the more important it is to consider the possible variation in that estimate.

Further, an estimate of the variation possible in a factor, no matter how judgmental it may be, is always better than a simple average estimate, since it includes more information about what is known and what is not known. This very lack of knowledge may distinguish one investment possibility from another, so that for rational decision making it must be taken into account.

This lack of knowledge is in itself important information about the proposed investment. To throw any information away simply because it is highly uncertain is a serious error in analysis that the new approach is designed to correct.

Computer runs

The next step in the proposed approach is to determine the returns that will result from random combinations of the factors involved. This requires realistic restrictions, such as not allowing the total market to vary more than some reasonable amount from year to year. Of course, any suitable method of rating the return may be used at this point. In the actual case, management preferred discounted cash flow for the reasons cited earlier, so that method is followed here.

A computer can be used to carry out the trials for the simulation method in very little time and at very little expense. Thus for one trial 3,600 discounted cash flow calculations, each based on a selection of the nine input factors, were run in two minutes at a cost of $15 for computer time. The resulting rate-of-return probabilities were read out immediately and graphed. The process is shown schematically in Exhibit 14.2.

Data comparisons

The nine input factors described earlier fall into three categories:

1 *Market analyses* – Included are market size, market growth rate, the company's share of the market, and selling prices. For a given combination of these factors sales revenue may be determined for a particular business.

2 *Investment cost analyses* – Being tied to the kinds of service-life and operating-cost characteristics expected, these are subject to various kinds of error and uncertainty; for instance, automation progress makes service life uncertain.

3 *Operating and fixed costs* – These also are subject to uncertainty but are perhaps the easiest to estimate.

These categories are not independent, and for realistic results my approach allows the various factors to be tied together. Thus if price determines the total market, we first select from a probability distribution the price for the specific computer run and then use for the total market a probability distribution that is logically related to the price selected.

We are now ready to compare the values obtained under the new approach with those obtained by the old. This comparison is shown in Exhibit 14.3.

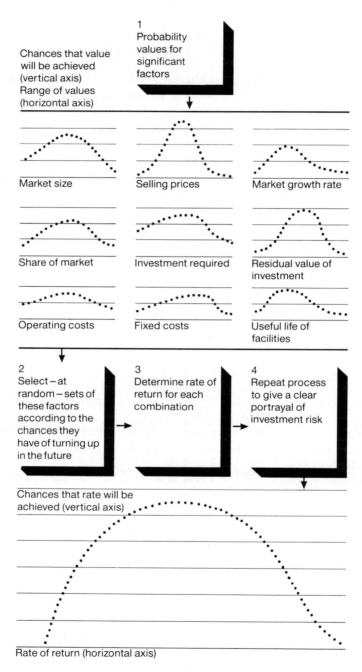

Exhibit 14.2 Simulation for investment planning

	Conventional 'best estimate' approach	New approach
Market analyses		
1 Market size		
Expected value (in tons)	250,000	250,000
Range	–	100,000–340,000
2 Selling prices		
Expected value (in dollars/ton)	$510	$510
Range	–	$385–$575
3 Market growth rate		
Expected value	3%	3%
Range	–	0–6%
4 Eventual share of market		
Expected value	12%	12%
Range	–	3%–17%
Investment cost analyses		
5 Total investment required		
Expected value (in $ millions)	$9.5	$9.5
Range	–	$7.0–$10.5
6 Useful life of facilities		
Expected value (in years)	10	10
Range	–	5–15

Exhibit 14.3 Comparison of expected values under old and new approaches

Exhibit 14.3 (*cont.*):

7 Residual value (at 10 years)		
Expected value (in $ millions)	$4.5	$4.5
Range	–	$3.5–$5.0
Other costs		
8 Operating costs		
Expected value (in dollars/ton)	$435	$435
Range	–	$370–$545
9 Fixed costs		
Expected value (in $ thousands)	$300	$300
Range	–	$250–$375

Note: Range figures in right-hand column represent approximately 1% to 99% probabilities. That is, there is only a 1-in-100 chance that the value actually achieved will be respectively greater or less than the range.

Valuable results

How do the results under the new and old approaches compare? In this case, management had been informed, on the basis of the one-best-estimate approach, that the expected return was 25.2% before taxes. When we run the new set of data through the computer program, however, we get an expected return of only 14.6% before taxes. This surprising difference results not only from the range of values under the new approach but also from the weighing of each value in the range by the chances of its occurrence.

Our new analysis thus may help management to avoid an unwise investment. In fact, the general result of carefully weighing the information and lack of information in the manner I have suggested is to indicate the true nature of seemingly satisfactory investment proposals. If this practice were followed, managements might avoid much overcapacity.

The computer program developed to carry out the simulation allows for easy insertion of new variables. But most programs do not allow for dependence relationships among the various input factors. Further, the program used here permits the choice of a value for price from one distribution, which value determines a particular probability distribution (from among several) that will be used to determine the values for sales volume. The following scenario shows how this important technique works:

Suppose we have a wheel, as in roulette, with the numbers from 0 to 15 representing one price for the product or material, the numbers 16 to 30 representing a second price, the numbers 31 to 45 a third price, and so on. For each of these segments we would have a different range of expected market volumes – for example, $150,000–$200,000 for the first, $100,000–$150,000 for the second, $75,000–$100,000 for the third. Now suppose we spin the wheel and the ball falls in 37. This means that we pick a sales volume in the $75,000–$100,000 range. If the ball goes in 11, we have a different price, and we turn to the $150,000–$200,000 range for a sales volume.

Most significant, perhaps, is the fact that the program allows management to ascertain the sensitivity of the results to each or all of the input factors. Simply by running the program with changes in the distribution of an input factor, it is possible to determine the effect of added or changed information (or lack of information). It may turn out that fairly large changes in some factors do not significantly affect the outcomes. In this case, as a matter of fact, management was particularly concerned about the difficulty in estimating market growth. Running the program with variations in this factor quickly demonstrated that for average annual growth rates from 3% to 5% there was no significant difference in the expected outcome.

In addition, let us see what the implications are of the detailed knowledge the simulation method gives us. Under the method using single expected values, management arrives only at a hoped-for expectation of 25.2% after taxes (which, as we have seen, is wrong unless there is no variability in many input factors – a highly unlikely event).

With the proposed method, however, the uncertainties are clearly portrayed, as shown in Exhibit 14.4. Note the contrast with the profile obtained under the conventional approach. This concept has been used also for evaluation of product introductions, acquisition of businesses, and plant modernization.

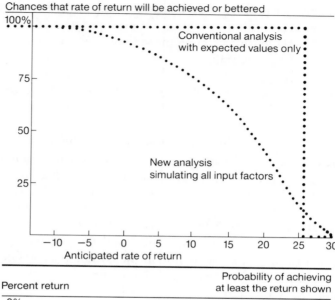

Percent return	Probability of achieving at least the return shown
0%	96.5%
5	80.6
10	75.2
15	53.8
20	43.0
25	12.6
30	0

Exhibit 14.4 Anticipated rates of return under old and new approaches

Comparing opportunities

From a decision-making point of view one of the most significant advantages of the new method of determining rate of return is that it allows management to discriminate among measures of (1) expected return based on weighted probabilities of all possible returns, (2) variability of return, and (3) risks.

To visualize this advantage, let us take an example based on another actual case but simplified for purposes of explanation. The example involves two investments under consideration, A and B. With the investment analysis, we obtain the tabulated and plotted data in Exhibit 14.5. We see that:

- Investment B has a higher expected return than Investment A.
- Investment B also has substantially more variability than Investment A.

There is a good chance that Investment B will earn a return quite different from the expected return of 6.8% – possibly as high as 15% or as low as a loss of 5%. Investment A is not likely to vary greatly from the anticipated 5% return.

• Investment B involves far more risk than does Investment A. There is virtually no chance of incurring a loss on Investment A. However, there is 1 chance in 10 of losing money on Investment B. If such a loss occurs, its expected size is approximately $200,000.

Clearly, the new method of evaluating investments provides management with far more information on which to base a decision. Investment decisions made only on the basis of maximum expected return are not unequivocally the best decisions.

Selected statistics	Investment A	Investment B
Amount of investment	$10,000,000	$10,000,000
Life of investment (in years)	10	10
Expected annual net cash inflow	$ 1,300,000	$ 1,400,000
Variability of cash inflow		
1 chance in 50 of being *greater than*	$ 1,700,000	$ 3,400,000
1 chance in 50 of being *less than**	$ 900,000	($ 600,000)
Expected return on investment	5.0%	6.8%
Variability of return on investment		
1 chance in 50 of being *greater than*	7.0%	15.5%
1 chance in 50 of being *less than**	3.0%	(4.0%)
Risk of investment		
Chances of a loss	Negligible	1 in 10
Expected size of loss	Negligible	$200,000

*In the case of negative figures (indicated by parentheses) *less than* means *worse than*.

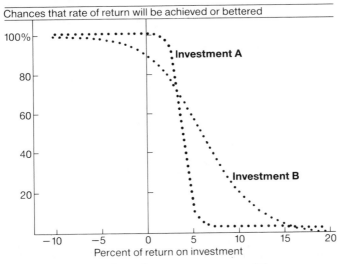

Chances that rate of return will be achieved or bettered

Exhibit 14.5 Comparison of two investment opportunities

Summary of new approach

After examining present methods of comparing alternative investments, the author reports on his firm's experience in applying a new approach to the problem. Using this approach, management takes the various levels of possible cash flows, return on investment, and other results of a proposed outlay and gets an estimate of the odds for each potential outcome.

Currently, many facilities decisions are based on discounted cash flow calculations. Management is told, for example, that Investment X has an expected internal rate of return of 9.2%, while for Investment Y a 10.3% return can be expected.

By contrast, the new approach would put in front of the executive a schedule that gives him the most likely return from X, but also tells him that X has 1 chance in 20 of being a total loss, 1 in 10 of earning from 4% to 5%, 2 in 10 of paying from 8% to 10%, and 1 chance in 50 of attaining a 30% rate of return.

From another schedule he learns what the most likely rate of return is from Y, but also that Y has 1 chance in 10 of resulting in a total loss, 1 in 10 of earning from 3% to 5% return, 2 in 10 of paying between 9% and 11%, and 1 chance in 100 of a 30% rate of return.

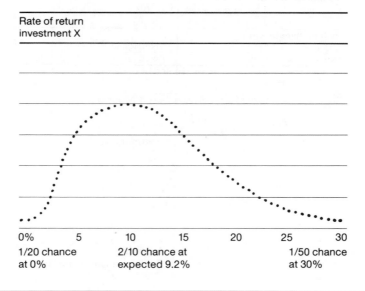

Rate of return
investment X

0%   5   10   15   20   25   30
1/20 chance   2/10 chance at   1/50 chance
at 0%   expected 9.2%   at 30%

Concluding note

The question management faces in selecting capital investments is first and foremost: What information is needed to clarify the key differences

In this instance, the estimates of the rates of return provided by the two approaches would not be substantially different. However, to the decision maker with the added information, Investment Y no longer looks like the clearly better choice, since with X the chances of substantial gain are higher and the risks of loss lower.

Two things have made this approach appealing to managers who have used it:

1 Certainly in every case it is a more descriptive statement of the two opportunities. And in some cases it might well reverse the decision, in line with particular corporate objectives.

2 This is not a difficult technique to use, since much of the information needed is already available – or readily accessible – and the validity of the principles involved has, for the most part, already been proved in other applications.

The enthusiasm with which managements exposed to this approach have received it suggests that it may have wide application. It has particular relevance, for example, in such knotty problems as investments relating to acquisitions or new products and in decisions that might involve excess capacity.

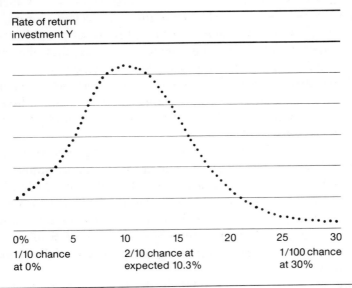

Rate of return
investment Y

| 0% | 5 | 10 | 15 | 20 | 25 | 30 |

1/10 chance   2/10 chance at   1/100 chance
at 0%   expected 10.3%   at 30%

among various alternatives? There is agreement as to the basic factors that should be considered – markets, prices, costs, and so on. And the way the future return on the investment should be calculated, if not agreed on, is at least limited to a few methods, any of which can be consistently used in a given company. If the input variables turn out as estimated, any of the methods customarily used to rate investments should provide satisfactory (if not necessarily maximum) returns.

In actual practice, however, the conventional methods do not work out satisfactorily. Why? The reason, as we have seen earlier in this article and as every executive and economist knows, is that the estimates used in making the advance calculations are just that – estimates. More accurate estimates would be helpful, but at best the residual uncertainty can easily make a mockery of corporate hopes. Nevertheless, there is a solution. To collect realistic estimates for the key factors means to find out a great deal about them. Hence the kind of uncertainty that is involved in each estimate can be evaluated ahead of time. Using this knowledge of uncertainty, executives can maximize the value of the information for decision making.

The value of computer programs in developing clear portrayals of the uncertainty and risk surrounding alternative investments has been proved. Such programs can produce valuable information about the sensitivity of the possible outcomes to the variability of input factors and to the likelihood of achieving various possible rates of return. This information can be extremely important as a backup to management judgment. To have calculations of the odds on all possible outcomes lends some assurance to the decision makers that the available information has been used with maximum efficiency.

This simulation approach has the inherent advantage of simplicity. It requires only an extension of the input estimates (to the best of our ability) in terms of probabilities. No projection should be pinpointed unless we are certain of it.

The discipline of thinking through the uncertainties of the problem will in itself help to ensure improvement in making investment choices. For to understand uncertainty and risk is to understand the key business problem – and the key business opportunity. Since the new approach can be applied on a continuing basis to each capital alternative as it comes up for consideration and progresses toward fruition, gradual progress may be expected in improving the estimation of the probabilities of variation.

Lastly, the courage to act boldly in the face of apparent uncertainty can be greatly bolstered by the clarity of portrayal of the risks and possible rewards. To achieve these lasting results requires only a slight effort beyond what most companies already exert in studying capital investments.

15

Creating Shareholder Value

ALFRED RAPPAPORT

*C*reating Shareholder Value *is a truly great book. Every business-man should read it. Its concepts are as relevant to the chief executive of a multidivisional international corporation as to the sole trader of a single high-street shop. The writing is lucid, the central concept is simple, the small amount of maths not difficult.*

We all know that historic accounting measures – whether of the management or statutory variety and whether based upon trends, ratios or both – are deeply flawed indicators of the worth of a business or of its trading performance. We continue to use such measures because they are the best available. However, Rappaport's shareholder value approach means that we no longer have any excuse for continuing to use such measures for the strategic management of our businesses.

This McKinsey anthology would not be complete without including an extract from Creating Shareholder Value. *It is not a long book and is easy to digest. I urge you to go out and buy a copy – and don't just leave it on your home or office bookshelf: read it.*

Shareholder value concepts are clearly superior to existing historic accounting measures. Why, then, have Rappaport's ideas not been more widely adopted or publicized? My view is that the new concepts will take over from the old only as the old ideas are discovered to be inferior to the new practice. *In the United Kingdom, the era of tough trading conditions coupled with high interest rates – which many young business managers have not experienced before – may indirectly provide the stimulus for change that has not been present until now.*

Those who adopt Rappaport's concepts 'ahead of the crowd' will avail themselves of one of the simplest and most effective competitive advantages in existence.

R. H. H. Nellist,
St Albans

Chapter 5: Value-Creating Business Strategies

IN today's fast-changing, often bewildering business environment formal systems for strategic planning have become one of top management's principal tools for evaluating and coping with uncertainty. Corporate board members are also showing increasing interest in ensuring that the company has adequate strategies and that these are tested against actual results. While the organizational dynamics and the sophistication of the strategic planning process vary widely among companies, the process almost invariably culminates in projected (commonly five-year) financial statements.

This accounting format enables top managers and the board of directors to review and approve strategic plans in the same terms that the company uses to report its performance to shareholders and the financial community. Under current practice the projected financial statements, particularly projected earnings-per-share performance, commonly serve as the basis for judging the attractiveness of the strategic or long-term corporate plan.

The conventional accounting-oriented approach for evaluating the strategic plan does not, however, provide reliable answers to such basic questions as:

- Will the corporate plan create value for shareholders? If so, how much?
- Which business units are creating value and which are not?
- How would alternative strategic plans affect shareholder value?

The three case studies below illustrate for top management and board members a theoretically sound, practical approach for assessing the contributions of business unit plans and overall corporate strategic plans toward creating shareholder value. The first covers valuation issues both at the business unit and corporate levels. The second case illustrates how value can be created by exploiting intracompany synergies. The last case contrasts the shareholder value approach to product mix analysis with the more conventional approach.

Business unit/corporate strategy valuation[1]

Econoval, a diversified manufacturing company, divides its operations into three business units – telecommunications, industrial systems, and automotive parts (see Table 15.1).

Table 15.1 Strategic overview of Econoval's business units

Business Unit	Product Life Cycle Stage	Strategy	Risk	Current Year's Sales ($ in millions)
Telecommunications	Embryonic	Invest aggressively to achieve dominant market position	High	50
Industrial systems	Expanding	Invest to improve market position	Medium	75
Automotive parts	Mature	Maintain market position	Low	125

Before beginning their detailed analysis, Econoval managers must choose appropriate time horizons for calculating the value contributed by each business unit's strategy. The product life cycle stages of the various units should determine the length of the forecast period. If we were to measure value creation for all businesses arbitrarily in a common time horizon, say five years, then embryonic businesses with large capital requirements in early years and large payoffs in later years would be viewed as poor prospects even if they were expected to yield exceptional value over the life cycle. Therefore, in this case, the projections for the telecommunications unit were extended to ten years and projections for the industrial systems and auto parts units were limited to five years.

The telecommunications unit designs, manufactures, and sells sophisticated computerized PBX systems. Its customers (end users, distributors, and independent telephone companies) are particularly attracted to its least-cost routing software features which can lead to significant savings in usage-sensitive communication costs. The recent development of the ability to handle voice and data transmission simultaneously gives the telecommunications unit an early technological lead. Despite this lead, the telecommunications unit can expect serious competition as the PBX technology moves from its current third generation stage to fourth generation switches. In addition, the threat of substitute technology is ever present in the competition for office-of-the-future dollars.

Once business unit managers have developed and analyzed their initial planning projections, they can prepare more detailed analyses for evaluating alternative planning scenarios. Table 15.2 shows the telecommunications unit's planning parameters for conservative, most likely, and optimistic scenarios.

The worst case, or conservative scenario, assumes significant market penetration by other producers via major technological advances

Table 15.2 Telecommunications unit's forecasts for three scenarios (in percent)

	Year									
	1	2	3	4	5	6	7	8	9	10
Sales Growth Rate										
Conservative	25	25	20	20	18	18	18	18	18	18
Most likely	30	28	25	22	20	20	20	20	20	20
Optimistic	32	30	30	25	25	25	25	25	25	25
Operating Profit Margin										
Conservative	11.5	12	12.5	13	13.5	13.5	13.5	13.5	13.5	13.5
Most likely	12	12.5	13	13.5	14	14.5	15	15	15	14.5
Optimistic	12.5	13	14	14.5	15	15	15	15	15	15
Incremental Working Capital Investment										
Conservative	20	20	20	20	20	20	20	20	20	20
Most likely	20	20	20	20	20	20	20	20	20	20
Optimistic	18	18	18	18	18	18	18	18	18	18
Incremental Fixed Capital Investment										
Conservative	42	42	42	40	40	35	35	35	35	35
Most likely	45	45	44	42	42	40	38	38	35	35
Optimistic	40	38	38	36	36	35	35	35	35	35
Cash Income Tax Rate										
Conservative	41	41	41	41	41	41	41	41	41	41
Most likely	40	40	40	40	40	40	40	40	40	40
Optimistic	39	39	39	39	39	39	39	39	39	39

coupled with aggressive price competition. The most likely scenario assumes the telecommunications unit's continued dominance in the PBX market, substantial R&D expenditures to enable it to maintain its competitiveness in the learning curve race, and gradual technological parity, which will place pressure on operating profit margins. The optimistic scenario projects more rapid industry growth and greater success in the unit's effort to carve out high-margin proprietary niches.

Table 15.3 presents the shareholder value contribution for each of these three scenarios and for a range of discount rates.

Table 15.3 Shareholder value created by the telecommunications unit under different scenarios and discount rates ($ in millions)

	Cost of Capital (Discount Rate)				
Scenario	*14%*	*14.5%*	*15%*	*15.5%*	*16%*
Conservative	$ 9.30	$ 6.96	$ 4.87	$ 2.99	$ 1.30
Most likely	16.92	13.59	10.60	7.91	5.48
Optimistic	39.64	34.53	29.93	25.79	22.05

Econoval expects the telecommunications unit's ten-year plan for the most likely scenario to contribute $10.6 million to shareholder value. The range of value creation from conservative to optimistic scenarios is from $4.87 million to $29.93 million for the estimated cost of capital or discount rate of 15 percent. An assessment of the likelihood of each scenario will provide further insight into the relative riskiness of business unit investment strategies. For example, if all three scenarios are equally likely, the situation would be riskier than if the most likely scenario is 60 percent probable and the other two are each 20 percent probable.

Table 15.4 presents the cash flows and shareholder value calculations for the 'most likely' scenario. The combination of fast growth and relatively large working capital and fixed capital investment requirements results in negative cash flows throughout the forecast period. Despite this, as can be seen from the 'increase in value' column the business is operating above its cost of capital in all years except years 2 and 10. Over the entire ten-year period the value created by the strategy amounts to $10.6 million. Table 15.5 provides further insight into the unit's value creation process. The 'operating profit margin' column reproduces the

Table 15.4 Cash flows and shareholder value for telecommunications – most likely scenario (cost of capital = 15.0%) ($ in millions)

Year	Cash Flow	Present Value	Cumulative Present Value	Present Value of Residual Value	Cumulative PV + Residual Value*	Increase in Value
1	$(5.1)	$(4.4)	$ (4.4)	$24.4	$20.0	$0.2†
2	(5.6)	(4.2)	(8.6)	28.3	19.7	(0.3)
3	(5.2)	(3.4)	(12.0)	32.0	20.0	0.3
4	(3.9)	(2.2)	(14.2)	35.2	21.0	1.0
5	(2.9)	(1.5)	(15.7)	38.1	22.4	1.4
6	(2.4)	(1.0)	(16.7)	41.2	24.5	2.1
7	(1.5)	(0.5)	(17.3)	44.5	27.2	2.7
8	(1.8)	(0.6)	(17.9)	46.4	28.5	1.3
9	(0.5)	(0.2)	(18.1)	48.5	30.4	1.9
10	(1.8)	(0.4)	(18.5)	48.9	30.4	0.0
						$10.6

CORPORATE VALUE	$30.4
Less: Market value of debt	5.0
SHAREHOLDER VALUE	$25.4

* Assumes a 46 percent residual value income tax rate.
† Operating profit margin in year 0 = 11 percent.

Table 15.5 Profit margins for telecommunications – most likely scenario (in percent)

Year	Operating Profit Margin	Threshold Margin	Threshold Spread
1	12.0	11.9	0.1
2	12.5	12.6	(0.1)
3	13.0	12.9	0.1
4	13.5	13.2	0.3
5	14.0	13.6	0.4
6	14.5	13.9	0.6
7	15.0	14.2	0.8
8	15.0	14.6	0.4
9	15.0	14.5	0.5
10	14.5	14.5	0.0

projections for the forecast period. The 'threshold margin' entries provide management with minimum acceptable margins the business must attain in each period for value to be created in that period. The difference between the projected and threshold margins is the 'threshold spread.' Consistent with Table 15.4, the threshold spread is positive, thus indicating value creation, in all years except years 2 and 10.

Once the initial value creation calculations have been completed and reviewed, it becomes important to identify which of the value drivers have the greatest impact on shareholder value. Table 15.6 presents the changes in shareholder value resulting from a 1 percent increase in each of the value drivers. Note that the 1 percent increase represents a change in a variable from, say, 10 percent to 10.1 percent, not to 11 percent; that is, it represents a point elasticity for each item, assuming other items are held constant.

Table 15.6 Relative impact of key variables on shareholder value for telecommunications – most likely scenario

A 1% Increase in:	Increases Shareholder Value Created by
Sales growth rate	$ 94,000
Operating profit margin	1,135,000
Incremental fixed capital investment	(555,000)
Incremental working capital investment	(276,000)
Cash income tax rate	(431,000)
Residual value income tax rate	(416,000)
Cost of capital	(1,033,000)

Understanding the aspects of the business that are most critical to value creation enables management to focus its analysis more efficiently on key elements of a strategy. Telecommunications' strategy value is most sensitive to changes in operating profit margin and cost of capital. In addition, because most business decisions involve tradeoffs between two or more value drivers, establishing the relative impact of value drivers can provide useful direction for decision making. To illustrate, suppose the telecommunications unit wishes to evaluate the attractiveness of a proposed promotional campaign. The campaign is expected to stimulate product demand and thereby increase sales growth, but the campaign costs would result in a decrease in operating profit margin. Table 15.6 shows that a 1 percent increase in the sales growth rate would increase shareholder value created by $94,000 and a 1 percent increase in operating profit margin would increase value by $1,135,000, respectively. The analysis proceeds as follows:

Step 1: Compare the relative impacts of changes in sales growth rate and operating profit margin.

$$\frac{\text{Impact of 1\% change in operating profit margin}}{\text{Impact of 1\% change in sales growth rate}} = \frac{\$1,135,000}{94,000} = 12$$

Shareholder value creation is about twelve times more sensitive to a change in operating profit margin than to a change in the sales growth rate. The relative insensitivity of value creation to sales growth is not surprising since the business is operating relatively close to the threshold margin throughout the forecast period (as shown by the small threshold spreads in Table 15.5).

Step 2: Estimate the anticipated change in the more critical variable. In this case, the promotional campaign is projected to reduce operating profit margin by 0.5 percent.

Step 3: Evaluate whether the decision is advisable. To justify the promotional campaign, the sales growth rate would need to increase by more than 6 percent, that is, twelve times 0.5 percent.

The relative impact analysis tests only a 1 percent change in each of the value drivers and is very useful for an initial understanding of the financial dynamics of the business. Invariably managers want to test the sensitivity of shareholder value to changes in the value drivers for ranges other than 1 percent as well as using pairs of value drivers to conduct 'what if' analysis. Table 15.7 illustrates this type of analysis. (In these sensitivity exhibits percentage changes are additive, i.e., a 1 percent increase represents an increase in a variable from, say, 10 to 11 percent not to 10.1 percent.)

The telecommunications unit is actively considering the possibility of increasing its capital investment outlays to gain laborsaving production efficiencies that should improve operating profit margin. It estimates that to gain a 1 percent improvement in margin it will have to increase its capital expenditures by 5 percent for each dollar of sales increase. Table 15.7a presents the results of the analysis. The center cell reflects the most likely scenario value contribution of $10.6 million. The combination of a 5 percent increase in incremental capital expenditures and a 1 percent margin improvement results in a strategy value of $11.7 million

Table 15.7

a Sensitivity of shareholder value created by strategy for telecommunications

		Operating Profit Margin ($ in millions)		
		−1.00%	0.00%	1.00%
Increm. Fixed Capital Invest.	−5.00%	9.5	17.5	25.5
	0.00%	2.6	10.6	18.6
	5.00%	(4.3)	3.7	11.7

b Sensitivity of internal rate of return for telecommunications

		Operating Profit Margin		
		−1.00%	0.00%	1.00%
Increm. Fixed Capital Invest.	−5.00%	18.13	20.58	22.90
	0.00%	15.83	18.34	20.50
	5.00%	13.61	16.15	18.34

Internal rate of return uses prestrategy residual value as investment ($19.8 million).

– an improvement of just over $1 million. If the unit makes the outlays and no margin improvement is forthcoming, then the value of the strategy decreases significantly to only $3.7 million.

The identical analysis is performed in Table 15.7b except that now the results are expressed in terms of discounted cash flow rates of return, that is, internal rates of return. Because the most likely strategy does create value ($10.6 million), we can be certain that it yields a rate greater than its 15 percent cost of capital. As shown in the centre cell, the rate of return is 18.34 percent. If the capital outlays are made without margin improvement, the rate of return falls to 16.15 percent.

Econoval performed similar analyses for the industrial systems and automotive parts units.[2] Table 15.8 summarizes the results for most likely scenarios. To ensure consistency in comparing or consolidating scenarios of various business units, it is important for the corporate planning group to establish that such scenarios share common assumptions about critical environmental factors such as inflation and energy prices.

The analysis in Table 15.8 provides support for corporate level management's concern about the automotive unit's performance. While the unit now accounts for 50 percent of Econoval's sales, the company expects it to create only $3.57 million, or about 15 percent of the total increase in shareholder value.

Table 15.8 Shareholder value, sales growth, and earnings growth rates by business unit for most likely scenarios

Business Unit	Years in Plan	$ in millions	*Shareholder Value Increase* Per Discounted $ of Sales (Value ROS) %	Per Discounted $ of Investment (Value ROI) %	*Growth Rates* Sales %	Earnings %
Telecommunications	10	10.60	7.7	12.8	22.4	26.1
Industrial systems	5	8.79	17.5	43.8	15.0	17.7
Automotive parts	5	3.57	6.8	19.4	10.0	11.9
Consolidated		22.96				

On the basis of traditional criteria such as sales and earnings growth rates, the telecommunications unit clearly emerges as the star performer. However, its high investment requirements and risk vis-à-vis its sales margins combine to limit its value-creating potential. Despite the fact that the telecommunications unit's sales and earnings growth rates are substantially greater than those of the industrial systems unit, the telecommunications unit is expected to contribute only modestly more shareholder value in ten years than the industrial systems unit in five years.

The shareholder value increase per discounted dollar of investment provides management with important information about where it is realizing the greatest benefits per dollar of investment. Indeed, this value ROI, rather than the traditional accounting ROI, enables management to rank various business units on the basis of a substantive economic criterion.

Value ROI, oftentimes referred to as the 'profitability index,' is simply the amount of shareholder value created per dollar of investment.

$$\text{Value ROI} = \frac{\text{Value created by strategy}}{\text{Present value of investment}}$$

When value ROI is equal to zero, the strategy yields exactly the cost of capital, and when value ROI is positive, the strategy yields a rate greater than its cost of capital. Telecommunications, for example, creates 12.8 cents of value per dollar of investment. Recall that the telecommunications strategy is forecasted to yield a rate of return of 18.34 percent while its cost of capital is 15 percent. Note, however, that the telecommunications unit ranks last, even behind the auto parts unit, in this all-important performance measure.

Ranking units on the basis of value ROI can be particularly helpful to corporate headquarters in capital-rationing situations where the various parts of the company are competing for scarce funds. In the final analysis, however, corporate resources should be allocated to units so as to maximize the shareholder value creation of the company's total product-market portfolio.

Once the company has established a preliminary plan, it should test its financial feasibility, that is, whether it is fundable. This involves integrating the company's planned investment growth strategies with its dividend and financing policies. In this case, Econoval management concluded that the strategic plan was financially feasible. The analysis did, however, raise two concerns. First, the current dividend payout rate could not be sustained without issuing additional equity or issuing debt in excess of its target capital structure unless the plans fully materialized. The company would be particularly vulnerable if actual operating margins were lower than those projected. Second, management was concerned about the riskiness of the telecommunication unit's aggressive competitive positioning and the related high level of investment requirements. This unit's large cash requirements, coupled with its relatively modest value ROI, prompted Econoval management to launch a study of alternative product portfolio strategies and related restructuring activities.

Increasingly, companies are adding financial self-evaluation to their strategic planning process. A financial evaluation poses two fundamental questions: How much is the company and each of its major lines of business worth? How much would each of several plausible scenarios involving various combinations of future environments and management strategies affect the value of the company and its business units?

The following types of companies would especially benefit from conducting a financial evaluation:

- Companies that wish to sell and need to establish a minimum acceptable selling price for their shares
- Companies that are potential takeover targets
- Companies considering selective divestments
- Companies evaluating the attractiveness of repurchasing their own shares

- Private companies wanting to establish the proper price at which to go public
- Acquisition-minded companies wanting to assess the advantage of a debt-financed versus an equity-financed offer

The shareholder value of any business unit, or the entire company, is the sum of the estimated shareholder value contributed by its strategic plan and the current cash flow level discounted at the risk-adjusted cost of capital (i.e., prestrategy value) less the market value of outstanding debt. Table 15.9 summarizes these values for Econoval and its three major business units. For example, the telecommunications unit's current cash flow perpetuity level is $2.97 million, which, when discounted at its risk-adjusted cost of capital of 15 percent produces a value of $19.8 million. Subtracting the $5 million of debt outstanding provides the $14.8 million prestrategy shareholder value. To obtain the total shareholder value of $25.4 million for the telecommunications unit, simply add the $10.6 million value created by the strategic plan.

Table 15.9 Business unit and corporate financial evaluation summary for most likely scenarios ($ in millions)

	Telecommunications	Industrial Systems	Automotive Parts	Consolidated
Prestrategy shareholder value	$14.80	$20.93	$25.10	$60.83
Shareholder value created by strategy (see Table 15.8)	10.60	8.79	3.57	22.96
Shareholder value	$25.40	$29.72	$28.67	$83.79
Percent of total shareholder value	30.3%	35.5%	34.2%	
Econoval shareholder value at corporate cost of capital of 14%				$87.57

The sum of the three business unit values is $83.79 million. Combining the cash flows of the individual businesses and discounting them at the 14 percent corporate cost of capital yields a value of $87.57 million. In this case, the differences between the value of the whole and the sum of the parts is relatively small. However, this may not always be the case.

Aggregating the values of the company's business units is consistent with the assumption that the riskiness of each unit must be considered separately. If, however, the company's entry into unrelated businesses reduces the overall variability of its cash flows, then the lower expected probability of bankruptcy can decrease its cost of debt and increase its unused debt capacity.

What happens to the company's overall cost of capital naturally depends on any changes in the cost of equity as well as on the cost of debt. Analysis of the impact of business units on the overall risk of the company is generally a difficult and subjective exercise.

A more attractive alternative is to (1) assume risk independence in establishing the cost of capital for business units and (2) interpret the difference between the value of the company and the aggregate value of its individual businesses as a broad approximation of the benefits or costs associated with the company's product portfolio balancing activities.

Value creation by exploiting synergies[3]

The purpose of this case is to illustrate the shareholder value approach for choosing between two strategies involving organizationally independent operating units which have potentially synergistic relationships.

This case deals with a manufacturer of telephones. The company has two operating divisions: (1) Home Phones, which makes state-of-the-art telephones for home use; and (2) Biz Phones, which makes sophisticated equipment for businesses. Some common core components are used in both product lines, although each division currently manufactures the components separately for its own use. The buyers of Home Phones' products are extremely price sensitive, while Biz Phones' buyers are much less price sensitive.

Each of the two divisions has prepared a plan to submit to the corporate office. First, I will examine how the Home Phones division would assess its own value creation opportunities. This will be followed by a discussion of how the corporate office would make its funding allocation decision in light of both divisions' plans.

The manager of the Home Phones division begins the analysis by preparing forecast data for a 'base scenario' (i.e., Strategy 1) that would assess Home Phones' value contribution if the division continues 'business as usual' – that is, without making any significant changes to its current strategy. A summary of value driver forecasts appears below:

			Year		
	1	2	3	4	5
Sales growth rate	15%	15%	15%	15%	15%
Operating profit margin	20	20	20	20	20
Incremental fixed capital investment (as a percentage of each dollar of sales increase)	40%	40%	40%	40%	40%
Incremental working capital investment (as a percentage of each dollar of sales increase)	18%	18%	18%	18%	18%
Cash income tax rate	38%	38.4%	38.7%	38.9%	39.2%
Residual value income tax rate	45	45	45	45	45
Cost of capital	14	14	14	14	14

Table 15.10 presents the cash flows and Table 15.11 shows that if Home Phones pursues basically a 'business as usual' strategy, it can expect to increase its shareholder value by $35.5 million, resulting in a total shareholder value of $106.2 million. An analysis of the relative impact of the value drivers reveals that shareholder value is most sensitive to changes in the operating profit margin.

Because Home Phones' market is so price sensitive, it is considering a price-cutting strategy to gain market share. To get a preliminary estimate of how much sales would need to increase to offset a 1 percent decline in profit margin, a sensitivity analysis is performed (Table 15.12).

This exhibit shows that if prices were cut (and the operating profit margin declined by 1 percent, from 20 to 19 percent), even a 4 percent increase in sales (from 20 to 24 percent) would not offset the reduction in profit margin: as the upper right-hand corner of the matrix indicates, shareholder value would decline by $85,000. Sales would need to increase by almost 5 percent before there begins to be any significant increase in shareholder value, offsetting the 1 percent decline in the profit margin.

Home Phones is also considering a strategy that would entail investing $25 million in a new, more efficient production process that would reduce the cost of making the core components. The cost savings would enable the division to lower its prices and thereby obtain a much larger

Table 15.10 Cash flow statement for Home Phones Division

	($ in millions) Year				
	1	2	3	4	5
Sales	$115.000	$132.250	$152.087	$174.901	$201.136
Cost of goods sold	48.875	56.206	64.637	74.333	85.483
Gross profit	66.125	75.044	87.450	100.568	115.653
Selling, general & administrative expense	43.125	49.594	57.033	65.588	75.426
Taxable operating profit	23.000	26.450	30.417	34.980	40.227
Depreciation expense	10.000	10.600	11.290	12.083	12.996
Funds from operations before tax	33.000	37.050	41.708	47.064	53.223
Cash income taxes	8.750	10.152	11.765	13.620	15.753
Funds from operations after tax	$ 24.250	$ 26.897	$ 29.942	$ 33.443	$ 37.470
Incremental working capital investment	2.700	3.105	3.571	4.106	4.722
Fixed capital investment	16.000	17.500	19.225	21.209	23.490
Cash flow from operations	$ 5.550	$ 6.292	$ 7.146	$ 8.128	$ 9.258

Table 15.11 Cash flows and shareholder value for Home Phones division – Strategy 1 (cost of capital = 14%) ($ in millions)

Year	Cash Flow	Present Value	Cumulative Present Value	Residual Value	Cumulative PV + Residual Value	Increase in Value
1	$5.550	$4.868	$ 4.868	$79.261	$ 84.129	$13.415
2	6.292	4.842	9.710	79.956	89.666	5.537
3	7.146	4.824	14.534	80.657	95.191	5.525
4	8.128	4.813	19.347	81.365	100.711	5.520
5	9.258	4.808	24.155	82.079	106.233	5.522
						$35.519

Marketable securities	0.000
DIVISION VALUE	$106.233
Less: Market value of debt	0.000
SHAREHOLDER VALUE	$106.233

Note: Neither division carries any marketable securities or debt on its balance sheet.

share of its price-sensitive market – while still maintaining its profit margins.

However, these savings can be realized only if the division sells enough units to take advantage of economies of scale. A Home Phones study showed that the new production line would be too large for Home Phones to use efficiently on its own. But the combined volume of production by both Home Phones and Biz Phones would be sufficient to make full use of the new production line.

The strategy would involve a $25 million investment, shared equally by the divisions in year 1 (each would pay $7.5 million) and in year 2 (each would pay $5 million). The resulting cost savings would enable

Table 15.12 Sensitivity of changes in shareholder value creation for Home Phones division – Strategy 1 ($ in millions)

		Sales Growth Rate		
		−4.00%	0.00%	4.00%
Operating Profit Margin	−1.00%	(13.596)	(7.253)	(0.085)
	0.00%	(7.323)	0.000	8.278
	1.00%	(1.050)	7.253	16.642

Home Phones to cut its prices without reducing its operating profit margin and also achieve a sharp increase in sales. (The impact on Biz Phones will be explored later.)

Home Phones developed a forecast for the new strategy involving a shared investment in the new production facilities. The projections shown below reflect Home Phones' portion of the fixed capital investment as well as the increased sales growth that could result when Home Phones cuts its prices. All other forecasts from Strategy 1 are unchanged except for the cash tax rates which are less because of the increase in depreciation. The new forecast is shown following the earlier Strategy 1 projections.

	Year				
	1	2	3	4	5
Sales Growth Rate					
Strategy 1	15%	15%	15%	15%	15%
Strategy 2	15	25	30	30	30
Incremental Fixed Capital Investment (as a percentage of each dollar of sales increase)					
Strategy 1	40%	40%	40%	40%	40%
Strategy 2	90	57.4	40	40	40
Cash Income Tax Rate					
Strategy 1	38%	38.4%	38.7%	38.9%	39.2%
Strategy 2	34.8	34.3	34.9	35.4	35.7

The valuation summary for Strategy 2 (Table 15.13) shows that the shareholder value contributed by the new strategy is almost $53 million or $17.5 million more than the $35.5 million that would be generated under Strategy 1. Based on this analysis, Home Phone has decided it would like to pursue the new strategy. The division therefore proposed that the two divisions invest jointly in the new production process to manufacture the common component.

The corporate staff recognizes that the Biz Phones Division, whose buyers are not nearly as price-sensitive, has no interest in sharing the investment because the cost savings would not improve their profit margins enough to offset the negative effect of the increased investment. When the managers at Biz Phones had conducted a similar analysis of

Table 15.13 Valuation summary for Home Phones division – Strategy 2, five-year forecast ($ in millions)

Cumulative present value of cash flows	$ (5.176)
Present value of residual value	128.878
Shareholder value	$123.702
Less: Prestrategy shareholder value	70.714
Value created by strategy	$ 52.988

the shared-investment project, they found that the shared-investment strategy would generate $1 million less value. Moreover, Biz Phones is reluctant to undertake such a project because it perceives that the benefits would accrue to Home Phones, while Biz Phones would only lose control over its production process without getting much credit for contributing to Home Phones' success.

Corporate management is considering two alternatives:

1 Turning down the project, consistent with current policy of assessing the operating divisions' plans on a stand-alone basis (i.e., Home Phones cannot justify the $25 million investment solely on the benefits that would accrue to itself)
2 Evaluating the investment decision in terms of its contribution to shareholder value of the overall company

The issue is whether the benefits to Home Phones of the shared investment would more than offset the detriment to Biz Phones by improving the shareholder value of the corporation as a whole. In this case the value created for the overall company is about $16.5 million higher under Strategy 2 compared to Strategy 1. Thus, it would benefit the corporation to have Home Phones and Biz Phones jointly build and use the new production process.

The treatment of the subsidiaries as autonomous business units (as reflected in Strategy 1) would result in sacrificing opportunities offered by potential synergies between the businesses. The shared-investment strategy would help the Home Phones division but would not be as favorable for the Biz Phones division. By applying the shareholder value approach to evaluation of a funding allocation decision, one could assess what the overall impact of the shared-investment strategy would be on the corporation as a whole in order to select the strategy that would maximize overall shareholder value creation. Exploiting the opportunity to share activities in the value chain by related divisions is an essential aspect of strategies that seek to gain competitive advantage.

Product-line value creation

A manufacturer of personal computers sells through its own sales force to major corporate accounts and also sells to retail computer stores. While there is general agreement that direct sales to corporations and the retail channel of distribution are complementary rather than competitive, there is a keen interest in analyzing the relative contributions of the two segments. The most recent year's contribution statements for the corporate and retail segments are presented in Table 15.14.

Table 15.14 Contributions of corporate and retail segments ($ in millions)

	Corporate	%	Retail	%	Total	%
Sales	$250	100	$250	100	$500	100
Variable manufacturing costs	100	40	100	40	200	40
MANUFACTURING CONTRIBUTION MARGIN	150	60	150	60	300	60
Variable selling and administrative expenses	50	20	35	14	85	17
CONTRIBUTION MARGIN	100	40	115	46	215	43
Other expenses directly traceable to segments	45	18	45	18	90	18
SEGMENT OPERATING CONTRIBUTION	$ 55	22	$ 70	28	$125	25
Unallocated common expenses					45	9
EARNINGS BEFORE TAXES					$ 80	16

The computers sold directly to corporations and those sold to retail dealers are identical. In both markets discounts from list price have averaged about 25 percent. Thus, the manufacturing contribution ratio for each segment is also an identical 60 percent. Due to relatively greater selling expenses (e.g., the direct sales force) and order processing costs, the contribution margin ratio for the corporate segment is just 40 percent compared to 46 percent for the retail segment. Other expenses directly traceable to the respective segments such as advertising and promotion were 18 percent of sales last year. As a consequence, the segment operating contribution ratio for retail (28 percent) remains a significant six percentage points greater than corporate (22 percent). On the basis of the contribution statement, management concluded that even though each segment generated the same level of sales, the retail segment was clearly more profitable, with an operating contribution of $70 million versus $55 million for the corporate segment. Indeed, this analysis along with some pressure from retail chains has moved management to consider the possibility of distributing exclusively through the retail channel.

There are several limitations associated with the foregoing contribution statement. First, it is historical rather than forward-looking. Second, it ignores the investments in working and fixed capital needed to generate the sales. Finally, it does not consider the possible differences in risk related to the corporate versus retail segments. To transform the conventional contribution analysis to a shareholder value creation analysis the three limitations listed above must be overcome.

Assume the following constant projections over the five-year forecast period:

	Corporate	Retail
Sales growth rate	18%	18%
Operating profit margin	22	24
Incremental working capital investment	12	30
Cost of capital	14	15

The projected operating profit margin for retail of 24 percent continues to be better than the 22 percent margin projected for the corporate segment. Retail's incremental working capital requirements of 30 percent, however, are two and a half times greater than those of the corporate segment. This is due, in part, to the substantially slower inventory turnover realized in the retail segment particularly for smaller dealers. In addition, the company has used liberal collection policies as a competitive vehicle in gaining acceptance among dealers. As a result, retail averages sixty days of outstanding receivables in contrast to forty days for the corporate segment. The higher cost of capital, 15 percent, assigned to retail is based on a relatively higher expected variability in demand in response to economy-wide factors than might be expected for sales to corporations. Furthermore, because the company is not yet well established in the extremely competitive retail channel, management believes it to be a relatively risky business at this time.

Table 15.15 Cash flows and shareholder value for corporate segment (cost of capital = 14%) ($ in millions)

Year	Cash Flow	Present Value	Cumulative Present Value	Present Value of Residual Value	Cumulative PV + Residual Value	Increase in Value
1	$ 59.500	$52.193	$ 52.193	$406.642	$458.835	$ 65.977
2	70.210	54.024	106.217	420.910	527.127	68.292
3	82.848	55.920	162.137	435.678	597.816	70.689
4	97.760	57.882	220.019	450.965	670.985	73.169
5	115.357	59.913	279.932	466.789	746.721	75.736
						$353.864

Table 15.15, in sharp contrast to the earlier analysis, shows that the corporate segment will create about $36 million more value than the retail segment, that is, $353.864 million versus $317.440 million. The reversal in results is due to the higher working capital requirements and relatively higher risk associated with the retail channel. These results have strongly altered management's view of possibly distributing exclusively through the retail channel.

If management wishes to estimate the combined value creation of the two segments, then unallocated common expenses as well as fixed capital investment in shared production and warehouse facilities must be incorporated into the analysis. At this consolidated level, income taxes need also to be considered.

Operating profit margins are projected to decrease by four percentage points when unallocated common expenses are considered. The income tax rate is expected to approximate 46 percent. Incremental fixed capital investment is projected at 15 percent. With these additional forecasts, the value created by the combined segments totals $188 million compared to $671 million (see Table 15.16) before consideration of capital investment, common expenses, and income taxes.

The shareholder value approach has much to offer in ensuring successful implementation of complex strategies. The shareholder value approach provides organizations with a consistency of analysis across functions, levels, and types of business decisions. In this way, those who are competing for resources in a company will share the same framework for analyzing their businesses and can also speak to other business units in the same 'language.' In addition, this approach is not more difficult to implement because it requires only a modest amount of new data (such as the cost of capital). It also offers the benefit of

Table 15.16 Cash flows and shareholder value for retail segment (cost of capital = 15%) ($ in millions)

Year	Cash Flow	Present Value	Cumulative Present Value	Present Value of Residual Value	Cumulative PV + Residual Value	Increase in Value
1	$ 57.300	$49.826	$ 49.826	$410.435	$460.261	$ 60.261
2	67.614	51.126	100.952	421.142	522.094	61.833
3	79.785	52.460	153.412	432.128	585.540	63.446
4	94.146	53.828	207.240	443.401	650.641	65.101
5	111.092	55.232	262.472	454.968	717.440	66.799
						$317.440
	Total shareholder value created					$671.304

overcoming the limitations of traditional accounting-based financial statements.

Notes and References

1 This section is adapted from my article 'Selecting Strategies That Create Shareholder Value,' *Harvard Business Review*, May–June 1981, pp. 139–149.
2 Five-year projections are as follows:

	Sales Growth Rate %	Operating Profit Margin %	Incremental Fixed Investment %	Incremental Working Capital Investment %	Cash Income Tax Rate %	Cost of Capital %
Industrial systems	15	11	20	20	42	14
Automotive parts	11	7.5	15	20	44	13

In these analyses different costs of capital (14 percent for industrial systems and 13 percent for automotive parts) were used. The company's cost of capital is not the appropriate rate for discounting the cash flow projection of individual business units. The use of a single discount rate for all parts of the company is valid only in the unlikely event that they are identically risky. Executives who use a single discount rate companywide are likely to have a consistent bias in favor of funding higher-risk businesses at the expense of less risky businesses. To provide a consistent framework for dealing with different investment risks and thereby increasing shareholder value, management should allocate funds to business units on a risk-adjusted return basis.

The process of estimating a business unit's cost of capital inevitably involves a substantial degree of executive judgment. Unlike the company as a whole, ordinarily the business unit has no posted market price that would enable the analyst to estimate systematic or market-related risk. Moreover, it is often difficult to assign future financing (debt and equity) weights to individual business units. One approach to estimating a business unit's cost of equity is to identify publicly traded stocks in the same line of business that might be expected to have about the same degree of systematic or market risk as the business unit. After establishing the cost of equity and cost of debt, the analyst can calculate a weighted-average cost of capital for the business unit in the same fashion as for the company.

3 This section is adapted from Michael L. Blyth, Elizabeth A. Friskey, and Alfred Rappaport, 'Implementing the Shareholder Value Approach,' *Journal of Business Strategy*, Winter 1986, pp. 48–58.

16

Why Do Mergers Miscarry?

JOHN KITCHING

Marvin Bower sent me a note after this article had appeared, saying that it had been shortlisted for a McKinsey Foundation Award. (The ration was one per year in those days.)

Then, as now, I could not think why. The data base is small. Top management's evidence was mainly anecdotal. And the conclusions missed some vital points.

Yet it was widely quoted and widely translated. This was partly because it was a contrariant view, launched against a riptide of acquisitions, and top management could readily take its message on board. (It also coined – or more likely re-coined – the concept of 'managers of change'.) And it was partly because some countries – particularly France – were at that time re-structuring industry into larger business units and were interested in 'track records'.

What would one add with hindsight? Well, after writing a book (based this time on 18 months' work, covering 407 acquisitions), and after 20 years of setting strategies and implementing mergers and acquisitions, I have some new points to make.

Firstly, post-merger growth is a dominant cause of success. You get that from buying into growth industries; or acquiring turnarounds; or from great managers.

Secondly market-segment share is crucial – see the findings in the book. (Can anyone tell us how to find a defensible niche? Weinstock says that the trouble with niches is that they can become tombs.)

Thirdly, if your strategy is to go for growth in earnings per share (EPS) by financial engineering, rather than organically, you will follow the (Lorenz) 'S' curve. Great – at the beginning. Then the 'sea anchor' effect starts to work (where 'the only acquisition that will make an impact on our EPS would have to be Belgium'). Eventually, the behemoth stalls. At the end, it's the chop shop: leveraged acquisitions; spinoffs; LBOs; and the Corporate Raiders Squadron on the horizon, flying Jolly Rogers.

But by the time the M&A industry reaches the top of each 'S' curve, a new generation of managers has started up. (This probably explains why the percentage of failures stayed the same in both my 1967 and 1974 surveys and in Egon Zehnder's 1984 survey.) Plus ça change, plus c'est la même chose.

Which, of course, is good for management consultants who advise on these matters!

John Kitching,
J. Kitching Associates,
Paris

Why Do Mergers Miscarry?

A CQUISITIONS are in fashion. Large corporations are creating special posts with titles like 'director of acquisitions.' Smaller companies now list the responsibility for acquisitions high among the duties of the vice president for corporate planning and investment. A host of fashionable terms have sprung up in connection with the acquisitions movement – for instance, 'conglomerate,' 'concentric,' 'defensive,' and 'a key part of diversification strategy.' Academics argue learnedly about 'synergy' in acquisitions. And there is even a journal devoted to mergers and acquisitions.*

In isolated incidents, growth and diversification by means of acquisitions has led to Justice Department investigation. But, generally, the progress toward more and bigger acquisitions seems inevitable, and socially and economically acceptable. It's about time, therefore, that someone took a close look at this royal progress and asked the question, 'Has the king any clothes?' Or, putting it more plainly, are companies really getting what they paid for?

Research aims

This article is based on discussions with top executives of 22 companies, and draws on their experience in acquiring and managing a total of 181

* *Mergers and Acquisitions* is published by Mergers and Acquisitions, Inc., 1725 K Street, N.W., Washington, D.C.

companies in the period 1960–1965. It audits in detail the *actual results* of 69 acquisitions made by 20 of the 22 companies sampled.

Research scope and methods

The research was divided into two parts – a survey of the management literature and field interviews with executives of 22 companies.

It focused on the experience of companies two to seven years following an acquisition, since that amount of time is required for an acquisition to become stable enough to be evaluated accurately.

The field research was done with the generous cooperation of 25 top-level executives. Company chief executives, senior vice presidents for finance, controllers, treasurers, directors of corporate planning, and directors of acquisitions all contributed their time and experience.

The industries covered included textiles, electronics, communications, automotive supply, marketing, recreation products, toiletries, food, aviation products, tobacco, finance, retailing, rubber goods, building supplies, and chemicals. The sales volume of these companies ranged from $25 million to $2 billion. Acquisitions were classified as follows:

Horizontal – Same industry as buying company, with approximately the same customers and suppliers.

Vertical integration – Major supplier or customer of the buying company and in the same industry.

Concentric marketing – Same customer types as buying company but different technology.

Concentric technology – Same technology as buying company but different customer types.

Conglomerate – Customers and technology different from those of buying company.

The names of the companies contributing to this study have been withheld in order to protect their confidence. Instead, they are designated by initials, such as 'Company M,' and their various subsidiaries are differentiated by subscripts, such as 'M_1,' 'M_2,' and so on.

The scope and methods of the research are described in the ruled insert ['Research scope and methods']. Two considerations influenced the approach which I took:

1 The top executives I interviewed seemed uneasy about their companies' acquisition activities. In the use of mergers, their companies had a fashionable tactic, and one which looked good to stockholders – either as a strategy for growth or as a defensive move. But the executives were uneasy about the relatively high degree of risk associated with investment in an acquisition compared with an equivalent investment in, say, a new plant. They wished to know what the 'track record' of other companies had been, before attempting to undertake or expand their own acquisition programs. And if there were any general rules to be learned from the experience of others – either about avoiding pitfalls or about taking positive action to help ensure success – then they wanted to know about them.

2 The research seemed important from the standpoint of testing out unproven academic hypotheses. For example, to what extent do acquisitions lead to economies of scale? Can the concept of synergy, so widely held, be proved out in practice? And is there any relationship between the type of acquisition and its success or failure?

Performance patterns

Analysis of the data gathered in the study shows some interesting facts, many of which are summarized in Exhibit 16.1. Although, as earlier indicated, a larger sample is needed for definitive statements, it is quite probable that these results present a fair picture of the total acquisition movement in the United States.

Varying failure rates

Exhibit 16.2 shows the breakdown of the sample among the various categories of acquisition, as well as the incidence of failure for each type. (Acquisition types are defined in the ruled insert 'Research scope and methods.')

Interestingly, the greatest proportion (45%) of acquisitions consists of the conglomerate type. This suggests that the move to diversify and spread risk is well under way. But this strategy is in itself risky, as the exhibit shows, since 42% of all the failures occurred in this group. Risk reduction evidently bears its own risks!

The proportion of horizontal acquisitions is surprisingly high (25%), inasmuch as this type is the one most likely to be accused of having a restraining effect on trade. However, the Justice Department does not generally discourage horizontal mergers among smaller units of an

Exhibit 16.1 Results of mergers

Key to synergy scores: H = High   M = Medium   L = Low   O = Nil

Subsidiary code name	Date of merger	Type of merger	Performance	Management of acquired company — Organization	Management of acquired company — Subsidiary manager reports to:	Sales volume as percent of parent sales volume	Synergy released in organization [ease of achievement] — Motivation	Synergy released in organization [ease of achievement] — Efficiency	Synergy released in other functions [ease of achievement/dollar payout] — Finance	Marketing	Technology (including R&D)	Production
A_1	1960	Conglomerate	Failure	Autonomous; then grouped	President at first; then group vice president	0.5%	O	M	H/$L	O/$O	O/$O	O/$O
A_2	1961	Horizontal	Success	Grouped	Group vice president	2.0%	M	M	H/$L	L/$L	O/$O	O/$O
B_1	1963	Conglomerate	Success	Autonomous		29.0%						
B_2	1963	Conglomerate	Success	Autonomous	'Face to face' meetings with holding company	9.0%	H	M	H/$H	M/$M	O/$O	L/$L
B_3	1963	Conglomerate	Success	Autonomous (formed own group)	executive team	31.0%						
B_4	1965	Conglomerate	Success	Autonomous		4.2%						
C_1	1965	Concentric technology	Success	Autonomous	President	7.0%	H	M	H/$H	M/$L	L/$L	O/$O
D_1	1964	Conglomerate	Success	Autonomous	Senior vice president	3.0%	H	O	H/$H	L/$M	O/$O	O/$O
E_1	1960	Concentric marketing	Failure	Merged with parent	Group vice president at first, then president, North America	6.7%	O	M	H/$L	M/$O	O/$O	O/$O
E_2	1963	Concentric marketing	Failure	Merged with E_1	President, North America	0.2%	O	M	H/$O	M/$O	O/$O	O/$O
E_3	1963	Concentric marketing	Failure	Merged with parent	President of international corporation	0.4%	O	M	H/$L	L/$O	O/$O	O/$O
E_4	1962	Horizontal	Success	Grouped with existing company in Canada		3.6%	M	L	H/$H	M/$M	L/$L	O/$O
F_1	1965	Conglomerate	Success	Parent company officer appointed chairman of subsidiary's executive committee	Senior vice president	12.3%*	M	O	H/$H	O/$O	O/$O	O/$O
F_2	1964	Conglomerate	Success			5.3%**	M	O	H/$H	O/$O	O/$O	O/$H
F_3	1965	Conglomerate	Success			1.8%*	M	O	H/$H	O/$O	O/$O	O/$O
G_1	1962	Conglomerate	Success	Grouped	Group vice president	16.0%	H	L	H/$H	L/$O	L/$M	O/$O
G_2	1965	Conglomerate	Failure	Grouped & merged with another company	Group vice president	10.0%	H	L	H/$L	M/$L	M/$L	L/$O
H_1	1965	Vertical	Success	Autonomous	Area vice president	2.0%	M	L	H/$O	M/$O	O/$O	H/$H
I_1	1961	Horizontal	Success	Merged	Senior vice president	35.0%	O	L	H/$H	H/$H	M/$L	M/$L
I_2	1963	Concentric marketing	Success	Merged	Senior vice president	12.0%	H	L	L/$L	H/$M	M/$L	L/$L
J_1	1961	Concentric technology	Failure; then success	Autonomous; then merged	President at first; now area vice president	29.0%	H	L	L/$L	H/$H	L/$M	L/$L

Case	Year	Type	Outcome	Organization	Position	Net income*							
K_1	1961	Concentric technology	Success	Autonomous	Snior vice president, operations	37.0%	H	L	H/$M	L/$L	L/$L	H/$L	O/$O
K_2	1965	Concentric technology	Success	Autonomous	Senior vice president, operations	66.0%	H	L	H/$M	L/$L	L/$L	M/$M	O/$O
L_1	1961	Horizontal	Success	Merged	Executive committee	8.0%	M	M	H/$O	O/$O	O/$O	O/$O	O/$O
L_2	1965	Horizontal	Failure	Merged	Executive committee	10.5%	M	M	H/$O	O/$O	O/$O	O/$O	O/$O
M_1	1962	Conglomerate	Failure	Autonomous	Executive committee & 3 separate officers	1.0%	L	L	H/$L	O/$O	O/$O	M/$O	?/$O
N_1	1965	Horizontal	Success	Merged	Division manager	0.2%	H	H	H/$M	H/$H	H/$M	M/$M	M/$M
N_2	1964	Horizontal	Failure	Autonomous; then merged	Corporate headquarters at first; then division manager	0.3%	O	O	L/$O	L/$L	L/$L	L/$O	O/$O
N_3	1964	Horizontal	Success	Merged	Division manager	0.5%	M	M	M/$M	H/$H	H/$H	H/$H	L/$L
N_4	1961	Concentric technology	Failure	Grouped as a division	Group vice president at first; then corporate vice president	0.6%	O	L	O/$O	O/$O	M/$O	H/$O	H/$O
N_5	1961	Concentric technology	Failure	Grouped as a division	Group vice president at first; then corporate vice president	0.6%	O	L	O/$O	O/$O	M/$O	H/$O	H/$O
N_6	1961	Concentric technology	Failure	Grouped as a division	Group vice president at first; then corporate vice president	0.5%	O	L	O/$O	O/$O	M/$O	H/$O	H/$O
N_7	1962	Conglomerate	Success	Merged	Division manager	0.6%	L	H	M/$L	M/$M	M/$M	L/$L	M/$M
N_8	1964	Concentric technology	Failure	Merged; then autonomous	Division manager at first; then group president	1.8%	O	L	O/$O	O/$O	O/$O	M/$O	O/$O
N_9	1965	Conglomerate	Success	Autonomous	Group vice president	6.0%	M	M	H/$H	O/$O	O/$O	L/$L	O/$O
N_{10}	1965	Conglomerate	Success	Grouped		—	L	M	H/$H	M/$M	M/$M	L/$L	M/$M
N_{11}	1965	Conglomerate	Success	Grouped		2.0%	L	M	H/$M	M/$M	M/$M	L/$L	M/$M
N_{12}	1965	Conglomerate	Success	Grouped	Group manager	—	L	M	H/$M	M/$M	M/$M	L/$L	O/$O
O_1	1963	Vertical	Failure; then success	Autonomous; then merged	Parent company president	1.0%	O	L	H/$L	H/$L	L/$O	L/$O	O/$O
P_1	1961	Concentric marketing	Success	Autonomous; then grouped		0.1%	H	H	H/$L	H/$L	O/$O	O/$O	H/$L
P_2	1960	Conglomerate	Success			10.0%	H	M	H/$H	H/$H	L/$L	L/$L	M/$H
P_3	1960	Conglomerate	Failure		President at first; after 1965, group vice president	0.5%	H	M	H/$H	H/$H	L/$L	L/$L	H/$H
P_4	1960	Conglomerate	Success			2.0%	H	H	H/$H	H/$H	L/$L	L/$L	H/$H
P_5	1960	Horizontal	Success			3.0%	H	H	H/$H	H/$H	M/$H	M/$H	H/$H
P_6	1960	Concentric technology	Success			2.0%	M	M	H/$H	H/$H	L/$L	L/$L	H/$M
Q_1	1962	Conglomerate	Failure	Autonomous	Two different parent company executives	1.0%	O	L	H/$L	H/$L	O/$O	O/$O	O/$O
R_1	1965	Concentric marketing	Success	Grouped semiautonomous	Group manager	10.0%	M	M	H/$H	H/$H	M/$L	O/$O	M/$H
R_2	1965	Conglomerate	Failure		(Several reporting relationships)	0.4%	O	O	H/$L	H/$L	H/$M	O/$O	O/$O
S_1	1965	Conglomerate	Success		Product group vice president†	2.7%	H		—	—	—	—	—
S_2	1963	Conglomerate	Success		Product group manager†	3.8%		M	H/$H	L/$H	O/$O	O/$O	O/$O
S_3	1964	Conglomerate	Success		Product group manager†				—	—	—	—	—

* Net income as % of parent net income.

Exhibit 16.1 Results of mergers (continued)

Key to synergy scores: H = High   M = Medium   L = Low   O = Nil

Subsidiary code name	Date of merger	Type of merger	Performance	Management of acquired company — Organization	Subsidiary manager reports to:	Sales volume as percent of parent sales volume	Synergy released in organization [ease of achievement] — Motivation	Efficiency	Synergy released in other functions [ease of achievement/dollar payout] — Finance	Marketing	Technology (including R&D)	Production
S_4	1963	Concentric marketing	Success		Group vice president at first; then product group manager	4.6%	—	—	—	—	—	—
S_5	1963	Horizontal	Success		Product group manager†	2.2%	H	H	H/$H	M/$H	O/$O	O/$O
S_6	1965	Conglomerate	Failure		Various group vice presidents	0.1%	L	O	H/$L	O/$O	O/$O	O/$O
S_7	1965	Conglomerate	Success		Executive vice president	3.3%	—	—	—	—	—	—
S_8	1963	Conglomerate	Success		Product group manager†	0.7%	—	—	—	—	—	—
S_9	1961	Conglomerate	Success		Group vice president at first; then product group manager		H	H	H/$H	L/$H	O/$O	L/$L
S_{10}	1963	Horizontal	Success		Group executive	3.1%	—	—	—	—	—	—
S_{11}	1964	Horizontal	Success		Product group manager†	0.6%	—	—	—	—	—	—
S_{12}	1961	Horizontal	Success		Product group manager†	1.8%	—	—	—	—	—	—
S_{13}	1962	Concentric marketing	Failure		Product group manager†	0.3%	M	H	H/$M	M/$M-$L	M/$H	H/$H
S_{14}	1965	Horizontal	Success		Group vice president	1.8%	—	—	—	—	—	—
S_{15}	1964	Concentric technology	Success		Product general manager	0.1%	—	—	—	—	—	—
S_{16}	1965	Horizontal	Failure; then success		Product group manager†	0.1%	M	M	H/$L	M/$M	O/$O	O/$O
S_{17}	1964	Horizontal	Success		Product group manager†	0.1%	H	M	H/$H	M/$H	O/$O	O/$O
S_{18}	1965	Concentric marketing	Failure		Product group manager†	0.01%	—	—	—	—	—	—
S_{19}	1965	Horizontal	Success		(Merged with existing division)	0.6%	—	—	—	—	—	—
T_1	1963	Conglomerate	Failure	Various forms of grouping	Vice president, automotive group	1.1%	H	O	M/$L	L/$L	O/$O	O/$O
T_2	1960	Conglomerate	Success	Semiautonomous	Executive vice president	4.0%	H	M	H/$H	M/$M	M/$M	L/$L

† After period of autonomy

Exhibit 16.2 Which types of acquisition have the highest incidence of failure? [As reported by executives]

Acquisition type	Percent of total	Percent of failures
Vertical integration	3%	0%
Horizontal	25	11
Concentric marketing	13	26
Concentric technology	14	21
Conglomerate	45	42

industry. The results shown here are probably indicative of a continuing movement among firms with smaller market shares in the direction of merging with larger companies to improve their industry standing. The encouragingly low incidence of failure in this group is probably due to the fact that the parent company is familiar with the market and the technology.

The greatest incidence of failure occurs in the concentric acquisition. Those companies with common customers, the 'concentric marketing' group, represent only 13% of the sample, but their failures constitute 26% of the sample total. Similarly, the 'concentric technology' group had 21% of the failures, although it represented only 14% of the sample. Apparently, what happens is that the parent company, feeling it 'knows the market backwards,' gets lulled into a false sense of security and neglects the technology aspect, or vice versa.

The *type* of merger, however, is not the determining factor in the success or failure of an acquisition. The primary cause must be sought elsewhere.

Size mismatches & organization

Several executives attributed acquisition failures to mismatches of size. For example, frequent comments were made to the effect that the acquired company 'was so small no one in corporate headquarters could get interested in it,' or 'we couldn't get these little entrepreneurs to think like big businessmen.'

In 84% of the failures, as previously stated, the acquired company's sales volume is less than 2% of the parent company's at the time of acquisition. Certainly, where there is a great difference in size between the parent company and the acquired company, management needs to be particularly thorough in developing its plans for integrating the new company. As an example of the consequences of mismatch when the acquired company is not carefully meshed with its new parent, take this comment from a top manager in Company N:

> This little group of companies didn't cost much to buy, but since 1961 I reckon they have lost us $10 million, plus the drain on management time.

Size mismatch *can* be overcome with the use of the right organizational structure and reporting relationships, as we shall see later, but frequently the wrong action seems to be taken. It is worth noting that in 81% of the failures, the organization structure has been changed – usually in the direction of greater consolidation – or else the chief executive's reporting relationship has been altered. The danger is that such action will create confusion at the subsidiary level and a lack of knowledge at the parent company level – two factors which help to explain the failures of these acquisitions. Moreover, such changes are usually symptomatic of a lack of adequate planning at an earlier stage. What usually happens is that when failure appears imminent, re-organization efforts are made to 'try to get the mixture right.' But it is poor planning, and poor appraisal of executive talent, which caused the mixture of the two organizations to go wrong in the first place.

Synergy – fact or fiction?

Everyone knows about synergy. Putting 2 and 2 together to make 5 sounds like 'a good 20% return' to the businessman. But do such happy results ever actually occur? To quote an experienced acquirer, the senior vice president for finance of Company K:

> We are quite skeptical about the existence of synergy. When we are testing the potential earnings of a company, we don't place any value on the benefits which might accrue from synergy.

The survey probed both the ease with which synergy is released and the dollar value of the synergy in each of five business functions. The objective results contradict the usual notions about synergy.

Most managers would consider the potential for synergy highest in the case of production mergers. This is because of the economies of scale that can be achieved as a consequence of longer runs, the increased purchasing power made possible (quantity discounts), the justification of more expensive, more efficient machinery, and the opportunity to close down inefficient lines and transfer production to other factories.

Technology would appear to be the next most profitable area for mergers because of the possibilities of sharing R&D know-how and of transferring technical processes. Mergers of marketing organizations, where there are opportunities to sell two complementary product lines through one distribution channel and with one sales force, would seem to have the third greatest synergistic potential. And mergers in the organization area might rank fourth, since they provide opportunities for eliminating duplicated functions and releasing human creativity through improved motivation. Finally, financial mergers appear to offer possibilities of achieving synergy, since additional capital may enable high-risk, high-payoff projects to get off the ground; and, with two sets of assets as collateral, borrowing power goes up and the cost of money goes down. But there was a general impression that the synergistic potential of financial mergers is not as high as that of the other types just mentioned.

However, the research findings show that practice just about reverses hypothesis. As Exhibit 16.3 shows, far from producing the biggest payoff, production and technology are at the bottom of the list of dollar

Exhibit 16.3 Which functions produce the biggest dollar payoff from synergy after acquisition?
[As scored by executives]

Type of merger	Finance	Marketing	Technology [including R&D]	Production
Conglomerate	100	58	20	32
Concentric technology	100	72	72	27
Concentric marketing	100	100	57	72
Horizontal	96	100	41	29
All categories	100	74	33	36

Note: Executives scored the dollar payoff of synergy as 'high,' 'medium,' 'low,' or 'none' for each acquisition case. The scores were converted into arbitrary units, with 100 representing the score for the highest rated function. Thus the table shows *relative* payoff values for each function. Vertical integration is excluded because the sample is too small. Organizational efficiencies are excluded from the payoff area because they are too difficult to quantify, and management motivation is similarly excluded because it is the prime cause of the dollar payoffs in the other areas.

producers through synergy; marketing shows up better; and finance is clearly the area where synergy has the biggest payoff.

Finance: Why should finance have the greatest payoff? Part of the answer is revealed in Exhibit 16.4, which relates to the ease of synergy release. In financial mergers, synergy is achieved with greater ease than in any other type of merger. This is understandable when we consider that additional funds are much easier to obtain when the asset backing of the merged companies is larger. And the cost of capital – due to lower interest rates and longer repayment times – can be lowered. Frequently, too, the parent company has surplus capital which can be used to finance what the senior vice president for finance of Company T calls 'the subsidiaries' frustration list' of projects previously denied funds. The resultant growth usually occurs in the area of high-margin sales and may lead the subsidiary to the 'take-off' point of generating its own substantial profits. Little wonder, then, that top managers see financial synergy as having achieved the greatest payoff.

Other functions: Marketing seems to have the next biggest dollar payoff. This again is related to the ease of achievement. It is not difficult to train a sales force to sell another product line, or to get the distribution channels to handle the acquired company's products (although several horror stories were told to me about product lines which produced the opposite of a synergetic effect in the distribution channels or among the sales force). Advertising economies can still be found. And it is relatively easy to save money in physical distribution, too, when one is able to take advantage of lower unit costs or to eliminate duplicate field sales offices. Furthermore, product lines sometimes reinforce each other, as in the case of Company I and its subsidiary, I_2, where the previously separate product lines are now marketed together as a package deal to appeal to one sector of the leisure market.

Technology and production – the two areas which theoretically should pay off most handsomely – do not do so in fact. Although the whole point of the technology-based concentric merger is to pool R&D knowledge and to transfer any specialized process know-how, the actual dollar payoff of so doing is rated, in Exhibit 16.3, below that of finance and equal to that of marketing.

With regard to the area where traditional economics suggests that synergy should be greatest – namely, in production – many of the managers echoed these comments of an executive of Company I:

Economies of scale are a highly overrated concept. They do occur. For example, certain technologies are possible when certain volume breaks occur; that is, the trade-off between hand labor and mechanical methods is worthwhile at certain volume levels. But most of the so-called fixed costs are actually volume variable, so that the profit leverage in expanding production volume in one factory or the·other after acquisition is actually limited.

Motivation & efficiency: One of the most interesting aspects of Exhibit 16.4 relates to the gains in organizational efficiency and the extent to which the motivation of the subsidiary managers is seen to be changed. (These payoffs can be included in Exhibit 16.4 because we are dealing here with opinions and impressions, not financial performance.)

There are two ways in which organization change can release synergy. One way is to centralize control, legal, public relations, and other services at the corporate level. To quote an executive of Company T, this move 'frees up the managers of subsidiaries to do the things they are best at.' The second way of releasing synergy is to change the management environment so that previously conservative or frustrated men are now motivated to become managers of change and to make more effective and profitable use of resources.

One cautionary note should be sounded in connection with the findings obtained in this study. The sample deals with companies acquired two to seven years ago. It probably takes longer to effect production economies than any other type. For example, closing down a factory or transferring a production line is a lengthy process. Conceivably, therefore, the relatively low dollar payoff in production may in time improve as major changes are decided and implemented. Also, conglomerates constitute 45% of the sample, and these acquisitions by definition do not combine companies with the exact same production or technological skills. In these particular cases, the synergistic effects in production or technology cannot be expected to rank very high.

Causes of success & failure

What are the primary reasons that acquisitions succeed or fail? While the judgments of the executives interviewed cannot be quantified, a common pattern or thread runs through their beliefs. This pattern can be summarized in six main points.

Exhibit 16.4 In which function of a business is it easiest to release synergy? [As scored by executives]

Type of merger	Finance	Organization			Technology [including R&D]	Production
		Motivation	Efficiency	Marketing		
Conglomerate	100	67	42	42	18	24
Concentric technology	65	70	55	75	100	65
Concentric marketing	100	52	79	74	21	47
Horizontal	100	73	70	67	33	24
All categories	100	68	55	59	33	34

Note: Scores are tabulated as explained in Exhibit 16.3

1 *Managers of change*

In the time period immediately following the merger, the quality of management talent determines the success or failure of the venture, and it is at this time that careful planning allows the synergy potential to be released, if it is released at all.

An interesting finding of the survey is that few top managers regard synergy as being inherent in a situation; most feel that synergy is a product or result of superior management. As the director of acquisitions in Company S puts it, 'The key variable for success is managing the company better after the acquisition than it was managed before.'

As for the ease of achieving synergy release, consider this comment of the senior vice president for operations of Company T: 'Don't think it's hard to release synergy; it's not. It's damn near impossible.' This executive went on to say that it required stock option incentives in front and 'a red hot poker behind' to motivate his line managers sufficiently to do the hard work, make the changes, and produce a synergistic effect.

It does not matter whether these managers of change are provided by the parent company or by the subsidiary. But whichever company provides them, the supply of managerial talent must be carefully husbanded. I was told by an executive of the highly successful Company G:

> We appraised our position when we started on the acquisition trail and found that our major strength was in management, whereas we had a negative working capital position. So we used preferred stock to buy companies in trouble at distress prices. Then we put our superior management in and turned the situations around. The results were so successful that we are now able to borrow long-term and pay for our acquisitions in cash. Now we have a very positive working capital position – *but no managers to spare.* So we buy well-managed companies these days.

Sometimes a pruning operation to remove dead wood at the top is necessary. Many of the success stories with acquisitions started this way. By the same token, failures are often characterized by the presence of old or conservative managements who will not, or cannot, change.

2 *Skills for the task*

The sum of management skills must be greater than the joint management task. A common mistake is to underestimate the demands a merger will make on management time; executives erroneously believe that, because the company to be acquired is smaller than the buying company, its problems will require proportionately less management time. The consequences of believing in this fallacy are revealed in these comments by the senior vice president of Company Q:

> We made the great mistake with Q_1 of thinking that its problems – and therefore its demands on our top management time – were proportional to its size. It didn't get the attention it needed, and it died on us.

How, then, to guard against the danger of not having enough competent managers to do the job? Consider:

• The first step is to have a policy based on recognition of the problem. Note how managerial manpower resources are specifically taken into account in the strategy of Company K, as described by one of its executives:

> We just don't have enough managers up here at headquarters to send in to turn a poor situation around. Our policy therefore is one of autonomy. We buy the company for its management. We don't intend to push managers around after we have acquired a company. We will be neither wreckers nor resurrectors.

• An acquisition policy must include some good method of appraising subsidiary company management before the purchase is made. An executive of Company T, which is a highly successful conglomerate, describes the 'track record' approach used by his company:

> We can't spare anybody from headquarters to go in and operate a company. So the managements of the companies we acquire have to have a good track record – on the down side of the business cycle as well as the up side. Their performance, judged on the basis of return on assets, must be as good as, or better than, the industry average. We buy demonstrated performance – because we don't have enough spare management talent to do anything else.

• A final refinement is to make an independent audit of subsidiary management's competence before the merger takes place. This step is expensive, and it involves delay. But it reinforces the 'track record' approach, providing a detailed evaluation of individual managers. This is how an executive of Company F, which diversified from a service to a manufacturing industry, describes his company's reasons for using this approach:

We couldn't tell you which men have what competence level. Sure, we know if the company is a leader or laggard in its industry. But we don't have the industrial know-how to say that Jones is weak while Smith is strong. So what we do is to hire some consultants to make an organization study. The company we're negotiating with invites the consulting firm in, but we pick up the tab. After the study, we know whom we'll want to keep, and where we'll need fresh talent.

3 *Management relationships*

The most successful acquisitions seem to be distinguished by three characteristics in the relationships between the parent company management and the subsidiary management.

'*Riding herd*': First, the parent company appoints a top executive to 'ride herd' *immediately* after the acquisition. The necessity of appointing a key person to this post, and of doing so right away, can be seen in this account of Company H's experience with H_2 (a subsidiary not included in Exhibit 16.1 because of insufficient data), as related by an executive of the parent company:

> When Company H bought H_2, it discovered several skeletons in the closet. There had been a good deal of dishonesty at the time of negotiations. Luckily, Mr. X [a parent company vice president] was assigned the responsibility for the company. We didn't see him around H for several months – he was full time in the acquired company. And now H_2 is coming around. Experience shows us how important key people are in the acquired company, and so are those assigned to ride herd on the new acquisition.

Reporting procedures: The second characteristic of successful mergers is that the reporting relationship between key people in both the acquired company and the parent is immediately made clear. When subsequent changes in reporting relationships occur, they are made on a planned basis.

There are many different ways of handling this matter after a company has been acquired. Clearly, there is no one ideal method; the approach chosen must be tailored to the environmental conditions encountered and the capabilities of the executives concerned. What *must* be avoided, however, is the setting up of unclear reporting relationships and the temptation to change them often; such action was present in 81% of the failures. An executive in Company M states:

> During the first three years, Company M left the original top manager of M_1 in command. In that time he reported to *three* different people or committees in Company M. And he had two different parent company managers ride herd on him.

When Company R acquired its subsidiary, R_2, there was split reporting in the R&D function. In this case, as in many other cases of failure, R_2 was geographically remote from its parent. An executive from Company R reports:

> We had an extraordinary situation. R_2 was spending a great deal of money on R&D and producing nothing. The R&D department in R_2 was headed by two men, neither of whom would speak to the other. Each reported to a different R location – one man reported to the engineering department, and the other to the research department.

Plans & controls: The third distinguishing characteristic of successful acquisitions is the approach of the buying companies to installing a system of controls. At the outset they place major emphasis on *information reporting* rather than on budgets. This system is put into operation immediately. But no hard-and-fast rule is followed. Successful companies vary their requirements according to the situation.

4 *Reactors vs. planners*

The study shows a distinct difference in the success rate of companies with a strategy for growth and diversification, of which an acquisition program may be only a part, and that of companies which merely react to opportunities to buy.

The two different approaches were neatly characterized by one executive as 'crystal ball mergers' and 'golf course mergers,' respectively.

'Golf course' mergers: The react-to-opportunity approach is illustrated by the actions of Company O. According to one of its executives:

> Representatives of O_1 came to us with a proposal that we buy their company. It seemed a pretty good idea. O_1's product was a major part of the manufacturing cost of sales of our product, and I could see the

economies to be obtained from this vertical integration. The research people in O_1 looked pretty good – all kinds of academic qualifications. And the product samples they gave us all worked beautifully.

'So we bought the company and gave its product range the full marketing treatment. O_1's products sold through our sales force like hotcakes – once. Then the complaints came in. The manufactured items just didn't meet the specs that the laboratory 'one-offs' had. And all those Ph.D.'s weren't worth a damn when it came to making the production item perform. Eventually we had to close down the company, redesign the product, and redo the production engineering. Now we make the line ourselves, under our own roof. It's a success; but was the effort worth it?

Many companies still operate – and quite successfully – on this philosophy. Nevertheless, the 'golf course' approach seems to be going slowly out of style.

'Crystal ball' mergers: There is a noticeable trend toward treating acquisitions as a part of the overall corporate strategy. Decisions are influenced by the answers given to these questions: What business are we in? What business *should* we be in? Instead of reacting to offers to sell, in other words, management focuses on the recommendations made by such a person as a director of corporate planning; he indicates desirable fields for entry and suggests specific companies whose purchase would open the gate to these fields. Here [is an] example as described by [an executive] I interviewed:

Company N used to count mainly on reacting to offers to sell. All this has changed. I now have a plan which details the areas of greatest potential. These are not expressed in terms of products but, rather, in terms of human needs. For example, we don't say that closed-circuit TV or teaching machines are the products with the greatest potential. Instead, we see the area of educational aids as a whole as the greatest field of potential. Closed-circuit TV and learning machines are just two ways of entering this field. If we are going to offer a well-rounded product line, however, we are going to have to acquire much more competence than these two items will give us. For instance, we will need a book publishing company, someone who can write programmed learning texts, and so on.

There is probably a greater chance of success when the responsibility for developing an acquisition program is some top executive's main job – resting with, say, a vice president of corporate development, rather than with a senior vice president of finance. The reason is that when a corporate officer has his own full-time job to do in addition to this new job, the task of evaluating a proposed acquisition – from the standpoint both of its 'fit' with corporate goals and of its intrinsic worth – can easily be skimped. As the president of Company P said, 'An acquisition is equally as important as building a new plant. But most managements do not give the acquisition a fraction of the time or the analysis that goes into putting up a new plant.'

5 *Effective criteria*

A key factor for success is having acquisition criteria that are consistent and that are rigorously applied. Otherwise, acquisition decisions are likely to be distorted by impulses and emotions, and acquiring companies victimized by the environment which typically surrounds purchase negotiations. This environment, with its atmosphere of necessary secrecy, of cards being held close to the chest, and the outside world (especially the financial press) being kept firmly at bay, has a low emotional flash point. The acquiring company is playing for high stakes; the performance record of the managers concerned will be greatly affected by the results of the deal. The management team of the potential subsidiary is wondering what will happen to it afterwards, and perhaps is playing for a high payoff (where the managers own the stock). Unlike most sale-purchase situations with high risk (e.g., house buying, or bidding on large contracts), the lifetime careers of top executives are bound up in the results.

It is hardly an atmosphere conducive to rigorous application of objective criteria. Yet successful acquirers manage to do a thorough job. The first, and most important, task is to develop a set of acquisition criteria beforehand. Armed with this, the successful acquiring company *selects* rather than *reacts*. An example is Company T. A top executive of that company outlines its criteria as follows:

> 1   Management's track record in the company being considered for acquisition should be better than the industry average in terms of return on assets - on the down side, as well as on the up side, of business cycles.
> 2   We will only buy into old industries which are 'nonglamor.'
> 3   We will buy companies with low price-earnings ratios. [The actual average in this case is 6.5 times earnings!]
> 4   We seek to buy assets which are readily convertible into cash.
> 5   The top executive of the company in question *must* stay on.

6 These shall be our minimum sales volume criteria:
(a) For entry into a new field – $100 million.
(b) For entry into a new market – $20 million.
(c) To round out a product line, if already in market – $1 million.

Companies which have made a success of their acquisitions are distinguished by their top managements' ability to weigh the strengths and weaknesses of potential acquisitions in a short period of time. Time pressures are great for two reasons. First of all, the secrecy necessarily surrounding negotiations dictates that lengthy visits and conversations with the top management of a potential subsidiary be ruled out. Secondly, long delays may be costly. As Company T's senior vice president of finance says, 'The longer we wait, the less chance there is of making a deal' – and the survey results certainly bear him out. Only an estimated 10% of the companies were 'courted' over several months. If the pre-merger evaluation is not thorough, however, postmarital problems can result. One regret frequently voiced is, 'If only subsidiary managers looked as good now, when they are on our side of the table, as they did on theirs when we were bargaining.'

The need for both speed and thoroughness poses an apparent dilemma. Fortunately, it has been neatly solved by the more experienced companies. One technique often used where both companies' stocks are publicly traded is to peg the level at which any stock will be exchanged, using as the basis the figures put out by the company to be bought. Since the 'exchange rate' between the two stocks is fixed, a leisurely – and public – evaluation of the opportunity will not cause the acquiring company any additional expense. Room can be left for subsequent adjustment, usually on a contingent basis.

Another technique is for management to hold a portion of the purchase price 'in escrow' until the acquired company makes the profits it has forecasted (assuming such a forecast enters into purchase price negotiations). For instance, Company R pays the price its estimators feel is 'right.' Then, if and when the acquired company reaches the profit target on which it based its asking price (which is invariably higher), Company R pays over the difference between the bid price and the price asked.

6 *Analysis of future needs*

Finally, this study shows that *successful companies make a careful analysis of their subsidiaries' future requirements for parent company funds*. Statements

of financial results of a number of the acquisitions were compared with
the returns projected at merger time. This provided a check on the
failure-success rating given the acquisition (see Exhibit 16.1). But it also
brought to light a really significant finding – that is, the great extent to
which the future capital requirements of the acquired company are often
underestimated. As an executive of Company K noted sadly:

> We made the sales and profit targets for K_1 easily. But I underestimated
> the capital requirements of the new company by a factor of two.

Clearly, companies acquiring smaller companies in the future would do
well to pay more attention to their estimates of the capital required for
plant and machinery, as well as that needed to finance additional sales.
This finding reinforces the earlier one on the necessity of establishing
appropriate plans and controls. When decent budgetary control has not
been set up, it is all too easy for the new acquisition to say, in effect,
'Papa is rich. Let's go buy four new tape-controlled machine tools.' And
when the investment half of the ROI fraction goes up, in such cases, the
ROI itself usually goes down.

Conclusion

What, then, are the general implications of these research findings for
management? The study points to the following suggestions for
analyzing an acquisition:

● Above all, match the managers of change available with the tasks in the
newly merged enterprise. This requirement makes it important to:

1 Identify the nature of the management tasks.
2 Evaluate the managers in the new organization against the tasks to be
  accomplished, and decide which managers should be let go.
3 Specify which managers in the buying corporation can be spared to take
  care of the new acquisition, and decide whom to hire in addition.
4 Also motivate the new team to manage change.

● Specify the control system to be used, and stick to it. Name the top
executive who is to ride herd. Put in the appropriate planning and control
systems. Decide on the right organization structure, keeping in mind that
problems of size mismatch can probably be avoided by grouping the new
organization with other subsidiaries having similar product lines, marketing
structures, or other vital operations. (In this event, get group management
involved at the negotiating stage.)

● Allocate the strategic planning responsibility, preferably on a full-time basis, to a top-level officer, and ask him to develop acquisition criteria which are consistent with overall corporate policy. When a specific acquisition opportunity arises which looks interesting, ask each executive in charge of a major function for a formal appraisal of the company.

● In evaluating the ROI projections for the new company:

1 Treat the forecasts of production and technology dollar payoff with skepticism.

2 Make sure that the marketing synergisms (especially those expected to arise out of combining the two companies' sales forces, distribution channels, and advertising) can be realized in practice.

3 Give the greatest weight to the dollar payoff expected in the finance area (through cheaper borrowing, liquidating unused assets, and financing new ventures formerly starved for capital).

4 Finally, if the acquiring corporation is new to the game, why not tap the skills and experience of the sophisticated acquirers, especially their knowledge in the area of risk reduction at negotiation time?

Part V

Calls to Arms

Introduction

OSCAR Wilde once said, 'It is personalities, not principles, that move the age.' We have already seen many names that support this hypothesis. Personalities such as Levitt, Drucker, Porter, Ohmae and Chandler have certainly had a part to play in 'moving the age' over the past 30 years.

In this section, we look at the work of some observers and commentators who, in most cases unexpectedly, have left an indelible mark on management and business thinking.

In 1978 I completed a consulting assignment with two colleagues that was concerned with identifying the characteristics of those corporations that seemed to be outstanding innovators in their fields. We travelled around the world and interviewed executives representing many industries and many cultures.

After we had presented our conclusions, my colleagues suggested that it would be interesting to pursue this research and write a short book about our conclusions. I was not enthusiastic but told them to go ahead, without getting their expectations too high. Nine million copies later, Tom Peters' and Bob Waterman's book, *In Search of Excellence*, has been translated into 16 languages and has become a classic whose simple findings have given birth to several new generations of ideas with their concomitant truisms – 'stick to your knitting', 'stay close to the customer', 'simple form, lean staff' and 'hands on, value driven'. While these sayings did not perhaps originate in the book, they certainly became well established credos for management action as a result of its success.

Another idea that was rejuvenated – or, some may say, resurrected – by a writer whose work appears in this Part began life in Japan just after the end of World War II. A somewhat obscure academic, George Deming, went to Japan at the request of the US occupying government concerned with rebuilding the country and introduced the notion of the importance of quality. Not unlike those of many prophets, his words passed relatively unnoticed 'in his own land'. The opposite was the case in Japan, and, metaphorically speaking, monuments to his contribution exist in almost every factory in that country. *Quality is Free* appeared some 29 years later. In it, Philip Crosby has tried to do for the West what Deming was so successful in doing for the East.

While *In Search of Excellence* clearly had an upbeat message, full of sometimes embarrassingly simple home truths, 'Managing Our Way to Economic Decline', written by two distinguished Harvard Business School professors, was the synopsis of a carefully researched programme designed to find some explanations for the depressing performance of the US economy. Its message might be paraphrased as follows: 'You have no one to blame but yourselves – and no one but yourselves can get you out of this mess!'. A useful message to post in board rooms around the world, perhaps.

When I first arrived in Great Britain in 1962, I came across a modestly produced book called *Thrusters and Sleepers*. Published by PEP, it was a simple report card on the attitudes, practices and policies of enterprises in various categories of business. A total of 396 companies were studied in six major industrial sectors. The list of differing approaches and attitudes was succinctly summarized in matched pairs of quotations. This book is a true, timeless gem. The theme of extremes in an array of managerial activities – marketing, planning, manufacturing – could have been written on again and again in each of the 30 years covered by this anthology.

Finally, an early clarion call to arms was sounded in Europe in *The American Challenge* [*Le Défi Américain*]. In his introduction to that piece, Michael Allen poses an intriguing array of questions. And, as we move through the last decade of the twentieth century, from whom will the challenge come? Will it be a revitalized, united, business-driven European region? Will it be Japan, with a seemingly insatiable appetite for growth and the will and determination to go with it?

17

The American Challenge
[Le Défi Américain]

JEAN-JACQUES SERVAN-SCHREIBER

O ver 20 years after its publication in 1968, Jean-Jacques Servan-Schreiber's book raises many questions about the contemporary world of international business. Did the eloquent 'call to arms' with which it concluded result in a swing of the pendulum of multinational corporate power? Did it galvanize governments, managements and educational thinking in Europe? Have we seen, as a result, the demise of the unstoppable American multinationals of the 1960s and the emergence of a new breed of European mega-corporations that are winning in the markets of the 1980s? If so, can Servan-Schreiber's analysis of the ingredients of modern economic power explain the shift? Has Europe turned the tide of technology supremacy, information management, management education and entrepreneurship? Does Europe have a new global success formula of its own, rooted in unity, a long-term perspective and balanced socio-economic values? Will Europe be the continent of the 1990s . . . setting new standards of achievement?

How well are European multinationals doing in the global economy that Servan-Schreiber brilliantly predicted? How do they rank in the 'economic Olympics' of telecommunications, computers, health care, food, energy, financial services, transportation, travel, entertainment, media or environmental management? Are they moving towards global supremacy in any of these areas? Are they closing the McNamara gap?

To pursue Servan-Schreiber's diagnosis of Europe's problems further, has the European value system become more business-driven and has its educational infrastructure been renewed? Is there a European management renaissance? Is a new breed of entrepreneur emerging in Europe that can win in the individualized, sophisticated service markets of the 1990s, while many change-resistant US corporate superpowers retrench, restructure and decline?

Is there now a 'défi européen'?

Jean-Jacques Servan-Schreiber gave us both a cri du coeur and a model for considering these issues.

Michael Allen,
Center for Strategic Management,
Rowayton, Connecticut

Introduction

THIS book develops an inquiry that began with a factual observation but has far-reaching implications.

Starting with a rather matter-of-fact examination of American investment in Europe, we find an economic system which is in a state of collapse. It is our own. We see a foreign challenger breaking down the political and psychological framework of our societies. We are witnessing the prelude to our own historical bankruptcy.

At times like this we naturally think about reinforcing the barricades to hold back the invader. But purely defensive measures might well make us even weaker. In trying to understand why this is so, we stumble across the key element. This war – and it is a war – is being fought not with dollars, or oil, or steel, or even with modern machines. It is being fought with creative imagination and organizational talent.

At least a dozen European authorities have known this, and have been trying to tell us for some time. But no one has been paying any attention. This inquiry is based on what these men have seen, explained, and analysed.

Those whose job it is to lead us and keep us informed have been casually looking at each individual piece of the puzzle. Now it is time to concentrate on the problem as a whole. This strange phenomenon, so dangerous, so massive in its size and power, is hypnotizing and over-whelming. From our present ignorance we could sink into total despair.

The day may indeed come when we can only sit by helplessly and watch Europe disappear as a centre of civilization. But that day is not yet here, and there is still time to act.

Act how? Fight against what? We have less to fear from the absence of a European will than from its lack of direction.

General Motors, after all, isn't the Wehrmacht. The fight for the ownership of Machines Bull isn't Munich. And the supersonic Concorde jet isn't the battle of Sedan. This is the first full-scale war to be fought without arms or armour. If we had another André Malraux today, he would tug our heartstrings not with tales of the heroism of the fighters at Terruel, but with the fabulous struggle for the conquest of Titan's metal, or the ferocious effort to master the mental world of integrated circuits.

Even without a great lyric poet to recount them, the facts themselves are charged with power and emotion. It is enough to watch American investment skim gently across the earth like the fabled swallow, and watch what it takes away, how 'it thrusts, twists, enfolds, tears away, carries off, breaks open, and attacks'. Here is how it is done.

Part 2, Chapter 8: McNamara on the 'Gap'

Excerpts from remarks by Robert McNamara at Millsaps College, Jackson, Mississippi, 27 February 1967.

In the modern world, national defence and security are based on economic and scientific development. This is sometimes difficult for us to understand, since we have some stereotyped views which translate security into a purely military term. Security has, of course, a military component. But we make a dangerous and myopic mistake to believe that security and military power are synonymous.

History is full of human folly. And surely one of the most foolish features of man all through history is his almost incurable insistence on spending more energy and wealth on waging war than in preventing it.

It has not proved to be a very good bargain.

We read a great deal today about the crisis of the economic gap between the underdeveloped countries of Asia, Africa and Latin America, and the more favoured nations of the northern hemisphere.

The average annual per capita income in some 40 of the world's poorest countries today is roughly $120. That is less than 35c a day. The annual per capita income in the United States is nearly $3,000. That is almost $8.00 a day. That is a difference of 2,000 per cent.

This is no mere economic gap. It is a seismic fissure, driving deep into the earth's sociological crust to a certain, if hidden, fault line. It can produce – and it *will* produce – thunderous earthquakes of violence if rich and poor countries alike do not do more to meet the threat.

But seismic sociological explosions are much more damaging and deadly than natural volcanic explosions – and the real difference between them is that the former can be predicted.

Not only can they be predicted theoretically, they can often be practically prevented.

Let us be blunt. If the wealthy nations of the world do not do more to close this sundering economic split which cleaves the abundant northern half of the planet from the hungering southern hemisphere, none of us will ultimately be secure.

The seismic social shocks will reach us all – and with them will come the inevitable tidal waves of violence. The economic chaos that is foreseeable when we are faced with such disparity is as threatening to the security of the United States as Chinese nuclear weapons. It is as simple and as sobering as that.

Now, let me say a word about the second gap.

Unlike the first one, this second gap is between the *developed* nations: specifically between the highly industrialized nations of Europe, and ourselves.

The Europeans have termed it the Technological Gap. Their complaint is that we are so surpassing them in industrial development that we will eventually create a kind of technological colonialism.

Prime Minister Harold Wilson of Great Britain used some rather pointed language at a recent meeting of the Council of Europe at Strasbourg. He warned of 'an industrial helotry under which we in Europe produce only the conventional apparatus of a modern economy, while becoming increasingly dependent on American business for the sophisticated apparatus which will call the industrial tune in the 70s and 80s.'

And at the last meeting, in Paris, of the Atlantic Pact, the subject that dominated the debates was this technological gap. It is the major problem of our time; but I believe that the technological gap is misnamed. It is not so much a technological gap as it is a managerial gap. And the brain drain occurs not merely because we have more advanced technology here in the United States but rather because we have more modern and effective management.

God is clearly democratic. He distributes brain power universally. But He quite justifiably expects us to do something efficient and constructive with that priceless gift. That is what management is all about. Management is, in the end, the most creative of all the arts – for its medium is human talent itself.

What, in the end, is management's most fundamental task? It is to deal with change. Management is the gate through which social, political, economic and technological change – indeed, change in every dimension – is rationally and effectively spread through society.

Some critics, today, keep worrying that our democratic, free societies are becoming over-managed. The real truth is precisely the opposite. As paradoxical as it may sound, the real threat to democracy comes from under-management, not from over-management. Society cannot survive and develop unless management continues to make progress.

The under-organization, the under-management of a society is not the respect of liberty. It is simply to let some force other than reason shape reality. That force may be unbridled emotion. It may be greed, it may be aggressiveness, it may be hatred, it may be ignorance, it may be inertia, it may be anything *other* than reason. But whatever it is, if it is *not* reason that rules man, then man falls short of his potential.

Vital decision-making, in policy matters as well as in business, must remain at the top. That is partly – though not completely – what the top is for. But rational decision-making depends on having a full range of rational options from which to choose. Successful management organizes the enterprise so that this process can best take place. It is a mechanism whereby free men can most efficiently exercise their reason, initiative, creativity and personal responsibility.

This is the great human adventure of our time. And to create the necessary organization for a precise formulation of the different options which underlie our decisions is an exalting adventure. All reality can be reasoned about. And *not to* quantify, classify, measure what can be dealt with in this way is only to be content with something less than the full range of reason.

The argument against modern tools like the computer is, in the end, an argument against reason itself. Not that a computer is a substitute for reason. Quite the contrary, it is the product of reason and it assists us in the application of reason.

But to argue that some phenomena transcend precise measurement – which is true enough – is no excuse for neglecting the arduous task of carefully analysing what *can* be measured.

A computer does not substitute for judgment any more than a pencil substitutes for literacy. But writing ability without a pencil is not a particular advantage.

Modern creative management of huge, complex phenomena is

impossible without both the technical equipment and the technical skill which the advance of human knowledge has brought us.

In my view, the industrial gap that is beginning to widen between Europe and the United States is due precisely to what we have been discussing here.

Now, how can that gap be closed?

Ultimately, it can be closed only at its origin: education.

Europe is weak educationally. And that weakness is seriously crippling its growth. It is weak in its general education; it is weak in its technical education, and it is particularly weak in its managerial education.

In the United Kingdom, France, Germany and Italy, about 90 per cent of the 13- and 14 year-old students are enrolled in school. But after age 15, there is a tremendous drop-off. Then, less than 20 per cent remain in school.

In the United States, 95 percent of all the 13- and 14 year-olds are in school. But what is more important is that at age 18 we still have more than 45 per cent pursuing their education. We have more than 4 million students in college, and this represents some 40 per cent of our college-age population. In Western Europe this percentage ranges between 65 per cent and 15 per cent. But what is also to the point is that modern managerial education, for private enterprise as well as government, is almost unknown in industrialized Europe.

Technological advance has two bedrock requisites: broad general knowledge, and modern managerial competence. It cannot come into being without improving the foundation of it all, which is education of the young, as well as adults. If Europe really wants to close the technological gap, it has to improve its education, both general and special, and both quantitatively and qualitatively. There is just no other way to get to the fundamental root of the problem.

Science and technology, and modern management, do not sum up the entire worth of education. Developing our human capabilities to the fullest is what ultimately matters most. Call it humanism or call it whatever you like, but that is clearly what education in the final analysis is all about.

But without modern science and technology – and the generalist and managerial infrastructure to go with it – progress of any kind, spiritual, humanistic, economic or otherwise, will become increasingly less possible everywhere in the world.

Without this kind of progress, that is, without progress in education, the world is simply going to remain explosively backward, unbalanced and provincial.

Part 6, Conclusion

For societies, as for men, there can be no growth without challenge. Progress is a battle, just as life is a struggle. We have never been able to forget these truths, because so far human history has been nearly indistinguishable from military history.

Today the industrially advanced societies – the United States, the Soviet Union, Europe – are bringing that era of history to a close. Military confrontations between these great powers can be only hypothetical or thermonuclear. We cannot, of course, exclude the possibility of annihilation. But our point of departure for thought and action must be a hypothesis of atomic peace. The war we face will be an industrial one.

The conflict in Vietnam, that absurd and barbarous residue of the Crusades, will inevitably come to an end. The great majority of Americans are eagerly supporting efforts to reach a negotiated peace so that they may bring to an end an expedition whose sole rational objective was long ago achieved; halting the spread of Chinese imperialism in Asia, as Stalinist imperialism was contained in Europe.

Now we are beginning to discover what was concealed by twenty years of colonial wars, wars that dominated our thoughts and our behaviour: the confrontation of civilizations will now take place in the battlefield of technology, science, and management.

The American expeditionary corps will leave Vietnam, where there is nothing more to gain and everything to lose. But American industry will not leave Europe, where it has made new conquests and increased its formidable power. Even if we were not faced with such a challenge by the Americans, we ought to find in ourselves the power and the desire to build a more intelligent and bountiful post-industrial society. Technological duels and organizational prowess appeal to us, but are less enthralling than the vision of a higher form of civilization. The American challenge really only adds an external pressure to what is an internal necessity.

This unprecedented challenge has found us alone and unprepared, but not without resources. When power was measured by the number of men in arms and the number of legions, Europe was a leader. When power became industrial and was applied to the transformation of raw materials, Europe was still in the front ranks. In 1940 nothing would have been able to defeat a coalition of Germany, Britain, and France, if they were really united. Even when plunged into the most terrible civil war of her history by Hitler's folly, this Europe, her body bled and her spirit drained, revived to make an extraordinary recovery after 1950, and can still aspire to a role of leadership. What our leaders have lacked in this postwar period is a rational ambition – an ambition that can be achieved.

During the years when American industry began its conquest of advanced technology, our political leaders were blind to new realities and the potential of the future. So blind that Britain and France were no better off than defeated Germany and Italy when confronted with the real winner who knew how to exploit his success and is now preparing his greatest triumph.

This new conquest is the perfect definition of 'intangible'. This no doubt explains why it has been misunderstood by leaders accustomed to think in terms of tons of steel, machinery, and capital. The signs and instruments of power are no longer armed legions or raw materials or capital. Even factories are only an external symbol. Modern power is based on the capacity for innovation, which is research, and the capacity to transform inventions into finished products, which is technology. The wealth we seek does not lie in the earth or in numbers of men or in machines, but in the human spirit. And particularly in the ability of men to think and to create.

The scientist accepts this, but the politician, the civil servant, and the businessman understand it only with difficulty. It is fashionable today to praise profit indiscriminately. But as the French economist François Perroux has shown, it is a catch-all for everything: returns on a business, monopoly gains, killings on a speculation. Healthy profit, real profit, for a business as for society as a whole, lies in the *fruits of innovation*.

The training, development, and exploitation of human intelligence – these are the real resources, and there are no others. The American challenge is not ruthless, like so many Europe has known in her history, but it may be more dramatic, for it embraces everything.

Its weapons are the use and systematic perfection of all the instruments of reason. Not simply in the field of science, where it is the only tool, but also in organization and management, where Europeans are used to the irrational – the fetishism of precepts passed down from father to son, the weight of routine, the divine right of authority, and the unjustified priority of flair over systematic thought. In contrast with these entrenched forces, human reason is flexible, light, and mobile.

We can no longer sit back and wait for the renaissance. And it is not going to be evoked by patriotic rhetoric or clarion calls left over from the age of military battles. It can come only from subtle analysis, rigorous thought, and precise reasoning. It calls for a special breed of politicians, businessmen, and labour leaders.

How much time do we have to find them? It would be foolish to set a date. But we know, since each area can be measured, that there is a point of no return, and that it is not far away. There are only a few years left, and if we take electronics as a gauge, very few.

In some areas it is already too late, such as full-scale space exploration and supersonic aviation. But these are not the really vital sectors. The new frontiers of human creativity in every area lie in information systems and their utilization, and the Americans themselves do not seem to fully realize this yet. We must forge ahead into this area before it is taken over by others.

This would be an enormous undertaking. It means utilizing the intelligence of all the qualified men our society can train and equip. Above all, it means they must fight to the full limit of their ability or their skills, and *for their own sake*. This is the political problem par excellence.

In a free society like our own, there is no single political path to follow. Each man should express his ideas, as we have given ours. The debate that follows will shed light and build the strength to follow through. The only condition is that everyone recognize and accept the subject of the debate. This time it is fairly simple. It is not for us to choose, for it is imposed upon us – it is the American challenge. We have only to understand it, to close in upon it, to study it.

This book has no other ambition than to contribute to that task. It is true that it offers no conclusion, for if tragedy is upon us, the final act has not yet been written. In any case, this is not a history book, but, with a little luck, a call to action.

18

Quality is Free

PHILIP B. CROSBY

The most powerful lesson that we have learnt from the Japanese in the 1980s has been that it is actually cheaper to make products of the highest quality than to make inferior ones. Ironically, though, the seminal thinking on this subject has been done by Americans. In my view, the most influential of these has been Philip Crosby. His now famous book on the subject, Quality is Free, explains the proposition of its own title in clear and arresting terms.

As a business strategist, I was sceptical at first. Not because what he said did not make sense, but because I thought that in many organizations benefits of this order would be blocked by those operating managers who had spent their careers saying the opposite. But evidence began to accumulate that Crosby's ideas really work on a practical level.

I recall attending a conference a few years ago at which the corporate quality programme leader of a large and diversified continental company spoke of savings of the order of 25 to 30 per cent of sales! Like me, the rest of the audience was jarred, but he defended his position persuasively. Since then, the experience of those involved in the 'quality wars' has further confirmed this enormous potential in one company after another.

It is becoming clear that the most far-reaching improvements in the way that professionals manage their businesses are arising from their efforts to harness the unexploited energies of highly motivated people. Examples include: the productivity improvements in automobile assembly derived from rethinking the role of the individual worker on the line; the spectacular returns being realized from management buy-outs; and the consistently superior performance in all sectors of Japanese industry, arising in large measure from participative decision-making systems.

The competitive and financial benefits from an obsession with quality at all organizational levels are probably the most telling example of all. Commitment to the pursuit of quality as a corporate way of life is becoming a prerequisite for competitive survival in the industries and companies of the future.

David R. Sadtler,
Sadtler Associates,
London

Chapter 7: Cost of Quality

L ET'S eavesdrop on the Management Monthly Status Review of our favorite company. The comptroller is providing his overview:

'Inventory increased $270,358 this month for a total of $21,978,375.18. This is still $9981 below budget, but I think it requires a good look because the rate of increase is getting steeper.'

'Good point,' says the boss, who then directs purchasing to see if they are bringing material in quicker than needed and asks material control to give him a detailed report on in-process versus finished-goods inventory.

'Sales are directly on budget except for the hotel operation, where occupancy is falling off. During the week occupancy is running 98 percent, but this is dragged down by the weekend rate of 35 percent.'

'Hmmm,' says the boss. 'Marketing better get hopping on putting together some weekend specials. 'Take the little lady away from it all' sort of thing. Give them a special rate and a bottle of bubbly. That should take care of it.'

'Employee compensation is overbudget. We've been paying too much overtime in the foundry and electronic test operations. This is caused by delinquent schedules in the assembly group. They got 2 days late last month and haven't been able to catch up.'

'Production,' frowns the boss, 'hasn't been paying enough attention to scheduling. I think it's all due to that new and expensive computer operation. Set up a task team to find out what's wrong and give me a daily report.'

'Our quality is falling off – we've had several customer complaints.'

'There's no excuse for low quality. The quality department has to get on the ball,' growls the boss. 'Maybe we need a new quality manager. I want high quality. Meeting adjourned.'

Abridged from Philip B. Crosby: *Quality is Free* (New York: McGraw-Hill, 1979). Reproduced by kind permission of McGraw-Hill Publishing Company.

Now you'll notice that everything in the above report is quite precise, even down to the last 18 cents of inventory. All things are measured, evaluated calmly, and dispositioned. All, that is, except quality, which is merely 'falling off.' How come that portion of the company is not reported in numbers? Why is it left dangling in midair? Why is the quality manager suddenly considered inadequate when the other functional managers who have troubles are not? Why wasn't he there?

How come there wasn't a report on *quality*? Something like this:

'Our receiving inspection rejection rate has climbed from 2.5 to 4 percent in the last month. This is due to purchase orders on standard hardware not calling out the proper plating requirements. Printed circuit board rejections have risen from 4 to 6 percent due to untrained assemblers being placed on the line. Production has pulled them back for training. Customer returns have dropped from 3 to 1.2 percent, but this has cost us $35,491 in overtime due to the additional testing required. An engineering error was responsible for the defect. Changes have been issued and the problem will be corrected by the 18th of next month. The cost of quality is running at 6.1 percent of sales, and we plan to meet the year-end objective of 5.9 percent.'

'Great,' beams the boss. 'As long as we can find these situations early and take action, we will be able to have confidence in our conformance. Quality is doing a fine job.'

Quality is free, but no one is ever going to know it, if there isn't some sort of agreed-on system of measurement. Quality has always suffered from the lack of an obvious method of measurement in spite of the fact that such a method was developed by General Electric in the 1950s as a tool for determining the need for corrective action on a specific product line. I remember a case history in a course I took that compared two product lines using the cost of quality as the basis of comparison.

The quality profession, however, clings to the very management concepts that allow them to be inadequate, so cost-of-quality measurement was never really implemented except by a radical here and there. The first instance of using a companywide quality measurement, actually calculated and reported by the comptroller was probably in the ITT program we instituted in the mid-60s.

By bringing together the easily assembled costs like re-work, scrap, warranty, inspection, and test, we were able to show an accumulation of expense that made the line management listen to us. This led us to install more sophisticated quality management programs, which uncovered costs in areas such as change notices, installation, and supplier in-plant operations. At present we are learning how to measure 'service' costs of quality. This applies not only to operations like insurance or hotels, where there are no milling machines or printed circuit assembly areas, but to manufacturing plants themselves. It took a long time to get around to the realization that half the people in the most manufacturing of manufacturing plants never touch the product. And of course, as individuals we are all service people. Unless we are blood donors – then we are manufacturing plants.

All you really need is enough information to show your management that reducing the cost of quality (COQ) is in fact an opportunity to increase profits without raising sales, buying new equipment, or hiring new people. The first step is to put together the fully loaded costs of (1) all efforts involved in doing work over, including clerical work; (2) all scrap; (3) warranty (including in-plant handling of returns); (4) after-service warranty; (5) complaint handling; (6) inspection and test; and (7) other costs of error, such as engineering change notices, purchasing change orders, etc. It is normal to obtain only one-third of the real cost the first time you try it.

Many quality management people start out with the thought that it is a good thing for them personally if the company has a very low figure for cost of quality. They tend to come up with readings like 1.3 percent of sales. Then they run to the boss for applause. A few years later their successor finds that it is really 12.6 percent of sales and embarks on a well-rewarded campaign to reduce this needless waste. The first person just refused to understand that the cost of quality has little to do with the operation of the quality department.

To make the total calculation more understandable to other managements it is a good idea to relate it to a significant base. Most people use a percent of sales. However, if you are in a company where there are unusually high costs of distribution like the food industry, you may want to measure COQ as a percentage of cost of sales, or just plain manufacturing costs. In insurance, banks, hotels, and similar businesses the cost of operations makes a good base. What is really important is that the number be something that quality management can use to communicate the importance of the concept. That is what the whole business of COQ is all about.

Many managers wait, and fiddle, and never really do get a workable COQ system installed. They collect endless lists and classifications of things that should be considered. They are too concerned with trying to obtain an exact cost figure, and don't really understand the reason for doing the calculation in the first place.

All this just delays the rest of their program. As I said, the purpose of calculating COQ is really only to get management's attention and to provide a measurement base for seeing how quality improvement is doing. If managers spend all their time getting ready and attending endless conferences searching for the secret, they will be disappointed.

Once an operation knows its COQ, or a good approximation, goals for reducing that cost can be set. Ten percent a year is a good, attainable goal that people can relate to. As you go along, and become more adept in determining things that belong in the COQ, you will find the base number growing. This means that you must go back and apply this information to figures obtained in the past if you want apples to look like apples.

All calculations should be produced by the accounting department; that ensures the integrity of the operation. Naturally, they are going to ask you for a list of those costs which must be included. The following list should be of some help, although you will have to add any items that are unique to your business. These three categories should be sufficient at first; don't search for additional details until you absolutely need them. That is what creates bureaucracy.

Prevention costs

Prevention costs are the cost of all activities undertaken to prevent defects in design and development, purchasing, labor, and other aspects of beginning and creating a product or service. Also included are those preventive and measurement actions conducted during the business cycle. Specific items are:

Design reviews
Product qualification
Drawing checking
Engineering quality orientation
Make Certain program
Supplier evaluations
Supplier quality seminars
Specification review
Process capability studies
Tool control

Operation training
Quality orientation
Acceptance planning
Zero Defects program
Quality audits
Preventive maintenance

Appraisal costs

These are costs incurred while conducting inspections, tests, and other planned evaluations used to determine whether produced hardware, software, or services conform to their requirements. Requirements include specifications from marketing and customer, as well as engineering documents and information pertaining to procedures and processes. All documents that describe the conformance of the product or service are relevant. Specific items are:

Prototype inspection and test
Production specification conformance analysis
Supplier surveillance
Receiving inspection and test
Product acceptance
Process control acceptance
Packaging inspection
Status measurement and reporting

Failure costs

Failure costs are associated with things that have been found not to conform or perform to the requirements, as well as the evaluation, disposition, and consumer-affairs aspects of such failures. Included are all materials and labor involved. Occasionally a figure must be included for lost customer credibility. Specifics are:

Consumer affairs
Redesign
Engineering change order
Purchasing change order
Corrective action costs
Rework

Scrap
Warranty
Service after service
Product liability

Once you and the comptroller have calculated the COQ for your operation, the next step is to figure out what to do with it. This calculation is the only key you will ever have to help your company properly implement quality management. Seize an opportunity and make a speech like the following:

> A prudent company makes certain that its products and services are delivered to the customer by a management system that does not condone rework, repair, waste, or nonconformance of any sort. These are expensive problems. They must not only be detected and resolved at the earliest moment, they must be prevented from occurring at all. To give you an idea of how expensive these problems are, let me show you some of the actual costs we are incurring at this moment. (At this point, show them.)
>
> To remove these costs and to prove that quality is free, we must implement our quality management system to its fullest. That way we can turn what is sometimes considered a necessary evil into a profit center. Our cost of quality is now X percent of sales. It only needs to be Y percent of sales. The difference is pretax profit.
>
> Thank you.

Used as a management tool for the purpose of focusing attention on quality management the COQ is a positive blessing and serves a unique purpose. Used as an accounting measurement, like the calculation of nuts-and-bolts inventory, it becomes a useless pain. When the concern becomes which operation has come up with the most accurate figures, the purpose of keeping the figures gets lost. It is like someone on a tight budget keeping neat records of overspending. Make certain you keep your eye on the true reason for the calculation. Don't get lost in statistical swamps.

19

Managing Our Way to Economic Decline

Robert H. Hayes and William J. Abernathy

The salutary tale of the 'boiling frog' has become almost a cliché in the world of management over the past 20 years. Yet it is remarkable how often executives ignore its significance to their own particular situation.

A reminder, in case it is needed: if you put a frog in a pan of cold water and heat the pan gently until the water boils, the poor creature will sit there until it dies. But if you plunge the frog straight into boiling water, it will have the sense to jump out.

To mix metaphors, 'Managing Our Way to Economic Decline' provided the boiling water for many Americans – and, indirectly, for plenty of Europeans too. Not before time.

In late 1979, nine months before Hayes & Abernathy's devastating thesis hit the streets, I attended a star-studded symposium at the Massachusetts Institute of Technology on US innovation and manufacturing productivity. Speaker after speaker reeled off statistics about America's declining competitiveness versus Japan, West Germany and even Italy – an alarming phenomenon that was already starkly evident to anyone who had bothered to notice the declining trade performance of the United States, especially in automobiles and consumer electronics.

Yet, despite this clear 'writing on the wall' – and the obviously serious impact that the 1979 oil crisis was bound to have on industry – most of the industrialists in the MIT audience were astoundingly complacent. In the corridors and coffee breaks of the conference, there was constant muttering that 'these academics are scare-mongering'.

At that stage, much of US business was still blithely simmering to death.

A return visit to the United States exactly a year later told a very different story. Suddenly, the frog was realizing its dire situation and taking evasive action.

The change in attitude was due in part to the effects of the oil shock, which were now patently obvious to one and all. But the most discussed trigger was the article by Hayes & Abernathy.

Its remarkable influence was by no means confined to that watershed year. Throughout the 1980s it was cited constantly in business, academia, government and the media to underline the vital importance to America's well-being of a resurgence in manufacturing. The force of the article's demolition of stock market short-termism towards industry *was made manifest in study after study that followed – and in the very vitriol with which several of Hayes & Abernathy's Harvard colleagues, across the mental Rubicon in finance, condemned the 'Managing Our Way' thesis as allegedly unfounded.*

Abroad, the article did – and continues to do – much to explode the facile argument, still fashionable in certain countries, that manufacturing is no longer an important activity in a so-called post-industrial society. In Great Britain, in particular, it has given authoritative support to local defenders of well-run manufacturing companies against the myopia of many brokers and institutional investors only interested in the next quarter's corporate earnings statements and their own monthly trading performance.

As a still strong-selling Harvard Business Review *reprint, 'Managing Our Way' stands as a fine tribute to the memory of Bill Abernathy, a universally admired and loved man who died tragically early, but whose brainpower had already exerted a tremendous influence over business decision-makers and fellow scholars alike. Through the person of Bob Hayes, now Philip Caldwell Professor of Business Administration in Harvard's Production and Operations Management area, it represents an unusual ability to bridge the gap between the worlds of academic rigour and business reality through its combination of erudition and popular style. To a professional writer, as to a policy-maker in business or government, it is a model of thoughtful and long-lasting evangelism.*

Christopher Lorenz,
Management Page Editor, *Financial Times*,
London

Managing Our Way to Economic Decline

DURING the past several years American business has experienced
a marked deterioration of competitive vigor and a growing unease
about its overall economic well-being. This decline in both health and
confidence has been attributed by economists and business leaders to
such factors as the rapacity of OPEC, deficiencies in government tax
and monetary policies, and the proliferation of regulation. We find these
explanations inadequate.

They do not explain, for example, why the rate of productivity growth
in America has declined both absolutely and relative to that in Europe
and Japan. Nor do they explain why in many high-technology as well as
mature industries America has lost its leadership position. Although a
host of readily named forces – government regulation, inflation,
monetary policy, tax laws, labor costs and constraints, fear of a capital
shortage, the price of imported oil – have taken their toll on American
business, pressures of this sort affect the economic climate abroad just
as they do here.

A German executive, for example, will not be convinced by these
explanations. Germany imports 95% of its oil (we import 50%), its
government's share of gross domestic product is about 37% (ours is
about 30%), and workers must be consulted on most major decisions.
Yet Germany's rate of productivity growth has actually increased since
1970 and recently rose to more than four times ours. In France the
situation is similar, yet today that country's productivity growth in
manufacturing (despite current crises in steel and textiles) more than
triples ours. No modern industrial nation is immune to the problems

and pressures besetting U.S. business. Whey then do we find a disproportionate loss of competitive vigor by U.S. companies?

Our experience suggests that, to an unprecedented degree, success in most industries today requires an organizational commitment to compete in the marketplace on technological grounds – that is, to compete over the long run by offering superior products. Yet, guided by what they took to be the newest and best principles of management, American managers have increasingly directed their attention elsewhere. These new principles, despite their sophistication and widespread usefulness, encourage a preference for (1) analytic detachment rather than the insight that comes from 'hands-on' experience and (2) short-term cost reduction rather than long-term development of technological competitiveness. It is this new managerial gospel, we feel, that has played a major role in undermining the vigor of American industry.

American management, especially in the two decades after World War II, was universally admired for its strikingly effective performance. But times change. An approach shaped and refined during stable decades may be ill suited to a world characterized by rapid and unpredictable change, scarce energy, global competition for markets, and a constant need for innovation. This is the world of the 1980s and, probably, the rest of this century.

The time is long overdue for earnest, objective self-analysis. What exactly have American managers been doing wrong? What are the critical weaknesses in the ways that they have managed the technological performance of their companies? What is the matter with the long-unquestioned assumptions on which they have based their managerial policies and practices?

A failure of management

In the past, American managers earned worldwide respect for their carefully planned yet highly aggressive action across three different time frames:

- *Short term* – using existing assets as efficiently as possible.
- *Medium term* – replacing labor and other scarce resources with capital equipment.
- *Long term* – developing new products and processes that open new markets or restructure old ones.

The first of these time frames demanded toughness, determination, and close attention to detail; the second, capital and the willingness to take sizable financial risks; the third, imagination and a certain amount of technological daring.

Our managers still earn generally high marks for their skill in improving short-term efficiency, but their counterparts in Europe and Japan have started to question America's entrepreneurial imagination and willingness to make risky long-term competitive investment. As one such observer remarked to us:

> 'The U.S. companies in my industry act like banks. All they are interested in is return on investment and getting their money back. Sometimes they act as though they are more interested in buying other companies than they are in selling products to customers.'
>
> In fact, this curt diagnosis represents a growing body of opinion that openly charges American managers with competitive myopia: 'Somehow or other, American business is losing confidence in itself and especially confidence in its future. Instead of meeting the challenge of the changing world, American business today is making small, short-term adjustments by cutting costs and by turning to the government for temporary relief. . . . Success in trade is the result of patient and meticulous preparations, with a long period of market preparation before the rewards are available. . . . To undertake such commitments is hardly in the interest of a manager who is concerned with his or her next quarterly earnings reports.[1]

More troubling still, American managers themselves often admit the charge with, at most, a rhetorical shrug of their shoulders. In established businesses, notes one senior vice president of research: 'We understand how to market, we know the technology, and production problems are not extreme. Why risk money on new businesses when good profitable low-risk opportunities are on every side?' Says another: 'It's much more difficult to come up with a synthetic meat product than a lemon-lime cake mix. But you work on the lemon-lime cake mix because you know exactly what that return is going to be. A synthetic steak is going to take a lot longer, require a much bigger investment, and the risk of failure will be greater.'[2]

These managers are not alone; they speak for many. Why, they ask, should they invest dollars that are hard to earn back when it is so easy – and so much less risky – to make money in other ways? Why ignore a ready-made situation in cake mixes for the deferred and far less certain prospects in synthetic steaks? Why shoulder the competitive risks of making better, more innovative products?

In our judgment, the assumptions underlying these questions are prime evidence of a broad managerial failure – a failure of both vision and leadership – that over time has eroded both the inclination and the capacity of U.S. companies to innovate.

Familiar excuses

About the facts themselves there can be little dispute. Exhibits 19.1–4 document our sorry decline. But the explanations and excuses commonly offered invite a good deal of comment.

It is important to recognize, first of all, that the problem is not new. It has been going on for at least 15 years. The rate of productivity growth in the private sector peaked in the mid-1960s. Nor is the problem confined to a few sectors of our economy; with a few exceptions, it permeates our entire economy. Expenditures on R&D by both business and government, as measured in constant (noninflated) dollars, also peaked in the mid-1960s – both in absolute terms and as a percentage of GNP. During the same period the expenditures on R&D by West

Exhibit 19.1 Growth in labour productivity since 1960 (United States and abroad)

	Average annual percent change	
	Manufacturing 1960–1978	*All industries 1960–1976*
United States	2.8%	1.7%
United Kingdom	2.9	2.2
Canada	4.0	2.1
Germany	5.4	4.2
France	5.5	4.3
Italy	5.9	4.9
Belgium	6.9*	—
Netherlands	6.9*	—
Sweden	5.2	—
Japan	8.2	7.5

* 1960–1977
Source: Council on Wage and Price Stability, *Report on Productivity* (Washington, D.C.: Executive Office of the President, July 1979).

Exhibit 19.2 Growth of labor productivity by sector, 1948–1978

Time sector	Growth of labor productivity (annual average percent)		
	1948–65	*1965–73*	*1973–78*
Private business	3.2%	2.3%	1.1%
Agriculture, forestry, and fisheries	5.5	5.3	2.9
Mining	4.2	2.0	−4.0
Construction	2.9	−2.2	−1.8
Manufacturing	3.1	2.4	1.7
Durable goods	2.8	1.9	1.2
Nondurable goods	3.4	3.2	2.4
Transportation	3.3	2.9	0.9
Communication	5.5	4.8	7.1
Electric, gas, and sanitary services	6.2	4.0	0.1
Trade	2.7	3.0	0.4
Wholesale	3.1	3.9	0.2
Retail	2.4	2.3	0.8
Finance, insurance, and real estate	1.0	−0.3	1.4
Services	1.5	1.9	0.5
Government enterprises	−0.8	0.9	−0.7

Source: Bureau of Labor Statistics
Note: Productivity data for services, construction, finance, insurance, and real estate are unpublished.

Germany and Japan have been rising. More important, American spending on R&D as a percentage of sales in such critical research-intensive industries as machinery, professional and scientific instruments, chemicals, and aircraft had dropped by the mid-1970s to about half its level in the early 1960s. These are the very industries on which we now depend for the bulk of our manufactured exports.

Investment in plant and equipment in the United States displays the same disturbing trends. As economist Burton G. Malkiel has pointed out: 'From 1948 to 1973 the [net book value of capital equipment] per unit of labor grew at an annual rate of almost 3%. Since 1973, however, lower rates of private investment have led to a decline in that growth rate to 1.75%. Moreover, the recent composition of investment [in 1978] has been skewed toward equipment and relatively short-term projects and away from structures and relatively long-lived investments. Thus our industrial plant has tended to age. . . .'[3]

Other studies have shown that growth in the incremental capital equipment-to-labor ratio has fallen to about one-third of its value in the early 1960s. By contrast, between 1966 and 1976 capital investment as a percentage of GNP in France and West Germany was more than 20% greater than that in the United States; in Japan the percentage was almost double ours.

Exhibit 19.3 National expenditures for performance of R&D as a percent of GNP by country, 1961–1978*

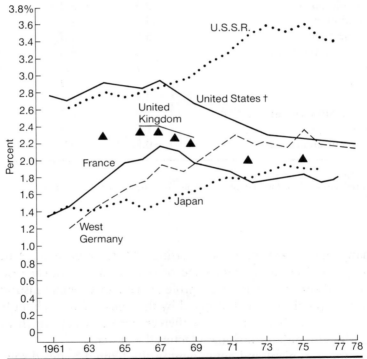

*Gross expenditures for performance of R&D including associated capital expenditures

†Detailed information on capital expenditure for R&D is not available for the United States. Estimates for the period 1972–1977 show that their inclusion would have an impact of less than one-tenth of 1% for each year.

Source: *Science Indicators – 1978* (Washington, D.C. : National Science Foundation, 1979), p.6

Note: The latest data may be preliminary or estimates.

Exhibit 19.4 Industrial R&D expenditures for basic research, applied research, and development, 1960–1978 (in $ millions)

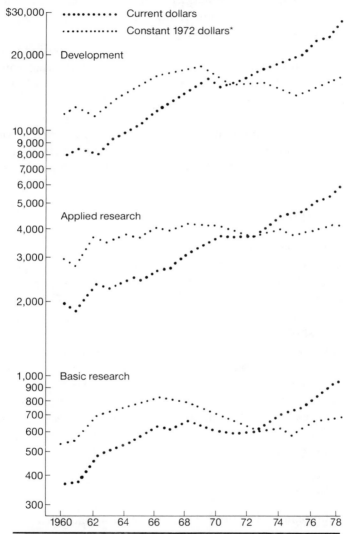

*GNP implicit price deflators used to convert current dollars to constant 1972 dollars.
Source: Science Indicators – 1978, p.87
Note: Preliminary data are shown for 1977 and estimated for 1978.

To attribute this relative loss of technological vigor to such things as a shortage of capital in the United States is not justified. As Malkiel and others have shown, the return on equity of American business (out of which comes the capital necessary for investment) is about the same today as 20 years ago, *even after adjusting for inflation*. However, investment in both new equipment and R&D, as a percentage of GNP, was significantly higher 20 years ago than today.

The conclusion is painful but must be faced. Responsibility for this competitive listlessness belongs not just to a set of external conditions but also to the attitudes, preoccupations, and practices of American managers. By their preference for servicing existing markets rather than creating new ones and by their devotion to short-term returns and 'management by the numbers,' many of them have effectively forsworn long-term technological superiority as a competitive weapon. In consequence, they have abdicated their strategic responsibilities.

The new management orthodoxy

We refuse to believe that this managerial failure is the result of a sudden psychological shift among American managers toward a 'super-safe, no risk' mind set. No profound sea change in the character of thousands of individuals could have occurred in so organized a fashion or have produced so consistent a pattern of behavior. Instead we believe that during the past two decades American managers have increasingly relied on principles which prize analytical detachment and methodological elegance over insight, based on experience, into the subtleties and complexities of strategic decisions. As a result, maximum short-term financial returns have become the overriding criteria for many companies.

For purposes of discussion, we may divide this *new* management orthodoxy into three general categories: financial control, corporate portfolio management, and market-driven behavior.

Financial control

As more companies decentralize their organizational structures, they tend to fix on profit centers as the primary unit of managerial responsibility. This development necessitates, in turn, greater dependence on short-term financial measurements like return on investment (ROI) for evaluating the performance of individual managers and management groups. Increasing the structural distance between those entrusted with exploiting actual competitive opportunities and those who must judge the quality of their work virtually guarantees reliance on objectively quantifiable short-term criteria.

Although innovation, the lifeblood of any vital enterprise, is best encouraged by an environment that does not unduly penalize failure, the predictable result of relying too heavily on short-term financial measures – a sort of managerial remote control – is an environment in which no one feels he or she can afford a failure or even a momentary dip in the bottom line.

Corporate portfolio management

This preoccupation with control draws support from modern theories of financial portfolio management. Originally developed to help balance the overall risk and return of stock and bond portfolios, these principles have been applied increasingly to the creation and management of corporate portfolios – that is, a cluster of companies and product lines assembled through various modes of diversification under a single corporate umbrella. When applied by a remote group of dispassionate experts primarily concerned with finance and control and lacking hands-on experience, the analytic formulas of portfolio theory push managers even further toward an extreme of caution in allocating resources.

'Especially in large organizations,' reports one manager, 'we are observing an increase in management behavior which I would regard as excessively cautious, even passive; certainly overanalytical; and, in general, characterized by a studied unwillingness to assume responsibility and even reasonable risk.'

Market-driven behavior

In the past 20 years, American companies have perhaps learned too well a lesson they had long been inclined to ignore: businesses should be customer oriented rather than product oriented. Henry Ford's famous dictum that the public could have any color automobile it wished as long as the color was black has since given way to its philosophical opposite: 'We have got to stop marketing makeable products and learn to make marketable products.'

At last, however, the dangers to too much reliance on this philosophy are becoming apparent. As two Canadian researchers have put it:

'Inventors, scientists, engineers, and academics, in the normal pursuit of scientific knowledge, gave the world in recent times the laser, xerography, instant photography, and the transistor. In contrast, worshippers of the marketing concept have bestowed upon mankind such products as new-fangled potato chips, feminine hygiene deodorant, and the pet rock. . . .'[4]

The argument that no new product ought to be introduced without managers undertaking a market analysis is common sense. But the argument that consumer analyses and formal market surveys should dominate other considerations when allocating resources to product development is untenable. It may be useful to remember that the initial market estimate for computers in 1945 projected total worldwide sales of only ten units. Similarly, even the most carefully researched analysis of consumer preferences for gas-guzzling cars in an era of gasoline abundance offers little useful guidance to today's automobile manufacturers in making wise product investment decisions. Customers may know what their needs are, but they often define those needs in terms of existing products, processes, markets, and prices.

Deferring to a market-driven strategy without paying attention to its limitations is, quite possibly, opting for customer satisfaction and lower risk in the short run at the expense of superior products in the future. Satisfied customers are critically important, of course, but not if the strategy for creating them is responsible as well for unnecessary product proliferation, inflated costs, unfocused diversification, and a lagging commitment to new technology and new capital equipment.

Three managerial decisions

These are serious charges to make. But the unpleasant fact of the matter is that, however useful these new principles may have been initially, if carried too far they are bad for U.S. business. Consider, for example, their effect on three major kinds of choices regularly faced by corporate managers: the decision between imitative and innovative product design, the decision to integrate backward, and the decision to invest in process development.

Imitative vs. innovative product design

A market-driven strategy requires new product ideas to flow from detailed market analysis or, at least, to be extensively tested for consumer reaction before actual introduction. It is no secret that these requirements add significant delays and costs to the introduction of new products. It is less well known that they also predispose managers toward developing products for existing markets and toward product designs of an imitative rather than an innovative nature. There is increasing evidence that market-driven strategies tend, over time, to dampen the general level of innovation in new product decisions.

Confronted with the choice between innovation and imitation, managers typically ask whether the marketplace shows any consistent preference for innovative products. If so, the additional funding they require may be economically justified; if not, those funds can more properly go to advertising, promoting, or reducing the prices of less-advanced products. Though the temptation to allocate resources so as to strengthen performance in existing products and markets is often irresistible, recent studies by J. Hugh Davidson and others confirm the strong market attractiveness of innovative products.[5]

Nonetheless, managers having to decide between innovative and imitative product design face a difficult series of marketing-related trade-offs. Exhibit 19.5 summarizes these trade-offs.

By its very nature, innovative design is, as Joseph Schumpeter observed a long time ago, initially destructive of capital – whether in the form of labor skills, management systems, technological processes, or capital equipment. It tends to make obsolete existing investments in both marketing and manufacturing organizations. For the managers concerned it represents the choice of uncertainty (about economic returns, timing, etc.) over relative predictability, exchanging the reasonable expectation of current income against the promise of high future value. It is the choice of the gambler, the person willing to risk much to gain even more.

Conditioned by a market-driven strategy and held closely to account by a 'results now' ROI-oriented control system, American managers have increasingly refused to take the chance on innovative product/market development. As one of them confesses: 'In the last year, on the basis of high capital risk, I turned down new products at a rate at least twice what I did a year ago. But in every case I tell my people to go back and bring me some new product ideas.'[6] In truth, they have learned caution so well that many are in danger of forgetting that market-driven, follow-the-leader companies usually end up following the rest of the pack as well.

Exhibit 19.5 Trade-offs between imitative and innovative design for an established product line

Imitative design	Innovative design
Market demand is relatively well known and predictable.	Potentially large but unpredictable demand; the risk of a flop is also large.
Market recognition and acceptance are rapid.	Market acceptance may be slow initially, but the imitative response of competitors may also be slowed.
Readily adaptable to existing market, sales, and distribution policies.	May require unique, tailored marketing distribution and sales policies to educate customers or because of special repair and warranty problems.
Fits with existing market segmentation and product policies.	Demand may cut across traditional marketing segments, disrupting divisional responsibilities and cannibalizing other products

Backward integration

Sometimes the problem for managers is not their reluctance to take action and make investments but that, when they do so, their action has the unintended result of reinforcing the status quo. In deciding to integrate backward because of apparent short-term rewards, managers often restrict their ability to strike out in innovative directions in the future.

Consider, for example, the case of a manufacturer who purchases a major component from an outside company. Static analysis of production economies may very well show that backward integration offers rather substantial cost benefits. Eliminating certain purchasing and marketing functions, centralizing overhead, pooling R&D efforts and resources, co-ordinating design and production of both product and component, reducing uncertainty over design changes, allowing for the use of more specialized equipment and labor skills – in all these ways and more, backward integration holds out to management the promise of significant short-term increases in ROI.

These efficiencies may be achieved by companies with commoditylike products. In such industries as ferrous and nonferrous metals or petroleum, backward integration toward raw materials and supplies tends to have a strong, positive effect on profits. However, the situation is markedly different for companies in more technologically active industries. Where there is considerable exposure to rapid technological advances, the promised value of backward integration becomes problematic. It may provide a quick, short-term boost to ROI figures in the next annual report, but it may also paralyze the long-term ability of a company to keep on top of technological change.

The real competitive threats to technologically active companies arise less from changes in ultimate consumer preference than from abrupt shifts in component technologies, raw materials, or production processes. Hence those managers whose attention is too firmly directed toward the marketplace and near-term profits may suddenly discover that their decision to make rather than buy important parts has locked their companies into an outdated technology.

Further, as supply channels and manufacturing operations become more systematized, the benefits from attempts to 'rationalize' production may well be accompanied by unanticipated side effects. For instance, a company may find itself shut off from the R&D efforts of various independent suppliers by becoming their competitor. Similarly, the commitment of time and resources needed to master technology back up the channel of supply may distract a company from doing its own job well. Such was the fate of Bowmar, the pocket calculator pioneer, whose attempt to integrate backward into semiconductor production so consumed management attention that final assembly of the calculators, its core business, did not get the required resources.

Long-term contracts and long-term relationships with suppliers can achieve many of the same cost benefits as backward integration without calling into question a company's ability to innovate or respond to innovation. European automobile manufacturers, for example, have typically chosen to rely on their suppliers in this way; American companies have followed the path of backward integration. The resulting trade-offs between production efficiencies and innovative flexibility should offer a stern warning to those American managers too easily beguiled by the lure of short-term ROI improvement. A case in point: the U.S. auto industry's huge investment in automating the manufacture of cast-iron brake drums probably delayed by more than five years its transition to disc brakes.

Process development

In an era of management by the numbers, many American managers – especially in mature industries – are reluctant to invest heavily in the development of new manufacturing processes. When asked to explain their reluctance, they tend to respond in fairly predictable ways. 'We can't afford to design new capital equipment for just our own manufacturing needs' is one frequent answer. So is: 'The capital equipment producers do a much better job, and they can amortize their development costs over sales to many companies.' Perhaps most common is: 'Let the others experiment in manufacturing; we can learn from their mistakes and do it better.'

Each of these comments rests on the assumption that essential advances in process technology can be appropriated more easily through equipment purchase than through in-house equipment design and development. Our extensive conversations with the managers of European (primarily German) technology-based companies have convinced us that this assumption is not as widely shared abroad as in the United States. Virtually across the board, the European managers impressed us with their strong commitment to increasing market share through internal development of advanced process technology – even when their suppliers were highly responsive to technological advances.

By contrast, American managers tend to restrict investments in process development to only those items likely to reduce costs in the short run. Not all are happy with this. As one disgruntled executive told us: 'For too long U.S. managers have been taught to set low priorities on mechanization projects, so that eventually divestment appears to be the best way out of manufacturing difficulties. Why?

'The drive for short-term success has prevented managers from looking thoroughly into the matter of special manufacturing equipment, which has to be invented, developed, tested, redesigned, reproduced, improved, and so on. That's a long process, which needs experienced, knowledgeable, and dedicated people who stick to their jobs over a considerable period of time. Merely buying new equipment (even if it is possible) does not often give the company any advantage over competitors.'

We agree. Most American managers seem to forget that, even if they produce new products with their existing process technology (the same 'cookie cutter' everyone else can buy), their competitors will face a relatively short lead time for introducing similar products. And as Eric von Hipple's studies of industrial innovation show, the innovations on which new industrial equipment is based usually originate with the user of the equipment and not within the equipment producer.[7] In other words, companies can make products more profitable by investing in the development of their own process technology. Proprietary processes are every bit as formidable competitive weapons as proprietary products.

The American managerial ideal

Two very important questions remain to be asked: (1) Why should so many American managers have shifted so strongly to this new managerial orthodoxy? and (2) Why are they not more deeply bothered by the ill effects of those principles on the long-term technological competitiveness of their companies? To answer the first question, we must take a look at the changing career patterns of American managers during the past quarter century; to answer the second, we must understand the way in which they have come to regard their professional roles and responsibilities as managers.

The road to the top

During the past 25 years the American manager's road to the top has changed significantly. No longer does the typical career, threading sinuously up and through a corporation with stops in several functional areas, provide future top executives with intimate hands-on knowledge of the company's technologies, customers, and suppliers.

Exhibit 19.6 summarizes the currently available data on the shift in functional background of newly appointed presidents of the 100 largest U.S. corporations. The immediate significance of these figures is clear. Since the mid-1950s there has been a rather substantial increase in the percentage of new company presidents whose primary interests and expertise lie in the financial and legal areas and not in production. In the view of C. Jackson Grayson, president of the American Productivity Center, American management has for 20 years 'coasted off the great R&D gains made during World War II, and constantly rewarded executives from the marketing, financial, and legal sides of the business while it ignored the production men. Today [in business schools] courses in the production area are almost nonexistent.'[8]

In addition, companies are increasingly choosing to fill new top

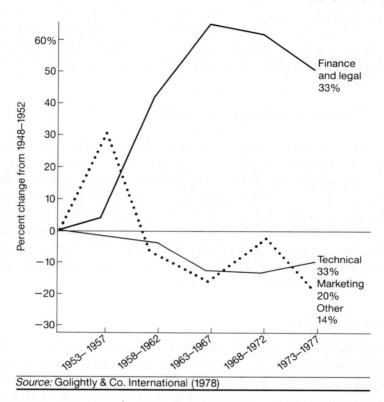

Exhibit 19.6 Changes in the professional origins of corporate presidents (percent changes from baseline years [1948–1952] for 100 top U.S. companies)

management posts from outside their own ranks. In the opinion of foreign observers, who are still accustomed to long-term careers in the same company or division, 'High-level American executives . . . seem to come and go and switch around as if playing a game of musical chairs at an Alice in Wonderland tea party.'

Far more important, however, than any absolute change in numbers is the shift in the general sense of what an aspiring manager has to be 'smart about' to make it to the top. More important still is the broad change in attitude such trends both encourage and express. What has developed, in the business community as in academia, is a preoccupation with a false and shallow concept of the professional manager, a 'pseudo-professional' really – an individual having no special expertise in any particular industry or technology who nevertheless can step into an unfamiliar company and run it successfully through strict application of financial controls, portfolio concepts, and a market-driven strategy.

The gospel of pseudo-professionalism

In recent years, this idealization of pseudo-professionalism has taken on something of the quality of a corporate religion. Its first doctrine, appropriately enough, is that neither industry experience nor hands-on technological expertise counts for very much. At one level, of course, this doctrine helps to salve the conscience of those who lack them. At another, more disturbing level it encourages the faithful to make decisions about technological matters simply as if they were adjuncts to finance or marketing decisions. We do not believe that the technological issues facing managers today can be meaningfully addressed without taking into account marketing or financial considerations; on the other hand, neither can they be resolved with the same methodologies applied to these other fields.

Complex modern technology has its own inner logic and developmental imperatives. To treat it as if it were something else – no matter how comfortable one is with that other kind of data – is to base a competitive business on a two-legged stool, which must, no matter how excellent the balancing act, inevitably fall to the ground.

More disturbing still, true believers keep the faith on a day-to-day basis by insisting that as issues rise up the managerial hierarchy for decision they be progressively distilled into easily quantifiable terms. One European manager, in recounting to us his experiences in a joint venture with an American company, recalled with exasperation that 'U.S. managers want everything to be simple. But sometimes business situations are not simple, and they cannot be divided up or looked at in such a way that they become simple. They are messy, and one must try to understand all the facets. This appears to be alien to the American mentality.'

The purpose of good organizational design, of course, is to divide responsibilities in such a way that individuals have relatively easy tasks to perform. But then these differentiated responsibilities must be pulled together by sophisticated, broadly gauged integrators at the top of the managerial pyramid. If these individuals are interested in but one or two aspects of the total competitive picture, if their training includes a very narrow exposure to the range of functional specialties, if – worst of all – they are devoted simplifiers themselves, who will do the necessary integration? Who will attempt to resolve complicated issues rather than try to uncomplicate them artificially? At the strategic level there are no such things as pure production problems, pure financial problems, or pure marketing problems.

Merger mania

When executive suites are dominated by people with financial and legal skills, it is not surprising that top management should increasingly allocate time and energy to such concerns as cash management and the whole process of corporate acquisitions and mergers. This is indeed what has happened. In 1978 alone there were some 80 mergers involving companies with assets in excess of $100 million each; in 1979 there were almost 100. This represents roughly $20 billion in transfers of large companies from one owner to another – two-thirds of the total amount spent on R&D by American industry.

In 1978 *Business Week* ran a cover story on cash management in which it stated that 'the 400 largest U.S. companies together have more than $60 billion in cash – almost triple the amount they had at the beginning of the 1970s.' The article also described the increasing attention devoted to – and the sophisticated and exotic techniques used for – managing this cash hoard.

There are perfectly good reasons for this flurry of activity. It is entirely natural for financially (or legally) trained managers to concentrate on essentially financial (or legal) activities. It is also natural for managers who subscribe to the portfolio 'law of large numbers' to seek to reduce total corporate risk by parceling it out among a sufficiently large number of separate product lines, businesses, or technologies. Under certain conditions it may very well make good economic sense to buy rather than build new plants or modernize existing ones. Mergers are obviously an exciting game; they tend to produce fairly quick and decisive results, and they offer the kind of public recognition that helps careers along. Who can doubt the appeal of the titles awarded by the financial community; being called a 'gunslinger,' 'white knight,' or 'raider' can quicken anyone's blood.

Unfortunately, the general American penchant for separating and simplifying has tended to encourage a diversification away from core technologies and markets to a much greater degree than is true in Europe or Japan. U.S. managers appear to have an inordinate faith in the portfolio law of large numbers – that is, by amassing enough product lines, technologies, and businesses, one will be cushioned against the random setbacks that occur in life. This might be true for portfolios of stocks and bonds, where there is considerable evidence that setbacks *are* random. Businesses, however, are subject not only to random setbacks such as strikes and shortages but also to carefully orchestrated attacks by competitors, who focus all their resources and energies on one set of activities.

Worse, the great bulk of this merger activity appears to have been absolutely wasted in terms of generating economic benefits for stockholders. Acquisition experts do not necessarily make good managers. Nor can they increase the value of their shares by merging two companies any better than their shareholders could do individually by buying shares of the acquired company on the open market (at a price usually below that required for a takeover attempt).

There appears to be a growing recognition of this fact. A number of U.S. companies are now divesting themselves of previously acquired companies; others (for example, W. R. Grace) are proposing to break themselves up into relatively independent entities. The establishment of a strong competitive position through in-house technological superiority is by nature a long, arduous, and often unglamorous task. But it is what keeps a business vigorous and competitive.

The European example

Gaining competitive success through technological superiority is a skill much valued by the seasoned European (and Japanese) managers with whom we talked. Although we were able to locate few hard statistics on their actual practice, our extensive investigations of more than 20 companies convinced us that European managers do indeed tend to differ significantly from their American counterparts. In fact, we found that many of them were able to articulate these differences quite clearly.

In the first place, European managers think themselves more pointedly concerned with how to survive over the long run under intensely competitive conditions. Few markets, of course, generate price competition as fierce as in the United States, but European companies face the necessity of exporting to other national markets or perishing.

The figures here are startling: manufactured product exports represent more than 35% of total manufacturing sales in France and Germany and nearly 60% in the Benelux countries, as against not quite 10% in the United States. In these export markets, moreover, European products must hold their own against 'world class' competitors, lower-priced products from developing countries, and American products selling at attractive devalued dollar prices. To survive this competitive squeeze, European managers feel they must place central emphasis on producing technologically superior products.

Further, the kinds of pressures from European labor unions and national governments virtually force them to take a consistently long-term view in decision making. German managers, for example, must negotiate major decisions at the plant level with worker-dominated works councils; in turn, these decisions are subject to review by supervisory boards (roughly equivalent to American boards of directors), half of whose membership is worker elected. Together with strict national legislation, the pervasive influence of labor unions makes it extremely difficult to change employment levels or production locations. Not surprisingly, labor costs in Northern Europe have more than doubled in the past decade and are now the highest in the world.

To be successful in this environment of strictly constrained options, European managers feel they must employ a decision-making apparatus that grinds very fine – and very deliberately. They must simply outthink and outmanage their competitors. Now, U.S. managers also have their strategic options hedged about by all kinds of restrictions. But those restrictions have not yet made them as conscious as their European counterparts of the long-term implications of their day-to-day decisions.

As a result, the Europeans see themselves as investing more heavily in cutting-edge technology than the Americans. More often than not, this investment is made to create new product opportunities in advance of consumer demand and not merely in response to market-driven strategy. In case after case, we found the Europeans striving to develop the products and process capabilities with which to lead markets and not simply responding to the current demands of the marketplace. Moreover, in doing this they seem less inclined to integrate backward and more likely to seek maximum leverage from stable, long-term relationships with suppliers.

Having never lost sight of the need to be technologically competitive over the long run, European and Japanese managers are extremely careful to make the necessary arrangements and investments today. And their daily concern with the rather basic issue of long-term survival adds perspective to such matters as short-term ROI or rate of growth. The time line by which they manage is long, and it has made them painstakingly attentive to the means for keeping their companies technologically competitive. Of course they pay attention to the numbers. Their profit margins are usually lower than ours, their debt ratios higher. Every tenth of a percent is critical to them. But they are also aware that tomorrow will be no better unless they constantly try to develop new processes, enter new markets, and offer superior – even unique – products. As one senior German executive put it, 'We look at rates of return, too, but only after we ask "Is it a good product?" '[9]

Creating economic value

Americans traveling in Europe and Asia soon learn they must often deal with criticism of our country. Being forced to respond can be healthy, for it requires rethinking some basic issues of principle and practice.

We have much to be proud about and little to be ashamed of relative to most other countries. But sometimes the criticism of others is uncomfortably close to the mark. The comments of our overseas competitors on American business practices contain enough truth to require our thoughtful consideration. What is behind the decline in competitiveness of U.S. business? Why do U.S. companies have such apparent difficulties competing with foreign producers of established products, many of which originated in the United States?

For example, Japanese televisions dominate some market segments, even though many U.S. producers now enjoy the same low labor cost advantages of offshore production. The German machine tool and automotive producers continue their inroads into U.S. domestic markets, even though their labor rates are now higher than those in the United States and the famed German worker in German factories is almost as likely to be Turkish or Italian as German.

The responsibility for these problems may rest in part on government policies that either overconstrain or undersupport U.S. producers. But if our foreign critics are correct, the long-term solution to America's problems may not be correctable simply by changing our government's tax laws, monetary policies, and regulatory practices. It will also require some fundamental changes in management attitudes and practices.

It would be an oversimplification to assert that the only reason for the decline in competitiveness of U.S. companies is that our managers devote too much attention and energy to using existing resources more efficiently. It would also oversimplify the issue, although possibly to a lesser extent, to say that it is due purely and simply to their tendency to neglect technology as a competitive weapon.

Companies cannot become more innovative simply by increasing R&D investments or by conducting more basic research. Each of the decisions we have described directly affects several functional areas of management, and major conflicts can only be reconciled at senior executive levels. The benefits favoring the more innovative, aggressive option in each case depend more on intangible factors than do their efficiency-oriented alternatives.

Senior managers who are less informed about their industry and its confederation of parts suppliers, equipment suppliers, workers, and customers or who have less time to consider the long-term implications of their interactions are likely to exhibit a noninnovative bias in their choices. Tight financial controls with a short-term emphasis will also bias choices toward the less innovative, less technologically aggressive alternatives.

The key to long-term success – even survival – in business is what it has always been: to invest, to innovate, to lead, to create value where none existed before. Such determination, such striving to excel, requires leaders – not *just* controllers, market analysts, and portfolio managers. In our preoccupation with the braking systems and exterior trim, we may have neglected the drive trains of our corporations.

Notes

1 Ryohei Suzuki, 'Worldwide Expansion of U.S. Exports – A Japanese View,' *Sloan Management Review*, Spring 1979, p. 1.
2 *Business Week*, February 16, 1976, p. 57.
3 Burton G. Malkiel, 'Productivity – The Problem Behind the Headlines,' *HBR* May–June 1979, p. 81.
4 Roger Bennett and Robert Cooper, 'Beyond the Marketing Concept,' *Business Horizons*, June 1979, p. 76.
5 J. Hugh Davidson, 'Why Most New Consumer Brands Fail,' *HBR* March–April 1976, p. 117.
6 *Business Week*, February 16, 1976, p. 57.
7 Eric von Hippel, 'The Dominant Role of Users in the Scientific Instrument Innovation Process,' MIT Sloan School of Management Working Paper 75–764, January 1975.
8 *Dun's Review*, July 1978, p. 39.
9 *Business Week*, March 3, 1980, p. 76.

20

In Search of Excellence

Thomas J. Peters and Robert H. Waterman, Jr

W e can safely judge a culture by its clichés: indeed, politicians and others who need to communicate via the mass media are now reduced to speaking in 30-second pre-rehearsed 'sound bites'; serious public discussion of complex issues is a near impossibility.

And the clichés of the business world in the late 1970s were particularly revealing. They indicated a society preoccupied with money; with short-term results (what have you done for me lately?); with rationality, analysis and problem-solving; and with winning. After all, did not 'nice guys finish last'; and was not 'winning not only the most important thing – but the only thing'? It was a world in which people were seen as machines; leadership was something best left to the generally discredited military. There was no business problem that would not succumb to the rigour of the Baker Scholar's analysis. It was the era of the model builder, the optimizer.

Bob Waterman and Tom Peters stood this world on its head. They advocated attention to things that were difficult for accountants to measure, let alone evaluate – such as management style. They showed that solving the business problem was the easy part; implementation was far more difficult and important. They suggested that the Japanese (or German) engineering tortoise might well beat the American or British financial hare in the long run – and that confusing financial engineering with the real thing could have seriously damaging consequences in the not so long run. They indicated that people were perhaps the only source of sustainable competitive advantage in a world where virtually everything else can be purchased: technology; raw materials; market access; even money, if you are prepared to pay the necessary rate of interest.

They were right; and, a decade later, the lessons implied by In Search of Excellence are as fresh and relevant as ever.

John M. M. Banham,
Director General, Confederation of British Industry,
London

Part II, Chapter 2: The Rational Model

Analytic ivory towers

THE reason behind the absence of focus on product or people in so many American companies, it would seem, is the simple presence of a focus on something else. That something else is overreliance on analysis from corporate ivory towers and overreliance on financial sleight of hand, the tools that would appear to eliminate risk but also, unfortunately, eliminate action.

'A lot of companies overdo it,' says Ed Wrapp. 'They find planning more interesting than getting out a salable product. . . . Planning is a welcome respite from operating problems. It is intellectually more rewarding, and does not carry the pressures that operations entail. . . . Formal long-range planning almost always leads to overemphasis of technique.' Fletcher Byrom of Koppers offers a suggestion. 'As a regimen,' he says, 'as a discipline for a group of people, planning is very valuable. My position is, go ahead and plan, but once you've done your planning, put it on the shelf. Don't be bound by it. Don't use it as a major input to the decision-making process. Use it mainly to recognize change as it takes place.' In a a similar vein, *Business Week* recently reported: 'Significantly, neither Johnson & Johnson, nor TRW, nor 3M – all regarded as forward thinking – has anyone on board called a corporate planner.'

David Ogilvy, founder of Ogilvy and Mather, states bluntly: 'The majority of businessmen are incapable of original thought because they are unable to escape from the tyranny of reason.' Harvard's renowned marketing professor Theodore Levitt said recently: 'Modelers build intricate decision trees whose pretension to utility is exceeded only by the awe in which high-level line managers hold the technocrats who construct them.' Finally, we have a recent account of a Standard Brands' new product strategy that was an abject failure. The reason, according to a *Business Week* cover story, was that Standard Brands hired a bevy of GE planners and then gave them something akin to operating responsibility. After letting most of them go, the chairman noted: 'The guys were bright, [but they] were not the kind of people who could implement the programs.'

Now, all of this is apparently bad news for many who have made a life's work of number crunching. But the problem is not that companies ought not to plan. They damn well should plan. The problem is that the planning becomes an end in itself. It goes far beyond Byrom's sensible dictum to use it to enhance mental preparedness. Instead, the plan becomes the truth, and data that don't fit the preconceived plan (e.g., real customer response to a pre-test market action) are denigrated or blithely ignored. Gamesmanship replaces pragmatic action. ('Have you polled the corporate staffs yet about the estimate?' was a common query in one corporate operating committee that we observed for years.)

Business performance in the United States has deteriorated badly, at least compared to that of Japan, and sometimes to other countries – and in many cases absolutely, in terms of productivity and quality standards. We no longer make the best or most reliable products and we seldom make them for less, especially in internationally competitive industries (e.g., autos, chips).

The first wave of attack on the causes of this problem focused on government regulators. That, however, seemed to be an incomplete answer. Then, in mid-1980, the quest for root causes took thoughtful executives, business reporters, and academics alike into the heartland of management practice, all trying to figure out what had gone wrong. Not surprisingly, America's recent dependence on overanalysis and a narrow form of rationality bore the brunt of the attack. Both seemed especially at odds with the Japanese approach to the work force and to quality – even allowing for cultural differences.

The inquiry ran into two formidable roadblocks. The first was inherent defensiveness. The businessman's intellect and soul were finally under attack. Until then he had been encouraged by the press simply to increase his finger pointing at others, namely, the government. Second, the attack ran into a language problem. It wasn't seen as an attack on 'a narrow form of rationality,' what we have termed the 'rational model,' thereby calling for a broader form. It was seen as an attack on rationality and logical thought per se, thus implicitly encouraging escape into irrationality and mysticism. One was led to believe that the only solution was to move Ford board meetings to the local Zen center. And, obviously that wasn't going to be the solution.

But let us stop for a moment and ask: What exactly do we mean by the fall of the rational model? We really are talking about what Thomas Kuhn, in his landmark book *The Structure of Scientific Revolutions*, calls a paradigm shift. Kuhn argues that scientists in any field and in any time possess a set of shared beliefs about the world, and for that time the set constitutes the dominant paradigm. What he terms 'normal science' proceeds nicely under this set of shared beliefs. Experiments are carried out strictly within the boundaries of those beliefs and small steps toward progress are made. An old but excellent example is the Ptolemaic view of the universe (which held until the sixteenth century) that the earth was at the center of the universe, and the moon, sun, planets, and stars were embedded in concentric spheres around it. Elaborate mathematical formulas and models were developed that would accurately predict astronomical events based on the Ptolemaic paradigm. Not until Copernicus and Kepler found that the formula worked more easily when the sun replaced the earth as the center of it all did an instance of paradigm shift begin.

After a paradigm shift begins, progress is fast though fraught with tension. People get angry. New discoveries pour in to support the new belief system (e.g., those of Kepler and Galileo), and scientific revolution occurs. Other familiar examples of paradigm shift and ensuing revolution in science include the shift to relativity in physics, and to plate tectonics in geology. The important point in each instance is that the old 'rationality' is eventually replaced with a new, different, and more useful one.

We are urging something of this kind in business. The old rationality is, in our opinion, a direct descendant of Frederick Taylor's school of scientific management and has ceased to be a useful discipline. Judging from the actions of managers who seem to operate under this paradigm, some of the shared beliefs include:

- Big is better because you can always get economies of scale. When in doubt, consolidate things; eliminate overlap, duplication, and waste. Incidentally, as you get big, make sure everything is carefully and formally coordinated.
- Low-cost producers are the only sure-fire winners. Customer utility

functions lead them to focus on cost in the final analysis. Survivors always make it cheaper.

- Analyze everything. We've learned that we can avoid big dumb decisions through good market research, discounted cash-flow analysis, and good budgeting. If a little is good, then more must be better, so apply things like discounted cash flow to risky investments like research and development. Use budgeting as a model for long-range planning. Make forecasts. Set hard numerical targets on the basis of those forecasts. Produce fat planning volumes whose main content is numbers. (Incidentally, forget the fact that most long-range forecasts are bound to be wrong the day they are made. Forget that the course of invention is, by definition, unpredictable.)

- Get rid of the disturbers of the peace – i.e., fanatical champions. After all, we've got a plan. We want one new product development activity to produce the needed breakthrough, and we'll put 500 engineers on it if necessary, because we've got a better idea.

- The manager's job is decision making. Make the right calls. Make the tough calls. Balance the portfolio. Buy into the attractive industries. Implementation, or execution, is of secondary importance. Replace the whole management team if you have to to get implementation right.

- Control everything. A manager's job is to keep things tidy and under control. Specify the organization structure in great detail. Write long job descriptions. Develop complicated matrix organizations to ensure that every possible contingency is accounted for. Issue orders. Make black and white decisions. Treat people as factors of production.

- Get the incentives right and productivity will follow. If we give people big, straightforward monetary incentives to do right and work smart, the productivity problem will go away. Over-reward the top performers. Weed out the 30 to 40 percent dead wood who don't want to work.

- Inspect to control quality. Quality is like everything else; order it done. Triple the quality control department if necessary (forget that the QC force per unit of production in Japanese auto companies is just a third the size of ours). Have it report to the president. We'll show them (i.e., workers) that we mean business.

- A business is a business is a business. If you can read the financial statements, you can manage anything. The people, the products, and the services are simply those resources you have to align to get good financial results.

- Top executives are smarter than the market. Carefully manage the cosmetics of the income statement and balance sheet, and you will look good to outsiders. Above all, don't let quarterly earnings stop growing.

- It's all over if we stop growing. When we run out of opportunity in our industry, buy into industries we don't understand. At least we can then continue growing.

Much as the conventional business rationality seems to drive the engine of business today, it simply does not explain most of what makes the excellent companies work. Why not? What are its shortcomings?

For one, the numerative, analytical component has an in-built conservative bias. Cost reduction becomes priority number one and revenue enhancement takes a back seat. This leads to obsession with cost, not quality and value; to patching up old products rather than fooling with untidy new product or business development; and to fixing productivity through investment rather than revitalization of the work force. A buried weakness in the analytic approach to business decision making is that people analyze what can be most readily analyzed, spend more time on it, and more or less ignore the rest.

As Harvard's John Steinbruner observes, 'If quantitative precision is demanded, it is gained, in the current state of things, only by so reducing the scope of what is analyzed that most of the important problems remain external to the analysis.' This leads to fixation on the cost side of the equation. The numbers are 'hardest' there. The fix, moreover, is mechanical and easy to picture – buy a new machine to replace nineteen jobs, reduce paperwork by 25 percent, close down two lines and speed up the remaining one.

Numerative analysis leads simultaneously to another unintended devaluation of the revenue side. Analysis has no way of valuing the extra oomph, the overkill, added by an IBM or Frito-Lay sales force. In fact, according to a recent observer, every time the analysts got their hands on Frito's '99.5 percent service level' (an 'unreasonable' level of service in a so-called commodity business) their eyes began to gleam and they proceeded to show how much could be saved if only Frito would reduce its commitment to service. The analysts are 'right'; Frito would immediately save money. But the analysts cannot possibly demonstrate the impact of a tiny degree of service unreliability on the heroic 10,000-person sales force – to say nothing of the Frito's retailers – and, therefore, on eventual market share loss or margin decline. Viewed analytically, the overcommitment to reliability by Caterpillar ('Forty-eight-hour parts service anywhere in the world – or Cat pays') or Maytag ('Ten years' trouble-free operation') makes no sense. Analytically, purposeful duplication of effort by IBM and 3M on product development, or cannibalization of one P&G brand by another P&G brand is, well, just that, duplication. Delta's family feeling, IBM's respect for the individual, and McDonald's and Disney's fetish for cleanliness make no sense in quantitative terms.

The exclusively analytic approach run wild leads to an abstract, heartless philosophy. Our obsession with body counts in Viet Nam and our failure to understand the persistence and long-time horizon of the Eastern mind culminated in America's most catastrophic misallocation of resources – human, moral, and material. But McNamara's fascination with numbers was just a sign of the times. One of his fellow whiz kids at Ford, Roy Ash, fell victim to the same affliction. Says *Fortune* of his Litton misadventures, 'Utterly abstract in his view of business, [Ash] enjoyed to the hilt exercising his sharp mind in analyzing the most sophisticated accounting techniques. His brilliance led him to think in the most regal of ways: building new cities; creating a shipyard that would roll off the most technically advanced vessels the way Detroit builds automobiles.' Sadly, *Fortune's* analysis speaks not only of Ash's Litton failure but also of the similar disaster ten years later that undid AM International under his leadership.

The rationalist approach takes the living element out of situations that should, above all, be alive. Lewis Lapham, the editor of *Harper's*, describes the fallacy of the numerative bias in an Easy Chair piece entitled 'Gifts of the Magi': 'The magi inevitably talk about number and weight – barrels of oil, the money supply – always about material and seldom about human resources; about things; not about people. The prevailing bias conforms to the national prejudice in favor of institutions rather than individuals.' John Steinbeck made the same point about lifeless rationality:

> The Mexican Sierra has 17 plus 15 plus 9 spines in the dorsal fin. These can easily be counted. But if the sierra strikes hard on the line so that our hands are burned, if the fish sounds and nearly escapes and finally comes in over the rail, his colors pulsing and his tail beating the air, a whole new relational externality has come into being – an entity which is more than the sum of the fish plus the fisherman. The only way to count the spines of the sierra unaffected by this second relational activity is to sit in a laboratory, open an evil-smelling jar, remove a stiff colorless fish from the formalin solution, count the spines and write the truth. . . . There you have recorded a reality which cannot be assailed – probably the least important reality concerning either the fish or yourself. . . . It is good to know what you are doing. The man with this pickled fish has set down one truth and recorded in his experience many lies. The fish is not that color, that texture, that dead, nor does he smell that way.

To be narrowly rational is often to be negative. Peter Drucker gives a good description of the baleful influence of management's analytic bias:

'Professional' management today sees itself often in the role of a judge who says 'yes' or 'no' to ideas as they come up. . . . A top management that believes its job is to sit in judgment will inevitably veto the new idea. It is always "impractical." John Steinbruner makes a similar point commenting on the role of staffs in general: 'It is inherently easier to develop a negative argument than to advance a constructive one.' In his analysis of the MLF (NATO's proposed shared nuclear multi-lateral force) decision, Steinbruner recounts an exchange between a conservative academic and a real-world statesman. Secretary of State Dean Acheson said to the Harvard-trained presidential adviser Richard Neustadt, 'You think Presidents should be warned. You're wrong. Presidents should be given confidence.' Steinbruner goes on to analyze the roles of 'warners' versus 'bolsterers.' Notwithstanding his attempt to present a balanced case, it is clear that the weight of the neutrally applied analytic model falls on the side of the warning, not the bolstering.

Mobil's chief executive, Rawleigh Warner, Jr., echoed the theme in explaining why his company decided not to bid on the 1965 offshore oil tracks in Prudhoe Bay: 'The financial people in this company did a disservice to the exploration people. . . . the poor people in exploration were adversely impacted by people who knew nothing about oil and gas.' Hayes and Abernathy, as usual, are eloquent on the subject: 'We believe that during the past two decades American managers have increasingly relied on principles which prize analytical detachment and methodological elegance over insight . . . based on experience. Lacking hands-on experience, the analytic formulas of portfolio theory push managers even further toward an extreme of caution in allocating resources.' Finally, George Gilder in *Wealth and Poverty* says, 'Creative thought [the precursor to invention] requires an act of faith.' He dissects example after example in support of his point, going back to the laying out of railroads, insisting that 'when they were built they could hardly be justified in economic terms.'

Today's version of rationality does not value experimentation and abhors mistakes. The conservatism that leads to inaction and years-long 'study groups' frequently confronts businessmen with precisely what they were trying to avoid – having to make, eventually, one big bet. Giant product development groups analyze and analyze until years have gone by and they've designed themselves into one home-run product, with every bell and whistle attractive to every segment. Meanwhile, Digital, 3M, HP, and Wang, amid a hotbed of experimentation, have proceeded 'irrationally' and chaotically, and introduced ten or more new products each during the same period. Advancement takes place only when we do something: try an early prototype on a customer or two, run a quick and dirty test market, stick a jury-rig device on an operating production line, test a new sales promotion on 50,000 subscribers.

The dominant culture in most big companies demands punishment for a mistake, no matter how useful, small, invisible. This is especially ironic because the most noble ancestor of today's business rationality was called *scientific* management. Experimentation is the fundamental tool of science: if we experiment successfully, by definition, we will make many mistakes. But overly rational businessmen are in pretty good company here, because even science doesn't own up to its messy road to progress. Robert Merton, a respected historian of science, describes the typical paper:

> [There is a] rockbound difference between scientific work as it appears in print and the actual course of inquiry. . . . The difference is a little like that between textbooks of scientific method and the ways in which scientists actually think, feel, and go about their work. The books on methods present ideal patterns, but these tidy, normative patterns . . . do not reproduce the typically untidy, opportunistic adaptations that scientists really make. The scientific paper presents an immaculate appearance which reproduces little or nothing of the intuitive leaps, false starts, mistakes, loose ends, and happy accidents that actually cluttered up the inquiry.

Sir Peter Medawar, Nobel laureate in immunology, flatly declares, 'It is no use looking to scientific 'papers,' for they do not merely conceal but actively misrepresent the reasoning which goes into the work they describe.'

Anti-experimentation leads us inevitably to overcomplexity and inflexibility. The 'home-run product' mentality is nowhere more evident that in the pursuit of the 'superweapon' in defense. A *Village Voice* commentator notes:

> The quickest way to understand the dread evoked in the Pentagon by Spinney [senior analyst with the Program Analysis and Evaluation division of the Department of the Defense] is to quote his bottom line: 'Our strategy of pursuing ever-increasing technical complexity and sophistication has made high-technology solutions and combat readiness mutually exclusive.' That is, the more money the U.S. presently spends on defense, the less able it is to fight. . . . More money has produced fewer

but more complex planes which do not work much of the time. Deployment of fewer planes means a more elaborate and delicate communication system which is not likely to survive in war conditions.

Caution and paralysis-induced-by-analysis lead to an anti-experimentation bias. That, in turn, ironically leads to an ultimately risky 'big bet' or the 'superweapon' mentality. The screw turns once more. To produce such superproducts, hopelessly complicated and ultimately unworkable management structures are required. The tendency reaches its ultimate expression in the formal matrix organizational structure. Interestingly, some fifteen years before the mid-seventies matrix heyday, the researcher Chris Argyris identified the key matrix pathologies:

> Why are these new administrative structures and strategies having trouble?... The assumption behind this [matrix] theory was that if objectives and critical paths to these objectives were defined clearly, people would tend to cooperate to achieve these objectives according to the best schedule they could devise. However, in practice, the theory was difficult to apply. . . . It was not long before the completion of the paperwork became an end in itself. Seventy-one percent of the middle managers reported that the maintenance of the product planning and program review paper flow became as crucial as accomplishing the line responsibility assigned to each group. . . . Another mode of adaptation was to withdraw and let the upper levels become responsible for the successful administration of the program. 'This is their baby – let them make it work.' . . . Still another frequently reported problem was the immobilization of the group with countless small decisions.

One can beat the complexity syndrome, but it is not easy. The IBM 360 is one of the grand product success stories in American business history, yet its development was sloppy. Along the way, chairman Thomas Watson, Sr., asked vice-president Frank Cary to 'design a system to ensure us against a repeat of this kind of problem.' Cary did what he was told. Years later, when he became chairman himself, one of his first acts was to get rid of the laborious product development structure that he had created for Watson. 'Mr. Watson was right,' he conceded. 'It [the product development structure] will prevent a repeat of the 360 development turmoil. Unfortunately, it will also ensure that we don't ever invent another product like the 360.'

The excellent company response to complexity is fluidity, the administrative version of experimentation. Reorganizations take place all the time. 'If you've got a problem, put the resources on it and get it fixed,' says one Digital executive. 'It's that simple.' Koppers's Fletcher Byrom adds support: 'Of all the things that I have observed in corporations, the most disturbing has been a tendency toward over-organization, producing a rigidity that is intolerable in an era of rapidly accelerating change.' HP's David Packard notes, 'You've got to avoid having too rigid an organization. . . . If an organization is to work effectively, the communication should be through the most effective channel regardless of the organization chart. That is what happens a lot around here. I've often though that after you get organized, you ought to throw the chart away.' Speaking on the subject of American organizational rationality, our Japanese colleague Ken Ohmae says: 'Most Japanese companies don't even have a reasonable organization chart. Nobody knows how Honda is organized, except that it uses lots of project teams and is quite flexible. . . . Innovation typically occurs at the interface, requiring multiple disciplines. Thus, the flexible Japanese organization has now, especially, become an asset.'

The rationalist approach does not celebrate informality. Analyze, plan, tell, specify, and check up are the verbs of the rational process. Interact, test, try, fail, stay in touch, learn, shift direction, adapt, modify, and see are some of the verbs of the informal managing processes. We hear the latter much more often in our interviews with top performers. Intel puts in extra conference rooms, simply to increase the likelihood of informal problem solving among different disciplines. 3M sponsors clubs of all sorts specifically to enhance interaction. HP and Digital overspend on their own air and ground transportation systems just so people will visit one another. Product after product flows from Patrick Haggerty's bedrock principle of 'tight coupling' at TI. It all means that people talk, solve problems, and fix things rather than posture, debate, and delay.

Unfortunately, however, management by edict feels more comfortable to most American managers. They shake their heads in disbelief at 3M, Digital, HP, Bloomingdale's, or even IBM, companies whose core processes seem out of control. After all, who in his right mind would establish Management By Wandering Around as a pillar of philosophy, as HP does? It turns out that the informal control through regular, casual communication is actually much tighter than rule by numbers, which can be avoided or evaded. But you'd have a hard time selling that idea outside the excellent companies.

The rational model causes us to denigrate the importance of values. We have observed few, if any, bold new company directions that have come from goal precision or rational analysis. While it is true that the good companies have superb analytic skills, we believe that their major decisions are shaped more by their values than by their dexterity with numbers. The top performers create a broad, uplifting, shared culture, a coherent framework within which charged-up people search for appropriate adaptations. Their ability to extract extraordinary contributions from very large numbers of people turns on the ability to create a sense of highly valued purpose. Such purpose invariably emanates from love of product, providing top-quality services, and honoring innovation and contribution from all. Such high purpose is inherently at odds with 30 quarterly MBO objectives, 25 measures of cost containment, 100 demeaning rules for production-line workers, or an ever-changing, analytically derived strategy that stresses costs this year, innovation next, and heaven knows what the year after.

There is little place in the rationalist world for internal competition. A company is not supposed to compete with itself. But throughout the excellent companies research, we saw example after example of that phenomenon. Moreover, we saw peer pressure – rather than orders from the boss – as the main motivator. General Motors pioneered the idea of internal competition sixty years ago; 3M, P&G, IBM, HP, Bloomingdale's, and Tupperware are its masters today. Division overlap, product-line duplication, multiple new product development teams, and vast flows of information to spur productivity comparison – and improvements – are the watchwords. Why is it that so many have missed the message?

Again, the analyze-the-analyzable bias is ultimately fatal. It is true that costs of product-line duplication and nonuniformity of manufacturing procedures can be measured precisely. But the incremental revenue benefits from a steady flow of new products developed by zealous champions and the increment of productivity gains that comes from continuous innovation by competing shop floor teams are much harder, if not impossible, to get a handle on.

Misplaced emphasis

Perhaps the most important failing of the narrow view of rationalists is not that it is wrong per se, but that it has led to a dramatic imbalance in the way we think about managing. Stanford's Harold Leavitt has a wonderful way of explaining this point. He views the managing process as an interactive flow of three variables: pathfinding, decision making, and implementation. The problem with the rational model is that it addresses only the middle element – decision making. In explaining the differences in the three activities, Leavitt has his classes first think of political leaders whose stereotypes most neatly fit the categories. For example, a typical class would suggest President John Kennedy as a pathfinder. For the decision-making stereotype, they might pick Robert McNamara in his role of Secretary of Defense or Jimmy Carter as ˙President. For the prototypical implementer, everyone thinks of Lyndon Johnson ('Let us reason together,' or 'I'd rather have him inside the tent pissing out, than outside the tent pissing in.')

To add understanding, Leavitt has his class associate various occupations with his three categories. People who fall into the decision-making category include systems analysts, engineers, MBAs, statisticians, and professional managers – strange bedfellows, but very much alike in their bias for the rational approach. Implementing occupations would be those in which people essentially get their kicks from working with other people – psychologists, salesmen, teachers, social workers, and most Japanese managers. Finally, in the pathfinding category we find poets, artists, entrepreneurs, and leaders who have put their personal stamp on some business.

Obviously, the three processes are interconnected, and emphasis on any one trait to the exclusion of the other two is dangerous. The business ranks are full of would-be pathfinders – artists who can't get anything done. Likewise, implementers abound – compromising salesmen who have no vision. And the pitfalls of those who overemphasize decision making have been the subject of this chapter. The point of all this is that business management has at least as much to do with pathfinding and implementation as it does with decision making. The processes are inherently different, but they can complement and reinforce one another.

Pathfinding is essentially an aesthetic, intuitive process, a design process. There is an infinity of alternatives that can be posed for design problems, whether we are talking about architectural design or the guiding values of a business. From that infinity, there are plenty of bad ideas, and here the rational approach is helpful in sorting out the chaff. One is usually left with a large remaining set of good design ideas, however, and no amount of analysis will choose among them, for the final decision is essentially one of taste.

Implementation is also greatly idiosyncratic. As Leavitt points out,

'People like their own children a lot, and typically aren't that interested in other people's babies.' As consultants, we repeatedly find that it does the client no good for us to 'analytically prove' that option A is the best – *and to stop at that point.* At that phase in the consulting process, option A is our baby, not theirs, and no amount of analytical brilliance is going to get otherwise uncommitted people to buy it. They have to get into the problem and understand it – and then own it for themselves.

As we've said, we don't argue for drastically tilting the balance toward either pathfinding or implementation. Rationality *is* important. A quality analysis will help to point a business in the right direction for pathfinding and will weed out the dumb options. But if America is to regain its competitive position in the world, or even hold what it has, we have to stop overdoing things on the rational side.

21

Thrusters and Sleepers

PEP REPORT

Thirty years ago, a major study concluded that 'the chief impediment to a faster growth of the British economy is that we do not want it enough'. Shocked, perhaps, by this conclusion, the author of this extract set out to examine 'the attitudes and practices of the men who manage industry'. The key conclusion – that management practices must be improved and modernized if industrial efficiency and the rate of growth were to be increased rapidly – was supported by a series of classifications of management attitudes that allowed the companies researched to be divided into 'thrusters' and 'sleepers'. Three industries identified as sleepy – machine tools, shipbuilding and woollen textiles – have since confirmed beyond doubt the accuracy of their classification, while domestic appliances and earthmoving equipment have similarly resolved the ambivalence of their earlier classification.

Although the criteria of effective management used in the 1960 survey have a dated air in the light of the great increase in management studies in the intervening years, would a fresh study, with revised criteria, yield different results – and, in particular, alter the overriding conclusion that we are not prepared to make great enough efforts to achieve the economic results of our principal competitors?

The 1980s have seen great strides in the development of British management, but it is hard to deny that we are still mostly concerned with obtaining higher rates of pay for less work than our principal competitors. In the area of unit labour costs, improved productivity has consistently been more than offset by higher wage awards, and most workers, in the great range of distribution and service industries, have seen their pay double in a decade, for little or no increase in productivity – indeed only 30 per cent of the workforce is actually concerned about unit costs. Increases in management pay, long overdue in 1980, are now also too often tied to profits boosted artificially by inflation, with little resultant motivation to attack or at least control inflation itself.* And have the great fiscal reforms of the 1980s – elimination of exchange controls and the lowering of marginal tax rates – resulted in too many managements opting out of Britain's productivity problems by investing overseas, occasionally, it is true, importing back into the United Kingdom and perhaps swelling earnings per share, but doing little to tackle the problems identified 30 years ago?

John Woodthorpe,
Former Director, McKinsey & Company,
London

* A potential problem highlighted in 'How to Prod Managers', Management Today, November 1980, and earlier in 'How to Pay Managers', Management Today, January 1974.

Chapter 1: Introduction

IN the past few years there has been much criticism of Britain's economic performance, prompted mainly by the country's slow rate of economic growth and its failure to achieve an adequate increase in exports. An earlier PEP report, *Growth in the British Economy*, published in the autumn of 1960, had some influence in calling attention to Britain's economic shortcomings.

Much of the discussion about these problems has been based on 'league tables' comparing the performance of Western countries in respect of economic aggregates such as gross national product, total investment or exports. This has been a useful exercise and the value of such analysis, and the efficacy of policy measures to increase aggregates such as investment or exports, should not be underrated. But there has been a tendency to stress this global, macro-economic thinking at the expense of the study of decisions and actions in individual firms, which are the motive power of a decentralised economy such as Britain's.

In the last analysis, the growth of the economy as a whole depends on the efficiency and growth of the individual firms and these, in turn, are determined largely by the men who manage them. *Growth in the British Economy* had concluded that one major barrier to economic growth was that people are not sufficiently interested in it* – a conclusion that was

* 'It is probably true that the chief impediment to a faster growth of the British economy is that we do not want it enough. Both management and labour and, more widely, people in general, do not attach such a priority to material progress as might lead them to great enough efforts to achieve the economic results for example of the United States, or Western Germany or the Soviet countries.' (*Growth in the British Economy* (PEP), 1960, p. xi.)

particularly important in the case of managers in view of their special influence on economic activity. It appeared, therefore, that, before it would be possible to formulate a fully effective policy for a sustained increase in Britain's rate of economic growth, an examination should be made of the attitudes and practices of the men who manage industry. PEP accordingly decided to undertake a detailed study at the level of the individual firm.

One difficulty of this approach is how to cover the vast number of individual firms making up the British economy. Altogether there are more than 20,000 enterprises with twenty-five or more employees in a multitude of different industries, the qualities and levels of attainment of whose managers are so varied as to evade any comprehensive review.

Previous investigators in this field have adopted a variety of approaches but most have concentrated on a very small sector of industry, confining themselves to firms within a restricted locality or to a particular, limited segment of an industry.

The PEP study has approached the problem from a somewhat different angle. It has examined the attitudes and practices of managers in forty-seven firms in a number of industries. In this way it was hoped that the findings of the study would indicate which attitudes and practices are likely to be associated with a high and sustained growth in firms and thus in industry as a whole. It is important to be clear at this stage what is the connection between national growth and the growth of the individual firm. At the national level a growth rate in the gross national product which is higher than the increase in the total number of man hours worked must mean that productivity is rising. At the level of the individual firm, however, it does not necessarily follow that an increase in output entails higher productivity, since this could result merely from an increase in the labour force at the expense of some other firm. An individual firm may, therefore, increase its production without increasing its productivity, although in practice these two indicators very frequently go together. The major interest of this study is, however, in those firms which are in fact increasing their productivity and not merely their production, since it is only through such firms that the nation's productivity and thereby its output can steadily be raised.

It became apparent that many of the firms visited did not apply even comparatively simple techniques that should contribute to high productivity. This is demonstrated so frequently in the interviews that it seems likely that indifference to modern practices for improving productivity and efficiency is widespread within certain strata of British industry. It is probable that this criticism applies far less to the relatively small number of giant firms which can afford to run their own specialist departments. Such firms have problems, but they are not usually of this sort. The present study has, however, concentrated on rather smaller firms: few in the sample have more than 5,000 employees.

Chapter 10: Thrusters and Sleepers

The purpose of the study has been to report and evaluate through the extensive use of quotations the salient attitudes and practices encountered in the research. Frequently, in order to provide a direct contrast, quotations have been 'paired'. So that the contrasts may be more easily remembered, a summary is given below of the main thrusting and sleepy characteristics, each one of which has been, where possible, illustrated by a quotation.

Provision for effective management	Thruster	Sleeper
1 Recruitment of potential managers	Open-minded on all potential sources of management material – creating spirit of opportunity within the firm	Ignoring potential supply – little attempt to foster such spirit
2 Recruitment of middle and senior management	Ready to buy up other firms' top management without undue regard to feelings	Inaction because of understanding with competitors not to poach
3 Management education	Regularly using outside training courses or internal equivalent	Haphazardly indulging in occasional training, if any
4 Management development	Considered of greater importance and planned	Little or no attention paid to it – probably caught napping
5 Treatment of existing management	Ready to retire early, demote or overlook second-class management to make way for first-class	Unwilling to be so tough
6 Delegation by senior management	Appreciates importance of delegation of responsibilities	Clings too much to day-to-day operational work
7 Management structure	Individual managers' responsibilities defined in written job specifications. Organisation chart exists and is used	Managers uncertain of individual responsibilities. Organisation chart non-existent

Provision for effective management	*Thruster*	*Sleeper*
8 Management communication	All members of management, including foremen, informed and consulted where practicable on firm's policy	Members of management haphazardly informed and consulted. Management demarcation exists or managers deliberately misinformed and not consulted
Broad assessment of firm and its future		
9 Management consultants	Aware of all activities of consultants – felt to be of great help in assisting firm	Regard consultants as charlatans – at best contribute more paper work
10 Interfirm comparison at home and overseas	Belief in learning about and from others	Such comparisons meaningless
11 Market share	Aware of market share	Unaware of market share or the importance of assessing it
12 Objective of firm	Determined to grow	Not growth conscious
13 Assessment of performance	Measured in terms of profits, assets, turnover, square feet, number of scientists, etc. Aware of industry trends	No sure knowledge of 'performance' statistics or relative position
14 Statement of accounts	Important indices published	Minimum required by company law published
15 Diversification	Prepared to consider diversification or have diversified	Diversification not considered
16 Future of firm	Planned in terms of specific medium and long-term objectives, i.e. share of market, sales expansion, return on capital, research and development effort, labour relations improvement	Thought about in terms of coping with immediate problems
17 Long-range planning	Carried out by special department or individual executive	Ignored
Operational control of firm		
18 Use of budgetary control	Budgetary control in use with great emphasis attached to its importance	Not in use
19 Reviewing of operations	Regularly undertaken, feedback exists, control exercised where necessary	Spasmodically carried out and no proper system of feedback

Operational control of firm	Thruster	Sleeper
20 Capital budgeting	Undertaken together with full assessment of capital projects and alternative use of funds	No such forecasting or analysis carried out
Marketing at home and overseas		
21 Marketing	Seen as key aspect of firm's organisation	Same as sales or meaningless concept
22 Market research	Seen as vital activity the results of which help to determine the scope and direction of the firm's activities	Thought to be inapplicable or impossible
23 Sales	Forecast	Not forecast or estimates based on guesswork
24 Relationship of sales to production	Production based on sales requirements	Production dominates sales
25 Method of home selling	Assessing and experimenting with traditional methods of selling	Present and probably traditional methods of selling accepted uncritically
26 Salesmen	Selected for definable, assessable and proven abilities and qualifications	Selected on basis of vague generalisations with reference to such things as loyalty, energy, enthusiasm
27 Advertising and public relations	Seen as useful in creating public image of company	Belief that product will sell itself if good enough
28 Export motivation	Wish to be world-beater	Exporting because of tradition or not interested in exporting
29 Difference in profitability between home and export sales	Known from calculations as far as possible	Guessed or known intuitively
30 Method of export selling	Actively assessing and experimenting with various methods of exporting	Unwilling to change traditional methods
31 Management of agents	Attempt to assess agents' efforts	Little or no assessment
Production		
32 Capacity, efficiency and productivity	Are known	Are assumed to be appropriate or excellent
33 Plant	Regular assessment of plant with regard to cost and innovation	Systematic cost studies not undertaken. Plant kept in service until depreciated or broken down

Production	Thruster	Sleeper
34 Shift working	Ramifications of shift working assessed. Introduced where economic and possible	Ramifications unassessed. Not introduced
35 Buying function	Carried out by a member of management	Undertaken as a clerical activity
36 Suppliers	Pays special attention to and carries out analysis of suppliers to select best/cheapest	No such close examination carried out. Tends to remain with traditional suppliers
37 Decisions to buy out components and/or sub-contract	Taken on assessment of reliability, quality and price of components in conjunction with production schedule	No assessment carried out. Traditional methods continued
38 Operational research techniques	Uses various operational research techniques to assist in optimising plant efficiency	Unaware of such techniques or regarded as irrelevant
Labour relations		
39 Responsibility for creating positive labour relations	Belief that all management is responsible	Blaming history and/or labour force
40 Assessment of good labour relations	Numerous methods employed – sickness, accident, lateness rates, labour turnover, strikes, product quality, etc.	Number of strikes or other single indicators used
41 Grievance procedure	Carefully worked out, agreed by all parties, and adhered to	Roughly drawn-up and not always followed
42 Unions	Regarded as having constructive role to play	Discussed in terms of actual or potential nuisance
43 Workers' output	Belief that men will give of their best when treated as being responsible	Belief that men are lazy and must be browbeaten
44 Consultation	Exists and is seen as healthy and functional	Does not exist or has been abolished or is discussed in terms of nuisance value
45 Personnel function	Matters affecting all personnel dealt with at senior managerial level	Does not exist or duties confined to welfare work
46 Training and education of work-force	A variety of training schemes and/or people sent away on courses	Limited facilities for training – largely concentrated on apprentices. Little use of outside courses
47 Staff/works differentials	Have been ended or are being progressively reduced	Little or no action taken to this end

Labour relations	Thruster	Sleeper
48 Labour relations research	Curious about other firms' practices – carries out investigations	Insular, ignores other firms' practices
49 Shortage of skilled labour and/or other labour	Action to train up unskilled or acquire extra labour from abroad if necessary	Acceptance of shortage as limiting factor
50 Method of payment	Actively assessing and experimenting with various methods of payment – flat rate, piece rate, merit system, bonus system, profit sharing and share owning	Present and probably traditional methods of payment accepted uncritically
51 Revelation of financial results	Regularly and frequently given to shop floor workers	Restricted to top management
52 Employees	All employees considered to be actively contributing to success of firm	Staff (non-production workers) regarded with suspicion – an overhead

Research and development		
53 Overall plan	Decided in consultation with marketing	No research and development carried out, or on an *ad hoc* basis
54 Research association	Uses research association or other sources of advice, viz. universities, technical colleges	Ignores research association and alternative sources
55 Relationship of research department to production	Research and development activity departmentalised, budgeted and represented at board level	Research and development is dogsbody of production
56 Taking out and granting licences	Both actions regularly examined with regard to all benefits economic or otherwise accruing to the firm	Either or both possibilities ignored

General		
57 Problems of firm	Managers' readiness to blame themselves for any shortcomings	Readiness to blame others (Government, unions, labour, Communists, junior supervision) for lack of progress
58 Unprofitable products	Ready to cut out unprofitable products unless case for retention demonstrated	Unwilling to be so surgical
59 Competition	Regarded as healthy, necessary and functional	All right as long as it does not hurt, otherwise unfair

Part VI

Trends

Introduction

ONE convenient way of segmenting those who choose to write on subjects of interest to management is to place them into three quite separate baskets:

- Those who are preoccupied with exploring and commenting on the present situation.
- Those who prefer to look back and explain on the basis of historical analysis why we are what we are.
- Finally, those who prefer to look ahead and, if not actually to predict the future, to suggest how it may unfold.

Regardless of which approach they took, all the authors in this section did far more than just look ahead; they influenced nations, institutions and people to act and think a little differently from how they had been accustomed.

A unique example of the second category of writer is Antony Jay. What could sixteenth-century politics possibly have in common with twentieth-century management? The answer – in *Management and Machiavelli* – is, a lot.

During the past 30 years, the notion of growth has become so ingrained in every aspect of our lives that we take it for granted. Big cities, big aeroplanes, huge roads, global enterprises and world-scale factories seem acceptable solutions to many economic and social conundrums. Two separate, but closely related, books, *The Limits to Growth* and *Small is Beautiful*, set out to argue that unlimited, uncontrolled growth might have some unexpected and unwanted consequences.

The Limits to Growth was a report submitted by a blue ribbon collection of world acclaimed 'shakers and movers'. It was dismissed in much the same way that Malthus was dismissed when, 175 years earlier, he hinted at many of the same things. Twenty years after its publication the problems that its authors foresaw are upon us, at least in part. In *Small is Beautiful*, Schumacher, chief economist of the Coal Board, not only looked ahead but also prescribed how we should act and behave in order to preserve our planet. There is an appropriate scale for most human activities – and we need to understand how to determine that scale and then plan accordingly.

Don Schon looked ahead as well, but from a totally different perspective. *Beyond the Stable State*, based on his BBC Reith Lectures, was more concerned with the strategy of growth, its corresponding impact on various aspects of institutional growth, and its effect on firms and their employees.

Yet another view of how growth actually works in practice was highlighted in *Sources of Invention* by Jewkes, Sawers and Stillerman. While the authors tried to explain specifically how ideas for new inventions are developed, nurtured and eventually transformed into commercial reality, they also alluded to a much grander and more eloquent explanation of creativity, innovation and change.

Most writers on management topics over the last 30 years wrote seriously about serious subjects. However, there were exceptions. Few management writers can claim to have their names permanently inscribed in *Webster's Dictionary*; C. Northcote Parkinson is one! *Parkinson's Law* – based, interestingly enough, on hard statistical evidence – rapidly became the basis for explaining many administrative phenomena that had previously been mysteries.

22

Beyond the Stable State

Donald A. Schön

*I*n Beyond the Stable State, *Don Schön introduced a concept of the firm that emphasized its ability to transform itself in order to adapt to a changing environment. Noting that many firms produced multiple products and that these changed over time, Schön focused attention on the shift in the concept and function of the firm from an organization that made well-defined products with well-understood technologies to a business system that met evolving customer needs, using new technologies as they emerged.*

This emphasis on the firm as an innovative institution was markedly different from the picture presented by most other authors, who viewed firms in terms of the economic efficiency of a static set of undertakings. Later, Schön would focus his work on the ways in which learning could be facilitated. In this sense, he anticipated by more than a decade the notion of dynamic strategy and fast-cycle innovators that we associate with 'Japanese management'.

Professor Joseph L. Bower,
Harvard Business School,
Boston, Massachusetts

Chapter 3: Evolution of the Business Firm

Business firms as learning systems

AS we search for examples of learning systems, it is hard to find a more striking example than the business firm.

To begin with, business firms in western society have been primary vehicles for the diffusion of innovations and therefore, in a major sense, agents of social learning for society at large. Moreover, seen as a form evolving in relation to its changing environment, the business firm has been unsurpassed over the last fifty years in its ability to effect rapid, inventive transformations of itself without flying apart at the seams, without disappearing as a form, often without loss of identity even at the level of the individual firm.

This pattern of evolution has proceeded in stages – each marked by a characteristic 'defining concept' for the firm, and by characteristic patterns of organization, planning and management. The most recently emerging stages represent, in effect, paradigms of learning systems for the society as a whole.

The classical business firm

The classical business firm – the firm as it was understood in the first decades of this century – was organized around a product. Shoes are a case in point. A shoe as a product defines itself at the intersection of a particular kind of use of market and a particular technology. A company 'in the shoe business' had to have within it men who understood the technology of leather – who could tell, for example, by the feel, smell

Abridged from Donald A. Schön: *Beyond the Stable State* (London: Maurice Temple Smith Ltd, 1971). Copyright © 1971 by Donald A. Schön.

and look of a hide what its uses would be in manufacture; and such men came, not surprisingly, to dominate the industry. Within the firm, divisions formed around functions like production, sales, and accounting. The firm was an organizational pyramid with functional units under the control of functional managers and functional managers under the control of top management. The firm existed as an intermediate link in a chain of supply which fed into it raw and intermediate materials and manufacturing equipment, and a chain of distribution and marketing which carried its products to the ultimate consumer.

The classical business firm took as given its particular technology and the demand for its particular product. Planning, therefore, consisted primarily in the effort to match projected curves of supply and demand. The principal planning question was 'Will our capacity to produce match the readiness of the market to buy?'

From this early stage, the evolution of the business firm has had several major turning points.

The first of these occurred around World War II, a time in which certain broad transitional themes were announced: the shifts from static product-line to product innovation, from single product-line to product diversity, and from product-based to process-based definition of the firm. These transitions were brought about by a number of factors working together. They occurred in various industries at different rates and in different ways. And they brought about revolutionary changes in what it meant to be a business or an industry.

After World War II it began to become commonplace to think of invention as a necessary internal function of the firm. Previously, entrepreneurs had established businesses around inventions. Now it began to be an idea in good currency that regular and continuing invention was essential to the established firm. In part, this reflected the increasingly technological nature of industrial competition. In part, it responded to the twin ideologies of research and growth which had received much of their impetus from the example of the development and use of technology in the war. Finally, it reflected the increasing saturation of traditional markets and the need to create new markets by developing and marketing new products.

Business firms began to take seriously not only the improvement of technological and marketing systems associated with their existing product lines, but the internal generation of new businesses based on new product lines. The internalization of this development capability, initially seen as an instrument of corporate growth, turned out to require transformation of the nature of the firm itself; the tool transformed its user.

• *Firms raised the level of generality at which they defined their products.* 'Shoe companies' began to say that their business was 'footwear'; oil companies, 'energy'; business equipment firms, 'information processing'.

Where the change was not merely nominal, it signaled a broadening of the industrial base away from the manufacture and sale of traditional products. A footwear company has within its scope the manufacture and marketing of slippers, sneakers, rubbers and boots, each built on a *different* technology. These are separate businesses, depending on different materials, sources of supply, methods of production, outlets, and channels of distribution. No one could manage such a cluster of businesses and integrate them into an effective whole, unless he were able to give up the old 'shoe' mentality built on the social and intellectual systems linked to the technology of leather shoes. Such a business has a charter for innovation far broader than newer and better varieties of shoes. The marketing man is king and the planners ask, 'Within the broad domain of our market, what will they need? What will they come to buy?'

• *Science-based industries, advanced in their ability to undertake and use research, invaded traditional industries.* The invasion of traditional industries dating from the Industrial Revolution (textiles, shoes, paper, machine tools, graphics) by science-based industries (chemical and petrochemical, electronic, information-processing) represented one of the last half-century's major themes of technological innovation. The science-based industries pre-empted markets. They served as carriers of new technological systems. In the forties, for example, the chemical industry's invasion of textiles yielded synthetic fibers and finishes, and in the fifties virtually the entire range of new textile products based on synthetics. The effect was to lock clusters of industries together. New industrial complexes have made the Standard Industrial Classification Manual obsolete. Now we have not a textile industry, but a textile-chemical-paper complex; not a machine tool industry, but a 'materials-forming' industry. And individual firms have had to incorporate the elements of diverse technologies and businesses associated with these new definitions of industries. A major textile manufacturer has synthetic fiber, non-woven, and information-processing divisions. A large machine tool builder has divisions for plastics, precision-forging, chemical-forming and numerically controlled machine tools.

• *Research- and development-based companies worked out the logical consequences of the concept of technological innovation as an inherent business function.*

3M (Minnesota Mining and Manufacturing) began by making minerals. They ground up the minerals and deposited them on a substrate with glue and cut it into pieces and had sandpaper. Sandpaper was their classical business product. Around World War II a man named Cooke in their research department invented a tape which was transparent and which you could stick on things. He called it Scotch tape. The idea was that you were supposed to save money with it. You could mend books instead of throwing them away. But in fact, when they put Scotch tape on the market, they discovered quite differently. What do you do with Scotch tape? How do you use it? Well, you wrap up presents with it, you hang things on the wall. My teenage daughter fixes her hair with it. It turns out that Scotch tape is a projective test for consumers. And the 3M company has a marketing style that is beautifully adapted to that. They have now come up with hair-fixing Scotch tape, noticing what consumers have done. 3M in that sense has become a learning system.

All of these trends have combined to effect certain major shifts. In response to new technologies, industrial invasions and diversification away from saturated markets, *the firm has tended to evolve from a pyramid, built around a single relatively static product line, to a constellation of semi-autonomous divisions.*

The constellation firm can no longer be defined in terms of a class of products – however general the class may be. There is no set of properties which all and only the products of the firm possess. Instead, the products of the firm bear to one another a family resemblance, which reflects the processes of development through which one led to another.

The firm defines itself as the vehicle for carrying out a special kind of *process*. It defines itself through its engagement in entrepreneurship, the launching of new ventures, or in commercializing what comes out of development.

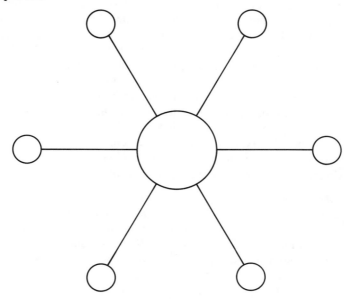

The constellation firm displays peculiar capabilities for adaptation. Each semi-autonomous unit may be discarded when it gets into trouble, and new units brought into being, without disturbing the other units and without requiring major shifts in the nucleus of the firm.

The principal figure in the firm becomes the manager of the corporate entrepreneurial process; and the central planning question is this: 'What are the potentials in development for new commercial ventures?'

From products to business systems

In the business firm's evolution over the last half-century, while the firm has acquired the capacity to diffuse whole industries and in some cases to sustain technological innovation within them, it has always defined itself around its product. At the present time, however, products are becoming obsolete. This is not to say merely that particular products are obsolescent, but that we are evolving away from the product as the unit around which business organizations are defined and towards integration around 'business systems'.

The potency of the concept of business systems owes a great deal to the aerospace and weapons systems of the last thirty years. NASA, for example, cannot be said to be in any traditional sense an industry. It is an immense organization, made up of government agencies, laboratories, and related contractors, all devoted (until recently) to the aim of getting man to the moon.

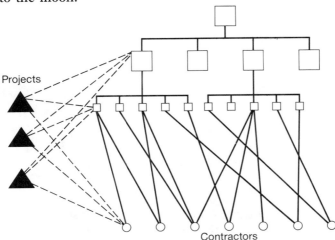

Contrast the manner in which the nation carries out another major function, which might be described as 'keeping us in clean clothes'.

The main thing about *this* function is that no person or agency is responsible for it. It is carried out through the interaction of elements of what are usually considered separate industries:

- The 'chain' of linked textile industries spins yarn from fiber or filament; makes, cuts and converts cloth; and manufactures, distributes and markets apparel.
- The soap and chemical complex manufactures, distributes and markets soaps, solvents, detergents and other cleaning materials.
- The appliance complex manufactures and distributes commercial and domestic equipment for laundering and cleaning garments.
- The service industry consists of laundering and dry-cleaning establishments.
- Consumers wear clothes, have them cleaned, and themselves perform many of the tasks of maintenance and cleaning.

This is an oversimple description. Nevertheless, the relations among its elements already appear to be extremely complex.

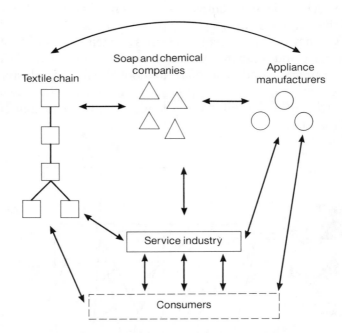

This complex of industries, organizations and institutions, all subsumed under the function of 'keeping us in clean clothes', we will call a business system. Any complex of firms related to one another in the performance of a major social function is a business system. On this particular business system the nation spends about $5 billion per year.

Within the system, 'innovation' turns out frequently to be a response, at a lag, in one part of the system to what another part of the system has done.

● In 1960 a group of consultants proposed to the Whirlpool Corporation that they produce a 'solvent washer' which would be, in effect, a home dry-cleaning machine for all kinds of garments. Whirlpool, it turned out, already had a version of the idea. But its market studies had convinced it that women would resist any increase in the amount of ironing they had to do; home dry-cleaners would simply produce more clothes to be ironed.

In the early sixties, however, 'wash-and-wear' gained acceptance. And wash-and-wear fabrics could in most cases be 'finished' acceptably without ironing. The introduction of wash-and-wear released the idea of the coin-operated dry-cleaner, which had been on Whirlpool's shelves. Norge had the same idea. And Whirlpool and Norge raced to be first to the market with the 'coin-ops'.

The introduction of the coin-ops confronted traditional private dry-cleaning establishments with a new form of competition. The result was to force such companies either to set up 'coin-op' concessions, to turn themselves into more industrialized dry-cleaning establishments better able to meet the new competition, or to specialize in 'craft' work highly geared to the needs of particular customers, so that in special areas they could outperform the 'coin-ops'.

In the meantime, people were cleaning their clothes in common equipment at room temperature. Bacterial problems arose which created the 'need' for new bacteriostats that could function effectively in 'coin-ops'.

The business system as a whole had been significantly transformed, but through a kind of systems-interaction managed by no one. An innovation in one part of the system had led to another, creating waves of new requirements to which others in the system had to respond in still different ways. To each element in the system, the wave brought requirements or opportunities for new products and services. The diffusion of product-innovation contributed to an overall transformation of the system whose character became clear only after the fact.

What emerges is a new strategy of growth. In the thirties, forties and fifties, businesses grew through 'horizontal' or 'vertical' integration. The vertical and horizontal integration of firms received its impetus from the pressures and opportunities for business growth: the expansion of markets, the increasing availability of capital, the transition from family to public ownership and from family to professional management. The industrial giants of the thirties and forties – the great steel, paper, automotive and chemical companies, for example – assumed this form. They aggregated and compressed similar product-centered firms and the business links which connected them, on the one hand, to sources of supply and, on the other, to end users. But throughout this process, the classical definition and organization of industries remained very much intact.

But the 'business system firm' has a kind of integration which is neither 'horizontal' nor 'vertical'. It takes different 'cuts' at business systems: it integrates a mix of the elements of a business system – elements which are neither horizontally nor vertically related to one another but which combine to perform a major social function. That is, it neither combines companies manufacturing similar end products nor links together the chains of companies that connect raw materials to consumer goods, but organizes sets of product and service companies that interact to make up a business system.

● Firms have grown up around 'institutional feeding'. They take on the function of providing meals to specification for certain numbers of people in certain institutions (hospitals, schools, airliners, hotels). They control not only the purchasing of raw materials, the preparation of intermediates, and the final preparation, but the design and manufacture of equipment, utensils, and maintenance equipment. They may be integrated back to agriculture, if that seems desirable, or to the steel in their forks. They retain, at each point, the freedom to decide to make or buy, own or franchise, employ one supplier or a number.

Such a firm stands an excellent chance of orchestrating the various innovations required to transform the feeding system. If the economic use of infra-red ovens depends, for example, on the uniform slicing of meat to certain thicknesses, the firm can assure that uniformity.

● In New York, a new firm combines a dredging service for New York harbor with a land development firm. The product of the dredging will provide fill for made land to be developed at the harbor's edge.

● A Danish pastor builds a business around a 'recreation system'. A travel service provides customers for a chain of hotels and restaurants dotted throughout Europe; bus and airline companies convey travellers from Denmark to these resorts and back; and a central computer-based information system makes reservations, projects demand, schedules trips, calculates costs. Control over *each* of these elements allows one to serve as customer for the other, permits full utilization of facilities, reduces costs – and leads, in turn, to increased demand.

The movement toward business systems further erodes the boundaries between private and public enterprise. Firms that have come to identify themselves with broad social functions ('providing shelter', 'feeding') have the capability to carry out functions usually reserved for public institutions.

In part, this reflects the growing market for public systems such as housing, transportation, waste management and the like. In part, it reflects recognition that, if a new technology is to be introduced into a public system, the whole system must be restructured.

Public systems, like business systems, are dynamically conservative social and intellectual systems built around prevailing technology. The established system will resist any significant technological innovation. A significant technological innovation will fail in a situation favorable to the introduction of a new *system* unless the other complementary components of the system can be made available.

● Firms like Raytheon, General Learning, and Xerox have organized divisions around 'educational systems' and claim the capability for initiating and managing all of the functions associated with an educational objective – for example, planning the junior college system of a community, developing curriculum and materials, training and recruiting teachers, and overseeing the construction of buildings.

● Westinghouse and Walt Disney Productions have entered the 'city business', which means that they have defined whole communities as their units of development and, beginning with land speculation, they are prepared to undertake land improvement, road-building, housing developments, construction of schools and community facilities, preparation of industrial sites and attraction of industry.

● Litton Industries and Corn Products Corporation have taken on, in developing countries, programs of agricultural and industrial development of a breadth usually associated only with big government. CPC, for example, is engaged in one Latin American country in performing a set of functions analogous to the work of the Agriculture Department in the United States – introduction of new crop varieties and methods, construction of 'packaged' food-processing plants, training of farmers, provision of technical assistance.

Such firms have under their control the elements required to permit the transformation of whole systems. If a firm controls the nature of the equipment to be used in preparing the food for its market, it can afford to introduce foods which need special preparation. If the firm can figure out how to modify or replace its preparation equipment economically, it need not wait for complementary innovation on the part of another element of the system, nor does it have to rely on persuasion. But the investments required to permit systems-wide control must be justified by the volume and profitability of the new forms of business to be generated.

The firm has internalized those elements of the business system (and the relationships between them) which would otherwise be split between separate industries and corporations. The firm gains capability, therefore, for initiating and managing the innovation and diffusion, not of products or techniques alone, but of whole new systems related to its central function.

The management of a business systems firm poses special problems, and it is not surprising that some firms seeking to organize around complex business systems have encountered major difficulties. For such a firm, 'management' now means the creation and maintenance of a network of components inside the firm which would have been handled through a variety of transactions with outside institutions. Changes of investment in one component produce chain reaction among others. Innovations in any one area penetrate all areas. The system must become capable of planning for all components in a balanced and comprehensive way, and its internal network of information and control must be adequate to detect and modulate events in one area which have significant implications for the system as a whole. As a diffusion system, the firm must take into account, and generate in each wave of expansion, all the elements required for the performance of the system's function. It cannot make decisions about expansion merely on the basis of an assumed market for its product. It cannot introduce a new product and let things take care of themselves. In order to make such decisions, it must assess the adequacy of a given functional system in a region, the problems associated with the introduction of a new system for performing that function, and the firm's own resources for carrying out that introduction – including the resulting dislocation of established firms and workers.

The firm has no stable base in the technologies of particular products or the systems built around them. It is, therefore, an internal learning system in which the system's interactions, illustrated by the example of the 'coin-op' dry-cleaner, must now become a matter of directed transformation of the whole system. These directed transformations are in part the justification for the business systems firm. But they oblige it to internalize processes of information flow and sequential innovation which have traditionally been left to the 'market' and to the chain reactions within and across industry lines – reactions in which each firm had only to worry about its own response as one component. The business firm, representing the entire functional system, must now learn to effect the transformation and diffusion of the system as a whole.

23

The Limits to Growth

Donella H. Meadows, Dennis L. Meadows,
Jørgen Randers and William W. Behrens III

The first report submitted to the Club of Rome, entitled The Limits of Growth, *bears the date 1972. Twenty years on, the 12 member countries of the EC are to constitute a single market encompassing 340 million Europeans. For the continent of Europe, the end of the twentieth century is doubly significant. Celebrations of the approach of the year 2000 will begin in 1992 – the quincentenary year of Christopher Columbus' discovery of America, which represented the first step towards establishing the geographical unity of the world and the concept of the 'global village'.*

The report of 1972, prepared by an interdisciplinary and multinational team from MIT using 'dynamic systems analysis', is still intellectually challenging today. Its concept of the 'state of global equilibrium' was criticized at the time as alarmist and apocalyptic and for its failure to take into account the great divide between the 'haves' and 'have nots'. Nonetheless, the equilibrium proposed did not imply zero growth. Progress was to result from technological advance, and higher productivity was to be aimed at achieving 'a higher standard of living or more leisure or more pleasant surroundings for everyone'. Growth was no longer to be an end in itself.

But originality is not the key feature here. The report acknowledges the fact that John Stuart Mill had recommended a stable wealth–population ratio as a basic ingredient in improving the quality of life in The Art of Living *in 1857. Its merit lies, rather, in its trail-blazing use of precise, quantifiable concepts – population, wealth, food, natural resources and pollution – and its contemporary approach to exploring their interrelationship and the likely consequences of anomalies in it if growth were to continue to occupy first place in the scale of priorities.*

The Limits to Growth *sounded a first and eloquent alarm call to a society that in the 1970s was attempting to 'stabilize' a throwaway culture on the basis of purely parochial attitudes. It pioneered the adoption of a global perspective by calling for better political and economic management on a worldwide basis. The Club of Rome was responsible for alerting the world to crisis on a planetary scale. Ecology, man's relationship with nature and with himself, became a major new issue for intellectual attention.*

Curiously enough, the MIT team's predictions echoed Saint-Just's trenchant revolutionary maxim, 'The present order is the disorder of the future'. At least in part, that future and that disorder are already upon us. The four macropollution phenomena referred to by Alexander King, current president of the Club of Rome – toxic waste, acid rain, the damaged ozone layer and the greenhouse effect – make it imperative that we should radically reassess our scale of values, rethink unlimited consumption-linked growth and work towards solidarity in achieving a global equilibrium.

Emilio Cassinello,
Presidente, Sociedad Estatal Para
La Exposicion Universal de Sevilla 1992,
Seville, Spain

Chapter V: The State of Global Equilibrium

Most persons think that a state in order to be happy ought to be large; but even if they are right, they have no idea of what is a large and what a small state. . . . To the size of states there is a limit, as there is to other things, plants, animals, implements; for none of these retain their natural power when they are too large or too small, but they either wholly lose their nature, or are spoiled.

Aristotle, 322 BC

POSITIVE feedback loops operating without any constraints generate exponential growth. In the world system two positive feedback loops are dominant now, producing exponential growth of population and of industrial capital.

In any finite system there must be constraints that can act to stop exponential growth. These constraints are negative feedback loops. The negative loops become stronger and stronger as growth approaches the ultimate limit, or carrying capacity, of the system's environment. Finally the negative loops balance or dominate the positive ones, and growth comes to an end. In the world system the negative feedback loops involve such processes as pollution of the environment, depletion of nonrenewable resources, and famine.

The delays inherent in the action of these negative loops tend to allow population and capital to overshoot their ultimately sustainable levels. The period of overshoot is wasteful of resources. It generally decreases the carrying capacity of the environment as well, intensifying the eventual decline in population and capital.

The Limits to Growth: A report for the Club of Rome's Project on the Predicament of Mankind, by Donella H. Meadows, Dennis L. Meadows, Jørgen Randers, William W. Behrens, III. A Potomac Associates book published by Universe Books, NY, 1972. Graphics by Potomac Associates. [Abridged.]

The growth-stopping pressures from negative feedback loops are already being felt in many parts of human society. The major societal responses to these pressures have been directed at the negative feedback loops themselves. Technological solutions have been devised to weaken the loops or to disguise the pressures they generate so that growth can continue. Such means may have some short-term effect in relieving pressures caused by growth, but in the long run they do nothing to prevent the overshoot and subsequent collapse of the system.

Another response to the problems created by growth would be to weaken the *positive* feedback loops that are generating the growth. Such a solution has almost never been acknowledged as legitimate by any modern society, and it has certainly never been effectively carried out. What kinds of policies would such a solution involve? What sort of world would result? There is almost no historical precedent for such an approach, and thus there is no alternative but to discuss it in terms of models – either mental models or formal, written models. How will the world model behave if we include in it some policy to control growth deliberately? Will such a policy change generate a 'better' behavior mode?

Whenever we use words such as 'better' and begin choosing among alternative model outputs, we, the experimenters, are inserting our own values and preferences into the modeling process. The values built into each casual relationship of the model are the real, operational values of the world to the degree that we can determine them. The values that cause us to rank computer outputs as 'better' or 'worse' are the personal values of the modeler or his audience. We have already asserted our own value system by rejecting the overshoot and collapse mode as undesirable. Now that we are seeking a 'better' result, we must define our goal for the system as clearly as possible. We are searching for a model output that represents a world system that is:

1 sustainable without sudden and uncontrollable collapse; and
2 capable of satisfying the basic material requirements of all of its people.

Now let us see what policies will bring about such behavior in the world model.

The equilibrium state

We are by no means the first people in man's written history to propose some sort of nongrowing state for human society. A number of philosophers, economists, and biologists have discussed such a state and called it by many different names, with as many different meanings.[1]

We have, after much discussion, decided to call the state of constant population and capital by the term 'equilibrium.' Equilibrium means a state of balance or equality between opposing forces. In the dynamic terms of the world model, the opposing forces are those causing population and capital stock to increase (high desired family size, low birth control effectiveness, high rate of capital investment) and those causing population and capital stock to decrease (lack of food, pollution, high rate of depreciation or obsolescence). The word 'capital' should be understood to mean service, industrial, and agricultural capital combined. *Thus the most basic definition of the state of global equilibrium is that population and capital are essentially stable, with the forces tending to increase or decrease them in a carefully controlled balance.*

There is much room for variation within that definition. We have only specified that the stocks of capital and population remain constant, but they might theoretically be constant at a high level or a low level – or one might be high and the other low. A tank of water can be maintained at a given level with a fast inflow and outflow of water or with a slow trickle in and out. If the flow is fast, the average drop of water will spend less time in the tank than if the flow is slow. Similarly, a stable population of any size can be achieved with either high, equal birth and death rates (short average lifetime) or low, equal birth and death rates (long average lifetime). A stock of capital can be maintained with high investment and depreciation rates or low investment and depreciation rates. Any combination of these possibilities would fit into our basic definition of global equilibrium.

What criteria can be used to choose among the many options available in the equilibrium state? The dynamic interactions in the world system indicate that the first decision that must be made concerns time. *How long should the equilibrium state exist?* If society is only interested in a time span of 6 months or a year, the world model indicates that almost any level of population and capital could be maintained. If the time horizon is extended to 20 or 50 years, the options are greatly reduced, since the rates and levels must be adjusted to ensure that the capital investment rate will not be limited by resource availability during that time span, or that the death rate will not be uncontrollably influenced by pollution or food shortage. The longer a society prefers to maintain the state of equilibrium, the lower the rates and levels must be.

At the limit, of course, no population or capital level can be maintained forever, but that limit is very far away in time if resources are managed wisely and if there is a sufficiently long time horizon in planning. Let us take as a reasonable time horizon the expected lifetime of a child born into the world tomorrow – 70 years if proper food and medical care are supplied. Since most people spend a large part of their time and energy raising children, they might choose as a minimum goal that the society left to those children can be maintained for the full span of the children's lives.

If society's time horizon is as long as 70 years, the permissible population and capital levels may not be too different from those existing today. The rates would be considerably different from those of today, however. Any society would undoubtedly prefer that the death rate be low rather than high, since a long, healthy life seems to be a universal human desire. To maintain equilibrium with long life expectancy, the birth rate then must also be low. It would be best, too, if the capital investment and depreciation rates were low, because the lower they are, the less resource depletion and pollution there will be. Keeping depletion and pollution to a minimum could either increase the maximum size of the population and capital levels or increase the length of time the equilibrium state could be maintained, depending on which goal the society as a whole preferred.

By choosing a fairly long time horizon for its existence, and a long average lifetime as a desirable goal, we have now arrived at a minimum set of requirements for the state of global equilibrium. They are:

1 *The capital plant and the population are constant in size.* The birth rate equals the death rate and the capital investment rate equals the depreciation rate.
2 *All input and output rates – births, deaths, investment, and depreciation – are kept to a minimum.*
3 *The levels of capital and population and the ratio of the two are set in accordance with the values of the society.* They may be deliberately revised and slowly adjusted as the advance of technology creates new options.

An equilibrium defined in this way does not mean stagnation. Within the first two guidelines above, corporations could expand or fail, local populations could increase or decrease, income could become more or less evenly distributed. Technological advance would permit the services provided by a constant stock of capital to increase slowly. Within the third guideline, any country could change its average standard of living by altering the balance between its population and its capital. Furthermore, a society could adjust to changing internal or external factors by raising or lowering the population or capital stocks, or both, slowly and in a controlled fashion, with a predetermined goal in mind. The three points above define a *dynamic* equilibrium, which need not and probably would not 'freeze' the world into the population-capital configuration that happens to exist at the present time. The object in accepting the above three statements is to create freedom for society, not to impose a straitjacket.

What would life be like in such an equilibrium state? Would innovation be stifled? Would society be locked into the patterns of inequality and injustice we see in the world today? Discussion of these questions must proceed on the basis of mental models, for there is no formal model of social conditions in the equilibrium state. No one can predict what sort of institutions mankind might develop under these new conditions. There is, of course, no guarantee that the new society would be much better or even much different from that which exists today. It seems possible, however, that a society released from struggling with the many problems caused by growth may have more energy and ingenuity available for solving other problems. In fact, we believe, as we will illustrate below, that the evolution of a society that favors innovation and technological development, a society based on equality and justice, is far more likely to evolve in a state of global equilibrium than it is in the state of growth we are experiencing today.

Growth in the equilibrium state

In 1857 John Stuart Mill wrote:

> It is scarcely necessary to remark that a stationary condition of capital and population implies no stationary state of human improvement. There would be as much scope as ever for all kinds of mental culture, and moral and social progress; as much room for improving the Art of Living and much more likelihood of its being improved.[2]

Population and capital are the only quantities that need be constant in the equilibrium state. Any human activity that does not require a large flow of irreplaceable resources or produce severe environmental degradation might continue to grow indefinitely. In particular, those pursuits that many people would list as the most desirable and satisfying activities of man – education, art, music, religion, basic scientific research, athletics, and social interactions – could flourish.

All of the activities listed above depend very strongly on two factors. First, they depend upon the availability of some surplus production after the basic human needs of food and shelter have been met. Second, they require leisure time. In any equilibrium state the relative levels of capital and population could be adjusted to assure that human material needs are fulfilled at any desired level. Since the amount of material production would be essentially fixed, every improvement in production methods could result in increased leisure for the population – leisure that could be devoted to any activity that is relatively nonconsuming and nonpolluting, such as those listed above. Thus, this unhappy situation described by Bertrand Russell could be avoided:

> Suppose that, at a given moment, a certain number of people are engaged in the manufacture of pins. They make as many pins as the world needs, working (say) eight hours a day. Someone makes an invention by which the same number of men can make twice as many pins as before. But the world does not need twice as many pins. Pins are already so cheap that hardly any more will be bought at a lower price. In a sensible world, everybody concerned in the manufacture of pins would take to working four hours instead of eight, and everything else would go on as before. But in the actual world this would be thought demoralizing. The men still work eight hours, there are too many pins, some employers go bankrupt, and half the men previously concerned in making pins are thrown out of work. There is, in the end, just as much leisure as on the other plan, but half the men are totally idle while half are still overworked. In this way it is insured that the unavoidable leisure shall cause misery all around instead of being a universal source of happiness. Can anything more insane be imagined?[3]

But would the technological improvements that permit the production of pins or anything else more efficiently be forthcoming in a world where all basic material needs are fulfilled and additional production is not allowed? Does man have to be pushed by hardship and the incentive of material growth to devise better ways to do things?

Historical evidence would indicate that very few key inventions have been made by men who had to spend all their energy overcoming the immediate pressures of survival. Atomic energy was discovered in the laboratories of basic science by individuals unaware of any threat of fossil fuel depletion. The first genetic experiments, which led a hundred years later to high-yield agricultural crops, took place in the peace of a European monastery. Pressing human need may have forced the application of these basic discoveries to practical problems, but only freedom from need produced the knowledge necessary for the practical applications.

Technological advance would be both necessary and welcome in the equilibrium state. A few obvious examples of the kinds of practical discoveries that would enhance the workings of a steady state society include:

- new methods of waste collection, to decrease pollution and make discarded material available for recycling;
- more efficient techniques of recycling, to reduce rates of resource depletion;
- better product design to increase product lifetime and promote easy repair, so that the capital depreciation rate would be minimized;
- harnessing of incident solar energy, the most pollution-free power source;
- methods of natural pest control, based on more complete understanding of ecological interrelationships;
- medical advances that would decrease the death rate;
- contraceptive advances that would facilitate the equalization of the birth rate with the decreasing death rate.

As for the incentive that would encourage men to produce such technological advances, what better incentive could there be than the knowledge that a new idea would be translated into a visible improvement in the quality of life? Historically mankind's long record of new inventions has resulted in crowding, deterioration of the environment, and greater social inequality because greater productivity has been absorbed by population and capital growth. There is no reason why higher productivity could not be translated into a higher standard of living or more leisure or more pleasant surroundings for everyone, if these goals replace growth as the primary value of society.

Equality in the equilibrium state

One of the most commonly accepted myths in our present society is the promise that a continuation of our present patterns of growth will lead to human equality. We have demonstrated in various parts of this book that present patterns of population and capital growth are actually increasing the gap between the rich and the poor on a worldwide basis, and that the ultimate result of a continued attempt to grow according to the present pattern will be a disastrous collapse.

The greatest possible impediment to more equal distribution of the world's resources is population growth. It seems to be a universal observation, regrettable but understandable, that, as the number of people over whom a fixed resource must be distributed increases, the equality of distribution decreases. Equal sharing becomes social suicide if the average amount available per person is not enough to maintain life. FAO studies of food distribution have actually documented this general observation.

> Analysis of distribution curves shows that when the food supplies of a group diminish, inequalities in intake are accentuated, while the number of undernourished families increases more than in proportion to the deviation from the mean. Moreover, the food intake deficit grows with the size of the households so that large families, and their children in particular, are statistically the most likely to be underfed.[4]

In a long-term equilibrium state, the relative levels of population and capital, and their relationships to fixed constraints such as land, fresh water, and mineral resources, would have to be set so that there would be enough food and material production to maintain everyone at (at least) a subsistence level. One barrier to equal distribution would thus be removed. Furthermore, the other effective barrier to equality – the promise of growth – could no longer be maintained, as Dr. Herman E. Daly has pointed out:

> For several reasons the important issue of the stationary state will be distribution, not production. The problem of relative shares can no longer be avoided by appeals to growth. The argument that everyone should be happy as long as his absolute share of wealth increases, regardless of his relative share, will no longer be available. . . . The stationary state would make fewer demands on our environmental resources, but much greater demands on our moral resources.[5]

There is, of course, no assurance that humanity's moral resources would be sufficient to solve the problem of income distribution, even in an equilibrium state. However, there is even less assurance that such social problems will be solved in the present state of growth, which is straining both the moral and the physical resources of the world's people.

The picture of the equilibrium state we have drawn here is idealized, to be sure. It may be impossible to achieve in the form described here, and it may not be the form most people on earth would choose. The only purpose in describing it at all is to emphasize that global equilibrium need not mean an end to progress or human development. The possibilities within an equilibrium state are almost endless.

An equilibrium state would not be free of pressures, since no society can be free of pressures. Equilibrium would require trading certain human freedoms, such as producing unlimited numbers of children or consuming uncontrolled amounts of resources, for other freedoms, such as relief from pollution and crowding and the threat of collapse of the world system. It is possible that new freedoms might also arise – universal and unlimited education, leisure for creativity and inventiveness, and, most important of all, the freedom from hunger and poverty enjoyed by such a small fraction of the world's people today.

Notes

1 See, for instance:
Plato, *Laws*, 350 B.C.
Aristotle, *Politics*, 322 B.C.
Thomas Robert Malthus, *An Essay on the Principle of Population*, 1798.
John Stuart Mill, *Principles of Political Economy*, 1857.
Harrison Brown, *The Challenge of Man's Future* (New York: Viking Press, 1954).
Kenneth E. Boulding, 'The Economics of the Coming Spaceship Earth', in *Environmental Quality in a Growing Economy*, ed. H. Jarrett (Baltimore, Md.: Johns Hopkins Press, 1966).
E. J. Mishan, *The Costs of Economic Growth* (New York: Frederick A. Praeger, 1967).
Herman E. Daly, 'Toward a Stationary-State Economy.' in *The Patient Earth*, ed. J. Harte and Robert Socolow (New York: Holt, Rinehart, and Winston, 1971).
2 John Stuart Mill, *Principles of Political Economy*, in *The Collected Works of John Stuart Mill*, ed. V. W. Bladen and J. M. Robson (Toronto: University of Toronto Press, 1965), p. 754.
3 Bertrand Russell, *In Praise of Idleness and Other Essays* (London: Allen and Unwin, 1935), pp. 16–17.
4 UN Food and Agriculture Organization, *Provisional Indicative World Plan for Agricultural Development* 2: 490.
5 Herman E. Daly, 'Toward a Stationary-State Economy,' in *The Patient Earth*, ed. John Harte and Robert Socolow (New York: Holt, Rinehart, and Winston, 1971), pp. 236–37.

24

Small is Beautiful

E. F. SCHUMACHER

In trying to keep things to 'the human scale', readers of Small is Beautiful *may try to relate its themes to their own experiences and seek trends in personal or professional activities that support or refute the author's view. Having done the same myself during a wide range of government and international development assignments in each of the geopolitical regions of the world, I find that, while much has changed in the intervening years (including United Nations membership growing to 159 states), the concepts contained in the extract remain as universally relevant and thought-provoking today as they were when it was first published.*

A re-read of this piece is indeed timely in this especially dynamic era, when massive scientific and technological developments are overshadowed by even greater political, social and environmental changes. Knowing the original book, subtitled 'A Study of Economics as if People Mattered', and a bit about Mr Schumacher, I was pleased to see that in the extract two inseparable propositions emerge: that human activity is directed at improving the lot of humankind, and that we need constantly to review how best to accomplish our objectives. Their relevance will certainly not disappear too quickly – unless we all do!

Margaret J. Anstee,
Director General, United Nations Office,
Vienna

Five: A Question of Size

I was brought up on an interpretation of history which suggested that in the beginning was the family; then families got together and formed tribes; then a number of tribes formed a nation; then a number of nations formed a 'Union' or 'United States' of this or that; and that, finally, we could look forward to a single World Government. Ever since I heard this plausible story I have taken a special interest in the process, but could not help noticing that the opposite seemed to be happening: a proliferation of nation states. The United Nations Organization started some twenty-five years ago with some sixty members; now there are more than twice as many, and the number is still growing. In my youth, this process of proliferation was called 'Balkanization' and was thought to be a very bad thing. Although everybody said it was bad, it has now been going on merrily for over fifty years, in most parts of the world. Large units tend to break up into smaller units. This phenomenon, so mockingly the opposite of what I had been taught, whether we approve of it or not, should at least not pass unnoticed.

Second, I was brought up on the theory that in order to be prosperous a country had to be big – the bigger the better. This also seemed quite plausible. Look at what Churchill called 'the pumpernickel principalities' of Germany before Bismarck; and then look at the Bismarckian Reich. Is it not true that the great prosperity of Germany became possible only through this unification? All the same, the German-speaking Swiss and the German-speaking Austrians, who did not join, did just as well economically, and if we make a list of all the most prosperous countries in the world, we find that most of them are very small; whereas a list of all the biggest countries in the world shows them to be very poor indeed. Here again, there is food for thought.

Taken from E. F. Schumacher: *Small is Beautiful* (London: Sphere Books, 1973). Reprinted by kind permission of Sphere Books Ltd. This material copyright © 1973 E. F. Schumacher.

And third, I was brought up on the theory of the 'economies of scale' - that with industries and firms, just as with nations, there is an irresistible trend, dictated by modern technology, for units to become ever bigger. Now, it is quite true that today there are more large organizations and probably also bigger organizations than ever before in history; but the number of small units is also growing and certainly not declining in countries like Britain and the United States, and many of these small units are highly prosperous and provide society with most of the really fruitful new developments. Again, it is not altogether easy to reconcile theory and practice, and the situation as regards this whole issue of size is certainly puzzling to anyone brought up on these three concurrent theories.

Even today, we are generally told that gigantic organizations are inescapably necessary; but when we look closely we can notice that as soon as great size has been created there is often a strenuous attempt to attain smallness within bigness. The great achievement of Mr Sloan of General Motors was to structure this gigantic firm in such a manner that it became, in fact, a federation of fairly reasonably sized firms. In the British National Coal Board, one of the biggest firms of Western Europe, something very similar was attempted under the Chairmanship of Lord Robens; strenuous efforts were made to evolve a structure which would maintain the unity of one big organization and at the same time create the 'climate' or feeling of there being a federation of numerous 'quasi-firms'. The monolith was transformed into a well-co-ordinated assembly of lively, semi-autonomous units, each with its own drive and sense of achievement. While many theoreticians – who may not be too closely in touch with real life – are still engaging in the idolatry of large size, with practical people in the actual world there is a tremendous longing and striving to profit, if at all possible, from the convenience, humanity, and manageability of smallness. This, also, is a tendency which anyone can easily observe for himself.

Let us now approach our subject from another angle and ask what is actually *needed*. In the affairs of men, there always appears to be a need for at least two things simultaneously, which, on the face of it, seem to be incompatible and to exclude one another. We always need both freedom and order. We need the freedom of lots and lots of small, autonomous units, and, at the same time, the orderliness of large-scale, possibly global, unity and co-ordination. When it comes to action, we obviously need small units, because action is a highly personal affair, and one cannot be in touch with more than a very limited number of persons at any one time. But when it comes to the world of ideas, to principles or to ethics, to the indivisibility of peace and also of ecology, we need to recognize the unity of mankind and base our actions upon this recognition. Or to put it differently, it is true that all men are brothers, but it is also true that in our active personal relationships we can, in fact, be brothers to only a few of them, and we are called upon to show more brotherliness to them than we could possibly show to the whole of mankind. We all know people who freely talk about the brotherhood of man while treating their neighbours as enemies, just as we also know people who have, in fact, excellent relations with all their neighbours while harbouring, at the same time, appalling prejudices about all human groups outside their particular circle.

What I wish to emphasize is the *duality* of the human requirement when it comes to the question of size: there is no *single* answer. For his different purposes man needs many different structures, both small ones and large ones, some exclusive and some comprehensive. Yet people find it most difficult to keep two seemingly opposite necessities of truth in their minds at the same time. They always tend to clamour for a final solution, as if in actual life there could ever be a final solution other than death. For constructive work, the principal task is always the restoration of some kind of balance. Today, we suffer from an almost universal idolatry of giantism. It is therefore necessary to insist on the virtues of smallness – where this applies. (If there were a prevailing idolatry of smallness, irrespective of subject or purpose, one would have to try and exercise influence in the opposite direction.)

The question of scale might be put in another way: what is needed in all these matters is to discriminate, to get things sorted out. For every activity there is a certain appropriate scale, and the more active and intimate the activity, the smaller the number of people that can take part, the greater is the number of such relationship arrangements that need to be established. Take teaching: one listens to all sorts of extraordinary debates about the superiority of the teaching machine over some other forms of teaching. Well, let us discriminate: what are we trying to teach? It then becomes immediately apparent that certain things can only be taught in a very intimate circle, whereas other things can obviously be taught *en masse*, via the air, via television, via teaching machines, and so on.

What scale is appropriate? It depends on what we are trying to do. The question of scale is extremely crucial today, in political, social and economic affairs just as in almost everything else. What, for instance, is the appropriate size of a city? And also, one might ask, what is the appropriate size of a country? Now these are serious and difficult questions. It is not possible to programme a computer and get the answer. The really serious matters of life cannot be calculated. We cannot directly calculate what is right; but we jolly well know what is wrong! We can recognize right and wrong at the extremes, although we cannot normally judge them finely enough to say: 'This ought to be five per cent more; or that ought to be five per cent less.'

Take the question of size of a city. While one cannot judge these things with precision, I think it is fairly safe to say that the upper limit of what is desirable for the size of a city is probably something of the order of half a million inhabitants. It is quite clear that above such a size nothing is added to the virtue of the city. In places like London, or Tokyo, or New York, the millions do not add to the city's real value but merely create *enormous* problems and produce human degradation. So probably the order of magnitude of 500,000 inhabitants could be looked upon as the upper limit. The question of the lower limit of a real city is much more difficult to judge. The finest cities in history have been very small by twentieth-century standards. The instruments and institutions of city culture depend, no doubt, on a certain accumulation of wealth. But how much wealth has to be accumulated depends on the type of culture pursued. Philosophy, the arts and religion cost very, very little money. Other types of what claims to be 'high culture' – space research or ultra-modern physics – cost a lot of money, but are somewhat remote from the real needs of men.

I raise the question of the proper size of cities both for its own sake but also because it is, to my mind, the most relevant point when we come to consider the size of nations.

The idolatry of giantism that I have talked about is possibly one of the causes and certainly one of the effects of modern technology, particularly in matters of transport and communications. A highly developed transport and communications system has one immensely powerful effect: it makes people *footloose*.

Millions of people start moving about, deserting the rural areas and the smaller towns to follow the city lights, to go to the big city, causing a pathological growth. Take the country in which all this is perhaps most exemplified – the United States. Sociologists are studying the problem of 'megalopolis'. The word 'metropolis' is no longer big enough; hence 'megalopolis'. They freely talk about the polarization of the population of the United States into three immense megalopolitan areas: one extending from Boston to Washington, a continuous built-up area, with sixty million people; one around Chicago, another sixty million; and one on the West Coast, from San Francisco to San Diego, again a continuous built-up area with sixty million people; the rest of the country being left practically empty; deserted provincial towns, and the land cultivated with vast tractors, combine harvesters, and immense amounts of chemicals.

If this is somebody's conception of the future of the United States, it is hardly a future worth having. But whether we like it or not, this is the result of people having become footloose; it is the result of that marvellous mobility of labour which economists treasure above all else.

Everything in this world has to have a *structure*, otherwise it is chaos. Before the advent of mass transport and mass communications, the structure was simply there, because people were relatively immobile. People who wanted to move did so; witness the flood of saints from Ireland moving all over Europe. There were communications, there was mobility, but no footlooseness. Now, a great deal of structure has collapsed, and a country is like a big cargo ship in which the load is in no way secured. It tilts, and all the load slips over, and the ship founders.

One of the chief elements of structure for the whole of mankind is of course *the state*. And one of the chief elements or instruments of structuralisation (if I may use that term), is *frontiers*, national frontiers. Now previously, before this technological intervention, the relevance of frontiers was almost exclusively political and dynastic; frontiers were delimitations of political power, determining how many people you could raise for war. Economists fought against such frontiers becoming economic barriers – hence the ideology of free trade. But, then, people and things were not footloose; transport was expensive enough so that movements, both of people and of goods, were never more than marginal. Trade in the pre-industrial era was not a trade in essentials, but a trade in precious stones, precious metals, luxury goods, spices and – unhappily – slaves. The basic requirements of life had of course to be indigenously produced. And the movement of populations, except in periods of disaster, was confined to persons who had a very special reason to move, such as the Irish saints or the scholars of the University of Paris.

But now everything and everybody has become mobile. All structures are threatened, and all structures are *vulnerable* to an extent that they have never been before.

Economics, which Lord Keynes had hoped would settle down as a modest occupation similar to dentistry, suddenly becomes the most important subject of all. Economic policies absorb almost the entire attention of government, and at the same time become ever more impotent. The simplest things, which only fifty years ago one could do without difficulty, cannot get done any more. The richer a society, the more impossible it becomes to do worthwhile things without immediate pay-off. Economics has become such a thraldom that it absorbs almost the whole of foreign policy. People say, 'Ah yes, we don't like to go with these people, but we depend on them economically so we must humour them.' It tends to absorb the whole of ethics and to take precedence over all other human considerations. Now, quite clearly, this is a pathological development, which has, of course, many roots, but one of its clearly visible roots lies in the great achievements of modern technology in terms of transport and communications.

While people, with an easy-going kind of logic, believe that fast transport and instantaneous communications open up a new dimension of freedom (which they do in some rather trivial respects), they overlook the fact that these achievements also tend to destroy freedom, by making everything extremely vulnerable and extremely insecure, unless conscious policies are developed and conscious action is taken, to mitigate the destructive effects of these technological developments.

Now, these destructive effects are obviously most severe in *large* countries, because, as we have seen, frontiers produce 'structure', and it is a much bigger decision for someone to cross a frontier, to uproot himself from his native land and try and put down roots in another land, than to move within the frontiers of his country. The factor of footlooseness is, therefore, the more serious, the bigger the country. Its destructive effects can be traced both in the rich and in the poor countries. In the rich countries such as the United States of America, it produces, as already mentioned, 'megalopolis'. It also produces a rapidly increasing and ever more intractable problem of 'drop-outs', of people, who, having become footloose, cannot find a place anywhere in society. Directly connected with this, it produces an appalling problem of crime, alienation, stress, social breakdown, right down to the level of the family. In the poor countries, again most severely in the largest ones, it produces mass migration into cities, mass unemployment, and, as vitality is drained out of the rural areas, the threat of famine. The result is a 'dual society' without any inner cohesion, subject to a maximum of political instability.

As an illustration, let me take the case of Peru. The capital city, Lima, situated on the Pacific coast, had a population of 175,000 in the early 1920s, just fifty years ago. Its population is now approaching three million. The once beautiful Spanish city is now infested by slums, surrounded by misery-belts that are crawling up the Andes. But this is not all. People are arriving from the rural areas at the rate of a thousand a day – and nobody knows what to do with them. The social or psychological structure of life in the hinterland has collapsed; people have become footloose and arrive in the capital city at the rate of a thousand a day to squat on some empty land, against the police who come to beat them out, to build their mud hovels and look for a job. *And nobody knows what to do about them.* Nobody knows how to stop the drift.

Imagine that in 1864 Bismarck had annexed the whole of Denmark instead of only a small part of it, and that nothing had happened since. The Danes would be an ethnic minority in Germany, perhaps struggling to maintain their language by becoming bilingual, the official language of course being German. Only by thoroughly Germanising themselves could they avoid becoming second-class citizens. There would be an irresistible drift of the most ambitious and enterprising Danes, thoroughly Germanised, to the mainland in the south, and what then would be the status of Copenhagen? That of a remote provincial city. Or imagine Belgium as part of France. What would be the status of Brussels? Again, that of an unimportant provincial city. I don't have to enlarge on it. Imagine now that Denmark a part of Germany, and Belgium a part of France, suddenly turned what is now charmingly called 'nats' wanting independence. There would be endless, heated arguments that these 'non-countries' could not be economically viable, that their desire for independence was, to quote a famous political commentator, 'adolescent emotionalism, political naïvety, phoney economics, and sheer bare-faced opportunism'.

How can one talk about the economics of small independent countries? How can one discuss a problem that is a non-problem? There is no such thing as the viability of states or of nations, there is only a problem of viability of people: people, actual persons like you and me, are viable when they can stand on their own feet and earn their keep. You do not make non-viable people viable by putting large numbers of them into one huge community, and you do not make viable people non-viable by splitting a large community into a number of smaller, more intimate, more coherent and more manageable groups. All this is perfectly obvious and there is absolutely nothing to argue about. Some people ask: 'What happens when a country, composed of one rich province and several poor ones, falls apart because the rich province secedes?' Most probably the answer is: 'Nothing very much happens.' The rich will continue to be rich and the poor will continue to be poor. 'But if, before secession, the rich province had subsidized the poor, what happens then?' Well then, of course, the subsidy might stop. But the rich rarely subsidize the poor; more often they exploit them. They may not do so directly so much as through the terms of trade. They may obscure the situation a little by a certain redistribution of tax revenue or small-scale charity, but the last thing they want to do is secede from the poor.

The normal case is quite different, namely that the poor provinces wish to separate from the rich, and that the rich want to hold on because they know that exploitation of the poor within one's own frontiers is infinitely easier than exploitation of the poor beyond them. Now if a poor province wishes to secede at the risk of losing some subsidies, what attitude should one take?

Not that we have to decide this, but what should we think about it? Is it not a wish to be applauded and respected? Do we not *want* people to stand on their own feet, as free and self-reliant men? So again this is a 'non-problem'. I would assert therefore that there is no problem of viability, as all experience shows. If a country wishes to export all over the world, and import from all over the world, it has never been held that it had to annex the whole world in order to do so.

What about the absolute necessity of having a large internal market? This again is an optical illusion if the meaning of 'large' is conceived in terms of political boundaries. Needless to say, a prosperous market is better than a poor one, but whether that market is outside the political boundaries or inside, makes on the whole very little difference. I am not aware, for instance, that Germany, in order to export a large number of Volkswagens to the United States, a very prosperous market, could only do so after annexing the United States. But it does make a lot of difference if a poor community or province finds itself politically tied to or ruled by a rich community or province. Why? Because, in a mobile, footloose society the law of disequilibrium is infinitely stronger than the so-called law of equilibrium. Nothing succeeds like success, and nothing stagnates like stagnation. The successful province drains the life out of the unsuccessful, and without protection against the strong, the weak have no chance; either they remain weak or they must migrate and join the strong; they cannot effectively help themselves.

A most important problem in the second half of the twentieth century is the geographical distribution of population, the question of 'regionalism'.

But regionalism, not in the sense of combining a lot of states into free-trade systems, but in the opposite sense of developing all the regions within each country. This, in fact, is the most important subject on the agenda of all the larger countries today. And a lot of the nationalism of small nations today, and the desire for self-government and so-called independence, is simply a logical and rational response to the need for regional development. In the poor countries in particular there is no hope for the poor unless there is successful regional development, a development effort outside the capital city covering all the rural areas wherever people happen to be.

If this effort is not brought forth, their only choice is either to remain in their miserable condition where they are, or to migrate into the big city where their condition will be even more miserable. It is a strange phenomenon indeed that the conventional wisdom of present-day economics can do nothing to help the poor.

Invariably it proves that only such policies are viable as have in fact the result of making those already rich and powerful, richer and more powerful. It proves that industrial development only pays if it is as near as possible to the capital city or another very large town, and not in the rural areas. It proves that large projects are invariably more economic than small ones, and it proves that capital-intensive projects are invariably to be preferred as against labour-intensive ones. The economic calculus, as applied by present-day economics, forces the industrialist to eliminate the human factor because machines do not make mistakes which people do. Hence the enormous effort at automation and the drive for ever-larger units. This means that those who have nothing to sell but their labour remain in the weakest possible bargaining position. The conventional wisdom of what is now taught as economics by-passes the poor, the very people for whom development is really needed. The economics of giantism and automation is a left-over of nineteenth-century conditions and nineteenth-century thinking and it is totally incapable of solving any of the real problems of today. An entirely new system of thought is needed, a system based on attention to people, and not primarily attention to goods – (the goods will look after themselves!). It could be summed up in the phrase, 'production by the masses, rather than mass production'. What was impossible, however, in the nineteenth century, is possible now. And what was in fact – if not necessarily at least understandably – neglected in the nineteenth century is unbelievably urgent now. That is, the conscious utilization of our enormous technological and scientific potential for the fight against misery and human degradation – a fight in intimate contact with actual people, with individuals, families, small groups, rather than states and other anonymous abstractions. And this presupposes a political and organizational structure that can provide this intimacy.

What is the meaning of democracy, freedom, human dignity, standard of living, self-realization, fulfilment? Is it a matter of goods, or of people? Of course it is a matter of people. But people can be themselves only in small comprehensible groups. Therefore we must learn to think in terms of an articulated structure that can cope with a multiplicity of small-scale units. If economic thinking cannot grasp this it is useless. If it cannot get beyond its vast abstractions, the national income, the rate of growth, capital/output ratio, input-output analysis, labour mobility, capital accumulation; if it cannot get beyond all this and make contact with the human realities of poverty, frustration, alienation, despair, breakdown, crime, escapism, stress, congestion, ugliness, and spiritual death, then let us scrap economics and start afresh.

Are there not indeed enough 'signs of the times' to indicate that a new start is needed?

25

Parkinson's Law

C. Northcote Parkinson

Thirty-two years have passed since the publication of Professor Parkinson's first set of satirical essays on the excesses of central administration and bureaucracy.

This extract covers the first law. The Professor's other laws, or really principles, also represent characteristic attacks on bureaucracy. Expenditure rises to meet income. Expansion means complexity, and complexity decay.

These arrows were put in flight in a humorous context. Subsequently, when others took up the lampooning of government departments and large institutions, they would often include references to Parkinson's Law. In contrast, there has been little reference to either the author or his laws in serious management and business books.

Perhaps the problem in achieving early converts was that in the late 1950s many people worked in large organizations. Moreover, the arrival of the large centralized computing operation, which offered the prospect of increased efficiency, was a disincentive to dispersal. There was also, in the 1960s, a strong tendency to encourage mergers and consolidation.

By the 1970s, the concern about public expenditure and the need for more entrepreneurial activity started to generate a wave of change. Smallness 'became beautiful' and privatization appeared on the political agenda. Could it be claimed that Parkinson's personal war on over-arching administration had been of influence?

Probably not, since he proposed neither a cure nor a means for prevention. His was only one of many voices that exposed the perils of restrictive practices, whether in his sphere of interest – headquarters bureaucracy – or in the form of production and employment inflexibilities. In the face of increasing competition from overseas, business leaders, politicians and academics recognized the need to concentrate on external factors – on markets, customers and competition.

Parkinson's maxims are perhaps unlikely to be seen as a significant milestone in management theory. However, he has created indelible impressions of the burden of bureaucratic over-conformity and the follies of inward thinking and aggrandizement. He has left us to work out the solutions: to challenge basic assumptions and customs, to adapt and continuously renew our approaches.

Keith W. Court,
Chairman, South West Water Plc,
Exeter, Devon

Parkinson's Law

WORK expands so as to fill the time available for its completion. General recognition of this fact is shown in the proverbial phrase 'It is the busiest man who has time to spare.' Thus, an elderly lady of leisure can spend the entire day in writing and dispatching a postcard to her niece at Bognor Regis. An hour will be spent in finding the postcard, another in hunting for spectacles, half an hour in a search for the address, an hour and a quarter in composition, and twenty minutes in deciding whether or not to take an umbrella when going to the pillar box in the next street. The total effort that would occupy a busy man for three minutes all told may in this fashion leave another person prostrate after a day of doubt, anxiety, and toil.

Granted that work (and especially paper-work) is thus elastic in its demands on time, it is manifest that there need be little or no relationship between the work to be done and the size of the staff to which it may be assigned. A lack of real activity does not, of necessity, result in leisure. A lack of occupation is not necessarily revealed by a manifest idleness. The thing to be done swells in importance and complexity in a direct ratio with the time to be spent. This fact is widely recognized, but less attention has been paid to its wider implications, more especially in the field of public administration. Politicians and taxpayers have assumed (with occasional phases of doubt) that a rising total in the number of civil servants must reflect a growing volume of work to be done. Cynics, in questioning this belief, have imagined that the multiplication of officials must have left some of them idle or all of them able to work for shorter hours. But this is a matter in which faith and doubt seem equally misplaced. The fact is that the number of the officials and the quantity of the work are not related to each other at all.

C. Northcote Parkinson: *Parkinson's Law* (Boston: Houghton Mifflin Co.; London: John Murray (Publishers) Ltd, 1957/8), Chapter 1. Copyright © C. Northcote Parkinson 1957.

The rise in the total of those employed is governed by Parkinson's Law and would be much the same whether the volume of the work were to increase, diminish, or even disappear. The importance of Parkinson's Law lies in the fact that it is a law of growth based upon an analysis of the factors by which that growth is controlled.

The validity of this recently discovered law must rest mainly on statistical proofs, which will follow. Of more interest to the general reader is the explanation of the factors underlying the general tendency to which this law gives definition. Omitting technicalities (which are numerous) we may distinguish at the outset two motive forces. They can be represented for the present purpose by two almost axiomatic statements, thus: (1) 'An official wants to multiply subordinates, not rivals' and (2) 'Officials make work for each other.'

To comprehend Factor 1, we must picture a civil servant, called A, who finds himself overworked. Whether this overwork is real or imaginary is immaterial, but we should observe, in passing, that A's sensation (or illusion) might easily result from his own decreasing energy: a normal symptom of middle age. For this real or imagined overwork there are, broadly speaking, three possible remedies. He may resign; he may ask to halve the work with a colleague called B; he may demand the assistance of two subordinates, to be called C and D. There is probably no instance, however, in history of A choosing any but the third alternative. By resignation he would lose his pension rights. By having B appointed, on his own level in the hierarchy, he would merely bring in a rival for promotion to W's vacancy when W (at long last) retires. So A would rather have C and D, junior men, below him. They will add to his consequence and, by dividing the work into two categories, as between C and D, he will have the merit of being the only man who comprehends them both. It is essential to realize at this point that C and D are, as it were, inseparable. To appoint C alone would have been impossible. Why? Because C, if by himself, would divide the work with A and so assume almost the equal status that has been refused in the first instance to B; a status the more emphasized if C is A's only possible successor. Subordinates must thus number two or more, each being thus kept in order by fear of the other's promotion. When C complains in turn of being overworked (as he certainly will) A will, with the concurrence of C, advise the appointment of two assistants to help C. But he can then avert internal friction only by advising the appointment of two more assistants to help D, whose position is much

the same. With this recruitment of E, F, G, and H the promotion of A is now practically certain.

Seven officials are now doing what one did before. This is where Factor 2 comes into operation. For these seven make so much work for each other that all are fully occupied and A is actually working harder than ever. An incoming document may well come before each of them in turn. Official E decides that it falls within the province of F, who places a draft reply before C, who amends it drastically before consulting D, who asks G to deal with it. But G goes on leave at this point, handing the file over to H, who drafts a minute that is signed by D and returned to C, who revises his draft accordingly and lays the new version before A.

What does A do? He would have every excuse for signing the thing unread, for he has many other matters on his mind. Knowing now that he is to succeed W next year, he has to decide whether C or D should succeed to his own office. He had to agree to G's going on leave even if not yet strictly entitled to it. He is worried whether H should not have gone instead, for reasons of health. He has looked pale recently – partly but not solely because of his domestic troubles. Then there is the business of F's special increment of salary for the period of the conference and E's application for transfer to the Ministry of Pensions. A has heard that D is in love with a married typist and that G and F are no longer on speaking terms – no one seems to know why. So A might be tempted to sign C's draft and have done with it. But A is a conscientious man. Beset as he is with problems created by his colleagues for themselves and for him – created by the mere fact of these officials' existence – he is not the man to shirk his duty. He reads though the draft with care, deletes the fussy paragraphs added by C and H, and restores the thing to the form preferred in the first instance by the able (if quarrelsome) F. He corrects the English – none of these young men can write grammatically – and finally produces the same reply he would have written if officials C to H had never been born. Far more people have taken far longer to produce the same result. No one has been idle. All have done their best. And it is late in the evening before A finally quits his office and begins the return journey to Ealing. The last of the office lights are being turned off in the gathering dusk that marks the end of another day's administrative toil. Among the last to leave, A reflects with bowed shoulders and a wry smile that late hours, like grey hairs, are among the penalties of success.

From this description of the factors at work the student of political science will recognize that administrators are more or less bound to multiply. Nothing has yet been said, however, about the period of time likely to elapse between the date of A's appointment and the date from which we can calculate the pensionable service of H. Vast masses of statistical evidence have been collected and it is from a study of this data that Parkinson's Law has been deduced. Space will not allow of detailed analysis but the reader will be interested to know that research began in the Navy Estimates. These were chosen because the Admiralty's responsibilities are more easily measurable that those of, say, the Board of Trade. The question is merely one of numbers and tonnage. Here are some typical figures. The strength of the Navy in 1914 could be shown as 146,000 officers and men, 3249 dockyard officials and clerks, and 57,000 dockyard workmen. By 1928 there were only 100,000 officers and men and only 62,439 workmen, but the dockyard officials and clerks by then numbered 4558. As for warships, the strength in 1928 was a mere fraction of what it had been in 1914 – fewer than 20 capital ships in commission as compared with 62. Over the same period the Admiralty officials had increased in number from 2000 to 3569, providing (as was remarked) 'a magnificent navy on land'. These figures are more clearly set forth in tabular form:

Admiralty statistics

Classification	Year 1914	1928	Increase or decrease %
Capital ships in commission	62	20	−67.74
Officers and men in R.N.	146,000	100,000	−31.50
Dockyard workers	57,000	62,439	+9.54
Dockyard officials and clerks	3,249	4,558	+40.28
Admiralty officials	2,000	3,569	+78.45

The criticism voiced at the time centred on the ratio between the number of those available for fighting and those available only for administration. But that comparison is not to the present purpose. What we have to note is that the 2000 officials of 1914 had become the 3569 of 1928; and that this growth was unrelated to any possible increase in their work. The Navy during that period had diminished, in point of fact, by a third in men and two-thirds in ships. Nor, from 1922 onward, was its strength even expected to increase; for its total of ships (unlike its total of officials) was limited by the Washington Naval Agreement of that year. Here we have then a 78 per cent increase over a period of fourteen years; an average of 5.6 per cent increase a year on the earlier total. In fact, as we shall see, the rate of increase was not as regular as that. All we have to consider, at this stage, is the percentage rise over a given period.

Can this rise in the total number of civil servants be accounted for except on the assumption that such a total must always rise by a law governing its growth? It might be urged at this point that the period under discussion was one of rapid development in naval technique. The use of the flying machine was no longer confined to the eccentric. Electrical devices were being multiplied and elaborated. Submarines were tolerated if not approved. Engineer officers were beginning to be regarded as almost human. In so revolutionary an age we might expect that storekeepers would have more elaborate inventories to compile. We might not wonder to see more draughtsmen on the payroll, more designers, more technicians and scientists. But these, the dockyard officials, increased only by 40 per cent in number when the men of Whitehall increased their total by nearly 80 per cent. For every new foreman or electrical engineer at Portsmouth there had to be two more clerks at Charing Cross. From this we might be tempted to conclude, provisionally, that the rate of increase in administrative staff is likely to be double that of the technical staff at a time when the actually useful strength (in this case, of seamen) is being reduced by 31.5 per cent. It has been proved statistically, however, that this last percentage is irrelevant. The officials would have multiplied at the same rate had there been no actual seamen at all.

It would be interesting to follow the further progress by which the 8118 Admiralty staff of 1935 came to number 33,788 by 1954. But the staff of the Colonial Office affords a better field of study during a period of imperial decline. Admiralty statistics are complicated by factors (like the Fleet Air Arm) that make comparison difficult as between one year and the next. The Colonial Office growth is more significant in that it is more purely administrative. Here the relevant statistics are as follows:

Colonial Office statistics

Year	1935	1939	1943	1947	1954
Staff	372	450	817	1,139	1,661

Before showing what the rate of increase is, we must observe that the extent of this department's responsibilities was far from constant during these twenty years. The colonial territories were not much altered in area or population between 1935 and 1939. They were considerably diminished by 1943, certain areas being in enemy hands. They were increased again in 1947, but have since then shrunk steadily from year to year as successive colonies achieve self-government. It would be rational to suppose that these changes in the scope of Empire would be reflected in the size of its central administration. But a glance at the figures is enough to convince us that the staff totals represent nothing but so many stages in an inevitable increase. And this increase, although related to that observed in other departments, has nothing to do with the size – or even the existence – of the Empire. What are the percentages of increase? We must ignore, for this purpose, the rapid increase in staff which accompanied the diminution of responsibility during World War II. We should note rather, the peacetime rates of increase: over 5.24 per cent between 1935 and 1939, and 6.55 per cent between 1947 and 1954. This gives an average increase of 5.89 per cent each year, a percentage markedly similar to that already found in the Admiralty staff increase between 1914 and 1928.

Further and detailed statistical analysis of departmental staffs would be inappropriate in such a work as this. It is hoped, however, to reach a tentative conclusion regarding the time likely to elapse between a given official's first appointment and the later appointment of his two or more assistants.

Dealing with the problem of pure staff accumulation, all our researches so far completed point to an average increase of 5.75 percent per year. This fact established, it now becomes possible to state Parkinson's Law in mathematical form: In any public administrative department not actually at war, the staff increase may be expected to follow this formula:

$$x = \frac{2k^m + l}{n}$$

where k is the number of staff seeking promotion through the appointment of subordinates; l represents the difference between the ages of appointment and retirement; m is the number of man-hours devoted to answering minutes within the department; and n is the number of effective units being administered, x will be the number of new staff required each year. Mathematicians will, of course, realize that to find the percentage increase they must multiply x by 100 and divide by the total of the previous year (y), thus:

$$\frac{100\,(2k^m + l)}{yn}\ \%$$

And this figure will invariably prove to be between 5.17 per cent and 6.56 per cent, irrespective of any variation in the amount of work (if any) to be done.

The discovery of this formula and of the general principles upon which it is based has, of course, no political value. No attempt has been made to inquire whether departments *ought* to grow in size. Those who hold that this growth is essential to gain full employment are fully entitled to their opinion. Those who doubt the stability of an economy based upon reading each other's minutes are equally entitled to theirs. It would probably be premature to attempt at this stage any inquiry into the quantitative ratio that should exist between the administrators and the administered. Granted, however, that a maximum ratio exists, it should soon be possible to ascertain by formula how many years will elapse before that ratio, in any given community, will be reached. The forecasting of such a result will again have no political value. Nor can it be sufficiently emphasized that Parkinson's Law is a purely scientific discovery, inapplicable except in theory to the politics of the day. It is not the business of the botanist to eradicate the weeds. Enough for him if he can tell us just how fast they grow.

26

Management and Machiavelli

ANTONY JAY

*I*t was, of course, the parallels between the practices of sixteenth-century *politics and twentieth-century management that formed the substance of* Management and Machiavelli. *But what really attracted me to the subject was something more profound. What made* The Prince *such a revolutionary, shocking and fascinating book was the way in which it divorced politics from morality. Whereas previous writers had assumed that political success was inseparable from moral probity, Machiavelli showed that villainy could be as effective as virtue. He did not advocate villainy, but he did not shrink from the discovery that it could work.*

The management theory of the mid-1960s was bedevilled by the same false assumption. Almost every writer seemed to assume that open, benevolent and enlightened practices were essential for business success and that mean, egotistical, grasping, bullying, secretive management could never work; that the qualities for a successful manager and for an admirable human being were identical.

I do not know where these writers had worked, but they cannot have worked in any institution of which I had personal experience. In the real world – mine and Machiavelli's – unpleasant people achieved just as good results as pleasant people. Some of the most impressive performances were achieved by near certifiable monomaniacs and manic depressives. I tried in Management and Machiavelli *to reflect and examine that world, and I hoped that other managers would recognize it. It seems that they did.*

Sir Antony Jay,
Chairman, Video Arts,
London

Chapter V: The King and the Barons

THE struggle between the king and the barons is the great recurrent theme in the domestic politics of medieval England. Sometimes the barons are up and the king is down (Stephen, John, Edward II) sometimes it is the king who is on top and the barons who are repressed or quiescent (Henry I, Henry II, Edward I). There was a time when I found it puzzling that England should have bouts of tearing itself to pieces in domestic strife, even when there were great dangers threatening (or great opportunities beckoning) from outside her borders. After all, they were all part of the same kingdom, weren't they? Surely they could see the advantages of all pitching in together? Now, after working with a number of large corporations, I find the behaviour of the rulers of medieval England just as unwise but far less surprising. Few employees of any large corporation are so naïve as to say 'After all, we're all part of the same company, aren't we? Why can't we all work together to beat our competitors instead of wasting our time on all these internal wrangles?' They are far too well aware of the strength of the internal rivalries and jealousies. I know of a case where one great company missed a marvellous opportunity to enlarge its share of the market by such a factor that it would have become the leader instead of the runner-up in its field. Their chief competitor ran into grave cash-flow troubles which they themselves, for special reasons, escaped. But they did nothing. It was not that they did not see the opening; they saw it, and they took action. But the actions were little more than gestures, and the reason was that their real energies were absorbed by a full-blown baronial war. One of the senior managers, with the known sympathy of some members of the board and an important corporate shareholder, was trying to get control of two other departments and some important production

Taken from Antony Jay: *Management and Machiavelli* (London: Hutchinson Business, 1967).
Copyright © Antony Jay 1967.

resources. Other managers were resisting bitterly. Long passionate memos were being placed before some executives and passed behind the backs of others. The talk in dining rooms and bars was of nothing except this all-absorbing internal conflict. Managers spent the journeys to work and back pondering nothing except the next move in the battle; they talked about it endlessly to their wives, and lay awake half the night thinking about it. Resignations were mooted and threatened, and preliminary secret approaches made to other companies. In short, all the thought and energy and passion that should have gone into the sales and promotion drive was diverted into the baronial war. When it was over, the opportunity had passed.

The reason, of course, was the same as in medieval history; when the king is strong the barons are weak, when the king is weak the barons are strong. And strong barons fight and plot to become stronger, at the expense of the king or other barons or both. In this case, strong leadership would have stopped the war before it started: the reorganization would have taken place at once or never, and the only criterion would have been the good of the company, not the relative strengths of feeling of various people within it. Instead, the king was playing politics. Kings should be free to play foreign politics; they should not have to play domestic politics.

There is a constant danger of baronial war in any large organization, and it is the first and surest sign of weakness at the top. The first duty of government, according to political and legal theorists, is to preserve order within the realm: the first duty of management is to prevent baronial warfare. Politically, we have learnt to suppress riot and civil strife, but industrially we have not. Frank Pace who took over General Dynamics from its founder, Jay Hopkins, in 1957 found himself virtually a prisoner of his own feudal barons. His total head office staff numbered 200, in a company of 106,000 made up of nine divisions which were all virtually corporations in their own right. Most of them had been independent enterprises before they joined, and had their own separate legal and financial staffs; and, of course, their tough baronial presidents. Pace decided to leave them more or less alone. 'The only way to succeed,' he said, 'is to operate on a decentralized basis.' If William I had thought that, the battle of Hastings would now be regarded as an unimportant raid instead of a turning point in history. As a result of its feudal, baronial structure, General Dynamics managed to lose 425 million dollars between 1960 and 1962, the biggest product loss ever sustained by any company anywhere. Britain, too, provides a spectacular case of strong warring baronies in the (aptly named) power industry. The three great nationalized boards who run Coal, Gas and Electricity are in constant and vicious competition with each other. Not just advertising and selling and lobbying against each other, either: householders on new estates are offered electricity installation at cut rates on condition that they do not install gas as well. It would take a powerful king to discipline three such barons: instead, their activities are coordinated by the Department of Energy, which is also responsible for North Sea oil and natural gas. Anyone who expects a smooth and integrated fuel policy for the UK under such a set-up must be totally ignorant of baronial emotions and practices, but connoisseurs of baronial warfare have watched the battles with reprehensible delight. The proposed privatization of the gas industry can only increase their glee.

Contact with large organizations also provides a useful corrective to the stereotype of the wicked, power-mad baron. I suppose there are people in management who seek power for the sheer pleasure of exercising it, but I have never encountered them. Most people who aspire to power within organizations will tell you that they want it so as to achieve objects they believe in, but even that does not go to the heart of the matter. The real pleasure of power is the pleasure of freedom, and it goes right back to one of man's most primitive needs, the need to control his environment. You get no great sense of freedom if you are liable at any time to starve or freeze or be devoured by wolves or speared by a neighbouring tribe, and so you set about securing a supply of food, shelter, warmth and defensive weapons. Gradually you increase the control, and one of the most important ways you increase it is by organization, by making your tribe the biggest and strongest in the area, and of course by doing so you submit yourself to the control of environment again – the environment now being the organization you belong to; a much more agreeable one than before, but still outside your control. However, if you become a respected and successful person within the organization, you may begin to be involved in the control of it. You taste what some people call power, but to you it tastes of freedom. Your life is still partly regulated by the actions and decisions of others, but now a part of it is regulated according to your own choice and by your own decisions. You are regaining control of your new environment. Finally, you become head of a whole division – production division, say. Only the chief executive stands between you and the sky: only his budget allocations, his overriding decisions, his general policy rulings, his overall plans, his vetoes, keep you from total control over your environment. He may see them as curbs on your power, but you see them as barriers to your freedom.

Suppose he is a new chief executive. At once you want to know how far he will restrict your freedom in practice. You have an important project which will cost more than the £1 million you are allowed to authorize, but only a little more. You know it is unlikely to be authorized for this year if you put it up. So you cost it at £980,000 and 'discover' later that it cost £1.1 million. What you are doing, in hippopotamus terms, is defecating on territory he has enclosed within his defecatory ring. (The colloquial term for this is very similar in its idiom.) Only just over the edge, but over it. His reaction will soon tell you if you can try it on again. If he is a weak king, you will quickly gauge that you can go further, and soon you will discover all the apparatus of baronial infringement of royal sovereignty that the English medieval barons became so expert at. They withheld tithes, you overspend your budget. They barred the king's officers from their castles, you withhold information and returns. They failed to contribute troops to the king's army, you cannot spare any staff to go and help start up the new subsidiary in Buenos Aires. They substituted feudal justice for royal justice, you pursue an independent personnel policy. And every time you get away with it, you take a little control of your environment away from him and appropriate it for yourself.

The trouble is, of course, that you are not the only one playing this game. The research and development manager is playing it too. So is the sales and marketing manager. And now it is not the weak king but the other strong barons who are the obstacles to your freedom. The stage is set for a first-class baronial war.

Suppose you are the king, and not a baron. What do you do about this situation? The obvious answer is that you do not let it arise, but the sad fact is that from time to time it does. After all, it is not only a problem of top management: it can happen with equal intensity, if diminishing significance, right down the management line. And if it is pointless to give advice to the man who has let it happen, there is still his successor to be considered. What do you do if you inherit a corporation or division or department which is in a state of baronial war?

There are of course the conventional exhortations: make it clear from the very start exactly where you stand, show them at once that you don't stand for any insubordination, etc., etc. The trouble is that you are likely to be on trial to some extent yourself, and if the barons who are divided in everything else are united on the fact that you are a menace, you are not likely to last long enough to reap the fruits of your firmness. There are however a number of techniques which have been employed by strong kings when succeeding weak ones, and they are all worth consideration.

To start with, it is essential to realize that you have a baronial problem, and that you are unlikely to achieve any real external success until you have quelled the internal strife. And then it is a great help if the baronial wars have been going on a long time. In the early stages each baron is anxious to try out his strength, and some may be strong enough to think they could emerge as top baron and become king. Some even do, which creates quite a different situation. But if you come in fresh to a war that has been going on a long time with no final victor, and especially when there is danger from overseas in the shape of competitors, products and sales drives, then there is likely to be a general wish for some sort of order and stability imposed from above.

Such timing cannot always be arranged. But it usually seems a good idea to direct attention firmly to real or potential threats from overseas, or to necessary offensive action to forestall them, so that internal conflict can be made to appear a sort of treachery. ('Look, if we can't get production up by twenty per cent we won't be in business at all next year. So for God's sake let's solve that one first and argue about who authorizes the staff increase later.') It is unwise to provoke any general issue of the king's power, as a question of principle, in the early stages. Much better to make an alliance with one baron and pick off the others singly for pragmatic, practical reasons. ('It's simply that if I don't get your capital expenditure forecast in more detail and earlier, it makes nonsense of the planning committee meeting.') The kings used to go out periodically and knock down the barons' castles: withheld information and unreferred decisions are the bricks that corporation barons build their castles with.

Another useful device is to take over, for a time, direct control of the least efficient barony. This is difficult and demanding for a king who has the whole realm to run, but Churchill combined the Ministry of Defence with the office of Prime Minister during the war. It may be risky for the king to go into battle himself, but if he fights bravely, and wins, it can secure his position like nothing else. If the chief executive takes over production for six months, sorts it out and gets it flowing smoothly, all the other corporation barons will suddenly fear that he might do the same to their division. Their strongest weapon, the threat of resignation, suddenly falls to pieces in their hand.

Some kings have also built up a royalist party. It is a dangerous game because, once it becomes apparent, the king is seen to be playing domestic politics, bidding for personal loyalties in return for personal favours. The ultimate aim of the corporation king is to command the complete trust, respect and loyalty of the whole board and management, and a royalist party is a great obstacle.

For many kings, the answer has been to turn to the great capitalists and enlist their aid against the barons. King and capitalist are natural allies: the king wants a kingdom at peace, and a kingdom at peace gives a better return on capital than a kingdom divided by civil strife and baronial faction. In the corporation kingdom, the large block-voting shareholders are the capitalists: if they support the Managing Director when he wants to sack the Director of Production, his hand is greatly strengthened for dealing with the other barons. The danger, in kingdom and corporation, is that the king may fall too much into their power: that he may merely exchange the military defiance of the barons for the financial compulsions of the capitalists. Nevertheless, most kings would probably think it a fair exchange.

The most powerful weapon in the war against the corporation barons, however, has usually turned out to be money. The sovereignty of parliament over the crown was established when parliament controlled the king's revenue, and the practical head of the government was for many years known simply as First Lord of the Treasury. So long as the corporation king retains that control, he is well armed. The corporation barons always want money – more money than they can have. The king will give it to them according to the overall needs of the corporation, but if he is clever he can tie it up with a wider plan which somehow involves the knocking of a few more bricks out of their castle wall – the supplying of more information, or the referring of more decisions. The money, after all, is their means of controlling their environment, of putting their plans into effect, running their division the way they want to. If it means trading in a less significant instrument of environment control, the deal is worth doing.

None of these devices can be applied to every situation, but I suspect that there are few successful chief executives who have not used them from time to time, even if they were unaware of their stately pedigree. The final aim is to get into a position where the barons can be moved, promoted or rotated at the wish of the king without any internal strife. This does not mean that he actually will move them: indeed, so long as they know that he can, they are likely to take pains to ensure that he does not have to.

27

Lateral Thinking

Edward de Bono

A gaggle of management gurus beat a path through the board rooms of big business in the late 1960s and early 1970s. Think big. Think small. Theory X or Theory Y. Stick to your knitting but, if you can't, remember 'If it ain't broke, don't fix it'. Competitive analysis will cure all ills but, if not, reach for the magic 'dogs', 'cows' and 'stars'.

All of these were prescriptions for doing better. Admonitions for every function were emerging in a variety of guises: checklists, case studies, true confessions, even secret revelations of world-class business giants – often written in their own fair hand.

Little time was devoted, it seems, to the subject of how to solve problems, how to be creative, how to increase innovation. Lateral Thinking, by Edward de Bono, came along and filled the vacuum. It audaciously challenged almost everything that was broadly regarded as common sense, and everything that was considered right was suddenly questioned.

Somehow, at just the same time as management organizational theory was becoming increasingly sophisticated, 'thinking' was unfortunately seldom included in the job description of the chief executive officer or the chairman. In fact, I remember reading those dreadful surveys carried out by journals on what top management actually did with its time, and it always struck me that thinking, problem-solving and reflecting were not even among the array of options.

Lateral thinking entered our vocabulary, and overnight de Bono was established as a welcome addition to the otherwise aging throng of corporate advisers. But, despite his popularity in the UK, de Bono's greatest impact was felt abroad. Very much like Deming's book Total Quality Control in the late 1940s, Lateral Thinking swept through Japan and was integrated into the culture of many Japanese board rooms.

Sir Christopher Wates,
Chairman, Wates Building Group Limited,
London

Chapter 2: Difference between Lateral and Vertical Thinking

SINCE most people believe that traditional vertical thinking is the only possible form of effective thinking, it is useful to indicate the nature of lateral thinking by showing how it differs from vertical thinking. Some of the most outstanding points of difference are indicated below. So used are we to the habits of vertical thinking that some of these points of difference may seem sacrilegious. It may also seem that in some cases there is contradiction for the sake of contradiction. And yet in the context of the behaviour of a self-maximizing memory system lateral thinking not only makes good sense but is also necessary.

Vertical thinking is selective, lateral thinking is generative

Rightness is what matters in vertical thinking. Richness is what matters in lateral thinking. Vertical thinking selects a pathway by excluding other pathways. Lateral thinking does not select but seeks to open up other pathways. With vertical thinking one selects the most promising approach to a problem, the best way of looking at a situation. With lateral thinking one generates as many alternative approaches as one can. With vertical thinking one may look for different approaches until one finds a promising one. With lateral thinking one goes on generating as many approaches as one can even *after* one has found a promising one. With vertical thinking one is trying to select the best approach but with lateral thinking one is generating different approaches for the sake of generating them.

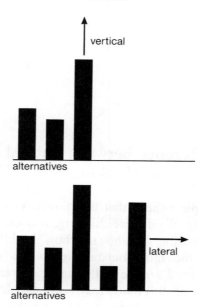

Vertical thinking moves only if there is a direction in which to move, lateral thinking moves in order to generate a direction

With vertical thinking one moves in a clearly defined direction towards the solution of a problem. One uses some definite approach or some definite technique. With lateral thinking one moves for the sake of moving.

One does not have to be moving towards something, one may be moving away from something. It is the movement or change that matters. With lateral thinking one does not move in order to follow a direction but in order to generate one. With vertical thinking one designs an experiment to show some effect. With lateral thinking one designs an experiment in order to provide an opportunity to change one's ideas. With vertical thinking one must always be moving usefully in some direction. With lateral thinking one may play around without any purpose or direction. One may play around with experiments, with models, with notation, with ideas.

The movement and change of lateral thinking is not an end in itself but a way of bringing about repatterning. Once there is movement and change then the maximizing properties of the mind will see to it that something useful happens. The vertical thinker says: 'I know what I am looking for.' The lateral thinker says: 'I am looking but I won't know what I am looking for until I have found it.'

Vertical thinking is analytical, lateral thinking is provocative

One may consider three different attitudes to the remark of a student who had come to the conclusion: 'Ulysses was a hypocrite.'

1 You are wrong, Ulysses was not a hypocrite.
2 How very interesting, tell me how you reached that conclusion.'
3 Very well. What happens next? How are you going to go forward from that idea?'

In order to be able to use the provocative qualities of lateral thinking one must also be able to follow up with the selective qualities of vertical thinking.

Vertical thinking is sequential, lateral thinking can make jumps

With vertical thinking one moves forward one step at a time. Each step arises directly from the preceding step to which it is firmly connected. Once one has reached a conclusion the soundness of that conclusion is proved by the soundness of the steps by which it has been reached.

With lateral thinking the steps do not have to be sequential. One may jump ahead to a new point and then fill in the gap afterwards. In the diagram below, vertical thinking proceeds steadily from A to B to C to D. With lateral thinking one may reach D via G and then having got there may work back to A.

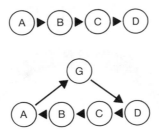

When one jumps right to the solution then the soundness of that solution obviously cannot depend on the soundness of the path by which it was reached. Nevertheless the solution may still make sense in its own right without having to depend on the pathway by which it was reached.

As with trial-and-error a successful trial is still successful even if there was no good reason for trying it. It may also happen that once one has reached a particular point it becomes possible to construct a sound logical pathway back to the starting point. Once such a pathway has been constructed then it cannot possibly matter from which end it was constructed – and yet it may only have been possible to construct it from the wrong end. It may be necessary to be on the top of a mountain in order to find the best way up.

With vertical thinking one has to be correct at every step, with lateral thinking one does not have to be

The very essence of vertical thinking is that one must be right at each step. This is absolutely fundamental to the nature of vertical thinking. Logical thinking and mathematics would not function at all without this necessity. In lateral thinking however one does not have to be right at each step provided the conclusion is right. It is like building a bridge. The parts do not have to be self-supporting at every stage but when the last part is fitted into place the bridge suddenly becomes self-supporting.

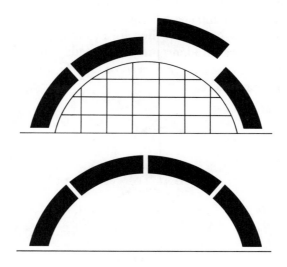

With vertical thinking one uses the negative in order to block off certain pathways. With lateral thinking there is no negative

There are times when it may be necessary to be wrong in order to be right at the end. This can happen when one is judged wrong according to the current frame of reference and then is found to be right when the frame of reference itself gets changed. Even if the frame of reference is not changed it may still be useful to go through a wrong area in order to reach a position from which the right pathway can be seen. This is shown diagrammatically below. The final pathway cannot of course pass through the wrong area but having gone through this area one may more easily discover the correct pathway.

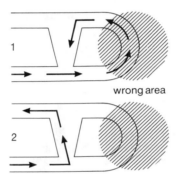

wrong area

With vertical thinking one concentrates and excludes what is irrelevant, with lateral thinking one welcomes chance intrusions

Vertical thinking is selection by exclusion. One works within a frame of reference and throws out what is not relevant. With lateral thinking one realizes that a pattern cannot be restructured from within itself but only as the result of some outside influence. So one welcomes outside influences for their provocative action. The more irrelevant such influences are the more chance there is of altering the established pattern. To look only for things that are relevant means perpetuating the current pattern.

With vertical thinking categories, classifications and labels are fixed, with lateral thinking they are not

With vertical thinking categories, classifications and labels are useful only if they are consistent, for vertical thinking depends on identifying something as a member of some class or excluding it from that class. If something is given a label or put into a class it is supposed to stay there. With lateral thinking labels may change as something is looked at now in one way and now in another. Classifications and categories are not fixed pigeonholes to aid identification but signposts to help movement. With lateral thinking the labels are not permanently attached but are used for temporary convenience.

Vertical thinking depends heavily on the rigidity of definitions just as mathematics does on the unalterable meaning of a symbol once this has been allocated. Just as a sudden change of meaning is the basis of humour so an equal fluidity of meaning is useful for the stimulation of lateral thinking.

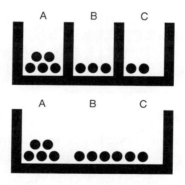

Vertical thinking follows the most likely paths, lateral thinking explores the least likely

Lateral thinking can be deliberately perverse. With lateral thinking one tries to look at the least obvious approaches rather than the most likely ones. It is the willingness to explore the least likely pathways that is important for often there can be no other reason for exploring such pathways. At the entrance to an unlikely pathway there is nothing to indicate that it is worth exploring and yet it may lead to something useful. With vertical thinking one moves ahead along the widest pathway which is pointing in the right direction.

Vertical thinking is a finite process, lateral thinking is a probabilistic one

With vertical thinking one expects to come up with an answer. If one uses a mathematical technique an answer is guaranteed. With lateral thinking there may not be any answer at all. Lateral thinking increases the chances for restructuring of the patterns, for an insight solution. But this may not come about. Vertical thinking promises at least a minimum solution. Lateral thinking increases the chances of a maximum solution but makes no promises.

If there were some black balls in a bag and just one white ball the chances of picking out that white ball would be low. If you went on adding white balls to the bag your chances of picking out a white ball would increase all the time. Yet at no time could you be absolutely certain of picking out a white ball. Lateral thinking increases the chances of bringing about insight restructuring and the better one is at lateral thinking the better are the chances. Lateral thinking is as definite a procedure as putting more white balls into the bag but the outcome is still probabilistic. Yet the pay off from a new idea or an insight from the restructuring of an old idea can be so huge that it is worth trying lateral thinking for there is nothing to be lost. Where vertical thinking has come up against a blank wall one would have to use lateral thinking even if the chances of success were very low.

Summary

The differences between lateral and vertical thinking are very fundamental. The processes are quite distinct. It is not a matter of one process being more effective than the other for both are necessary. It is a matter of realizing the differences in order to be able to use both effectively.

With vertical thinking one uses information for its own sake in order to move forward to a solution.

With lateral thinking one uses information not for its own sake but provocatively in order to bring about repatterning.

28

The Sources of Invention

JOHN JEWKES, DAVID SAWERS AND
RICHARD STILLERMAN

*I*t has been fascinating to read this extract from The Sources of Invention and to observe the continuing relevance of a number of the statements today, at a time when management of research and technology is receiving more and more attention in business and in the business schools.

However great the effort put into the planning and programming of research, chance still plays a large part in the process. It is surprising to observe that, despite the enormous increase in R&D planning, the great majority of ideas and inventions emerging from research programmes still fall into the category of 'originally unforeseen and untargeted opportunities', as opposed to the category of 'originally targeted opportunities'.

Of course, logical deduction continues to be as useful as it ever was, but the serendipity process of discovery is still a serious competitor for logic. It seems to me that this is too often overlooked by the planners, which further suggests that in planning research programmes we need somehow to find ways to deal with serendipity.

In planning technological innovation, it is often assumed that there is a straight-line progression from fundamental research through applied research and further technical development all the way to the marketplace. In reality, innovations often start with someone who, on the one hand, knows about market needs and opportunities and, on the other hand, is aware, through colleagues, of new scientific developments.

Therefore, I personally believe more in the so-called one-three-nine principle. For every three inventors, one needs, as a rule of thumb, one supporting colleague to keep the inventors informed of the latest scientific developments. Then, according to the same rule of thumb and almost as a penalty for success, one needs another three colleagues for every inventor, to develop ideas into products that can be marketed or processes that can be applied. This principle roughly corresponds to what one often finds in industrial laboratories, although many people outside industry implicitly assume that the straight-line progression is the natural one to follow.

Incidentally, I suspect that in Japan the 1:3:9 approach to invention is much more widely accepted than elsewhere, which perhaps explains Japanese successes in the field of technological innovation.

This extract from The Sources of Invention also touches upon the issue of technology assessment. Forecasting of future technology is one thing, forecasting of social development is another. Both are at best highly uncertain, while combining the two and thus attempting to forecast the social consequences of technological development surely can only be expressed as the product of the two levels of uncertainty.

My own inclination is to suggest that nowadays a more realistic approach to this difficult area lies in the use of scenario planning techniques.

Harry L. Beckers,
Former Director of Research, Royal Dutch Shell,
The Hague

Chapter IX: Conclusions and Speculations

I The continuity of things

THERE is nothing in the history of technology in the past century and a half to suggest that infallible methods of invention have been discovered or are, in fact, discoverable. It may be true that in these days the search for new ideas and techniques is pursued with more system, greater energy and, although this is more doubtful, greater economy than formerly. Yet chance still remains an important factor in invention and the intuition, will and obstinacy of individuals spurred on by the desire for knowledge, renown or personal gain the great driving forces in technical progress. As with most other human activities, the monotony and sheer physical labour in research can be relieved by the use of expensive equipment and tasks can thereby be attempted which would otherwise be wholly impossible. But it does not appear that new mysteries will only be solved and new applications of natural forces made possible by ever increasing expenditure. In many fields of knowledge, discovery is still a matter of scouting about on the surface of things where imagination and acute observation, supported only by simple technical aids, are likely to bring rich rewards.

The theory that technical innovation arises directly out of, and only out of, advance in pure science does not provide a full and faithful story of modern invention. As in the past three centuries, there is still a to-and-fro stimulus between the two; each has a momentum and a potential of its own. The case for scientific enquiry is not a utilitarian one. It may be that the flow of inventions is just as likely to be increased by stimulating the fuller exploitation of the myriads of technical possibilities

Abridged from John Jewkes, David Sawers and Richard Stillerman: *The Sources of Invention* (London: Macmillan, 1958). Reproduced by kind permission of Macmillan, London and Basingstoke.

inherent in the existing stock of scientific knowledge as by increasing that stock.

The history of invention shows no sharp break in continuity. The inventive drive continues to be found in people who, because of their temperament and outlook, are not easy to organize. The sharp contrasts sometimes drawn between the present and the last century seem to be the product of distortions, in the one direction, of what was happening in the nineteenth century and distortions, in the opposite direction, of what has been happening in this. The impression thereby created of the sharp passage from one epoch to another can be reinforced by comparing extremes – for example, an important discovery in a large modern industrial research laboratory contrasted with the struggles, such as would have called forth the sympathy and interest of Samuel Smiles, of some impoverished and obscure individual inventor of a hundred years ago. Extremes today are undoubtedly wider apart than they were. But the broad bank of middle cases provides little support for spectacular interpretations. In both periods there were inventors of scientific outlook, inventions of the intuitive and empirical type, men who worked in teams, men who worked essentially alone.

Of course, the immediate future may have something entirely different in store for us. It may be that we have now passed into a stage of very rapid transition (dating from about 1950 or perhaps the day when the first atom bomb blew off) which amounts to a violent break in the nature of technical change. But if this is to be the assumption made, and if public policy concerning innovation is to fly in the face of history, the onus for substantiating this assumption properly lies with those who make it.

II The prediction of invention

Nothing lends support to the view that inventions can be predicted or that forecasts of their consequences can provide secure grounds for anticipatory social action. Peering into the future is a popular and agreeable pastime which, so long as it is not taken seriously, is comparatively innocuous. But the claim that there is, or can be, a 'science of prediction' might easily do more harm than good.[1]

Experience suggests that most *specific* inventions were not foreseen: they had an element of the accidental in them, they represented the last, and therefore the crucial, step between the uncertain and the certain.

And the more revolutionary they were the less foreseeable they were. No one, least of all the inventors concerned, predicted the discovery of penicillin, nylon, polyethylene, the transistor, insulin, radio, the cyclotron, the zip fastener, the first aniline dye, the vulcanization of rubber or many other cases which could be quoted. More generally, in so far as specific inventions are empirical, they cannot be predicted.

But if the details of the future are hidden, are there reasons for believing that it is still possible to perceive in a broader way what is to come? Is there a valid parallel, for example, between plotting the broad surge of technology and drawing up (say) a table of the movements of the tides? An affirmative answer can be given here only if invention is accepted as a 'social process', as a movement which has a direction and a force independent of the influences of individuals. The reasons put forward for supposing that inventions will emerge, in their due and proper season, as the inevitable incidents in a forward sweep of history which is humanly comprehensible and can be tabulated may now be examined.

First, it is said that each new scientific discovery will reveal a new range of technical possibilities. This, in effect, is to admit that scientific discoveries cannot be foreseen, but to claim that their technical aftermath can. One possible objection to this is that many inventions do not, in fact, arise from recent prior scientific discovery. Another is that new scientific findings do not necessarily point to the uses to which they may ultimately be put. Even those in the best position to know have often been completely misled.[2]

Second, there is the argument derived from the phenomenon of 'simultaneous invention'. In a considerable number of cases inventions have been made at roughly the same time by different investigators apparently unaware of each other's work. It has therefore been suggested that inventions occur when the possibility of them is 'in the air', and many minds are being directed towards the same ends. Inventions are the product of deep-seated forces, of which the final inventor himself is but a creature; if these forces can be understood, the inventions arising from them can be forecast. This is a highly plausible line of reasoning but some of the links in it are weak. What is meant by simultaneous? In at least some quoted cases the simultaneous inventions were far enough apart in time to suggest the possibility of a transfusion of the idea from one point to another. What number of simultaneous inventions constitute a significant proportion of the whole? For every one simultaneous invention which could be named, certainly many more could be quoted as not falling into this category. Indeed a special group is often spoken about, 'inventions which come before their time', where one man has produced an idea which has aroused no general interest. Even, however, if the phenomenon of simultaneous invention were general why should it be supposed that simultaneous inventions are more predictable than isolated inventions? Their very nature suggests that they have broader origins but not necessarily origins more easily identifiable. Even if inventions of the simultaneous variety could be predicted in this way, what of the inventions not of this kind? And just as men may simultaneously stumble upon the truth, they may simultaneously fall into error: those who predict are still left with the task of deciding whether a certain concatenation of social forces will lead men towards the right answer or the wrong.

The third argument is that there is always a considerable period between the 'conception date' of an invention and the time when it comes into general use and begins to exert its effect upon standards of living and that this interim period will provide a favourable opportunity for studying the probable consequences of the invention and preparing to meet them. It will be noticed that two stages of prediction have now been dropped – that regarding the course of science and that concerning the emergence of inventions. In so far as inventions come into use slowly then it would seem less necessary to plan consciously for adjustments to them; such adjustments are more likely to take place spontaneously. In so far as the inventions make their impact speedily then this third argument falls to the ground.

Fourthly, it is argued that technology is now so versatile, there are so many different technical routes to the solution of a given problem, that once a general need has made itself evident it can be confidently assumed that this need will be met, that in one way or another an answer in the form of an appropriate invention will emerge. Here an entirely different predictive technique is being suggested: all unsatisfied human needs would presumably be surveyed and some picked out as exercising greater force than others. This in itself would be a formidable task and it carries with it a serious drawback for policy-making; for if it is predicted that *some* kind of invention will emerge to satisfy a given need but not exactly *what* kind, prognostications of its social consequences will be the more difficult to make. Another objection here is that it is simply not true that urgent needs automatically evoke a method of satisfying them. Inventions which have not been made, although there is an obvious need for them, are much more numerous and just as striking as those which have.

It seems quite as hazardous to try to anticipate the broad sweep of innovation as to spot future specific inventions. It is, however, at the second step – that of deducing the probable social consequences of any invention – that the proposals for a science of prediction seem most chimerical. For where policy-making is the aim, it would have to be decided how much the new products or processes will be utilized and this introduces all the uncertainties of the market: how rapidly and to what degree the new methods will supplant the old; how likely it is that the new methods may themselves have only a short life and be supplanted by something even newer. These hurdles having been surmounted, it would then be for the planners to assess the social consequences of the predicted technical and economic changes, to decide whether they should be welcomed and, if not, to design counter-measures and explain how to put them into operation. This is a nightmarish labyrinth which perhaps need not be followed any further. Except to note that it is often impossible to get agreement about the social consequences of an invention, as for example television, even after it has come into widespread use. And that, given the fashion in which, in democratic societies, important policy decisions on current and pressing national economic matters are arrived at, the suggestion that social planning for hypothetical conditions in the remote future would be seriously entertained or, if so, wisely and successfully conducted, appears unreal.

Against objections of this kind the defence is sometimes offered that, in fact, some outstanding successes in prediction have already been recorded and that, if such encouraging results have been achieved mainly by amateurs working in an embryonic science, much more could be hoped for from professionals with a more elaborately developed technique. It is, of course, true that many prophecies, often in the most unlikely quarters,[3] have been made of things which have come to pass. Considering the total volume of this prophecy it would have been surprising if the target had not been hit from time to time. The significance of such successes, however, depends upon the relation they bear to the number of failures, whether the proportion of successes is increasing, whether success can be repeated and the secret of it transmitted to other persons. At all these points there are grounds for extreme doubt.

A catalogue of errors in prediction, made even by unbiased and knowledgeable observers, would be an enormous document, limited only in size by the patience and available time of its compiler. The errors fall into two groups: the foretelling of things which in fact have not come to pass[4] and the denial of the possibility of things which have, in fact, made their appearance.

Most of the outstanding technical features of modern life have crept upon us almost unaware. In 1906 the Engineering Editor of *The Times* was asserting that 'all attempts at artificial aviation . . . are not only dangerous to human life but foredoomed to failure from an engineering point of view', and in 1910 the British Secretary of State for War could argue that 'we do not consider that aeroplanes will be of any possible use for war purposes'.[5] The possibility of radio broadcasting was overlooked until it happened. Until 1944 it would have been impossible to say with any confidence that atomic energy for peace-time purposes would be available in this century, and even now it is problematic how far it will be usefully employed. The use of electronic devices in industry was not talked about until after 1945. Up to 1930 it was generally believed that aeroplanes would never be suitable for the carriage of passengers over great sea areas and stubborn, but abortive, efforts were therefore made to develop the airship for this purpose.

Conversely, predictions made with confidence have often proved unsound. The idea that the diesel engine would be universally adopted for aircraft, especially large ones, was widely accepted in the 1920s. After the Second World War it was commonly assumed that the gas turbine would almost wholly replace other prime movers as a source of power, which has proved far too sweeping a conclusion. In 1945 it was generally supposed that the age of the private aeroplane was at hand; it was to replace the motor car just as the motor car had replaced the horse-drawn vehicle; nothing of the kind has happened. The views, strongly held but a few years ago, of the dominating rôle which would be taken by the chemical laboratory in the synthesizing of materials have recently been modified in important ways: medicinal plants may be preferred because they produce effects at present impossible for the chemist to reproduce, or because they are cheaper, and it is now realized that biochemical processes are sometimes so subtle and economical that artificial synthesis is unlikely to rival them. More generally, between the wars, much informed opinion held that rapid technical progress was coming to an end; no one forecast the technical advance after 1945, which was due largely to the effort to overcome the shortage of labour, itself an unpredicted phenomenon.

The balance between predictive successes and failures is important for, even if it is acknowledged that the successes might have some social value, it has to be borne in mind that, conversely, errors may do harm. For both over-optimism or over-pessimism would bring trouble. If, for example, it is wrongly assumed that some general need will shortly be catered for by a new invention, this may inhibit the efforts to improve the existing, older ways of meeting the need. Thus improvements in the more traditional methods of producing insulin were held up by the widespread belief that a synthesized product would soon be found. And exaggerated claims regarding the part to be played by atomic energy in the generation of electricity led to the comparative neglect of ways of improving traditional methods of generation. On the other side, pessimism may lead communities to impoverish themselves unnecessarily. Thus most policies for conserving natural resources have in the past been based either upon over-gloomy views about the probable future supply of such resources or about the possibility of substitute materials or methods; this has led to reduced consumption in the present without necessarily providing a *quid pro quo* for the future.

Finally, it may be asked, what body of men could be entrusted with the duties of prediction and of planning to change the shape of things which would otherwise come? How would they put themselves into a position in which they could establish such an overwhelming prestige and command such general confidence, on matters on which most people tend to regard themselves as experts, that communities would in the present patiently accept rearrangements, some of them painful, in order to avoid hypothetical future troubles? Scientists and technologists would hardly be suitable to act as the assessors; they are frequently among the most hardened sceptics about the possibilities of foreseeing the future for, by reason of their daily work, they are brought up sharply against the barriers to the unknown and the uncertainties about ever finding a way through them. Historians are for the most part inclined to fight shy of extrapolating into the future. Businessmen, toughened by their experience of the uncertainties in developing inventions, might well be reluctant to speculate too far ahead, particularly in unfamiliar fields.

It has been suggested that sociologists – standing back from the evidence, having no vested interests in these matters and no special reasons for optimism or pessimism – might carry out these duties, for, with their universal interest in the affairs of men, they could avoid the danger of not being able to see the wood for the trees. But their disabilities, too, are obvious. Not constituting a part of the active society of science and technology, they might fail to see even the trees. Up to now, their experiments in this field have not been free of serious mistakes. In any case it is doubtful whether it would be wise to entrust activities so highly charged with the possibilities of error to those who would carry no immediate and personal responsibility for the consequences of their mistakes.

The correct attitude would seem to be to accept the changes brought about by invention and to deal with these changes, as and when they occur, by methods adjusted on each occasion to the character of a specific and perceived problem. It is well to remember that, in the past, the prophets have tended to press upon us hasty and hysterical action because their views about the future have been founded upon a narrow and unsubtle picture of possibilities and an inadequate grasp of the power of communities to resolve their problems step by step. It is easy to list the major alarms that they have raised: progressively extensive unemployment as machines came to be more widely used; absolute shortages of raw materials because the use of natural resources was not being controlled; the social dangers of increased leisure as communities became richer; the spiritual and moral hazards of societies where more and more tasks were mechanized and less work left to the healthy use of hands and eyes; the prospects of science and technology being devoted wholly to the designs of individuals plotting to concentrate power in their own hands.

Some of these impending horrors have, in fact, proved to be nothing but shadows cast by the peculiar temperament of the prophet himself. It is by no means evident that those who have claimed the gifts of longest sight have proved to be the wisest counsellors. It may, of course, properly be argued that *if* men are determined to act now about events they believe to lie in the future, much better that they should so act with a sense of history and with as wide a knowledge as possible of all the different intertwined forces which are now creating their future. There is, however, a possible alternative. It might be better to recognize that all the knowledge of the past, even if it could be accumulated, provides no secure basis for seeing the future and that adjustment to observed change is an intricate enough task without piling upon it the confusions inseparable from the practice of soothsaying. For, as Francis Bacon put it:

> Men are wont to guess about new subjects from those they are already acquainted with, and the hasty and vitiated fancies they have thence formed: than which there cannot be a more fallacious mode of reasoning,

because much of that which is derived from the sources of things does not flow in their usual channels.

Notes

1 At the beginning of the century H. G. Wells advocated the encouragement of a science of prediction as part of a system for conscious social planning: 'In the past our kind had been hustled along by change; now it was being given the power to make its own changes'. He himself made many predictions of highly varying accuracy. More recently a group of distinguished sociologists associated with the University of Chicago developed these ideas in some detail. Their views are summarized in the Report of the United States National Resources Committee, *Technological Trends and National Policy*, 1936.
2 Up to his death Rutherford believed that the use of nuclear energy on a large scale was unlikely (A. H. Compton, *Atomic Quest*, p. 279). Robert A. Millikan, 'There is no appreciable energy available to man through atomic disintegration' *(Science and the New Civilization*, 1930, p. 163). Hertz did not think that the wireless waves he had discovered would have any practical application (W. R. Maclaurin, *Invention and Innovation in the Radio Industry*, p. 15.)

Even Sir Winston Churchill, whose prescience has been as outstanding as his distrust of long-range prediction, said of atomic energy in August 1939: 'It might be as good as our present-day explosives, but it is unlikely to produce anything very much more dangerous.' (*The Second World War*, vol. I, p. 301).
3 For example, Marie Corelli seems to have predicted the atom bomb in 1911, and Rudyard Kipling described Atlantic air transport with all the paraphernalia of radio communication and landing priorities in 1904.
4 In 1924 J. B. S. Haldane predicted that within fifty years light would cost one-fiftieth of its then price and there would be no more night in our cities (*Daedalus*, p. 18); this ought to be checked in 1974.
5 L. J. Ludovici, *The Challenging Sky*, pp. 40, 75.

Postscript

The future is tomorrow

Writing a few thousand words on what management thinking and practices might be like in 30 years' time initially sounded like a painless assignment. It wasn't.

In a world where disequilibrium is recognized as the steady state, where quantum leaps in technology are considered normal and where dramatic upheavals in social and political fundamentals have become the norm, the future indeed seems unclear. Consider just a few of the events of the past few years:

- In less than a year, the entire political structure of Eastern Europe, which took 45 years to create, has been effectively dismantled.
- The reality of a single European common market – a gleam in Monnet's eye a few decades ago – today takes its permanent place on the world's economic and political stage, along with the United States and Japan.
- Only three of the corporations that appeared in 1960 in the *Fortune* list of the top ten companies in the world survive today. Five of today's top ten – all Japanese – did not even exist 30 years ago.
- Half of all the students in higher education today come from countries officially designated as developing or less developed.
- Organized groups concerned with the environment, practically nonexistent 20 years ago, have proliferated and have the power today to close factories, move industries, change product specifications and directly affect the lives of millions of people.

If we define management simply as the process of arranging, coordinating and controlling resources to accomplish a specific task or set of objectives, each of these events clearly has had a direct impact on management thinking. However, in most cases, such thinking has followed events, rather than been the driving force behind them.

Thus, for example, much of the sophistication of the management of financial resources that we enjoy today was born of the necessity to cope with increasing pressures caused by massive industrial restructuring, major technical changes in communications and the concentration of power in the financial institutions.

Franco Modigliani and Merton Milles were two economists who were able to translate economic theories into pragmatic business guidelines. They postulated that debt-to-equity ratios must be a secondary consideration to future earning power and business risk profile. Both, 20 years after they had published their work, were recognized by being awarded the Nobel prize.

As the official caretaker of resources – both capital and human – management has become most adept at being creative and flexible in meeting the demands placed upon it. Theory often seems to follow practice. As a rule, many of the claims of management theory are after-the-fact rationalizations trying to explain why certain practical trends actually took place.

Paul Kennedy, in his perceptive book *The Rise and Fall of Great Powers*, summarizes this phenomenon: 'There exists a dynamic for change driven chiefly by economic and technological developments, which then impact upon social structures, political systems, military power and the position of individual states and empires.'

Looking ahead

Surprisingly, there is a number of important certainties about the future that at least partially reduce the unknowns that we must deal with.

The first of these certainties is that the people who will be in leadership positions in the year 2020 are already gainfully employed today, have already finished their formal education and, if we are to believe in the tenets of psychology, have established most of their patterns of behaviour and leadership styles.

Secondly, we can develop today a surprisingly accurate picture of the population profile of the globe or any particular geographic area. We can state, for example, that at least 25 per cent of the population of Europe in the year 2020 are likely to be over the age of 65; that the population of India will triple, making it more populous than China; and that there will need to be at least 20 cities in the world with populations of over 30 million. Today the largest city in the world has only 20 million inhabitants.

Finally, we might safely conclude that, while habits and practices might change, albeit slowly, the basic human needs of housing, shelter, food and social structures will somehow be met.

Against this background, it seems useful to consider the following questions from the perspective of management:

1   Will a predominant organizational structure or model emerge?
2   Will technological innovations dramatically change the way in which we do business?
3   Will there be a major change in the structure of industries?
4   Are there likely to be new forces at work, such as concern for the environment, that will have a disproportionate influence on our lives and, as a result, will require management to reconsider its function?
5   Will the 'Triad Powers' continue to be the dominant force in the world in terms of economic activity, technological change, political innovations and market power?

After considering these and related issues, I have postulated ten ideas that will dominate our thinking about management:

1   Structural freefall in relation to organization – more flexibility, more customization, more innovation. A steady, but systematic, and unsuccessful drive towards trying to find a single best solution.
2   Deglobalization – in effect, a reversal of the prevailing trend over the past few years. Local and regional influences will be more powerful than global forces.
3   Technological rampage – dramatic cross fertilization of scientific efforts leading to unexpected breakthroughs.
4   Micromanagement of human resources – recognition that people are *the* scarce resource and need to be managed.
5   Massive rationalization within most industries, leading to the creation of 'mega' entities on the one hand, and 'mini' ventures at the other extreme.
6   The acceptance of microprocessors, computers and modern communication technologies, not as a route to gaining competitive advantage but as a basic requirement for economic survival.
7   Creation of completely new enterprises to meet the challenge of global, regional and national problems that existing public institutions have been unable to resolve.
8   Much greater variety in ownership structure – the growth of family enterprises.
9   Permanent shortage of 'knowledge' workers.
10 Alliance management – a new skill identified as a crucial factor in reversing the trend of failures in mergers, acquisitions and cross-border agreements.

1   Structural freefall

Bob Waterman wrote a precursor to *In Search of Excellence* called *Structure Is Not Organization*, in which he noted that, 'It will not be possible (in the future) to define organizational structures in a few diagrams. The variations that we will create are so vast.'

We have already seen the beginnings of the move away from the classic command and control model of organization on which most post-war business structures were based. As Peter Drucker noted in the *Harvard Business Review*, this change was dictated first by the need for large businesses to innovate and become more entrepreneurial, but, perhaps, '. . . even more importantly by the opportunities and challenges brought about by the demands of information technology'.

What kind of structures can we expect in 2020?

The traditional nerve centre of a company – which we typically refer to as 'headquarters' or 'the centre' – will be relegated to the organizational history books. Already, many of the specialized skills and services that were husbanded away in these corporate pinnacles of power have been severely cut back.

Specialist departments dealing with functions such as public relations, legal affairs, advertising or communications will have disappeared. These services, skills and special advisory functions will, in 2020, be abundantly available from independent enterprises and practitioners. They will require such a high level of know-how that only the largest or richest companies will be able to afford to keep their specialist 'in house'.

In 2020 data will finally have become 'information'. Information flowing freely will, from a structural point of view, eliminate many of the layers in the typical organization, since tiers or layers in an organization were essentially introduced as span breakers of coordinating elements. All their activities will, in the future, be accomplished via the creative friendly real-time use of information.

By 2020 we shall need to have invented a new word to replace 'decentralization'. For the last 30 years the term has been rather imprecisely used to describe a wide range of actions surrounding the notion of devolving responsibility, pushing responsibility downward and creating autonomous profit-accountable units.

2 Deglobalization

We have developed elaborate matrices to describe the various types of global businesses and their likely development and evolution. The term globalization has been used so loosely that most management literature on the subject spends a disproportionate amount of time defining it.

Broadly speaking, globalization refers to the theory that customer needs for certain types of goods and services are so universal that no local adaptation is necessary. 'Wheaties' may be called by different names in different parts of the world but, in the 100 countries in which it is marketed, the product is basically the same.

In *Future Perfect*, Stanley Davis develops the notion of customized mass production – a seemingly contradictory idea that he suggests is one of the reasons for the continued success of Japanese companies in meeting consumer demand and winning and keeping the most lucrative markets in the world. Technology has indeed provided us with the means of manufacturing, for the same cost as a conventional product, or often for less, a mass-produced bespoke product that meets the *unique* needs of each and every separate customer. In Japan today, a new car with individual features can be ordered from a production line and delivered within 36 hours.

As our industrial enterprises learn to produce goods and services that are both uniquely designed to suit a specific microglobal market and cost less than a single global product, we shall gradually replace the notion of globalization by the concept of instant local adaptation.

3 Technological rampage

Most of the millions of words that have been written or spoken about modern technology – i.e. applied science – can be distilled into two propositions:

- That we are well into a period of rapid, accelerating technological change; and
- That our ability to cope with, let alone absorb or use, these developments is highly questionable.

I believe that these two propositions will still be true in 2020.

Consider, for example, the case of Enovid – a simple oral contraceptive introduced in 1960 and greeted as the solution to mankind's Malthusian curse. It has turned out to be something else. It initiated a sexual revolution, especially among the young, that is still causing tremors. It encouraged a decline in marriages and the creation of a novel civil state. It did help to reduce the birth rate, but in the wrong countries. And, paradoxically, it increased the demand for abortion, with all its searing implications and consequences. This is what a simple pill did in 1960. How shall we cope with applied science that is no longer science fiction but the basis for growing industries that did not even exist ten years ago?

How will management cope, for example, with developments such as:

- Factories without people.
- The collapse of strict hierarchical systems that have governed society for generations.
- The disappearance of familiar institutions, such as branch banks, that have become a permanent mosaic of our culture – but are, in effect, already redundant.
- A 10,000 fold increase in the capacity to transmit information.
- At-home medical facilities and monitoring devices activated by remote control that will allow many illnesses to be diagnosed and treated remotely – forcing us to rethink the role of hospitals, clinics and perhaps even the general practitioner.

Applied science – based on existing knowledge – will totally transform how our children learn and what they will be taught. It will prolong life, alleviate the miserable existence of a large part of the so-called underdeveloped world and will allow the 10 per cent of the globe's population that are now disabled to function more normally.

The challenge for management will be to keep up with the developments in applied science and to make certain that potential benefits are rapidly translated into realities.

4   Micromanagement of human resources

In relative terms, the development of the human resource function has, in most large corporations, significantly lagged behind other corporate activities. Too often, in the inevitable internal race to keep and attract future leaders, the personnel function turns out to be the consolation prize. As a result, while other corporate functions develop, mature, innovate and break new ground, comparatively speaking the personnel function has fallen behind in this unique marathon.

While there has been much lip service paid to the notion of human resource being a scarce corporate commodity, in practice the care, nurturing and maturing of managers is given the proper attention in only a few enterprises. This will change dramatically.

Systems for the recruitment, development, training, reward and career planning of all employees will undergo quantum leaps once this realization is understood and accepted. By 2020 the development of human resources will have caught up with, and raced ahead of, other corporate functions.

As we today are just beginning to take advantage of the technological (management information) tools that are available in, for example, consumer retailing, the next decades will demand that corporations should 'micromanage' their human resources.

5   Industrial end game

Since 1960 we have witnessed the extraordinary process of the birth, growth and death of major industries, first at a national level and most recently on a global scale. But, apart from the absolute increase in size, the most dramatic changes have been in geographic realignment. Shipbuilding is, perhaps, the best example. For instance, in 1960 almost 23 per cent of the world's shipbuilding capacity was in the UK. In 1990 Korea represented 65 per cent of that capacity, while the UK claimed less than 10 per cent.

In the next 30 years, the most far-reaching shifts in industry structure will be the growing importance of the biggest players, the continued entrance of new actors on the stage and the gradual, but systematic, disappearance one way or another of the great mass of middle sized companies. Whether one thinks of this as concentration or as rationalization is not as important as what this will mean in relation to management thinking and practice.

However much one can argue, as did Eli Ginzburg in *Beyond Human Scale*, that there is an optimum size for an industrial empire, we need only look at what has already happened to such industrial sectors as motor cars, soft drinks, mining and even financial institutions to see that we can expect larger and larger industrial entities to emerge. Notwithstanding the pressures from national and regional monopoly-control institutions, we will need to accept what will soon be seen as an inexorable drift towards larger and larger entities.

Concurrently, why should there occur a stream of brand new ventures, new companies, new commercial structures? I think that the answer lies in the realization that creative ideas, commercial innovations and breakthrough developments are not the unique property of large enterprises. In fact, the lessons of the last 30 years would suggest exactly the opposite. Likewise, there will always be a continuous flow of daring young men and women who simply are not, or feel that they are not, suited to life in a large corporation. However much these large entities try to behave like small independent units, they will never satisfy the base entrepreneurial instincts that often motivate people to produce heroic results.

Largeness per se will only be able to thrive and survive as and when we learn to live with this often unnatural phenomenon of the mega-corporation. We shall invent new structures to counterbalance the potentially inhuman qualities of large institutions. At the same time, information technology, which is a glorious catchphrase that we invented to include anything that is even remotely associated with 'black boxes' of any size or shape, will mature and stop being an end in itself. Instead, it will be bent and shaped to serve our needs, rather than forcing us to adjust our needs, our personal requirements, our style and our approach to decision-making.

Unfortunately, growth in employment and growth in the size of enterprises seem to be inversely proportional. In the past 30 years, the number of people employed by the world's 1,000 largest companies has in fact decreased by more than 20 per cent.

The clearest example of this phenomenon comes from an examination of agribusiness in the United States. One per cent of the total number of farms provides 30 per cent of the total agricultural production of the country and accounts for 45 per cent of net farm income. Armed with the most sophisticated equipment and computer-based planning, monitoring and control systems, these farms alone are able to meet the fickle demands of commodity markets and the changing patterns of consumer behaviour. In more and more sectors, we shall be able to claim to see similar patterns.

6 The 'management moron' comes of age

As we get closer to the turn of the millennium, predicting the future has become a growth industry. This 'art' – forecasting – is most mature in relation to the issue of our society's growing dependence on micro-processors.

I suspect that, taking the aggregate across all computers used today, less than 25 per cent of the available power is being effectively employed. By 2020 both the technical and cultural aspects impinging on the use of computers will have been dramatically changed:

- The phrase 'user friendly' will have real meaning, and applications will no longer require ordinary users to struggle with lengthy, unreadable tomes.
- We shall have machines with the ability to learn from their own experience, rather than from the experience imparted to them by humans. However, we shall still be a long way from duplicating the human brain's capacity to learn.
- The memory capacity of computers will no longer be a limiting factor in their applications. Memories now available only in back-to-back super computers will be available to everyone.
- A whole generation of our future leaders will have grown up in an environment where computers are no longer something to be regarded with suspicion and anxiety.
- Artificial intelligence systems will replace much of the management decision-making processes required, for example, to control an enterprise, plan a new product introduction or raise capital.

7   Privatized social responsibility

During the past 30 years, the world has had to cope with 160 wars, 25 million casualties, millions of people dying of starvation each year, endemic social injustice, gradual environmental deterioration and geometric growth in the incidence of untreatable diseases.

In the main, responsibility for dealing with the effects of these calamities has rested on national governments, regional country groups and international agencies – both governmental and nongovernmental. Their record, while commendable, has not been good enough. For example, while standards of living have risen, the fact is that more people go to bed hungry today than did 30 years ago. While there may well be edible salmon in the Thames, swimming off most of the world's beaches is still a little like playing Russian roulette.

Privately owned, profit-accountable corporations will be created · either as spinoffs from existing institutions or as totally new enterprises – to meet the increasing challenge of dealing with social problems. No one would dispute that, for example, had food distribution in Ethiopia been effectively subcontracted to a profit-making organization, the chances of food aid actually getting to where it was really needed would have been greatly increased – especially if compensation had been based on results achieved.

We shall see the creation of new enterprises designed to deal exclusively with the world's social problems. These institutions will be managed and led, not solely by a dedicated band of socially conscious people, many of whom have tried to make up for their lack of management and technical skills by determination and will-power, but by a new breed of professional managers as well. Thus, these new enterprises will be able to attract their share of the best and brightest.

Staffed with competent leaders and qualified staff, these new corporations will be able to utilize fully the rich armoury of competitive management tools and systems. Sophisticated logistical and distribution control systems developed, for example, by The Limited in the US must be able to make the distribution of food aid in the Sudan far more efficient. Well-developed early warning information systems used by commodity dealers would go some way towards relieving the devastating effects of some unexpected events that seem to create global emergencies – droughts, floods and crop failures.

8   Ownership structures and work patterns

Throughout the world there exist firms with a type of business structure that has, despite its importance, received little or no attention. These companies, for example, are seldom singled out in any traditional listing of the world's largest or most profitable enterprises. Each day of the year, at least five new books on management are published, and hardly any have recognized these businesses. Of all the business schools around the world, only 20 even give a course dealing with such enterprises.

Yet, today they account for 60 per cent of the gross national product of the US, and 75 per cent of *all* companies in America. The corresponding numbers in most highly industrialized countries – e.g. Germany, Canada, Italy, France – are probably even higher. These companies are what we have come to think of as family controlled businesses. Not all family firms are privately owned. Many today are public companies where outside investors hold important shares of outstanding stock. Yet, the real power and influence of companies such as Wang, Marriott and Anheuser-Busch are still clearly in the hands of the founding families. Pilkington and Sainsbury's, while 'public', are still controlled by the descendants of the founding fathers.

These family-controlled companies will grow and become more important. They will find ways of overcoming problems of continuity. Increasingly, they will become the subject of research and study. And new ways of merging family interests will appear, perhaps similar to the marriages, pacts and alliances that have produced the European royal houses.

9   Coping with a permanent cerebral worker shortage

Whether they are classified as 'knowledge workers', 'information employees' or 'cerebral staff', there seems to be little doubt that by the year 2020 most of those in employment will be professionals of this type. Today almost 40 per cent of all personal income – gross national product – is accounted for by knowledge workers. This figure will steadily increase and be as high as 75 per cent in 2020.

If that is the good news, the bad news is that, given the existing educational structure and propensity of many young people to shy away from higher education and vocational training, we shall need to learn how to live with a permanent shortage of cerebral workers. Part-time workers, home workers and telestaff will continue to proliferate, and management will invent new methods of making these resources more and more productive and responsive to an enterprise's needs.

10   A new skill – alliance management

Alliance is a term that has crept into the management lexicon late in the 30-year period covered in this anthology. It has been used to describe everything from joint ventures, research agreements, marketing consortia and cross licensing to distribution arrangements, manufacturing associations and logistical sharing schemes. Even those corporations that originally denigrated the notion of alliances have recently found that they indeed have extraordinarily valuable features of which they have decided to take advantage.

Notwithstanding numerous 'factual' studies about the post-alliance performance of companies, there does not appear to be any hard evidence about the success or failure of alliances. It is, of course, difficult to collect totally objective data, and the precise nature of the arrangements is often submerged under a sea of legal papers and memoranda of agreement. On balance, however, there seems to be a consensus that the results are 'not good enough'.

Alliances will continue to grow in importance. They represent an ownership pattern that is flexible, creative and easily adjusted to fit changing conditions.

What has apparently not been as flexible or creative has been the managerial, structural and systems capabilities of the enterprises that have been involved. Corporate marriages, whatever form they have taken, have tended to be fraught with difficulties. Bringing entities together, usually with common objectives, invariably has not been as straightforward as expected. Styles, cultures, systems, staffs and skills usually have not matched, and, as a result, major adjustments have been required.

Today the body of knowledge and experience that is available to help ensure a successful alliance is modest. In 2020 we shall have developed a rich base of experience and knowledge that will provide alliance patterns with tested approaches that will make these arrangements far more likely to succeed.

Which of these ideas discussed above will become realities? Shall we need to wait 30 years to see? Some of the ideas are extrapolations – we can be reasonably confident that these things will happen. Others fall more in the category of fundamental shifts in trends and accepted wisdom. Yet others are just mighty hopes for the future of a world that may be a better place to live in.